Airways

Smithsonian History of Aviation Series

On December 17, 1903, on a windy beach in North Carolina, aviation became a reality. The development of aviation over the course of little more than three-quarters of a century stands as an awe-inspiring accomplishment in both a civilian and a military context. The airplane has brought whole continents closer together; at the same time it has been a lethal instrument of war.

This series of books is intended to contribute to the overall understanding of the history of aviation—its science and technology as well as the social, cultural, and political environment in which it developed and matured. Some publications help fill the gaps that still exist in the literature of flight; others add new information and interpretation to current knowledge. While the series appeals to a broad audience of general readers and specialists in the field, its hallmark is strong scholarly content.

The series is international in scope and includes works in three major categories:

SMITHSONIAN STUDIES IN AVIATION HISTORY: *works that provide new and original knowledge.*

CLASSICS OF AVIATION HISTORY: *carefully selected out-of-print works that are considered essential scholarship.*

CONTRIBUTIONS TO AVIATION HISTORY: *previously unpublished documents, reports, symposia, and other materials.*

Airways

The History of

Commercial Aviation

in the United States

Henry Ladd Smith

Smithsonian Institution Press
Washington, D.C.

Reprinted 1991 in the Smithsonian History of
Aviation Series, Classics of Aviation History,
with new Editor's Introduction,
© 1991 by Smithsonian Institution.

Printed in the United States of America
96   95   94   93   92   91
5   4   3   2   1

⊗The paper used in this publication meets the
requirements of the American National Standard for Permanence of Paper for Printed Library materials Z39.48-1984.

This book is part of the Smithsonian History of
Aviation Series. Published in the United States
by the Smithsonian Institution Press, this series
of books is distributed in the United Kingdom,
Europe, the Middle East, and Africa by Airlife
Publishing Ltd.

Library of Congress Cataloging-in-Publication
Data

Smith, Henry Ladd, 1906–
    Airways : the history of commercial aviation
in the United States / Henry Ladd Smith.
        p.   cm.—(Smithsonian history of avia-
tion series. Classics of aviation history)
    Reprint. Originally published: New York :
Knopf, 1942.
    Includes bibliographical references and in-
dex.
    ISBN 1-56098-052-4
    1. Aeronautics. Commercial—United
States—History.   I. Title.   II. Series.
HE9803.A3S5   1991
387.7'0973—dc20   90-21853

Contents

Contents

Editor's Introduction

In his early 1942 *New York Herald-Tribune* review of *Airways: The History of Commercial Aviation in the United States*, Wolfgang Langeweische, himself no stranger to aviation, commented that "it is fitting that the story of the air lines should be written not by a historian but by a journalist. What Henry Ladd Smith, lecturer in journalism at the University of Wisconsin, reports in *Airways* is history only by the fast-moving time scale of aviation; by the standards of ordinary life, it is still contemporaneous, and thus the proper domain of the journalist."

Smith undoubtedly took exception to Langeweische's calling him a journalist. As he himself says in the introduction to *Airways*, "This book was not written as an expert's criticism of air transportation, nor with the idea of 'exposing' the industry. The only purpose was to tell the story as detachedly as possible, which is all the historian can hope to do." Nearly a half century later, the best history of the beginnings of commercial air lines in the United States is still contained in Smith's "journalistic" *Airways*.

Ironically, although the period Smith is writing about is now considered "historical," no professional historians have ventured onto Smith's turf. Academic historians have undertaken research in other areas of aviation, especially its military aspects, but commercial aviation seems not to be of interest to the historical community. This is not as surprising as it may appear. The reason, perhaps, is that since no one has been able to improve on *Airways*, it has stood the test of time and become a significant part of the literature.

In this book, Smith surveys the evolution of the air lines in the United States from the development of powered flight to the dawn of the air mail, progenitor of the commercial airlines, to the state of that industry just before World War II. The air lines may no longer be young and exciting, flying commercially now being a routine matter, but at the time Smith wrote his book, aviation was just beginning to be recognized as an economic and social-cultural force to be reckoned with, just as the railroads had been in the nineteenth century.

The strength of *Airways* lies in the telling portraits Smith paints of the early air lines pioneers. Some of them are familiar: Juan Terry Trippe, founder of Pan American Airways, for example, has received ample attention in Matthew Josephson's *Empire of the Air*, published in 1944, Robert Daley's *An American Saga: Juan Trippe and His Pan American Empire*, published in 1980, and Marilyn Bender and Selig Altschul's *The Chosen Instrument*, published in 1982.

Others, like Erle P. Halliburton, are not. Halliburton, a former oil wildcatter and controlling stockholder of a small regional air line called Southwest Air Fast Express (SAFE), Smith calls a "hard-boiled Oklahoman," who "was as colorful as his famous cousin, Richard Halliburton, author and traveler." So intent was Halliburton on competing head to head with the big operators and getting an air mail contract for his company that he is described as "flitting like a banshee through the corridors of the Old Post Office Building" to the consternation of Assistant Postmaster General [Walter] Glover, who "all but had him ejected bodily."

Smith's portrait of Walter Folger Brown, Postmaster General during Herbert Hoover's administration, is elucidating and perhaps the best and most reasoned of any piece ever written about Brown. This little-known man, who deserves a full-scale biography himself, continues to be a controversial figure. In conducting the so-called Spoils Conferences to divvy up airmail contracts in 1930, Brown has been vilified as a Republican Party hack, intent on business as usual. But now the wisdom of his insistence on rationalizing the air line structure in the United States is undeniable. Up to the time of the deregulation of the air lines a decade or so ago, the Big Four—American, United, TWA, and Eastern—which Brown was instrumental in creating, were the largest domestic carriers, each dominating a chunk of the United States airway map.

Smith's portraits of individuals are woven into the fabric of the larger story of what Langeweische says are the "conflicts and intrigues, the labors and maneuvers that went into the building of the system." All of Smith's work is solidly researched; he drew on a wealth of primary and secondary sources—personal interviews, published and unpublished accounts, congressional reports, archival records. The book is also rich in appendix material, including the text of important aviation legislation such as the Kelly Act of 1925, the McNary-Watres Act of 1930, a six-page chart (newly formatted for this edition) showing airmail route mileage, an annotated list of air lines in the United States, a chronology of important dates in the history of aviation, and bibliographical notes that list books, periodicals, newspapers, documents, and interviews.

In the final analysis, *Airways* is a book of enduring interest, quality and style, balance and proportion, clear and lively writing. It remains the bench mark by which any book to be written on the subject must be judged.

Dominick A. Pisano
Series Editor

Author's Introduction
to Original Edition

M EN have been piloting airplanes almost as long as they have been driving automobiles, but the flying machine has lagged far behind the motor car as an important vehicle until very recently. There were reasons for the slow development of the airplane, for aviation involved not only a new medium of transportation, but a whole new science. The very idea of taking off into space was revolutionary. Even today the world is not used to flying, and it was only a few years ago that whole neighborhoods could be thrown into turmoil by the cry of " Aeroplane, aeroplane! "

But if aviation was slow in getting started, it made up for lost time after 1925. It took the railroads half a century or more to complete a cycle of pioneering, merger, regulation, and stabilization. The air lines went through all this in about ten years. The history of the air lines is similar in many ways to that of the railroads, but it is a history compressed and streamlined. The air-line picture is a reproduction of that of the railroads, but it is as though we were viewing the scene through the finder of a miniature camera. If some of the details are lost by this compression, at least the general outlines are the same. Both the air lines and the railroads have had their pioneers and their heroes; their men of vision and their daring promoters. The " little fellow " was squeezed out as surely by the air-line manipulator as by the railroad robber baron. There was the same march from exciting small beginnings to methodical

Big Business. There was the same ruthlessness and the same public reaction.

True, the air lines had the advantage of being able to raise capital easily, which the railroads lacked. Early rail-road-builders had to go abroad to find financial backing, whereas the air-line magnate found no trouble in raising capital in the United States. Air lines started in boom times, while the railroad emerged during depression. Both systems had difficulty in surviving during their early years, however, and both had to overcome prejudices before they could become successful, so that, all in all, there is not so much difference in the organization of the railroads and air lines as one might suppose.

Today the air lines are on the verge of becoming vitally important carriers. The war has proved the value of the airplane as a weapon, but commercial aviation is only on the threshold of its greatness as this is written. Already two of the lines are listed in the first of the fifteen most pros-perous passenger carriers, which includes bus lines and railroads. That air transportation was important for the defense effort was proved by the special privileges granted by those in charge of priorities. And the big boom in com-mercial aviation is still to come. There may be a lag in the progress, following the war, but inevitably the airplane is to become the most popular means of fast transportation in this land of vast distances.

Perhaps if the public knew something of the background of commercial aviation there would not be the prejudices and misunderstandings that have delayed progress in times past. Because any new transportation system must depend upon government aid, the average citizen has had a direct connection with the growth of the air lines. The part that the government has played in the building of the air trans-portation system has never been clearly understood by the man in the street, and sometimes public reaction has been disastrous, as it was in 1934, when a new administration, with mistaken zeal, brought confusion to the aviation industry. Railroad and bus companies have had some of their bitterest battles with state legislatures, but because air lines transcend ordinary boundaries, much of the clashing between public and private interests over the airway system has been in Washington. This has only concentrated the strife.

Certain chapters in the story of commercial aviation have been intentionally left unwritten in this book. No attempt has been made to describe the development of lighter-than-air craft, because, although the dirigible balloon at one time gave promise of becoming important as a medium of transportation, it has not figured in the development of the domestic airways since the crash of the *Macon* on February 12, 1935. Nor would it appear to be fair to ignore the vast system of air lines radiating from this country. The part played by Pan American Airways System is a story in itself. Perhaps the development of our foreign routes should not be separated from this study of air lines in the United States, but the history of Pan American Airways is so complicated that it could not be included between these covers.

It was with the utmost humbleness that this work was undertaken. Having only a strictly unprofessional enthusiasm for flying, the writer may appear presumptuous in attempting to write an authoritative volume about aviation. On the other hand, the experts so far have neglected to paint the broad picture of commercial aviation. They have been so preoccupied with the military, economic, regulatory, or technical phases of the subject that invariably they present only one facet to the reader. This book was not written as an expert's criticism of air transportation, nor with the idea of " exposing " the industry. The only purpose was to tell the story as detachedly as possible, which is all the historian can hope to do. Almost any air-line veteran who reads this book will say that he would have written it differently, but since no two of them agree on all the

facts, the neutral observer can only use his own best judgment in setting down such a chronicle as honestly as he
knows how.

HENRY LADD SMITH

University of Minnesota
Minneapolis, November 1941

AIRWAYS

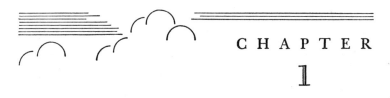

Kitty Hawk

Out of the darkness at the far end of the runway sweeps the air liner; running lights winking; the incredible organ note of the twin-Wasps tattering the atmosphere. For an instant the depot lights reflect from a gleaming, silver shape; long, lean, graceful. Then it disappears into the night: two thin blue streaks of flame scudding southward at two hundred miles an hour. It is Flight Seven out of Chicago, and six hours later it will alight safely and comfortably in the chill of a Texas morning.

Not many years ago the skeptic's stock expression was: " That's no more possible than for me to fly to Texas." Today that same skeptic may be on Flight Seven out of Chicago. He has had to find a new phrase to describe the impossible, for he has now so completely accepted the idea of flying to Texas that he does not rouse himself even for the take-off. To hundreds of travelers, flying to Texas is mere routine. Night after night, rain or clear, Flight Seven roars southward. During any second of each twenty-four-hour day, an average of 1,500 passengers and 18 tons of mail are rushing to their destinations in similar planes

3

throughout the country.[1] For this is the day of the skyliner.

Yet it is only in recent years that the public has learned to accept the airplane. Even today aviation is still strangely romantic. The airplane is almost as old as the automobile, yet long before Mr. Skeptic had summoned courage enough to take an air trip (it was probably an emergency), he had made the motor car as much a part of his life, almost, as his house.

Obviously, the airplane was too revolutionary for the public. The " gas buggy," any man could see, was simply an adaptation of an established means of locomotion. Machines had long moved across the earth powered by steam, and after a decent period of resistance to change, the public was willing to ride in vehicles propelled by electric or gasoline motors. Flying, however, was more than an adaptation. It was a whole new science. Furthermore, the airplane had to reach a high stage of development before the public could be coaxed into it, whereas the weaknesses of the early automobiles were not too much to tolerate. A ride in the horseless carriage might be thrilling, but a breakdown on a country road was only a matter of inconvenience, or, at most, of profanity. A breakdown in the air, however, was of considerable importance, not only to the pilot and his passengers, but quite possibly to the local undertaker.

Mass production made the automobile available to the average man, but limited demand, and the peculiarities of construction, kept up the price of the airplane. Aircraft were not dependable, even under the best of conditions. They were inefficient, because, for all their great cost, they could carry only small loads. Large hangars and landing fields added to the expense of flying. Above all, there was no *need* for commercial aircraft, since adequate means for fast, safe transportation already had been perfected.

In spite of his reluctance to leave the ground, man has thought about flying down through the ages. The Dædalus-Icarus myth is evidence that there is nothing new in the *idea* of flying. In literature the airplane is even older than the automobile, and men have experimented with flying machines for centuries. Yet when the airplane at last arrived, no one was ready for it.

Many factors have been important in the development of the air lines in this country. Public approval, financial backing, governmental regulation, and, above all, technical progress, have each played important parts in this development. One might say that when the first passenger paid for his transportation, public approval was won and the way opened for the air lines. Another historian might begin with the passage of the Kelly Bill on February 2, 1925, when transference of the air mail from government to private operation provided an attraction for sorely needed capital. Or, if early air lines were so dependent upon air mail subsidies, one might begin with the first air-mail flight in 1911, and the inauguration of regular service by the army in 1918. Others will say that the story of the air lines begins with the invention of the airplane. That completes the cycle, for until an invention has won public approval, it has little chance for commercial development.

Students of the pre-flight era will find many contributors to the science of aerodynamics, but one of the most ingenious of the early aeronautical engineers was Sir George Cayley, who conducted his experiments at the end of the eighteenth century.[2] The British scientist was an able engineer. He was the first to point out the advantages of " streamlining " and he understood the principles of flight, but even had he designed an aerodynamically perfect machine, he could not have flown with the motors available at that time. The crude steam engine of Cayley's day was too heavy and puny for aircraft. Sir George attempted to overcome this obstacle by inventing an internal-combustion motor, but chemists had not as yet developed the petroleum fuels necessary for such an engine, and nothing came of the experiment. Sir George Cayley was just too far ahead of his day, but already he had shown that the plane-designers and motor engineers were dependent upon each other, and that flight could not be achieved until the two worked out their problems together.

Others carried on the work. William Samuel Henson was a brilliant aeronautical engineer, and he was certain that his " aerial steam carriage " of 1843 would revolutionize transportation. Henson built a much lighter and more efficient steam engine for his craft, but, although its power-weight ratio had been brought down to thirty pounds per horsepower, it was still too heavy for its power output, and the ambitious plans of the inventor led only to failure. Henson's colleague, John Stringfellow, fared better. Stringfellow designed the first successful heavier-than-air flying machine. True, it was only a model, propelled by a small steam engine, but in 1848 it flew about forty yards. Stringfellow did not succeed in building a ship capable of carrying a man, however. Numerous experiments were conducted during the next fifty years, but the period from 1885 to 1900 was one of exceptional activity in aeronautics. Many of the great scientists believed they were on the verge of discoveries that would soon lead to the age of flying, but as the years rolled by, they experienced repeated disappointment. Hiram Maxim retired after spending more than $100,000. The Ader machine, heavily subsidized by the French government, was a failure.[3] Lilienthal and Pilcher, the famous German and British designers, were killed while making important gliding experiments. Octave Chanute, who built bridges in America, gave up his attempts to solve the problem of flight. Lastly there was the disappointing failure of the great Dr. Samuel Pierpont Langley.

Dr. Langley was the eminent secretary of the Smithsonian Institution. On May 6, 1896 he tested a steam-propelled model airplane on the Potomac River, near Washington.[4] Because the 26-pound craft stayed aloft for $1\frac{1}{2}$

minutes, the United States government encouraged further experimentation by an outright grant of $50,000. The scientist perfected a "whirling arm," or revolving table, to which he fixed various air foils and wing sections. Delicate instruments attached to the arm measured the effect of air resistance. With the aid of such data, Dr. Langley started construction of a man-carrying machine.[5]

Aiding the scientist was a genius named Charles M. Manly. Manly designed the gasoline engine that was the marvel of its day. Heretofore aircraft engines were too heavy for the horsepower they produced. Not until aircraft motors were designed with a power-weight ratio of around five pounds per horsepower was heavier-than-air flight practicable. The Manly engine was reduced to the unheard-of ratio of 3.6 pounds per horsepower, comparing favorably with motors of forty years later.[6] Manly reduced weight by cooling his cylinders with air instead of water. Since heat dissipates energy, cylinders were set around the hub of the motor like the spokes of a wheel, so as to present the greatest frontal area to the cooling air flow. This is the principle of the modern radial, used by Manly at the turn of the century.

Langley and Manly called their machine the "Aerodrome." On October 7, 1903 the Aerodrome was given its first test. Public curiosity in the machine was whetted by hundreds of fantastic newspaper and magazine articles, and because so important a figure as Dr. Langley was directing the experiments, spectators cannot be blamed for their reactions. For the experiment was a dismal failure, and the names of the courageous inventors were hooted in the streets. Manly was the pilot that day, and the launching took place from a barge anchored in the Potomac off Widewater, Virginia. Something went wrong with the catapult spring, which was to hurl the Aerodrome into the air, and when the signal was given, the clumsy contraption toppled ignominiously into the water.[7] Manly escaped with only a ducking, and the inventors set to work repairing the Aerodrome for a second launching.

Newspaper headlines reflected the disillusionment of the public. The following is typical of the reaction:

BUZZARD A WRECK
Langley Hopes Dashed
Costly Contrivance Utterly Unable to Take Wing
The Navigator Escapes with a Ducking
and has Shapeless Mass of Steel
and Cloth Stored Away [8]

The rebuilt Aerodrome was towed out on the launching barge for another trial on December 8, 1903. Knowing the limitations of his machine, Manly showed great courage when he took his place at the controls again. The signal was given. As the catapult spring was released, the lower front kingpost, to which was attached the launching rope, failed to release itself, and again the Aerodrome toppled into the river. With it toppled the hopes of Dr. Langley and Manly. The scientist never recovered from his humiliation. He died on February 27, 1906, of a broken heart, according to one report.

Several years later the Aerodrome did fly. In 1915 Glenn Hammond Curtiss rebuilt the Aerodrome, fitted it with a bigger engine, and lifted it from the water at Hammondsport, New York. The Smithsonian Institution brought the Aerodrome back to the National Museum in 1918, and in 1924 it was exhibited as the first heavier-than-air machine "capable" of flight, "in the opinion of many competent to judge."

When the Aerodrome experiments failed, the public was convinced that anyone who tried to fly must be mad. The average citizen believed that if the great Dr. Langley could not succeed in solving the problem of flight, no one could.

The amazing thing is that only nine days after the Aerodrome fiasco, man *did* fly.

On the night of December 17, 1903 the Reverend Dr. Milton Wright, Bishop of the United Brethren Church, notified the editor of the Dayton paper that he had an item if the paper cared to use it. Apparently the news was of little value, for the daily did not mention it until the late editions. The news on page one that day was concerned with the excellent Christmas trade in the Dayton stores; a labor meeting of no significance; the arrest of a Negro pickpocket; and the pardoning of a robber.[9] The story turned in by Bishop Wright merely stated that he had received a telegram from his two sons, who were then at Kitty Hawk, North Carolina, which read:

SUCCESS FOUR FLIGHTS THURSDAY MORNING ALL

AGAINST TWENTY-ONE MILE WIND STARTING FROM

LEVEL WITH ENGINE POWER ALONE AVERAGE SPEED

THROUGH AIR THIRTY-ONE MILES LONGEST FIFTY-

SEVEN SECONDS INFORM PRESS HOME CHRISTMAS

 OREVELLE [*sic*] WRIGHT 525P [10]

The Dayton editors had in their hands one of the great scoops of the century — and they dropped it. Offhand, their blindness seems inexcusable, but the events preceding the Bishop's announcement perhaps justify their indifference. Maxim, Bell, Lilienthal, Pilcher, and Ader had all gone down in defeat. Nine days before, the great Professor Langley had met disgrace, after a tremendous build-up by the press. The Dayton editor himself had been taken in by the Langley publicity, and he wasn't going to be caught again. It was recalled that the famous mathematician Simon Newcomb, builder of astronomical observatories, had proved conclusively in cold figures that it was *impossible* to fly. The editor was in no mood to make his paper a laughing-stock upon the unconfirmed report of two young men, who apparently believed they knew more than the world's greatest scientists.

And who were these Wright boys who disputed the impossibility of flight? The Wrights were not elderly scientists of international fame, but men in their early thirties with only a high-school education. They had no government subsidy to finance their experiments, but only the meager profits of a bicycle shop. Learned societies had not gone out of the way to lend them data and prestige, for the Wrights had gleaned their information from the public library, private correspondence, and the school of experience. The public did not even know about the Wrights, since they had done much of their work amid the wastes of the Carolina sand dunes. No wonder the editors " played down " the Bishop's offering. After Langley's fiasco at Widewater, Kitty Hawk was more than credulity could bear.

Yet these two Ohioans were the " fathers " of the modern airplane. The word " fathers " should be singular, for, as Mark Sullivan has pointed out, Wilbur and Orville were actually " one Wright raised to the Nth power." [11] Roy Knabenshue, pioneer American dirigible-builder and manager of the Wright Exhibition Company, agrees with Sullivan's description.[12] Knabenshue says that when he first went to work for the Wrights, he was amazed by the vehemence of their arguments.

" This can't go on," he once said to Katharine, sister of the inventors, after a particularly bitter verbal duel. " This partnership can't last much longer."

Katharine reassured him. She said that there was no real bitterness in the disputes and that the wrangling was only a way the brothers had of threshing out problems. Often, Knabenshue recalled, Wilbur and Orville Wright held opposite opinions during an argument, only to find, hours later, that each had convinced the other, so that they had to begin all over again. It was this perfect complement of minds and personalities that overcame all obstacles.

And there were many obstacles. The Wrights started from scratch. They made their own aircraft engine, since they could not afford to have a motor built according to their specifications for weight and power. They had to learn by themselves all the lore of meteorology and aerodynamics. They taught themselves to fly, since, of course, there were no flying instructors even for the elementary gliders. They worked out their own tables and formulæ — tables that refuted the findings of the world's greatest scientists — these young men who had left school at seventeen. Slowly, patiently, they learned about flight.

They had their first lesson in the autumn of 1878, when Bishop Wright brought home a present for his youngsters. The clergyman was hiding something in the palms of his hands as he entered the dining-room, where his family was gathered. As the children ran to him, he opened his hands. The object he held, instead of dropping, climbed to the ceiling, fluttered a moment, and fell lightly to the floor. This object, now on display in the National Museum, was a device known as a " heliocoptere " — a thing of cork and bamboo propelled by two air screws made of feathers. Wilbur and Orville recalled this incident often as they worked later upon their airplanes.

But it was not until 1896, when news of Lilienthal's death reached America, that the Wright boys began a serious study of aeronautics. At the library they obtained all the books they could find on flying, including Octave Chanute's *Progress in Flying Machines,* Langley's *Experiments in Aerodynamics,*[13] the *Aeronautical Annuals* of 1895–7, and some pamphlets by Lilienthal.

In 1900 there were two schools of aeronauts. Maxim and Langley represented the group that believed in power flight; Lilienthal and Chanute confined themselves to gliding experiments. Both groups had many followers, and at first the Wrights inclined toward the gliding school. They started gliding experiments more as a sport than as a study, but it was not long before they swung over to the other camp.

When the Wrights set out to design a plane, the most difficult problem was that of preserving balance. A few of the early designers placed the center of gravity far below the wings, in the belief that the weight would naturally seek to remain at the lowest point, like a pendulum. But like the pendulum, the hanging weight tended to swing, thereby destroying stability. A more satisfactory method, still in use, was to build the wings with the tips higher than the wing roots, so that weight was slung below the center of gravity. This " dihedral " theoretically provided automatic stability, but in practice it was effective only in calm air.

The Wrights ignored precedent by bending the wings down, so that they appeared to be sagging. This made the machine more inert, but since it destroyed inherent stability, some means had to be found to preserve equilibrium. Lilienthal and Chanute controlled their gliders by merely shifting their bodies, much as a child balances a seesaw by standing in the center with the weight first on one foot and then on the other; but this crude method of " trimming " the craft was inadequate for the more sensitive Wright machine. The brothers solved the problem by " warping " the wings — that is, by actually twisting them with levers and pulleys. Modern planes obtain the same results with a flap, or aileron, on the rear, or " trailing," edge of the wing tips. The Wright system of warping the wings provided the same kind of control. In fact the Wrights held that the aileron was an infringement of their warping patent. At any rate, the first Wright ships were more effectively controlled than any planes built theretofore.

The Wrights began their experiments in October 1900. The first machines were flown as kites, controlled from the ground, and as the United States Weather Bureau informed the brothers that the winds of the Carolina coast were ideal for such experiments, Orville and Wilbur decided to use the dunes of Kitty Hawk for their outdoor laboratory. By 1901 the Wrights had progressed to the " free gliding " stage, but flying was still a sport to them, not a life work. The Kitty Hawk experiments had attracted no attention, and the public was unaware of the Wrights; but soon the Dayton bicycle-makers were corresponding with the editors of foreign aviation magazines, and with glider experts all over the world. Octave Chanute was the leading authority on glider flight in this country. Chanute was an engineer by profession, but an aeronaut by preference. He had built bridges at Kansas City and St. Louis and had directed the construction of the Chicago stockyards. Chanute met Lilienthal on one of his trips to Europe, and before long the engineer had taken up gliding as an avocation. The Wrights corresponded with Chanute, and when he found that they were not in the least interested in financial gain, he visited them and gave them much valuable information. Chanute told them that their machines were aerodynamically superior to any built up to that time. The Wrights, however, were not satisfied. Having followed implicitly the mathematical tables of Chanute, Lilienthal, Langley, and others, the brothers were convinced that all these calculations were faulty. After two years of experimentation the Wrights cast aside all the learning of their illustrious predecessors, and from then on they relied upon their own tables. Flying had ceased to be a sport for them. It had become a science.

At first they rather resented exchanging fun for study, but the more they plunged into scientific experimentation, the more they were fascinated. By means of a small wind tunnel they worked out their own aerodynamic tables. These new calculations repudiated the findings of the famous scholars, but the revised tables proved to be correct. The results of their experiments were incorporated in the 1902 glider, and in September and October of that year the inventors made more than a thousand successful flights at Kitty Hawk. By 1903 the same machine, improved after further experiments, was making flights of more than a minute. With accurate data for making calculations and an effective system of balance-control, the brothers were now ready to install a motor in their craft.

On returning to Dayton from Kitty Hawk in 1902, the Wrights made inquiry for a suitable engine. None of the automobile-manufacturers could furnish a motor of the specified weight and horsepower, so the brothers decided to build their own power plant. Less than six weeks later the motor was on the test block, thanks to the mechanical genius of an assistant, C. E. Taylor. The Wrights demanded only eight horsepower, but it was evident that their engine would exceed that output, given the proper lubrication. When finished, it actually produced sixteen horsepower for short intervals, and could be counted upon for twelve. This increased power permitted the building of a slightly stronger and heavier ship. The engine was water-cooled, and it delivered only about one fourth the horsepower of the amazing Manly radial, used by Langley, but in a day when gasoline motors were rare and aviation power plants non-existent, the Taylor engine was nevertheless an engineering triumph. The motor was attached to the airplane on the right of the pilot, so that in case of a plunge to earth, he would not be crushed by its weight.

The machine itself was no problem, for the experiments of 1902–3 had proved the aerodynamic efficiency of the Wright design. The big problem was the propeller. There were no available data on air screws, but the Wrights had expected to learn the theory of marine propeller operation and then to substitute air pressure for water pressure. Much to their surprise, they found that marine propellers were manufactured, not according to formula, but almost entirely by the trial-and-error method. Again the Wrights were forced to calculate tables for propeller efficiency, but the air screw that they finally designed was superior to any ever made up to that time.

By the fall of 1903 the Wrights were ready for their greatest adventure. On the 25th of September they arrived at Kitty Hawk. The hangar, erected in 1901 and enlarged in 1902, had been blown from its foundation by the terrific winds of that locality, and while waiting for the plane to arrive, the brothers set to work repairing the building and erecting a smaller one to serve as workshop, kitchen, and bedroom. The crates of equipment, and one of the worst storms of the year, came at the same time. For several days it was too windy to fly, but occasionally there was a chance to practice on the 1902 glider, which had been stored in the older hangar. Chanute visited the brothers at this time, but because the weather and mechanical trouble caused considerable delay, he had to leave before the tests were completed.

The first run of the motor developed a flaw in one of the propeller shafts. The shaft was returned to Dayton for repairs and did not arrive back at Kitty Hawk until November 20. Then the chain sprockets, which were screwed to the shafts, persisted in shaking loose. Resorting to an old trick learned in their bicycle-building days, the brothers heated the shaft, poured tire cement into the threads, and screwed on the sprockets. There were no more loose sprockets.

While waiting for the wind and snow to abate, the Wrights rigged up an automatic timing device to record duration of the flight they were sure they would make. On the morning of November 28 the weather cleared and they trundled out the machine for a test. As the engine warmed up, Orville discovered that one of the propeller shafts had cracked again. There was nothing to do but to return to Dayton for repairs. Wilbur stayed in camp while

Orville went home to supervise the making of the new shafts. In place of the tubular shafts, solid metal rods were substituted. The solid shafts absorbed the shock of the engine and there was no more trouble of this nature.

It was the 11th of December before Orville returned. That was a Friday. On Saturday everything was ready, but this time the wind was too light to lift the machine from its monorail launching track and it was too late to carry the equipment to a near-by dune for a downhill take-off. Monday was another windless day. The brothers therefore decided to make their test from the steep Kill Devil hill. Members of the Kill Devil Lifesaving Station had agreed to answer a signal when help was needed, and soon the Wrights were joined by J. T. Daniels, Robert Westcott, Thomas Beachem, W. S. Dough, and " Uncle Benny " O'Neal. They laid the track down the side of the dune. With the slope of the track, the thrust of the propellers, and the sweep of a facing wind, the brothers expected the ship to rise easily from the sixty-foot monorail.

Both were eager to make the first test. They tossed a coin and Wilbur won. He took his place on the pilot's " bed," lying down to reduce wind resistance. Orville stood at a wing tip to balance the machine on the rail. The little motor went into a frenzy and the two chain-driven propellers bit into the wind until the whole machine quivered like a ship ready to slip its mooring. Wilbur pulled the launching release wire. Orville tried to hold the ship level, but the wing tip was wrenched from his grasp. After a 40-foot run the craft began to lift from the monorail. At that moment Wilbur made the mistake of pointing it up too steeply. It went into a stall and tumbled into the sand 105 feet below the starting-point. The spectators saw the fragile machine strike the ground on its left wing. It swung around and a landing skid dug into the sand, causing some damage.

Wilbur climbed out unhurt as Orville raced down the

slope. The timer had recorded a flight of just $3\frac{1}{2}$ seconds, but whether it was power flight or only a form of gliding, no one could say. At least the inventors were sure of their launching device.

It took two days to make repairs, but by December 16 the ship was ready again. That night a strong wind blew from the north. Ice formed on the rain puddles around the camp. The wind died down a little at dawn, but it was still sucking the top of the dunes at more than thirty miles an hour by mid-morning. Ten o'clock came and the brothers could stand the suspense no longer. They signaled their lifesaving-station friends and trundled out the biplane. Because of the high wind, the monorail was placed on level ground. Orville says that he still shudders when he thinks of his temerity in attempting to fly in such a breeze, but excitement and limited flying experience dulled caution that day.

The wind had dropped to twenty-seven miles an hour by the time the life guards arrived. Present, in addition to the Wrights, were Daniels and Dough, who had helped when Wilbur made his attempt; A. D. Etheridge, also of the Kill Devil station; W. C. Brinkley of Manteo; and little Johnny Moore from Nags Head. There was another spectator, although he was not on the spot. Robert Westcott, a life guard who had helped at the first trial, was on duty in the lookout tower, but from his perch three quarters of a mile away he could see everything clearly through his telescope.

Wilbur having had his turn on the 14th, it was now up to Orville to test the repaired machine. The engine was started and the younger Wright lay down on the lower wing next to the popping motor. Wilbur stood at the right wing tip.

Orville released the tether wire, and the ship began to move along the rail — much more slowly this time, because of the high wind. It began to lift almost at once, yet when it left the rail after/less than a forty-foot run, it was moving forward so slowly that Wilbur was almost able to keep up with it.

But was it *controlled flight?* That, Orville knew, he would soon find out. He was off the ground now. Cautiously he manipulated the controls, which did not react the same as in gliding flight. Back came the elevator lever, and suddenly Orville saw the blurred ground recede. He was flying.

CHAPTER

2

The Day of the Birdman

THE airplane was born on the sands of Kitty Hawk that winter day in 1903, but it was a feverish and recalcitrant infant. The machine staggered along its course in such an uncertain manner that spectators stood frozen with apprehension. The strong wind and the fact that the power craft was more sensitive to control than the gliders, partly accounted for its erratic performance. At any rate, only in a technical sense was Orville in control. Sometimes he was ten feet above the ground and sometimes he barely grazed the sand. A sudden dart downward ended the flight. Orville had been aloft just twelve seconds. His speed had been about one third that of an Olympic runner. The distance was only forty yards. In these days of transoceanic air service the Kitty Hawk flight seems unimpressive, yet it was one of the most significant events of the century, the opening of an entirely new frontier.

The Wright brothers completed four flights before noon, the last and longest being made by Wilbur, who kept the ship pitching along for fifty-nine seconds (the telegram said fifty-seven by mistake). Already there was progress, for Wilbur flew 284 yards before his craft got out of hand.

With a more favorable wind, even greater flights might have been made, for the brothers were acquiring skill with every attempt. The breeze was still at near-gale velocity, however, and while the group was discussing Wilbur's flight, a gust upset the resting ship and began rolling it over and over. Daniels, the life guard, who was as strong as any two ordinary men, grabbed a wing strut and tried to hang on. He was spun around within the wings until the wind slackened and he could emerge, bruised and shaken. The ship was so badly damaged that any more flights that year were out of the question.

The Wrights had solved the problem of flight, but it was five years before the man in the street, " taken in " once by the Langley failure, accepted the airplane as anything more than the wild dream of the Sunday newspaper feature writer. Not until 1908 did it dawn upon the average American that man could emulate the birds. In a reply to Mark Sullivan, who was writing Volume II of *Our Times,* Orville wrote in 1925:

You ask why it was that the public took so little notice of our 1903 flights and not until 1908 awoke to the fact that human flight had been accomplished. I think it was mainly due to the fact that human flight was generally looked upon as an impossibility and that scarcely anyone believed in it until he actually saw it with his own eyes. Only a few, probably less than a dozen, saw the first flight of 1903. In 1904 and 1905 the number of witnesses was increased to a hundred or two; in 1908 to thousands. Hundreds of people have told me that they saw the first real demonstration of mechanical flight, but as hardly any two of these had seen the same flight, I have come to the conclusion that almost no one ever really believed who had not himself actually seen a flight. It amuses me that practically everyone now thinks he has always believed in its possibility and that many think that before 1903 they had predicted its early accomplishment. At that time we couldn't find half a dozen such. This inability to believe without seeing probably accounts for the slowness of the general public to become interested, and also for the fact that today, after 20 years have passed to dull the edge of the novelty of it, the interest in aviation is greater than it has ever been before.[1]

Most of the experimentation after 1903 was carried on in Dayton. In the spring of 1904 Mr. Torrence Huffman gave the Wrights the use of a shed and a field at Sims Station, eight miles east of Dayton. The brothers built a new machine, heavier and stronger than the first, and when it was ready the newspapers were notified. A dozen reporters appeared for this first public demonstration, but the wind was light and the heavier machine did not lift from the short monorail. To add to the embarrassment, the engine stopped on the second attempt. The plane dropped to the ground at the end of the rail, and the exhibition had to be postponed. This performance reinforced the suspicions of the hard-boiled journalists. Only time could cure the press of its skepticism. Yet in 1904 and 1905 the Wrights flew regularly at Huffman Prairie within a few hundred feet of a well-traveled road and a trolley line.

When the newspapers were finally convinced that flight was possible, much of the credit went to designers other than the Wrights. To the undiscriminating eye of the reporter, the airplane was far less impressive than the dirigible balloon, and by 1908, when the press "discovered" aviation, critics had arisen who pointed out not only that the Wrights had merely adapted old principles to new uses, but that in other countries, notably France, the airplane appeared almost as early as it had in the United States. Orville Wright has an explanation of this:

After the Kitty Hawk flight, there were many persons who professed to have known the principles of flight all the time. It was said that the French made flights almost as soon as we did, and there was a tendency to minimize our contribution. But we were making known our plans all along, as you can see by referring to contemporary copies of such magazines as *L'Aérophile*.[2] Anyone could have followed our work, had he cared to take the trouble. The curious thing is that even after we showed the way, other designers were not as successful. Our experiments, for example, showed that a rather thick leading edge might seem to be more efficient. One of the French designers followed our plans, but in an attempt to surpass our performance, he constructed the leading edge of his wings so that they were almost razor-sharp. Of course the machine did not fly well. The builder blamed us. He thought the accounts of our flights must be exaggerated. But the fault was entirely his own.[3] [For further details, see note 3.]

Another reason for the lack of interest in flying up to 1908 was the reluctance of the Wrights to exhibit their machines until the invention was legally protected. They had offered the invention to the government at a very modest price, but the war bureaucrats were not interested. Accordingly the brothers did what they could to make their patents binding. By 1908, however, competitors were numerous, and within a year or so, airplane meets were popular all over the country.

There was nothing streamlined about those early planes. Wires and spars cluttered the space between the wings, and it was a standard saying that a sparrow released in the midst of the wing braces could not have squeezed its way to freedom. Enmeshed in this tangle, the pilot sat on the leading edge of the lower wing. His feet rested precariously on a flimsy bar, and under his knees there was nothing but altitude.

There were few instruments. On the front elevator, projecting like a cowcatcher, the pilot sometimes tied a cloth streamer. If the rag did not blow straight back, the airman knew that he was slipping on his turns. Most flyers looked upon instruments of any kind as sheer frippery. The successful pilot flew " by the seat of his pants," and if that part of his anatomy developed into a sensitive enough instrument, an airman might navigate safely for a considerable period.

" Fly at six — repair all day," was the slogan of the pioneer airman, for these early ships were as fragile as a dime-store toy. There were no 1,200-horsepower motors to pull one off a short field then, and it was years before power and weight could make friends with each other in the airplane engine. Biggest motor at the 1910 Boston air show was rated at 100 h.p., but none of the ships on exhibition could carry anything like that. In December of that year John B. Moisant was the favorite in the Michelin trophy race at New Orleans, and his power plant was only a 50-h.p. rotary.[4] Most pilots were content with 30–35 h.p., and if the motor just kept running, the airman asked nothing more.

The early planes could stand no more power. Constructed of bicycle parts, piano wire, and bamboo, they would have been torn apart by modern power plants. Small engines were adequate because the machines were extremely light. This lightness permitted a remarkably quick take-off, considering the low horsepower of that day, and landing speeds were correspondingly slow. Glenn Curtiss could get his 1910 pusher off the field in six and a half seconds, and even the heavy Farmans lifted at around thirty miles an hour.

Until ships could be built to carry more powerful motors, speed was not an attribute of the airplane. One thinks of the air liner today as the fastest means of transportation, but it was years before the airplane overtook more conventional vehicles. In describing the Esnault-Pelterie racing flyer of 1909–10, one writer said: " It is likely that the racing ship of the future will be a monoplane, speeds of *over 40 miles an hour* having already been attained." [5] Eight years after the birth of the airplane forty miles an hour was still considered adequate. The speed record set by Glenn Curtiss in 1910 was just under fifty miles an hour. That did not even approach the speed of the automobile, for on March 16, 1910 Barney Oldfield, driving against time with a racing start in a 200-h.p. Benz automobile of special design, dashed over the fastest mile ever traveled by a human being.[6] His speed at Daytona Beach was 131.7 miles an hour — a record that the airplane was not to reach officially until 1919. When the French army ordered an American airplane for delivery in 1911, not much was expected in the way of speed. Specifications were: " an airplane capable of carrying a weight of 661 pounds in a continuous flight of 186 miles at a minimum speed . . . of 37.26 miles an hour (about the landing speed of a modern light plane).[7] In 1910, motorcycles, automobiles, and locomotives were all capable of going at least twice as fast as the speediest flying machine.

Slowly and painfully airplanes became safer, faster, and better able to carry loads. Wilbur Wright was called " King of the Air " when he rose to 187 feet at Le Mans in 1908, but a year later Louis Paulhan had looked down on the world from an altitude of half a mile, and Louis Blériot had crossed the English Channel in a machine of his own design. By 1911 Louis Bréguet was able to boast that he had flown an airplane with twelve passengers, although his achievement was dimmed somewhat by the fact that his load consisted of small boys.[8] The same year C. P. Rodgers proved that the United States could be crossed by airplane.

Up to about 1908 the inventors and airplane-builders were the only flyers. They taught themselves the rudiments of aviation and demonstrated their own machines. The inventor-flyer was a man of vast patience and considerable caution. Such pilots flew with relative safety, and many of the pioneers had long careers, including Glenn Curtiss, the Farmans, Glenn Martin, Louis Bréguet, the Wrights, and Louis Blériot. After 1908, however, aviation produced a different type of airman. He was likely to be a youth with a strange light in his eyes — a former motorcycle racer, perhaps, or the breakneck driver of a Benz or Winton. Unlike the inventor-flyer, this new brood of fledglings knew little of patience, and nothing at all of caution. They began to appear with their machines at county fairs, golf caps turned backwards, a smudge of grease across the nose. Long before the word " aviator " was used, newspaper writers had coined a more appropriate name for these flyers. " Birdmen " the reporters called them.

The birdman flew, not to prove anything, but just for the hell of it. He tore the wings from his craft while testing it for speed and endurance. He evolved new flying techniques that were not always successful. He lived excitingly for a few months, and then he died — gloriously, foolishly, uselessly — no, not uselessly, although it appeared so at times. For every crash set the patient inventor to improving, redesigning, and perfecting this new contrivance, until the public, which shunned the air, was convinced at last that the airplane was worthy of patronage. The early birdmen are sometimes accused of retarding aviation by their recklessness and the bad name they gave to this newest form of transportation. Recklessness, however, is only an excess of daring, and without daring there could have been no aviation.

Most of these early flyers are long since forgotten, but a few won more lasting fame. There was Eugene Ely, who first flew to and from a boat, thereby foreshadowing the practicability of the aircraft carrier. Philip Parmelee and Charles F. Willard educated the army to the importance of the airplane. There was Lincoln Beachey, " the incomparable Beachey," who could scoop a handkerchief off the field with his wing tip; and John Moisant, who won races and designed ships. More typical of the birdman flyer, however, was Arch Hoxsey, almost forgotten today, but once the personification of reckless daring in the air. Because Hoxsey was so typical of the breed, a short account of his career may be the best way of describing the " day of the birdman."

It was Hoxsey's job to show the world that the airplane

was here to stay. Born of well-to-do landholders living in Staunton, Illinois, Hoxsey was transplanted to California at the age of six, following the death of his father. By 1905 Hoxsey owned the first automobile garage in Pasadena.

About that time there lived in near-by Los Angeles a flight-struck enthusiast, Roy Knabenshue, who was flying the first American dirigible balloon. Knabenshue's craft was an anemic-looking gas bag supporting a spindly girder, to which was attached a two-cylinder motorcycle engine. The pilot straddled the girder and by shifting his weight while pulling various levers he was able to direct his course to some degree, providing the wind was not too strong. Because Hoxsey knew more about motors than anyone else in the vicinity, Knabenshue asked his help, and the two became good friends.

Knabenshue exhibited his dirigible at county fairs all over the country, and so successful was he as a showman that the Wright brothers hired him as manager of the Wright Exhibition Company. The company traveled from city to city, demonstrating the advantages of the Wright machine in competition with rival craft. To provide pilots for their stable of air broncos, the Wrights had opened a flying school at Birmingham. Here were trained many of the outstanding pioneer airmen. Walter Brookins, the famous racer, was the first student, which is not surprising, inasmuch as he had been hanging around the Wrights' workshop since he was a boy. Soon after Knabenshue became manager of the Wright Exhibition Company, he invited Hoxsey to train at Birmingham as a Wright flyer. Hoxsey jumped at the chance.

He had his first airplane ride, appropriately enough, on April Fools' Day 1910. Within a month he was giving exhibitions. A pilot learned his business rapidly then. After a few days of tinkering and low ground hops, a man knew pretty well whether or not he could fly. Brookins had only two and a half hours of flight training before he soloed.

Four hours of dual instruction was average. Many of the Early Birds even taught themselves, for there were not many flying schools. Following his training, a student had before him the prospect of a short but extremely exciting life.

At Birmingham, Hoxsey and Brookins met Ralph Johnstone, who was the third member of what was to become a famous flying team. Johnstone, four years older than Hoxsey, was a former circus cyclist from Kansas City. Knabenshue had met him at a Western carnival and had persuaded him to become a pilot for the Wright Exhibition Company. In the summer of 1910 Brookins, Hoxsey, and Johnstone began a flying circuit that was to make their names familiar to every schoolboy. Brookins, a little superior because of his seniority as a pilot, was something of a lone wolf. Johnstone was the clown and inveterate vaudeville performer. Hoxsey was the gentleman — an immaculate dandy, balancing his pince-nez elegantly.

Almost at once Johnstone and Hoxsey, always the best of friends, became the bitterest of rivals. If Hoxsey performed a daring feat, Johnstone could not rest until he exceeded it. If trouble grounded Hoxsey while his rival was in the air, the Californian raged in his tent. The public was not long in finding out about this feud and it was delighted. One night during the Belmont Park races in late October, Frank Ward O'Malley, the wag of the New York *Sun,* went around to Hoxsey and intimated that Johnstone was planning the first moonlight flight. O'Malley then dropped over to Johnstone's tent and said the same thing about Hoxsey. A few moments later both flyers were found struggling to get their machines ready for flight, and only stern orders from their manager prevented the escapade.

It was at Belmont that Johnstone and Hoxsey were named the " Star Dust Twins." Both were striving to win the five-thousand-dollar prize offered for the first altitude flight of ten thousand feet. Every day they rose a little higher, each seeking to outfly the other. Late one afternoon the air was exceptionally calm, and both flyers took off for another attempt at the record. For an hour they spiraled upwards. The sun went down. Still they climbed. Neither would be the first to turn back. Night overtook them and only the throb of the straining motors reassured the anxious crowd. The mad contest ended when the fuel was exhausted. First one motor and then the other sputtered, picked up again as the last few drops of gasoline drained from the suddenly down-tilted tank, and lapsed finally into silence. Both machines landed safely in a Long Island potato patch, but in the intervening hour of suspense the exhibition officials aged perceptibly.

Occasionally the Wrights had to apply the brakes to their reckless protégés. The Chicago *Record-Herald* offered a prize of ten thousand dollars to the winner of a cross-country race from Chicago to Springfield, Illinois. Wilbur Wright picked Hoxsey to carry the honors of the company. Johnstone had had his fling at the Boston meet earlier in the year. Brookins had been picked twice before for important flights. Now it was Hoxsey's turn.

The " Star Dust Twins " were then flying at Detroit, and thither Wilbur went to bear the tidings. The Wrights were doing everything possible to promote safe flying, and the elder Wright was therefore horrified at what he found in the auto city. Hoxsey was acting like a madman in the air, and the newspapers were missing none of the fun. The pilots did not know that their employer was in Detroit, and without revealing his arrival Wilbur bought a seat in the grandstand. Johnstone took off on schedule that day, found the wind bad, and landed again under perfect control. Hoxsey thought this a fine time to show off. He flew according to orders for a short while, but suddenly the ship began to act like a defective skyrocket. Hoxsey was " flight drunk," and the crowd watched fascinated.

Wilbur returned to the hotel and left two notes. In one

he thanked Johnstone for obeying orders. In the other he rebuked Hoxsey in blunt terms and added that because of such recklessness Hoxsey was to forfeit the Chicago-Springfield race.

Brookins was selected for the flight. He won the prize by covering the 180-odd miles at an average speed of thirty-three miles an hour. Hoxsey, however, was only momentarily repressed by Wilbur's rebuke, for he followed Brookins within a few days, flew over his old home at Staunton, Illinois, and made a jump from Springfield to Clayton, Missouri, that almost eclipsed the official flight. No sooner had he completed his trip to Kinloch Park, outside St. Louis, than he broke into the headlines again.

Theodore Roosevelt arrived in St. Louis the first week in October to talk before a business club. One afternoon he was taken out to Kinloch to watch the flying. Teddy wanted to see an airplane, and the party drove up to the corner of the field where Hoxsey was warming up faithful old No. 9. The flyer and the ex-President were introduced.

" I was just getting ready for a flight," said Hoxsey. " Don't you want to come along? " [9]

To the surprise of everyone, Teddy accepted the invitation. Before his hosts could remonstrate, the chunky exponent of the strenuous life had climbed from the towering Packard to take his place next to Hoxsey. Someone called out a warning, but the engine was popping so loudly that Teddy did not hear, and while the startled business men were gathering their wits, the ship went bumping down the field. Hoxsey paid no attention to his passenger until he had his craft off the ground. They were up a hundred and fifty feet when the ship lurched violently. Hoxsey glanced to his right. Teddy was having the time of his life. He was waving wildly to the crowd and flashing his famous beaver-toothed grin. It was high time to curb this restless spirit.

" Be careful, colonel," shouted Hoxsey above the tur-

moil of wind, propellers, and engine. "Don't pull that
string," and he indicated the overhead cord that short-
circuited the engine — the equivalent of an ignition
switch.

Teddy turned. He was shouting enthusiastically, but
the sentences were torn away by the wind. Hoxsey understood only the words: "war . . . aeroplane . . . bomb,"
but there was little doubt as to the trend of his thought.

A few minutes later Hoxsey landed and the crowd
cheered. Teddy disembarked stern first, and for a moment
was caught like a great bluebottle fly in the spiderweb of
rigging. He shook hands with Hoxsey before rejoining his
hosts. Teddy never forgot the experience.

Johnstone was the first to die. On the whole, he was a
much more stable flyer than Hoxsey. He did not engage in
low-ground aerobatics. His one trick was the spiral glide,
and it was this that brought about his death at the Overland
Park meet in Denver on November 17, 1910.

Johnstone took off on his last flight and climbed steeply
until the plane began to get "soggy" in the rarefied air.
Then he started his spiral descent.

Within five hundred feet of the field something went
wrong. The left main spar snapped and the wing flapped
back as though on a hinge. Johnstone was hurled from the
controls, but he managed to grasp a bracing wire as he
fell and the crowd saw him climb back into his seat. He
strained at the long wooden main brace supporting the
upper wing and attempted to warp the trailing edges sufficiently to retard his fall. For a moment he seemed to succeed, for the football helmet he had been wearing was now
falling faster than the wreck. When the machine was still
two hundred feet from the ground, however, it turned over
completely. Now it was heading directly for the grandstand. Spectators fled screaming. Torn and splintered, the
broken bird landed in a cloud of dust on the edge of the
track.

The Wrights had been apprehensive about such trouble for some time.

" The day before Johnstone started for Denver I had a long talk with him in my office on Fifth Avenue," Wilbur told newspaper reporters shortly after the crash.[10] " I said to him, ' Ralph, you must obey orders from now on, or there will be trouble. You took unnecessary risks at Boston and at Belmont against definite orders, and you must stop that.'

" He said, ' I've made up my mind to obey orders. You don't seem to appreciate fancy flying, and I'm not going to do any more of it.' He was a little hot about it. I said, ' Ralph, you can't please me better than by sticking to that. We do not value a man by the number of times he outdoes his fellow aviators, but by the ability he has to restrain himself when the crowd yells for the uselessly sensational.'

" When Johnstone was killed, he was doing all right. On the day before, though, he had disobeyed a standing order by landing with the wind, instead of against it. ' Brooky ' [Walter Brookins] had come down, and by obeying the rule had landed some distance from the grandstand. Hoxsey followed and managed to light in front of the crowd by evading the injunction to fly against the wind. Of course Johnstone would have to do at least as well, and so he tried to do better. The result was that he ran into the fence.

" There may have been some detail omitted in making repairs. It was this, probably, that made the machine act so on the day Johnstone was killed. If the order to alight against the wind had been obeyed, the wing would not have been weakened and Johnstone would probably be alive today."

The death of his friend and rival sobered Hoxsey for a short time, but it did not discourage him as a flyer.

" Don't be afraid for me," he wrote his cousin at Staunton, adding, as many a flyer has added since that time:

" there is really no danger. When an airman has an accident while flying, he is careless with his machine. Besides I'm a fatalist." [11]

Two days before Christmas he broke all existing records by climbing to 11,474 feet. On the 27th he flew over Mount Wilson for an even greater unofficial record. So it was to him that all eyes turned on the last day of December 1910 at Dominguez Field, near Los Angeles. All the other pilots had been driven from the air. Hoxsey knew the risks he was taking in attempting a flight, but since Johnstone's death he felt a certain responsibility, and he hated to disappoint the crowd. He made his decision quickly.

" I'm going up," he told Hubert Latham, the British birdman.

" Don't do it, Hoxsey," warned Latham. " The air is as full of holes as a Swiss cheese."

If the air was too cheesy for Latham, it was unfit for any airman. Latham had taken up flying almost desperately, hoping to escape a consumptive's deathbed by a short, exciting career as a flyer. He gloried in taking long chances and he boasted that he had wrecked every part of his ship at one time or another. Strangely, after every crash Latham's health improved immeasurably, until by 1910 he was almost an athlete. (He never did die in a crash, or from consumption, but under the charge of a water buffalo in 1913, while hunting in Africa.)

In spite of Hoxsey's respect for the British flyer, the American refused to be swayed. He ordered his mechanic, Hazzard, to warm up No. 9.

Shortly before he took off, Hoxsey was notified of John Moisant's death that morning at New Orleans. Hoxsey knew Moisant as one of the world's great pilots, winner of many an important race, a former Central American filibusterer who had turned to the air for new thrills. Johnstone was dead only a month. And now Moisant. . . .

" Too bad," muttered Hoxsey. " I guess he was just tired

of driving." For Hoxsey still maintained that a careful " driver " never crashed.

He took his place at the controls. Everything was in good working order. The motor sang sweetly. Hoxsey raised his hand. Attendants released the wings. No. 9, a Series B Wright, scuttled down the field, twin screws blowing back a bank of dust and gravel. Slowly Hoxsey pulled back on the left lever. The plane left the runway, settled again for half a second, and then bounced two feet into the air, leaving behind a thin blue haze and the sickly odor of burning castor oil. A gust tilted the ship. The pilot warped the wings by pushing the right-hand lever, and the plane leveled out. At the far end of the field Hoxsey pulled back on this lever, at the same time bending down a short segment at the end of the stick, which controlled the rudder. No. 9 banked steeply at five hundred feet. Now it was climbing. Apparently Hoxsey was going to try for another altitude record. The wind was too bad, however, and at two p.m. he headed for the field. Off to the east the wind had kicked up a little funnel of dust (a " Santa Ana " they called it there), and evidently Hoxsey was racing to the field before the whirling sand made landing difficult. He was diving too steeply. At that very moment a gust stood the little ship on its nose.

" He's done for," cried Hazzard.

" Hoxsey, pull back," shouted Knabenshue, who had hurried to the field for the express purpose of forbidding a flight that day.

Had Hoxsey pulled back on the left lever, he might have righted his craft, although Knabenshue thinks Hoxsey must have had a heart attack. Perhaps the sudden drop from the high altitude had affected him. At any rate, the flyer sat motionless up to the moment of the crash.

Robert Lee, a spectator, was the first to reach the wreck. Hoxsey was pinned beneath the gasoline tank. His skull was fractured and his legs were doubled under him. Knabenshue, crying unashamedly, brought Dr. Sumner Quint running.

"Instant death," said the doctor.

Knabenshue took it upon himself to notify Hoxsey's mother. She saw him arrive in the nobby Buick roadster Arch had driven so proudly. A neighbor boy had already broken the news.

"Thank God he died and was not maimed," she said bravely. "I know Archie could not have stood that."

But though the proud mother seemed to bear the sorrow before her friends, she never recovered from the tragedy and eventually she died by her own hand.[12]

That was the life of the birdman. There were dozens like Hoxsey whose deeds are now all but forgotten. They lived spectacularly, flew for the love of it and for the high financial stakes, and died young. Hoxsey was only twenty-six when he crashed. It probably never occurred to him that he had a place in the development of aviation. But it was the Hoxseys who tested the theories of the inventors. They were the idols of the pre-war era. Not until 1914 was the birdman supplanted by another hero — the war pilot.

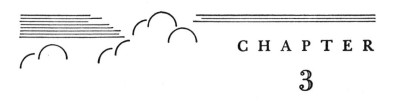

C H A P T E R

3

The Swivel-Chair Colonels

LINCOLN BEACHEY, most famous of the birdmen, was drowned in San Francisco Bay in 1915 when his plane broke up during an exhibition at the World's Fair. His death just about coincided with the end of the " Birdman Era " of aviation. After 1915 the World War began to shape the destiny of American flying. Measured by technical improvements, the war was a boon to the infant aircraft industry. During the four years of warfare planes were brought up to a new standard of performance.

The pre-war airplane was more efficient than is generally supposed, but it was clumsy, uncomfortable, and, above all, slow. Sixty miles an hour was good speed for a 1913 " kite," and that was fast enough when the pilot was so exposed to the elements. A few builders were leading the way with more advanced designs, but there were still plenty of Curtiss and Wright pushers churning the skies. Within five years all this had changed. The airplane of 1918 was a more streamlined machine, capable of darting through the air at speeds up to 130 miles an hour. Sputtering little pinwheel engines had been supplanted by powerful motors that could run for hours without faltering. The war brought this change. Nevertheless, the war was disastrous for commercial aviation.

The war put all the emphasis on military design, so that commercial development ceased. There was some prospect· in 1914 that the airplane was about to prove itself of economic value. The Postoffice Department seriously considered an aerial mail service over difficult routes,[1] and in January of that year the first air line was established in Florida. This enterprise was not very successful, but it showed that some thought was being given to the commercial possibilities of aircraft.[2] Glenn H. Curtiss, the seaplane-builder, even suggested regular transatlantic air service with his new cabin flying boat, the *America,* forerunner of the NC–4, which did make the first ocean crossing in 1919.[3] Curtiss was ahead of his day, but on the whole the aircraft industry was in a healthy condition. Most of the airplane companies were soundly financed, and this stability was conducive to slow, safe development.

War stimulated the industry like a drug, and the reaction (to carry out the comparison) was depressing and painful. Emphasis upon military craft raised standards of performance, but war pressure ended commercial progress. After 1914 the public thought of airplanes in terms of bombs and tracer bullets. War pilots were heroes, but they were not helpful in promoting a demand for air travel, following the war. Most damaging of all was the fact that war left this country with an enormous surplus of equipment. The airplanes glutting warehouses after 1918 were inefficient as transports, and yet designers had to wait for all this obsolete war equipment to be absorbed before there was any market for better ships. While the builders and designers waited, they went into bankruptcy. The four years of technical advance in wartime were therefore nullified by five years of virtual stagnation, with the result that many well-known companies disappeared between 1918 and 1923.

Soon after hostilities began in Europe, it became evident that the airplane was to become an important factor in battle tactics. Some of the experts even maintained that control of the air was equivalent to eventual victory. To gain supremacy, the Allies demanded planes from American manufacturers. The American is noted for his wholesale enthusiasm, once convinced, and the aircraft program outlined in 1917 reflected this quality. The program was stupendous, even for Americans, and the cost was correspondingly enormous.

In the short time this country was in the war, it appropriated a billion and a quarter dollars for aircraft. The amount of money is more impressive than the results, however, for, as many critics have pointed out, the United States was not able to place a single plane of its own design in active service. Aircraft production during the war years has been called as disgraceful an episode as Teapot Dome, the Star Route frauds, and similar "scandals." The fact is that the country seems to have expected too much of aviation, as it always has since the Wrights first flew in 1903.

The United States adopted the airplane for military use in 1908–9, but it was not until 1916 that it was called upon to demonstrate its usefulness under war pressure. In the so-called " Punitive Expedition " against the Mexican guerrilla Pancho Villa, scouting planes were brought into active service. General Pershing saw the Mexican campaign as an ideal proving ground for the new weapon, and he was all the more interested because of the growing dependence upon aircraft by European belligerents. He therefore ordered the First Aero Squadron to the border early in the 1916 campaign.

The squadron consisted of eight tractor biplanes manned by eleven pilots. In two weeks, with not a shot fired, all of the ships were out of the fight. Only a few flights were made, and the machines were so underpowered for the high altitude that it was suicide to fly in them.[4] Twelve more planes were sent down at great expense. They literally disintegrated before they could give any account of themselves. For more than two months the army was without any aircraft whatsoever, although a handful of planes might have tipped the scales between success and failure.

Indignation over the performance of the "Suicide Squadron" was so great that Congress threatened an investigation. To forestall this, an aviation board was appointed, headed by Lieutenant Colonel George O. Squier. Assistant to Colonel Squier was that Cassandra of military aviation, Major William (Billy) Mitchell, center of numerous controversies in years to come. The board discovered some peculiar practices in the procurement of aircraft.

Grover Loening, famous aeronautical engineer, quotes a salesman of the Sturtevant Aeroplane Company, to the effect:

Out of five radiators, we have only two that do not boil. I have kept changing the radiators in order to get the machines accepted. The navy does not know that I changed the radiators, as I did it at night. This is the only way that I could get the machines accepted.[5]

If the lessons of 1916 had been applied when the United States entered the World War, our first aircraft "scandal" might have had some value. As it was . . .

The United States declared war in April 1917. By the end of May, Congress appropriated $12,000,000 for the purchase of aircraft. This was an enormous order for such a new industry, but it was only a sop compared with orders that were to follow. In July $43,000,000 more were earmarked for aviation. By this time Congress was getting into the spirit of the war and in August it approved the largest appropriation ever passed for a specific purpose. Thrown to the undersized aircraft industry was an appropriation of $640,000,000. By the end of the war about a billion and a quarter dollars had been approved for the purchase of army aircraft alone. For this vast expenditure it was commonly believed that the industry produced only:

1. An aircraft engine that came out too late to do any good.
2. Less than two hundred defective observation craft, derisively called by pilots " flaming coffins."
3. A flurry in aviation manipulations that brought enormous profits to a few favored companies.

Granted that the above charges are true, there is another side to the picture. An industry that was less important financially than the toy-balloon business was suddenly ordered to produce 29,000 airplanes, although it had not yet produced 200 since the first flight in 1903.[6] Immediately after the declaration of war by this country, the Signal Corps had on order 334 planes. They were of *32 different designs,* and the orders were placed with sixteen companies, not more than six of which *had ever made more than ten planes before.*[7] There were only forty flying instructors in the entire country, and only a few of these were familiar with modern fighting planes. There were only about ten qualified designers available. There were no instrument companies and, what was worse, no engines.

Providing aircraft engines was a herculean job in itself. It took more than three thousand new tools, jigs, and dies to produce the famed Liberty motor, which had to be built from scratch. Ten years later Henry Ford, with a staff of experienced engineers and an organization of many years' growth, required more than a year merely to shift production from his Model T to his Model A car, yet American aviation had an even greater problem in 1917. The wonder is that American aviation produced any results at all in the nineteen months between the opening and closing of hostilities. Yet in that time the country saw:

1. Forty-eight large training fields, where formerly there were only two.

2. More than 20,000 trained aviation officers, where formerly there had been only 55.
3. More than 175,000 men trained as mechanics and ground force, where there had been 1,300.
4. A production line that started at a rate of 224 planes a year and ended with a potential rate of 17,000.
5. Adequate substitutes for castor oil (hitherto the only reliable lubricant), Irish linen (wing covering), and spruce (spars and frames).
6. The finest aviation motor produced up to that time.

Furthermore, only about half the money *appropriated* was *spent*. Based on its promises, the board in charge of aircraft production was a failure. Based on accomplishments, the record is far more impressive. There was plenty of chicanery, but it is only fair to present the qualifications. The Liberty motor will illustrate some of the misunderstanding that was common.

The Liberty motor received a bad name at the start because the first series, the Liberty 8, did not show up well. The Liberty 12, a later model with many of the " bugs " removed, can stand upon its record, however. It was still giving good service six years after the war, on many of the mail routes. It powered the first plane to cross the Atlantic Ocean. It served the army on the round-the-world flight. It appeared on one of our earliest, specially designed transport ships, the Stout all-metal monoplane. Today most engineers have acknowledged the worth of the Liberty motor, but its reputation has long been under a cloud.

Other critics admit the excellence of the Liberty motor but maintain it was useless because it did not appear until too late to do any good. These experts say that this country should have manufactured motors already battle-tested, such as the Hispano-Suiza and Hall-Scott. There may have been error in judgment, but the reasoning of those who favored the Liberty motor is at least understandable. European motors were mostly hand-made. With little retooling necessary, it was relatively easy to keep up with improvements, which were being made rapidly. America, however, was asked to produce engines in quantity, and in machine production every change means delay. American engineers thought they could bring out an engine so superior to anything known in Europe that it could be produced in quantity for a year or more before any rival could duplicate it. The remarkable thing is that by June 1918, only a year after the Liberty motor was nothing more than a blueprint, 1,243 motors were delivered. By October the production of Liberties exceeded the output of all other motors combined in any one country. In one year the United States surpassed *the total wartime production of motors* in Great Britain. This would hardly appear to be failure.[8]

On May 25, 1917 the Joint Army and Navy Technical Aircraft Board met and presented to the secretaries of the War and Navy Departments a procurement program of ambitious proportions. The board recommended that the army should have at once:

3,500 training planes of the Curtiss JN–4 type
1,700 De Haviland battle and observation planes
  600 Spad pursuits (standard equipment of the French)
  600 SE–5's (the British equivalent of the Spad)
  600 Sopwith scouts (another British design)
  200 Curtiss R–4's (a larger, more advanced trainer)
  175 Farman seaplanes

The board also recommended that 12,000 planes be ready for the spring drive of 1918. Later the quota was raised to 20,475 — all of which were to be ready in twelve months. That was a large order for the " industry " which had produced less than 200 planes in its entire existence.

The men who were asked to produce war planes were not in the least discouraged by the prospect, however. A group of " go-getters " who had never yet found a job too big for them, these men thrived on optimism — had used it as a kind of side-arm in their daily production battles. Many of the new aircraft bosses — " swivel-chair colonels " they were called — were former automobile-makers. Thinking in terms of Detroit production lines, they did not hesitate to tell the public what they intended to do with the picayune aviation industry, and they boasted that the skies would soon be filled with planes. They discovered, soon enough, that mass production was not adaptable to the manufacture of highly specialized and rapidly changing aircraft, and when their optimistic promises were not realized, the man in the street was bitterly disillusioned.

The influence of the financier and automobile-maker had begun to be felt by the aircraft industry even before the United States declared war. Wilbur Wright died of typhoid fever on May 30, 1912. Orville, left stranded by his brother's death, was harried by a series of patent suits. When the suits were settled in his favor, in 1914, the younger Wright was offered a large amount of money for his factory and patent rights; he sold his interest to a syndicate, which included in its membership such financiers as Richard F. Hoyt, of Hayden, Stone; Thomas Chadbourne and Harvey D. Gibson, of Manufacturers Trust Company; Albert H. Wiggin, of Chase National Bank; and others.[9] In 1916 the Wright factory was merged with Glenn L. Martin Company to form Wright-Martin Aircraft Company. Since the same syndicate also owned the Simplex automobile factory, Wright-Martin was one of the first to feel the influence of the motor-car industry.

The second oldest aircraft factory was also tied to the automotive interests. Curtiss Aeroplane and Motor Corporation was incorporated in 1916 to absorb the various properties of Glenn H. Curtiss. Within a few months of its reorganization the automobile financiers began boring in. John Willys, of Willys Car Company, acquired substantial holdings, and there were other auto men connected with the organizations.

But the most important company during the war period was Dayton-Wright Aeroplane Company. Dayton-Wright had no connection with Wright-Martin, although for a time Orville Wright was consultant for it. It was organized a year before the United States declared war, and its purpose was undoubtedly to win some of the fat war contracts being placed by the belligerents. Two groups gradually assumed control of it — the " Dayton group," and the " Detroit gang."

The Dayton group was headed by E. A. Deeds, general manager of the National Cash Register Company. Associated with him were Charles F. Kettering, H. E. Talbot, Sr., and H. E. Talbot, Jr. Deeds and Kettering had formed the Dayton Engineering Laboratories Corporation (Delco) in 1911 and had sold out to the United Motors Corporation in 1916. They made millions in the transaction and retained lucrative positions with Delco.[10] In April 1915 Deeds, Kettering, and the Talbots had organized Dayton Metal Products Company, which soon won profitable contracts to make fuses for the British. In 1917 Deeds and the elder Talbot were appointed on a fuse subcommittee of the Munitions Standards Board. While its organizers were on this important board, Dayton Metal Products received big orders from the United States government.[11] By the time the United States entered the war, Dayton Metal Products had bought a substantial interest in Dayton-Wright Aeroplane Company.

The other group interested in Dayton-Wright, the so-called " Detroit gang," was led by Howard E. Coffin, executive vice president of Hudson Motor Car Company; Jesse G. Vincent, of Packard; and Henry Leland, of Cadillac. With the declaration of war in 1917, Coffin was made chairman of the important Aircraft Production Board serving under Secretary of War Newton D. Baker. Coffin appointed Deeds to the board and later Deeds headed the vital Equipment Division. It was at this point that he was commissioned a colonel in aviation; the title he has retained ever since.

Regardless of his ability, Colonel Deeds has been criticized as not the best choice for the important position he was to occupy. While with the National Cash Register Company, he had been indicted in 1912 by the Federal District Court of Ohio for violation of the Sherman anti-trust law. He and several others were convicted, but the verdict was later set aside by the Circuit Court of Appeals, and the prosecution went no further.

Conceding his innocence, one cannot but feel that another man might have inspired more confidence in the important procurement post. That Colonel Deeds did little to improve his standing is indicated by the report of Charles Evans Hughes, chairman of a committee investigating the wartime activities of the Equipment Division director in 1918.[12] Hughes was a Republican, and the Republicans were, of course, eager to discredit the Wilson administration, but the findings of such a respectable citizen (later Chief Justice of the Supreme Court) must be of some significance.

The Dayton-Detroit groups gained control of the aviation industry just in time to benefit from the vast Congressional appropriations. Most of the contracts from Colonel Deeds's Equipment Division went to his associates in Dayton-Wright.[13] The company answered charges of favoritism by maintaining that Dayton-Wright was especially equipped for the tasks, and officials added that their profits were limited by law. Other companies might have been willing to install special equipment, however, if they had been assured a backlog of aircraft orders. As for the profit, Dayton-Wright had no cause for complaint. Contracts were let on a cost-plus basis, the amount involved being upwards of thirty million dollars. There was a fixed profit of $620 on each training plane and $875 on each battle plane. Total fixed profit amounted to about $3,750,000, exclusive of the profit on spare parts.[14]

Contracts also provided for a profit of twenty-five per cent of the saving under the " bogey." Bogey was the estimated cost of a plane. If the actual cost turned out to be $1,000 less than the bogey, Dayton-Wright collected $250 of the saving. That seemed fair enough. Trouble was that the bogey was too high. Bogey for the De Haviland battle plane was $7,000, and the amount so exceeded the actual cost that the profit on this item alone has been estimated at $2,600,000.[15] Later the bogey and fixed profit were reduced, but even then the profit on 4,000 planes was in the neighborhood of $3,500,000. All this profit came to a company whose capital was not even entirely paid in, and whose expansion costs were partly financed by the government.[16]

During this time, officers of Dayton-Wright were reaping a full harvest. Talbot Sr. and Kettering were down on the books for salaries of $35,000 a year, while twenty-nine-year-old Talbot Jr. received $30,000 a year. Considering the importance of their positions, such salaries do not seem particularly noteworthy, but these same officers received other salaries from companies also dependent upon government contracts. Talbot Sr. was receiving $60,000 from Dayton Metal Products, which was only the holding company for Dayton-Wright. From the same source Kettering received $25,000, and Talbot Jr. $18,000. Lastly, Kettering was paid $50,000 as an officer of Delco, which supplied ignition systems to Liberty motor manufacturers. Makers of such aircraft motors *had* to use Delco ignition, since it was stipulated in the contracts Colonel Deeds awarded, although this system had never before been used on an airplane engine.

Dayton-Wright had so much to do that it had to farm

out some of its contracts. Even here it made a profit. It collected a fee of one per cent of the contract price for the use of designs. Dayton-Wright maintained that it had a property right to these designs, although it would seem that such plans belonged to the government.

The huge expenditures, salaries, and fees might have gone unchallenged had the aircraft program shown tangible results. By the spring of 1918, however, the public was growing restive. Airplanes did not fill the skies, according to promise. Word of devious manipulations began to leak out. Sculptor Gutzon Borglum cried loudly for action. A Senate investigation (the Thomas Committee) dredged up buckets of alarming testimony.[17] Finally President Wilson appointed his erstwhile opponent, Charles Evans Hughes, to make a report of the aircraft situation. The Hughes report was bitter in its denunciation, but it came out too late to do much good, since it was not published until October 1918.[18]

Hughes accused Colonel Deeds of favoritism in awarding contracts to Deeds's former company, from which he was only temporarily separated. Eventually the colonel was exonerated of criminal charges, because it could not be proved that he had made any personal profit. Hughes recommended that Colonel Deeds be tried by court martial, however, since the aircraft executive was an army officer. The report was transmitted to President Wilson, who turned it over to Secretary Baker. Baker lost no time in whitewashing Colonel Deeds. Under the pressure of his work, said Baker, Colonel Deeds could not be bothered with such things as transference of stock (Colonel Deeds was shown to have held stock, which he had publicly declared he had transferred) and Baker said he was not going to have maligned a man who had sacrificed a lucrative position for war work in Washington.[19]

Near the end of the war Colonel Deeds was replaced by John D. Ryan, of Anaconda Copper, and the old board was reorganized into the Bureau of Aircraft Production. For the first time, aviation experts were called upon, and at once production increased. Glenn Martin brought out the American equivalent of the British Handley Page bomber. Grover Loening built the fastest pursuit ship in the world. Chance Vought began turning out advanced trainers. But it was too late. The war was over.

Peace was a devastating blow to an industry geared for the waste of battle. Aircraft plants were overexpanded to meet the emergency, but with peace came wholesale cancellation of contracts, a point that explains why aircraft-builders were so insistent upon fat profits during wartime. Without the forced feeding of government orders, most aircraft companies starved to death within a few months. There was nothing to cushion the shock, for with the government no longer a customer, there was no market. Surplus equipment filled the warehouses, and the few commercial operators who started up after the war were not interested in buying new planes as long as the cheap surplus stock was available. Wartime equipment was scarcely the way to lure the public to air travel, since battle planes were inefficient for civilian use, and so costly to operate that rates were of necessity sky-high.

The war made one big contribution to aviation, however, and that was as an educator. Thousands of boys had been taught to fly. Many of them hated to shed their wings when war was over, and, because war stock could be purchased cheaply, scores of them were able to turn their training into a career. No one knows how many more learned to fly after the war in the hundreds of surplus training planes, but the number was considerable. Many of these youngsters became " Gypsy Flyers."

Familiar to every wartime pilot was the Curtiss JN4D2, a temperamental but successful biplane trainer known affectionately as the Curtiss " Jenny." The " Canuck," or " Canadian Jenny," was another popular trainer. Any aviation magazine of the post-war period contains advertisements offering " Jennies " and " Canucks " for as little as' $300 complete. Slightly used motors, usually 90-h.p. Curtiss OX–5's (built in quantity for trainers) were sold for as little as $75. In some instances flying schools offered training and a new Jenny for only $500. The Gypsy Flyer purchased a cheap ship, selected a convenient cow pasture, and peddled flight to the public for whatever the traffic would bear. When business declined, or when an accident cooled the enthusiasm of his patrons, the Gypsy Flyer threw his tools into the aft compartment and moved to greener fields.

The main idea was to keep the ship in the air. The " Barnstormer," as the Gypsy Flyer became known in later years, paid the farmer five dollars for the use of a field, put aside a small amount for gas, oil, and repairs, and prayed against the inevitable crash or " washout " that would end business, at least temporarily. Makeshift fields were hard on the worn-out planes, and as the ship aged, it was repaired with home-made splints and old parts wired together. Engine overhauls were expensive, so rickety motors frequently " cut out " while in flight. Overloaded, flying from inadequate fields, the barnstorming Jenny might have been a menace to healthy progress had it not been for one thing: It was the only way that aviation was kept before the public in those lean years after the war. In all fairness, it should be said that the Gypsy Flyer was sometimes more careful than the government pilot, because he just couldn't afford to take chances that might result in expensive damage. Hundreds of civilians became aviation enthusiasts after their first trip with a Gypsy Flyer. If he did nothing else but bring on the legislation and control that were so sorely needed, the barnstormer was worth all the trouble he caused. He was the flying missionary of his day — the now forgotten promoter of municipal landing fields, beacon lights, and air services. From the Gypsy Flyer fraternity came some of our outstanding aviators, and in the acid test of barnstorming many a serious air-line pilot developed.

There was another effect of the war that was to have an influence on commercial flying. This was the air mail. Air mail is the very root of the modern air line. Most of the lines were started with the idea of carrying mail, not passengers, and the influence of the Postoffice Department continued long after the air line had been accepted by the public. The first regular air-mail service, conceived as a training method for future war pilots, was started while this country was deeply engrossed in the European conflict. It began a whole new era in American aviation.

CHAPTER

4

The Mail Flies Through

THE POSTOFFICE DEPARTMENT, since its organization in 1789, has always fostered better means of transportation. Americans were proud of the four-in-hand stagecoaches carrying the United States mails, and the old post roads were a transportation triumph in their day. The postoffice helped the early railroads and steamship lines. Sometimes it even developed its own transportation system in backward areas. But from the pony express to the modern skyliner, the mail has had an honorable place in the progress of communication and travel. The air lines of today stem directly from the early air-mail routes. Private capital could not be expected to assume the profitless risks of pioneer air transportation, and it was the Postoffice Department that charted the modern airways.

Air mail is much older than the airplane, with which it has been associated recently. Jean Pierre François Blanchard and the Bostonian Dr. John Jeffries carried messages in their first crossing of the English Channel by balloon, on January 7, 1785. One of the letters was for Benjamin Franklin, who thus became the first American to read a message sent by aerial post.[1] Similar letters were sent in this country as early as 1835, when Richard Clayton ascended from Cincinnati at a Fourth of July celebration.[2] Because these ascents were not authorized by the postal services, however, they are of no great significance to air-mail history.

More important was the flight of John Wise and John LaMountain. Wise was an exponent of the " west-wind theory." He believed that winds in the upper regions blew steadily from the west, and that if an aeronaut reached a level of about twelve thousand feet, he could travel eastward. So confident were these two Americans that in 1859 they formed the Trans-Atlantic Balloon Company. On July 1 of that year Wise and LaMountain put their theories to the test. They ascended from St. Louis with a sack of letters, and for the first time in this country " air mail " had a definite destination, as the balloonists were bound for New York. Unfortunately, they ran into a storm over Lake Ontario. The balloon was wrecked and the two aeronauts barely escaped with their lives. The mail had been carried by air 809 miles, however — a record that was to stand for more than half a century.[3]

The St. Louis flight was still unofficial, since the " mail " was not authorized by the Postoffice Department, but on August 17 of the same year Wise made another attempt in the giant balloon *Jupiter,* and this ascension has all the marks of the first official air-mail flight in history.[4] The *Jupiter* ascended from La Fayette, Indiana, but there was almost no wind that day, and after drifting for many hours, Wise dropped the mail sack near Crawfordsville, only about thirty miles from his starting-point. This earliest known " drop mail " was forwarded by train to its destination.[5]

No one has been able to prove conclusively that this was the first official air-mail flight. It was usual at that time to send letters by private means, in much the same way that we send express packages today. The internal evidence points to the Wise flight as under the sponsorship of the government postoffice, however. An advertisement in the local newspaper read:

> All persons who wish to send their letters to their friends in the East by balloon today must deliver them at the postoffice previous to 12 m., as the *Jupiter's* mail closes at that hour. The letters must be addressed " via Balloon Jupiter " added to the ordinary directions and prepaid. This mail will be conveyed by Mr. Wise to the place of landing with the balloon, when it will be placed in the nearest postoffice for distribution.[6]

The mail was received by Thomas Wood, the local postmaster, and was placed in sealed bags. Because it was received by a postoffice official, was to be marked " prepaid " *in addition to the ordinary directions,* and was to be transferred to the regular posts, it appears that this was an official undertaking. A letter envelope with a cancellation mark or notation would prove the point, but as such covers have now a market value of about ten thousand dollars and still have not appeared, there may be none in existence.

A Frenchman, H. Piquet, was the first to transport letters by airplane. On February 18, 1911 Piquet carried a sack of messages five miles at the Indian Exhibition at Allahabad. Piquet flew a Humber biplane (British Farman) and the proceeds of the flight were for the benefit of the Indian hospital. It was no more " official," however, than the balloon flights.[7] The first official airplane mail goes back to September 9 of the same year, when the Coronation Aerial Post was a feature of the celebration in honor of the new King, George V. The route was from London to Windsor, about twenty miles. Three planes continued the service for two weeks, traveling in this period about 720 miles, with some 100,000 pieces of mail.[8]

Earle L. Ovington was the first pilot in this country to carry official mail in an airplane. Ovington flew from September 23 until October 2, 1911, during an air meet on Long Island. His route was from Nassau Boulevard to

Garden City Estates, a distance of about ten miles. Letters were collected in special air-mail boxes for the first time, and mail sacks were dropped from the moving plane at Garden City, a method of delivery that was not to become common for nearly thirty years. Ovington's service was essentially a stunt, since mail was not much speeded, but it has some significance because of the part played by the Postoffice Department. For the first time the airplane was recognized as a responsible carrier, and already there was an indication that the postoffice might be the agency to sponsor early commercial aviation. For these reasons, and because Ovington was sworn in as a carrier by Postmaster General Frank Hitchcock, the Postoffice Department likes to think of 1911 as the birth of the air mail in the United States.

Actually, nothing much came of the experiment, but the Ovington flight, and others like it, stimulated interest in air mail, as the literature of the period indicates. When Rudyard Kipling allowed his fancy to play over the future of air travel, he called his story " The Night Mail," and a bibliography of aeronautics for these years contains 46 citations under the heading " Air Mail Service." [9]

A more ambitious venture was that of Calbraith P. Rodgers. In 1911 chain publisher William Randolph Hearst offered a prize of fifty thousand dollars for the first transcontinental flight completed within thirty days. Ovington was a contestant and again he asked the postoffice for permission to carry mail. He crashed before he had proceeded far, but his mail privileges were granted to some of his rivals. Rodgers was one of those who carried mail from city to city, and although he was not, strictly speaking, a mail-carrier, he was encouraged by C. P. Grandfield, the Assistant Postmaster General (who died in 1925, as his dream of transcontinental air transportation was about to come true) .

Rodgers was the first airman to cross the United States,

and his historic Wright-EX biplane is now on display in
the National Museum in Washington. Rodgers learned to
fly at the Wright school in June 1911, and he soloed after
only an hour and a half of instruction. He began his cross-
country flight from Sheepshead Bay, Long Island, on September 17, 1911. All of the other contestants eventually
dropped out of the race, and it was soon evident that
Rodgers himself could not reach the coast within the thirty-
day limit. An advertising contract with the makers of Vin
Fiz, a soda pop, provided expense money, however, and
Rodgers fought on. He crashed fifteen times and replaced
so many parts of his machine that only one strut and the
rudder survived the entire trip. As he was approaching
Pasadena on the forty-ninth day, Rodgers suffered his worst
crack-up and was in a hospital for a month, although he
was almost within sight of his goal. Finally, on December
10, 1911, he touched the Pacific Ocean with his wheels at
Long Beach. It had taken him 84 days to cross the country.
He had flown 4,321 miles, averaging less than 52 miles a
day. His longest flight had been only 265 miles. He was
badly injured in his many crashes. But he had proved that
the country could be crossed by air. Four months later this
gallant airman was killed in a crash at Long Beach.[10]

Mail flights were common after 1911 and began to receive some serious consideration by business men. The
report of the Second Assistant Postmaster General for 1912
mentions thirty-one orders issued in the period between
July 1, 1911 and June 30, 1912, permitting air-mail flights
in sixteen states.[11] The first mention of possible air-mail
service in the United States was on June 14, 1910, when
Representative Morris Sheppard of Texas introduced a bill
(HR 26833) "for an investigation to determine the practicability and cost of an aeroplane or airship mail route."
The bill was referred to the Committee on Post Offices and
Post Roads, but no action was taken.[12] The subject came
up again in 1912 when, in the debates over the Postoffice

Department appropriations, Representative Sharp of Ohio offered an amendment providing fifty thousand dollars for experimenting with air mail. Sharp predicted regular air-mail service within two years. That the Congressman was a little ahead of his time is revealed by the remark of a colleague, who cried out during the debate: " The Postoffice Department has been up in the air long enough, and now let us get down to terra firma for once." [13] The amendment was defeated, but the spark had been struck. When Woodrow Wilson took office as President, Sharp again introduced a bill authorizing air-mail contracts, and in his 1913 report Postmaster General A. S. Burleson also recommended such development.[14] This time the bill received favorable consideration, although it was eventually submerged by other business.

The next postoffice appropriation bill was actually amended so that air mail could be carried, and on February 12, 1916, bids on eight proposed routes were advertised.[15] Seven of the routes were in Alaska and the eighth was between New Bedford and Nantucket. Legislators and postoffice officials were under the impression that the airplane was to serve where other means of transportation were impossible or difficult. Fortunately for the safety of aviation, manufacturers were so busy with war orders that only one bid was submitted — on the line between Seward and Iditarod. The service was to cost $49,500 a year, which was a saving of $34,558 over the previous service by dog team. No bond was posted on the bid, however, and it was not accepted.[16]

Later in 1916 a group of Chicago business boomers proposed an overnight passenger service between New York and Chicago. The company hoped to be aided by postal appropriations, according to a pattern later applied to the air lines. The new company may or may not have had serious intentions, but late in the year officers proposed a nonstop flight between the two cities as a publicity stunt. The pilot of the plane was to be Victor " Swede " Carlstrom, a Curtiss-trained flyer of twenty-six, who had set a record in 1915 by flying from New York to Toronto. Although the New York *Times* and Chicago *Evening Post* in 1910 had offered twenty-five thousand dollars for the first non-stop flight between their respective cities, dangerous terrain and the short cruising range of the pre-war ships counteracted the financial stimulus.

The Carlstrom machine was an oversize Curtiss R (called an R–7) with a 200-h.p. Curtiss engine. It represented a considerable advance over the majority of planes in this country. Here was a craft to challenge the " hell stretch " of the Alleghenies. Carlstrom flew out of Chicago on November 2, 1916. The flight was to have been non-stop, but the big plane was forced down at Erie by a leaking oil line. Even so, this flight of 452 miles was a record. Carlstrom spent the night at Hammondsport. Next day he streaked into New York before a tail wind at 130 miles an hour and placed his foreign mail pouches aboard the German submarine *Deutschland*. He had failed to fly the route non-stop, but had indicated the speed and possibility of air service between the two cities.[17] Two weeks later Ruth Law eclipsed the feat by flying non-stop over the same route to Hornell, New York, which was 138 miles better than Carlstrom's flight. The stunt was remarkable not only because it was made by one of the few women flyers of that day, but also because Miss Law's ship was an antiquated Curtiss pusher, far inferior to the Carlstrom machine.

The Postoffice Department was given $100,000 for airmail experiments in its 1917–18 budget, and the National Advisory Committee for Aeronautics now stepped forward to suggest that Congress permit the postoffice to fly mail over less difficult routes than those specified in the first contracts. The NACA was an independent establishment of the government, authorized by an act in 1915. It was composed of three representatives from the War Department; three from the Navy Department, Weather Bureau, Bureau of Standards, and additional civilians experienced in aeronautics. The NACA merited respect, and when it recommended that the air-mail service be given a chance to obtain operating experience on practicable routes, those in authority listened. By now the war was taking all available planes and the air-mail plan was pigeonholed. Major General George O. Squier, in charge of army aviation, and a member of the NACA, was sympathetic, however, and when the United States entered the conflict he suggested that flying the mail might be negotiated by considering it as military training for future army pilots. At first his suggestion was ignored and the postoffice went ahead with its own plans. The outlook seemed hopeless until the War Department, apparently heeding General Squier, late in 1917 agreed to furnish motors if the postoffice could get the planes.

On February 11, 1918 the Postoffice Department advertised for five mail planes, and bids were opened ten days later. Deliveries were held up for three months because of war pressure, and the Postoffice Department, eager to start flying at once, accepted a plan of Colonel Deeds, who was then in charge of the Equipment Division of the Aircraft Production Board. Colonel Deeds saw a way to help both the War and Postoffice Departments. He recommended that the army carry mail in order to gain flying experience. Secretary of War Newton D. Baker was not enthusiastic over the proposal, but the Postoffice Department made it clear that if the army did not fly the mail, some other way would be found. The NACA also backed the proposal, and Secretary Baker finally agreed. Major Reuben H. Fleet, later to head the great Consolidated Aircraft Corporation, was put in command of the officers assigned to fly the air mail, and a bill was rushed through Congress authorizing air-mail postage up to twenty-four cents a half ounce.

At this rate, revenues were expected to reach $3,800 a

trip, which implied carrying about 500 pounds of mail in
each plane. This, as Warner remarks with superb under-
statement, " proved to have been a little over-sanguine." [18]
Actually each pilot might almost have carried the mail load
in his helmet, after the first day.[19] The faulty estimate was
no reflection upon the Postoffice Department, since it had
made a careful survey to determine the amount of potential mail traffic. Three weeks before the first mail flights,
the department queried the postmasters of Washington,
Philadelphia, and New York for an estimate of what mail
loads might be expected from those cities. The reports of
local postal officials were glowingly optimistic. Every business house wished to go on record as favoring this new,
romantic, speedy means of transportation, but when it
came to putting twenty-four cents postage on air-mail letters, enthusiasm dwindled. The Postoffice Department, on
the other hand, was misleading, probably without intention. It promised that a letter mailed in Washington in the
morning would be delivered that afternoon in New York
— an efficiency that twenty years later had not been realized. The department also stated that air mail sent from
New York via Washington would save eight hours on the
trip to Pittsburgh, St. Louis, and the West, although it is
obvious that a letter going from New York to Pittsburgh
would find itself far off the road if it were detoured by way
of Washington.[20]

Looking back on the historic moment when the first air-
mail service began in 1918, it is difficult to imagine a great
institution starting under more unfavorable circumstances.
The purpose was not so much the transportation of mail
as it was the training of pilots, and the personnel was therefore inexperienced for the hazardous task. Equipment was
only what the army could spare. Airports were inadequate;
the Washington terminus being the cramped polo field between the Tidal Basin and the Potomac River. Yet with all
its weaknesses, the system was amazingly successful. It was

75 per cent efficient the first fortnight and was soon completing 93 per cent of its schedules.

The New York-Philadelphia-Washington route was selected for the first test. Flying was relatively safe and easy between these points, and the heavy mail traffic was expected to be a yardstick for future operations. Service was to start not later than April 1918, but there were so many difficulties in getting planes, fields, and pilots that the inauguration was delayed nearly six weeks. On the afternoon of May 13, mail flyers were notified that their planes had arrived in crates and that the ships would be assembled the following day. On the 14th, two of the machines were set up and flown to Philadelphia and Washington to be in readiness, and by the 15th, mail planes were prepared to leave simultaneously from New York, Washington, and Philadelphia.

Wartime Washington was too busy to waste time on trivialities in 1918, but a sizable crowd gathered on May 15 to witness the start of regular air-mail service. President Wilson was present, along with members of his Cabinet and other dignitaries, including Japanese Postmaster K. Kambara and Captain Benjamin Lipsner, soon to become chief of the air-mail service. There was a little ceremony as Lieutenant George Boyle supervised the stowing of his cargo — four sacks of mail and a special letter from the President to be auctioned for the benefit of the Red Cross by Mayor Hylan of New York. The impressiveness of the occasion was marred somewhat when the motor failed to start. Before patience was quite exhausted, someone discovered that the gasoline tanks were empty, and after another delay for fueling, there were a few more farewell gestures. Lieutenant Boyle climbed into the cockpit again, taxied into the wind, waved, and pushed forward on the throttle. Gracefully and effortlessly the plane lifted from the turf. Air mail was off on its glorious adventure.

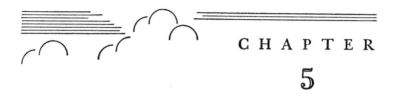

CHAPTER

5

The Night Riders

IN spite of a few minor mishaps, the service was successful from the start. Captain Torrey Webb left the old Belmont track on Long Island with the New York mail and arrived safely an hour later at Bustleton Field, which served Philadelphia as an airport. Lieutenant James C. Edgerton was waiting to pick up the relay, and three hours and twenty minutes after leaving New York, the mail sacks were in the custody of the Washington postmaster.

The northbound mail did not fare so well. Lieutenant Boyle had barely gained altitude before he lost his bearings and was forced to land on a farm near Waldorf, Maryland, scarcely twenty-five miles from his starting-point. On the second day the pilot out of Philadelphia lost his way and tangled with a paddock of horses when he landed at Bridgeton, New Jersey.[1] The mail was returned to Philadelphia, but the second plane was forced back by motor trouble. Lieutenant Edgerton saved the day. Returning from Washington with the northbound mail, he volunteered to carry the accumulated sacks on to New York. As chief pilot of the new service, he felt the responsibility, but it was already after sundown, and he realized the risk he was taking as he flew off into the gloom. A telephone call warned attendants at Belmont Field to be ready. The resourceful field manager commandeered every available automobile in the vicinity, and the pilot made a safe landing by the light of their headlamps.

Mail out of Washington was delayed again on the third day when the pilot followed instructions too closely. Unfamiliar with the route to Philadelphia, he was told to keep Chesapeake Bay on his right, and he followed directions so carefully that after reaching the northern end of the bay, he continued right on around to Cape Charles, where he landed " on making the dual discovery that he was out of fuel and that water was now not only on his right, but on his left and in front as well, and that only a narrow strip of land lay behind him." [2]

Despite these mishaps, the mail soon went through with railroad regularity. Lieutenant Edgerton turned in a perfect score of twenty completed trips at the end of the first month.[3] Edgerton, later an executive in the Civil Aeronautics Bureau, points out that the early mistakes were caused more by inexperience than by stupidity. Many a student flyer has known the strange sensation of being lost within sight of his home field, and many of these early mail pilots were little more than students.[4] As the young pilots gained experience, service improved. By midsummer, air mail was well established, although revenue still amounted to less than fifty dollars a trip.

But the Postoffice Department objected to using the service for training army fledglings. There was continual pressure to put air-mail service on its own merits. As long as war raged, there was apparently no hope of reorganizing the air mail, for in the summer of 1918 the Allies were hard pressed. The big German push of March had forced the defenders almost to the Channel ports. Every available plane and pilot was needed at the front. American squadrons girded for the battles that were to culminate in Châ-

teau-Thierry and the Meuse-Argonne. In the midst of all
this turmoil the Postoffice Department won the right to
have its own service, and, what is more, it wheedled the
equipment from a harassed procurement division. Strong
popular support undoubtedly helped the postoffice in effecting the reorganization, but it must have taken considerable pressure to pry loose the army. Captain Benjamin
B. Lipsner gave up his commission to take charge of the
new service and he began at once to improve equipment
and personnel. From now on, the postoffice would run its
own show.

Captain Lipsner received notice of his postal appointment on July 15, 1918. At the end of a month he had collected seventeen planes, some of which, like the Standard
JR1B's, were especially adaptable for mail service. There
were now nearly as many ships on the mail route as Pershing had commanded in the entire Mexican campaign.
Most of the pilots were picked from instructors at army
bases, and all of them had from 500 to 1,000 hours of flying experience. When the Postoffice Department took over
the operation of the mail routes on August 12, 1918, sea-
soned pilots were ready to man the ships.

During the first ninety days after the change of air-mail
administration, every trip went through on schedule — a
feat that the operators could scarcely duplicate twenty
years later.[5] So encouraged were the sponsors by the success of the venture that they determined to extend the service. Postmaster General Burleson told a Congressional
committee that he was ready at once to build a network of
air lines.[6] He envisioned a trunk route extending from New
York to San Francisco, with feeders from Cincinnati, Atlanta, and New Orleans. Two foreign routes out of Key
West — one to South America, and the other to Panama
via the West Indies — completed the plan. It was a decade
before such a grandiose scheme materialized, but America's

air empire was in the process of incubation as far back as 1918.

Meanwhile, the 218-mile run between Washington and New York was too short for a real test of air mail, since it provided few advantages over the railroad. For some time the department had considered a plan to start regular service between New York and Chicago. Serving the country's two largest metropolitan areas, and with many important trade centers along the way, the proposed route presented an irresistible challenge. In its haste to justify air mail, the Postoffice Department made the mistake of starting the route between Chicago and New York during the worst time of year. Even under ideal conditions the dreaded "hell stretch" over the Allegheny Mountains has taken its toll through the years, yet the postoffice was willing to inaugurate service in open ships over an uncharted, unlighted airway in the middle of winter.

The vision and boldness of these early air-mail officials are incredible. Postmaster General Burleson was a Texan, and Texans in the Postoffice Department have had an important place in the development of air commerce. Mr. Burleson had fought for air-mail appropriations since the day of his appointment. But the real force behind the air-mail service was Otto Praeger, the Second Assistant Postmaster General. Every postoffice administration hopes to be remembered for the progress it has fostered in communication, but Praeger was twenty years ahead of his time. In a day of open-cockpit planes, he dreamed of transoceanic airways and multi-engined ships; and a regular air-mail service between Chicago and New York seemed to Otto Praeger only a faltering step toward the goal he had set. " But here is the big thing," he told Congressmen:

In the spring we are going to fly at night, leaving Chicago about 9:30 or 9:40 p.m. with the afternoon accumulation of mail, and you will get all of your transactions on the stock exchange and everything will go out that night and be in New York in the morning in time for the first or second delivery. It replaces your night letter business on the wires.[7]

Night service over the " hell stretch " before there was a single beacon along the way — before the route had ever been flown regularly in daylight — preposterous!

But the obstacles did not deter the postal officials of 1918. The year before, when air mail was still a matter of debate, Postmaster General Burleson made a bargain with Mr. Praeger. Against the windows of the dingy old Postoffice Building beat a blinding snowstorm. The Postmaster General took Mr. Praeger by the arm and led him to the casement. Looking out at the storm, Mr. Burleson said:

If it can be shown that a dependable service can be maintained all the year round, I will authorize an air mail service . . . and remember, it must function dependably, even on a day like this.[8]

That may explain why Mr. Praeger defied hell and high water to extend the service. He had to prove its worth and dependability in order to get appropriations upon which the very life of the air mail depended.

The postoffice tried to blaze the Chicago and New York air trail not only during the worst season of the year, but also on one of the worst days of that season. On December 12, 1918, pilots set out from both ends of the proposed route, but every plane was forced down by the weather. The Postoffice Department, with its battle-cry: " The Mail Must Go Through," tried again on January 2, 1919. Again the machines were dashed to the ground. Pilots smoldered with a resentment that was soon to flare into the first airmen's strike. Once more too much was demanded of the airplane. Flimsy, open-cockpit ships were expected not only to compete with railroads, but even to surpass the older service. As one aeronautical expert put it:

The greatest service which the Postoffice Department expects from the air mail service in winter time will be keeping open the lines of written communication during those distressing periods following blizzards when the railroads are frozen up or are snowed in for days.[9]

Failure of these winter flights did not kill the enthusiasm of the officials. From time to time they made announcements of air-mail service over the mountains, but the Alleghenies were the same barrier to the airman that they had been to the pioneer wagon-driver, and it was spring before the frustrated postal authorities had much to show for their efforts. Not until May 15, 1919, the first anniversary of regular air mail, did planes fly the new route, and then a much chastened department was content to fly only over the Chicago-Cleveland section, where hazards were at a minimum. Not until the long days of summer did pilots fly the " Graveyard Run " over the mountains. By that time there were two emergency fields at Lehighton and Bellefont, Pennsylvania. On July 1, 1919, mail planes started regular service between America's two largest cities.

The press greeted the new service with loud approval, if we may judge by numerous editorials of the time, but the response of the public was disappointing. It cost twenty-four cents to send a letter by air mail. Reduction of the rate to sixteen cents did little to increase mail traffic. Then, from July 18, 1919 until July 1, 1924, the special air-mail rate was abandoned altogether until experts could determine the proper ratio of revenue and postage. During this period, planes were loaded with as much first-class mail as they could carry, a use of the mail plane that continued to have its proponents for years.

Not until air mail reached the west coast could its sponsors hope to interest the business man. There was not much advantage over the railroad in sending air mail short distances, but a transcontinental schedule might save considerable time. The Postoffice Department realized this only too well, and as fast as it could obtain appropriations it expanded westward. As before, the army blazed the trail. In October 1919 the Army Air Service sent a group of sixty-four daring pilots across the country and back, in competition. The press called it a race, although it was more of a military maneuver, and the winner was Lieutenant Belvin W. Maynard. His elapsed time was nine days, four hours, and twenty-five minutes for the round trip, which was no improvement over fast railroad schedules. Considering the type of equipment, unknown terrain, and utter lack of flying fields, however, the army flight was a creditable experiment.

The experiences of the army flyers demonstrated that there could be no westward expansion until there were adequate fields. In the summer of 1920, postal officials junketed all over the country demanding airports of city officials, and in some cases implying that the federal government might repay the municipality later. As far as can be determined, no city ever received a penny from the government for its airport. Queried about this some years later, Colonel Paul Henderson, who became Second Assistant Postmaster General, explained:

Well, our experience with that [repayment to the cities] has been rather sad. When the air mail service was first established, they were naturally anxious to get it going as quick as possible . . . and agents of the Postoffice Department went to the cities — I might use Salt Lake as an example. They urged the commercial clubs to provide a field and to provide hangars and that sort of thing. Without stating directly, they sort of half promised to pay the money back, don't you know, and in the case of Salt Lake they used Ogden as counterbait, you know, to state, "If you do not provide us with a field soon, we will go to Ogden; they are ready and they will be glad to do it," and we created a competition in that sort of thing. The result has been that it created a very bad taste in the mouths of those who put up the expense.[10]

On May 15, 1920, the first anniversary of regular service between Cleveland and Chicago and the second birthday of air mail, the postoffice extended the main line to Omaha. Already the mail time across the country was shortened by a day and a half. All summer long, while workmen graded intermediate fields, air pilots waited for word that would send them across the full breadth of the United States. On September 8, 1920 the postoffice began regular transcontinental service between San Francisco and New York. It should have been a day of triumph for Mr. Praeger, but unfortunately all was not well with transcontinental air mail.

In the first place, there was little saving in time, since the planes flew only by day. Mail was transferred to the railroad at night and the delay counteracted most of the advantages of air transportation. Moreover, the Wilson administration was on the way out, and all that it had stood for was about to be repudiated. President Harding had been elected on his slogan: " Back to Normalcy," and there was a strong tendency to let well enough alone. Air mail had been born and reared in Wilson's time, and there was every indication that the new Congress would reduce air-mail appropriations to the strangulation-point. The cost of the service and the limited use to which it was put seemed hardly to justify the expense. True, the service had demonstrated that the airplane, under wise and courageous management, could pile up an impressive record of schedule efficiency, but air mail had yet to prove its value to the nation and to the business man. In the last days of the Wilson administration air-mail officials attempted a desperate and daring experiment for the sake of their beloved service. They decided to inaugurate night flying over the transcontinental route.

The audacity of the order can scarcely be appreciated today. There were at that time no radio beams to guide the lonely pilot. There were no weather stations. All the navigation aids we accept so casually today were unknown in 1920. Radio communication, blind-flying instruments, even that irreducible minimum the lighted airway, were still far in the future. There weren't even landing fields in case the obsolete wartime planes failed in the darkness. To top it all, the department was initiating the night service during the worst season of the year, as usual. The test was to be made just before Wilson stepped out of office on March 4, 1921. Upon the success of night air mail depended future appropriations, perhaps even the continuance of the air-mail program.

The night air mail went through on Washington's Birthday. Four pilots started in the morning, two from New York and two from San Francisco. One of the Eastern pilots was downed before he had gone far from his home field; the other westbound plane was grounded by snow at Chicago. Captain Lewis, in the eastbound plane out of San Francisco, crashed to his death in Nevada. As darkness settled, the weather thickened. Apparently the test of transcontinental night mail was to be a tragic failure.

One ship was still in the air, however. At 4.29 a.m. Pilot Nutter had left the Golden Gate behind him in the clammy darkness. He headed eastward and climbed rapidly to twelve thousand feet in order to clear the jagged Sierras.[11] Day was breaking when Pilot Eaton took over the controls at Reno. Just before noon Pilot Murray picked up the relay, alighted at Rawlins for gas and oil, and found the Cheyenne field at 4.57 p.m. — just twelve hours after the mail had started east. Night began to blot out familiar landmarks as Frank Yeager roared toward North Platte. The lights of the little Nebraska city looked very good to Pilot Yeager as he taxied up to the apron at 7.48 p.m. Waiting on the line was Jack Knight, who was to make aviation history that wintry night in 1921.

Jack Knight in 1941 was still flying (for United Air Lines) after one of the longest flying careers of any man in the world. In all his experience, however, Pilot Knight never flew with heavier responsibilities than he did on that trip when the night mail went through back in February 1921. For in the last analysis Jack Knight was the hero of that episode, although the other airmen deserve their share of the glory. Knight waited almost three hours at North Platte while mechanics repaired a broken tail skid. It was 10.44 when No. 172, the big De Haviland 4, lifted heavily from the North Platte field. At two thousand feet the river was visible through holes in the clouds, but the surrounding countryside was a sea of darkness relieved only by the lights of occasional hamlets. At Lexington, Kearney, and Central City there were welcome beacons — bonfires lit by public-spirited citizens somehow stirred by the thought of that unseen ship buffeting the winds above them. It was 276 miles by air from North Platte to Omaha, and Knight was hungry and tired as he saw the city lights looming far ahead. It made him feel better to know that " Mother " Andrew Bahm would have a cup of steaming coffee waiting in the all-night beanery just across from the hangar. He looked at his watch. It was 1.15. Knight shivered. It was getting colder. He " jazzed " the motor, just to let them all know that he was glad to be in Omaha.

Bill Votaw, field manager at Omaha, let the pilot thaw out a minute or two before breaking the news. All the ships were down. The other eastbound flight was a washout in Nevada. The ship which was to have returned east with the Omaha mail was grounded at Chicago.

" Well, then," Knight wanted to know, " who's going to take her out of here? "

Votaw looked appealingly at Knight.

" I see," said the flyer.

Knight's father was ill in Michigan and Knight was impatient to get to him. But the Omaha-Chicago route was across 435 miles of unfamiliar territory. Knight had already flown his leg of 276 miles, and the weather was getting nasty. The meager weather reports promised more snow. It was no night to be flitting around in the clouds. But if Bill Votaw gave the word, Jack Knight was ready to go ahead.

They let him warm up a little longer while his plane was being serviced. Then he was off into the darkness again, "crabbing" a twenty-five-mile north wind that made navigation difficult, and with only a Rand-McNally automobile guide for a chart.[12] Near Des Moines there was fog and snow. With that quartering wind, he would be lucky to find the city. But the clouds opened up, and there, shining through the murk was the monstrous rococo dome of the Iowa Capitol. Knight had hit Des Moines "right on the nose" by dead reckoning. There was too much snow to risk a landing, and Knight headed on to Iowa City, following the railroad track. The faithful old Liberty 12 pounded away reassuringly, but there was fuel for only ten minutes' more flight when at last Iowa City appeared as a dull glow in the snow ahead. Knight was flying as low as possible to keep the few landmarks in view, but now he had to climb a little for safety. And where was the airport? Why weren't the lights guiding him in? He circled the city. Didn't they know he was almost out of gas? Had they all gone to bed?

The ground crew had done just that. The airport staff knew that the westbound flight had been grounded at Chicago and had thought that the eastbound trip must *ipso facto* be canceled. Only a night watchman remained at the field. He lit a red flare as he heard the plane circling haphazardly, and Knight landed just as his fuel tank ran dry. In the dark and sleet he refueled with the help of the watchman. Then he was on his way again. The snow gave way to a Mississippi Valley fog. The plane churned past cities too dark at this hour to serve as landmarks, and dawn was a heartening sight to the numbed pilot. At 8.30 he sighted Chicago and landed at Maywood Field ten minutes later.

Pilot Webster whisked the mail into Cleveland at 104 miles an hour and Ernest Allison landed at Hazelhurst Field, Long Island, just thirty-three hours and twenty minutes after the mail had left San Francisco. The time seems slow now, but it was a new record for transcontinental mail carriage. Even the skeptical were impressed by the feat. On April 12, President Harding recommended air mail and federal regulation of aviation. Congress had a change of heart and was willing to grant more money. Regular day and night service did not begin until the completion of the lighted airway in 1925, but the first night mail showed the feasibility of the service and paved the way for the beacons that were to make night flying routine. In the words of Mr. Praeger, the first night flight was " the most momentous step in the development of civil aviation." [13]

"Neither Rain, Nor Snow, Nor Gloom of Night..."

Such rapid expansion of the air-mail system was certain to produce unfortunate results, and 1921, with all its achievements, was a year of disastrous flying. During the fourth quarter of 1919, mail pilots flew 3,047 miles for each forced landing. During the same period of 1920 there was a forced landing every 1,373 miles.[1] Only two pilots crashed to their deaths in 1919, and there were only five fatalities in 1920, which, considering the extended routes and increased schedules, was not a heavy toll. But in 1921 there were twelve fatal accidents, and carrying the air mail became one of the most hazardous occupations. On the basis of the 1921 figures, a mail flyer could not expect to live more than four years. Of the forty mail pilots first engaged by the Postoffice Department, thirty-one lost their lives during the period of government operation.[2]

Pilots grumbled over the inadequate equipment. There were ninety-eight mail planes in service at the end of 1921, but only forty were of a standardized type. The department depended primarily upon the De Haviland (DH–4), an American adaptation of a 1917 British reconnaissance plane. " Flaming Coffins " the pilots called them, because the fuel tank between engine and cockpit frequently exploded in crash landings. Veteran pilots hated the original DH's. Actually, the De Haviland (the British spelling is "De Havilland," after the designer, Geoffrey De Havilland) was a fair enough ship for its day, but it was inefficient for commercial use. Other charges against the DH were that it was too heavy to climb out of small fields; that visibility was poor; that the landing gear was too weak to prevent "ground loops" on rough runways; that the ships landed at excessive speed and had "the gliding angle of a brick"; and that there were insufficient instruments for cross-country flying.

Postal authorities knew all this, but air-mail appropriations were so small that there was no money for equipment.[3] As long as the army provided such planes at cost, the post-office had to be content with what it could get. The worst of it was that there seemed to be no limit to the surplus equipment. When the United States entered the war, a group of experts (the Bolling Commission) recommended that American factories concentrate on producing the De Haviland battle plane, which was the only ship of stabilized design capable of taking the mass-produced Liberty motor. The result was that aircraft companies began manufacturing the De Haviland in enormous quantities, and the Post-office Department became the unwilling heir to the surplus stock. Not until 1924 did the department even consider more efficient designs for standard use, and not until after 1925 did the DH disappear from the mail routes.[4] Ten years after the war no airport was complete without two or three DH-4's tethered in the hangar, ready, like sturdy old plow-horses, to do any kind of disagreeable work, such as crop-dusting, or sky advertising.

The Postoffice Department rebuilt these De Havilands for mail service. Planes were uncrated in the Chicago shops of the department and engineers made more than six hundred structural changes in the design.[5] It cost the government about two thousand dollars to rebuild a DH for mail service. In the long run it would have been cheaper to buy more efficient ships than to struggle along with free but obsolete equipment.

There were other faults. Living up to Herodotus' accolade of the postal service, that " neither rain, nor snow, nor heat, nor gloom of night stays these couriers from the swift completion of their appointed rounds," [6] the postoffice sometimes ignored the human element and insisted upon a standard of air-mail operation that pilots considered suicidal. Flyers saw no reason to risk their lives in threatening weather " for the sake of a two-cent stamp," and as early as 1919 occurred the first air-line strike. Two pilots who refused to take off one foggy night were discharged. Both airmen were respected for their courage and skill, and when the department officials declined to reinstate the rebels, pilots organized and agreed to walk out. The strike was called for July 25, 1919. Pilots demanded the right to decide when conditions warranted cancellation of schedules. Postal officials, on the other hand, insisted that traditions of the service were based on iron-bound discipline. On July 27, spokesmen of both sides met and signed a compromise. The discharged pilots were to be reinstated. (One of them, E. Hamilton Lee, was still flying the mail in 1941.) Both sides relinquished the right to decide on cancellations and agreed to abide by the decisions of airport managers.[7]

It was not a perfect settlement, and service continued to deteriorate. In the closing days of the administration morale reached low ebb. Only about half the schedules were completed between Chicago and New York. The maintenance shop at the western terminus was overrun with incompetents and political lame ducks. Mechanics serviced the ships haphazardly, and the unlighted airway was marked with the twisted wrecks of planes. Even so, the air mail was a great achievement — an institution that appealed to the pride of every American.

The administration changed March 4, 1921, and Colonel E. H. Shaughnessy succeeded Otto Praeger as chief executive of the air-mail section. The ruthless driving of Mr. Praeger was largely responsible for making the United States air-mail service the envy of other nations, in spite of its defects, but unrest was becoming serious. Colonel Shaughnessy at once shut down the service for three days while he made a survey of conditions. He determined to raise the *esprit de corps* of the discouraged pilots by granting them additional privileges. They were given quasi-ownership of their planes, and it was remarkable how this unimportant item improved morale. Some of the pilots painted appropriate designs on their ships, such as Jiggs and Maggie, homeward-bound. Flyers began to have the same feeling for their planes that the cowboy might have for his horse. Colonel Shaughnessy issued no official orders to the effect, but he spread the word that pilots were to be consulted when weather threatened schedules. He reduced some of the feeder lines, such as the routes from Chicago to Minneapolis and to St. Louis, thereby saving $675,000, which could be put to better use.[8]

The air-mail service began to recuperate. Although only 3.4 per cent more miles were flown in 1923 than in 1922, the loads were 38.5 per cent heavier. Seventeen radio stations aided the pilot in navigating his course. Forced landings because of motor failure dropped from 810 in 1921 to 281 in 1922,[9] and the fatality record, which was 3.66 per million miles in 1921, dropped to 0.57 in 1922 — a figure not materially improved upon for more than ten years.[10] One reason for the better safety record was that Colonel Shaughnessy canceled night-flying operations. Insufficient appropriations no doubt made this move advisable, but after Colonel Shaughnessy was killed in the spring of 1922, when the Washington Knickerbocker Theater collapsed under heavy snow, there was again a change of policy.

The new chief of the air mail was Colonel Paul Henderson, a Chicago contractor and son-in-law of Representative Martin B. Madden. Colonel Henderson got into the Postoffice Department after serving as ordnance officer in the AEF. He was one of those who had convinced civic leaders that an airport-building program was important. It was Colonel Henderson who argued Cleveland officials into providing the first improved municipal airport for the use of the air mail.[11] From 1922 on, Colonel Henderson was to be an important figure in the story of American air transportation. And because he was convinced that air mail could never amount to much until it began a round-the-clock program of regular schedules, he has been called the father of the night mail service. Night mail was a kind of rebirth of the service. Mr. Praeger had tried it. Colonel Shaughnessy had considered it. Colonel Henderson accomplished it.

The air beacons which march single-file across mountain and desert don't mean much to the air-line pilot today, though the small-plane flyer still depends on them, but no step in the history of the service has been more significant than the completion of the lighted airways. According to E. P. Warner, an aviation authority, much of the credit goes to the army.[12] In 1921 Lieutenant Harold R. Harris, later an important air-line executive, and Lieutenant Donald L. Bruner built the first lighted airway across the eighty-mile stretch between Columbus and the army's experimental field at Dayton. For several months the military flyers tested the possibilities of night flying, and presumably air mail benefited by the experience. Colonel Henderson, who was in charge of air mail at this time, denies that the army had anything to do with the lighted airways. He maintains that the postoffice developed its own system, with the help of the General Electric and American Gas Accumulator companies.[13] At any rate, the Postoffice

Department did everything it could to push through its ambitious program.

The system eventually selected provided for emergency landing fields every twenty-five miles, connected by revolving searchlights that turned on automatically at night. These electric or acetylene beacons were spaced every ten miles, and were fitted with auxiliary blinker lights which told the pilot by the number of times they flashed how many miles he was from the next field.

The risks of emergency landings were reduced by providing ground obstructions with red lights and by fitting the planes themselves for night flying. Wartime flyers used to guide themselves in at night by dropping Holt flares, which were magnesium torches parachuted from the circling plane. These flares gave intense illumination, but sometimes the glare blinded the pilot. Field searchlights were helpful, but it was impossible to put searchlights at every cow-pasture emergency field, and they were far from perfect, anyway. In Europe, where there had been very little need for commercial night flight, there was some dependence upon the Hoenig Circles. Hoenig Circles were concentric rings of neon lights that appeared like this (⌀) when the pilot was off his course; like this (◎) when he was coming in at the proper angle; and like this (o) when it was time to flatten for the actual landing.[14] Air-mail engineers, however, found that landing lights on the wing tips were far more effective than any sort of ground lights. Wing-tip lights did not reflect from the whirling propeller and they could be turned on and off as needed. All of these developments played a part in the success of the night air mail.

The lighted airway was first tested on August 21, 1923. Four nights of uninterrupted flying gave every evidence that night mail was feasible, but Colonel Henderson withheld regular service until he could perfect all the details. Dur-

ing the next year the lighted airway crawled westward,
until by the summer of 1924 the beacons reached to Rock
Springs, Wyoming. On July 1, 1924, mail pilots began
regular night mail flights across the country, timing their
schedules so as to reach the end of the lighted airway by day-
break. There were now 1,886 miles of airway, constructed
at a cost of only half a million dollars.[15]

Every air-mail trip was an adventure in the days when
the lighted airway was still a luxury. The pilot sat in a wartime ship, cut off from earth as definitely as though he lived
on Mars. A few of the planes carried radio, but as late as
1926, pilots on feeder routes were without communication.
What it was like to fly under such conditions is described
by one of the country's greatest air heroes. Before fame
touched him, Charles Augustus Lindbergh was a mail pilot.
In the early days he was free of the publicity phobia that
later caused him so much trouble. In fact, Lindbergh at
one time was rather fond of publicity. Newspaper inter-
viewers found him agreeable and co-operative. Occasionally he even wrote up his own adventures for the aviation
magazines. The following account, which he wrote in his
early mail days, describes with laconic vividness conditions
of that era.

" Slim " Lindbergh took off with the mail from Lambert-
St. Louis Field one gray November day, and after stopping
briefly at Springfield, Illinois, he headed for Peoria. Night
was falling, and the conditions the flyer met from then on
were typical of countless trips during this period.

" The ceiling at Springfield was about 500 feet," wrote
Lindbergh, " and the weather report from Peoria, which
was telephoned to St. Louis earlier in the afternoon, gave
the flying conditions as entirely passable.

" I encountered darkness about 25 miles north of Springfield. The ceiling had lowered to around 500 feet and a
light snow was falling. At South Pekin, the forward visibility of ground lights from 150-foot altitude was less than

one-half mile, and over Pekin the town lights were indistinct from 200 feet above. After passing Pekin, I flew at an altimeter reading of 600 feet for about five minutes, when the lightness of the haze below indicated that I was over Peoria. Twice I could see lights on the ground and descended to less than 200 feet before they disappeared from view. I tried to bank around one group of lights, but was unable to turn quickly enough to keep them in sight.

" After circling in the vicinity of Peoria for 30 minutes, I decided to try to find better weather conditions by flying northeast towards Chicago. I had ferried a ship from Chicago to St. Louis in the early afternoon, and at that time the ceiling and visibility were much better near Chicago than elsewhere along the route.

" Enough gasoline for about one hour and ten minutes' flying remained in the main tank and twenty minutes in the reserve. This was hardly enough to return to St. Louis even had I been able to navigate directly to the field by dead reckoning and flying blind the greater portion of the way. The only lights along our route at present are on the field at Peoria, consequently, unless I could pick up a beacon on the transcontinental route, my only alternative would be to drop the parachute flare and land by its light, together with what little assistance the wing lights would be in the snow and rain. The territory towards Chicago was much more favorable for a night landing than that around St. Louis.

" I flew northeast at about 2,000 feet for 30 minutes, then dropped down to 600 feet. There were numerous breaks in the clouds this time, and occasionally ground lights could be seen from over 500 feet. I passed over the lights of a small town and a few minutes later came to a fairly clear place in the clouds. I pulled up to about 600 feet, released the parachute flare, whipped the ship around to get into the wind and under the flare, which lit at once, but, instead of floating down slowly, dropped like a rock,

For an instant I saw the ground, then total darkness. My ship was in a steep bank, and for a few seconds after being blinded by the intense light I had trouble righting it. I then tried to find the ground with the wing lights, but their glare was worse than useless in the haze.

" When about ten minutes' gas remained in the pressure tank and still I could not see the faintest outline of any object on the ground, I decided to leave the ship rather than to attempt to land blindly. I turned back southwest towards less populated country and started climbing in an attempt to get over the clouds before jumping.

" The main tank went dry at 7:51 and the reserve at 8:10. The altimeter then registered approximately 14,000 feet, yet the top of the clouds was apparently several thousand feet higher. I rolled the stabilizer back, cut the switches, pulled the ship up into a stall, and was about to go out over the right side of the cockpit, when the right wing began to drop. In this position the plane would gather speed and spiral to the right, possibly striking my parachute after its first turn. I returned to the controls and, after righting the plane, dove over the left side of the cockpit while the airspeed registered about 70 miles per hour and the altimeter 13,000 feet.

" I pulled the rip cord immediately after clearing the stabilizer. The Irving chute functioned perfectly. I had left the ship head first and was falling in this position when the risers whipped me around into an upright position and the chute opened.

" The last I saw or heard of the D.H. was as it disappeared into the clouds just after my chute opened. I placed the rip cord in my pocket and took out my flashlight. It was snowing and very cold. For the first minute or so the parachute descended very smoothly, then commenced an excessive oscillation which continued for about five minutes and which I was unable to check.

" The first indication that I was near the ground was a

gradual darkening of the space below. The snow had turned to rain and, although my chute was thoroughly soaked, its oscillation had greatly decreased. I directed the beam from the 500-foot spotlight downward, but the ground appeared so suddenly that I landed directly on top of a barbed wire fence without seeing it.

" The fence helped to break my fall and the barbs did not penetrate the heavy flying suit. The chute was blown over the fence and was held open for some time by the gusts of wind before collapsing. I rolled it up into its pack and started towards the nearest light. Soon I came to a road, which I followed about a mile to the town of Covell, Illinois, where I telephoned a report to St. Louis and endeavored to obtain some news of where the ship had landed. The only information that I could obtain was from one of a group of farmers in the general store, a Mr. Thompson, who stated that his neighbor had heard the plane crash, but could only guess at its general direction.

" I rode with Mr. Thompson to his farm and, after leaving the parachute in his house, we canvassed the neighbors for any information concerning the plane. After searching for over an hour without any result, I left instructions to place a guard over the mail in case it was found before I returned, and went to Chicago for another ship.

" On arriving over Covell the next morning I found the wreck, with a small crowd gathered around it, less than 500 feet back of the house where I had left the parachute. The nose and wheels had struck the ground at about the same time, and after sliding along for about 75 feet it had piled up in a pasture beside a hedge fence. One wheel had come off and was standing inflated against the wall on the inside of a hog house a hundred yards farther on. It had gone through two fences and the wall of the house. The wings were badly splintered, but the tubular fuselage, though badly bent in places, had held its general form

even in the mailpit. The parachute from the flare was
hanging on the tailskid.

" There were three sacks of mail in the plane. One, a full
bag, from St. Louis, had been split open and some of the
mail was oil soaked, but legible. The other two were only
partially full and were undamaged. I delivered the mail
to Maywood by plane, to be dispatched on the next ship
out." [16]

It was the second time in three weeks that Lindbergh
had saved his life by a parachute leap. That made him a
veteran of the Caterpillar Club, whose members owed their
lives to the parachute and hence to the silkworm. Jumping over the side of a doomed airplane was automatic initi-
ation into this exclusive, if nebulous, group. It was a club
whose waiting list was never published.

Often the oil-soaked envelopes could have told a tale of
adventure and heroism, but to the pilots navigating the
treacherous cloud-lanes, carrying the air mail was a business. There are no dramatics in the above account. The
airman coolly notes the very moment that the gas tanks go
dry. In the midst of his parachute leap he has presence of
mind to watch his disappearing plane, since on a previous
occasion the spiraling ship had nearly swooped into him.
And he ends with the matter-of-fact statement: " I delivered the mail to Maywood [Chicago terminus] to be dispatched on the next ship out."

The air mail had acquitted itself well. It had built a solid
foundation for the private capital that was soon to develop
a whole new era of air transportation in this country. The
air-mail pilot began to take the place of the war ace as the
hero of the small boy. This healthier state of mind is indicated by the recognition given to the Postoffice Department. In both 1923 and 1924 the United States Air Mail
was awarded the coveted Collier Trophy for the greatest
achievement in aeronautics.

C H A P T E R

7

The Mail Must Pay

ON July 1, 1924 the Postoffice Department divided the transcontinental route into three zones. They were: New York-Chicago, Chicago-Cheyenne, and Cheyenne-San Francisco. It cost eight cents to send a letter across each zone, and although the cross-country postage was still twenty-four cents, a large percentage of the mail traffic was within one or two of the zones, so that the average correspondent found he could send his letters by air mail at a reduced rate. At once mail traffic began to increase. Just a year later, on July 1, 1925, the Postmaster General authorized overnight service between New York and Chicago. The improved schedule between America's two largest cities, coupled with the zoning system, resulted in such an increase of mail traffic that, for the first time in air-mail history, revenues began to catch up with expenses. Using surplus wartime equipment obtained at very low cost, and operating on relatively high postal rates, the air-mail service began to show promise. The zone system was cumbersome; mail revenue was still inconsequential, and it was still below the actual cost of operation, but the results of the experiment were so encouraging that private investors began to scent possible profits in air mail.

It had always been the intention of the Postoffice Department to transfer air-mail routes to private operators as soon as such a change was practicable. As far back as 1911 Postmaster General Hitchcock had prophesied that air mail would one day be carried by private operators. The railroads hastened the process. As air-mail sacks grew heavier, railroads demanded that the government cease competing in a business that threatened their incomes. Colonel Henderson denies that there was any strong pressure exerted by the railroads for the termination of government operation of the air mail,[1] but there is no doubt that there was some such sentiment among business men.

Representative Clyde Kelly of Pennsylvania, voice of the railway mail clerks, was ready with an air-mail bill as early as 1924, but Assistant Postmaster Henderson asked that action be postponed one more year, until the government completed its program.[2] When the lighted airway made possible regular night service across the country, the Postoffice Department gladly gave its blessing to the proposed transference of air mail to private operation.

Private operators had tried before to establish air lines, but all attempts were doomed, without some kind of government help. The first scheduled passenger line in the United States was an aerial ferry across the twenty-three miles of bay between Tampa and St. Petersburg, Florida.[3] Called the St. Petersburg-Tampa Airboat Line, the company began operations on January 1, 1914, with Benoist flying boats as equipment. For three months the planes shuttled passengers between the two cities on a more or less regular schedule, but when tourists went north in the spring, the Tampa air line disappeared. After the Armistice there was talk of a nation-wide system of air lines, and promoters even set May 15, 1919 as the opening day. Nothing came of the proposal, however, and without air-mail payments, or some such government help, no private operator could have existed long, even if he had had the temerity to start such an enterprise.

There was, however, a precedent for air-mail routes operated by private contractors. In 1919 Edward Hubbard of Seattle convinced the Postoffice Department that there was need of an air-mail service between Seattle and Victoria, British Columbia. Hubbard's plan was to fly across Puget Sound with mail that had missed steamers outward-bound from Seattle. The plane would intercept the ships before they cleared from the Canadian port. Transpacific mail might thus be speeded as much as a week, depending upon the frequency of Seattle sailings. The flying boat would then scoot home with mail from incoming ships touching at Victoria, which would bring the Orient at least one day closer to Seattle. The postoffice would have gotten into border complications had it attempted to begin such a service, but there was nothing to prevent the United States and Canadian governments from paying a private operator for the work.

Hubbard began operations on March 3, 1919. His first plane was a Boeing C–700, open-cockpit biplane, equipped with pontoons. The passenger on that historic trip was the plane's builder, William E. Boeing, member of a wealthy lumber family. Boeing was destined to become one of the great names in American aviation. Late in 1919 Hubbard took delivery of a Boeing B–1, which was a flying boat of much greater carrying capacity than the spidery C–700. The B–1 clinched the reputation of Boeing as a plane-builder, for it was as rugged and reliable as a draft horse. Until 1927 the ship was still in service. Later it was replaced by faster equipment, but it stands today at Boeing Field, Seattle, where it was installed by the local chapter of the National Aeronautic Association.

Hubbard Air Transport (sometimes called the Seattle-Victoria Air Mail Line, or Hubbard Air Service) was suc-

cessful from the start. Day in and day out, the seaplane
scuttled across the Sound. Hubbard operated several
months on probation and then was awarded a contract.
On July 1, 1921 he completed one year of private air-mail
service *with a perfect schedule record*. Hubbard continued
his operation for seven years. He died in 1929.

A similar line, started only a short time after Hubbard
began service, was the route between New Orleans and
Pilottown, operating between New Orleans and the mouth
of the Mississippi River. Merrill K. Riddick received ninety
dollars each trip for carrying air mail to steamers that had
left the Louisiana port the day before. Both the Seattle and
the New Orleans enterprises were specialized services, depending entirely upon mail for revenue. More nearly corresponding to the modern air line were Aero Limited and
Aeromarine Sightseeing & Navigation Company, established primarily as passenger-carriers, but aided by air-
mail payments.

Aero Limited was organized in August 1919 to ferry passengers back and forth between New York and Atlantic
City. When traffic slackened at the end of the summer, the
operators moved to Miami and began a service to Nassau,
Bahama Islands, using six-place Curtiss naval-patrol flying
boats, acquired from the government at less than cost.
These ships were inefficient for passenger operation, but
they were larger than the Aeromarine seaplanes used on the
Atlantic City route, and their low first cost offset the high
maintenance charges. The Prohibition Act became effective June 30, 1919, and with the Bahamas a Mecca for
thirsty Americans, Aero Limited carried 2,200 passengers
to the islands during the first season. So optimistic were the
operators that they opened up an air-line ticket office, the
first air passenger agency in the history of American aviation.[4]

Aeromarine Sightseeing & Navigation Company, flying
to resort towns near New York, cast envious glances in the

direction of Aero Limited. Aeromarine was an offshoot of
a New Jersey aircraft factory that had disappeared with the
drying up of military orders after the war. It was backed by
Inglis M. Uppercu, once a New York automobile-distribu-
tor, but in 1919 one of the outstanding aviation leaders.
In the fall of 1919 Uppercu sent two Aeromarine naval-
patrol flying boats down to Florida to test the possibilities
of a route between Key West and that oasis of prohibition
days, Havana. West Indies Airways had been carrying passengers intermittently between these two points, but it
lacked capital. Aeromarine and West Indies merged to
form Aeromarine West Indies Airways, Incorporated. The
new company won a mail contract and began regular service on November 1, 1919, thus ranking with the Seattle and
New Orleans lines as a pioneer private mail-carrier. Aeromarine carried about three hundred passengers that winter.
In the next two years it expanded to include summer service between New York and Atlantic City, Cleveland and
Detroit, and Long Island resorts. In the winter it transferred operations to the run between Key West and Havana, and later absorbed the old Aero Limited route from
Miami to Nassau. On December 31, 1922 Aeromarine reported that it had carried 17,121 passengers more than a
million miles during the fiscal year. It had a spotless safety
record, due, no doubt, to ideal weather conditions and the
fact that over-water routes minimized emergency landing
hazards. Charles F. Redden of the Aeromarine company
told a House committee in 1925 that his company had carried thirty thousand passengers safely more than two million miles in four and a half years of operation.[5] Aeromarine found that it could maintain a solid passenger business
by keeping fares within reasonable comparison to railroad
charges,[6] but when the United States and Cuba withdrew
mail payments, the company did not earn enough profits
to warrant continuance. Nevertheless, Aeromarine had
pointed the way. It became a kind of measuring stick for

future passenger operations. The fact that such a well-managed line could not pay dividends without mail payments did much to discourage air-transportation promoters and directed attention more than ever to the necessity of government help, preferably in the form of an air-mail subsidy.[7]

There was not much money in flying in the twenties, and the annual reports of the Aeronautical Chamber of Commerce reflect the instability of air transportation. There were 88 " airline " operators listed in 1921; about 125 in 1922; and 129 in 1923. This appears to be normal development, until a breakdown of the figures shows that of the 88 operators listed in 1921, only 17 remained in 1923; and of 125 operators reporting in 1922, only 56 were in business a year later.[8] It is true that many of the companies listed as " airlines " were only taxi services operating from fixed bases, but even so, the mortality rate suggests the uncertainty of depending upon air passengers for revenue.

Until the public learned to appreciate the advantages of air transportation, something other than passenger traffic had to cushion the financial shock of establishing an air line. Many critics in this country were impatient because the United States was so far behind Europe in commercial air transportation, but European air lines were given outright payments, and in some cases this subsidy amounted to one fourth the cost of equipment. France was paying private operators as much as a thousand francs a year toward the salaries of each transport pilot. In short, the elaborate system of European airways could not have lasted a year without direct government subsidy out of all proportion to the service performed. The nations of the Old World, already looking to the next war, believed such expenditures were good defense investments.

There were groups in this country who believed the United States should do the same. In October 1919 a board of army officers went so far as to suggest outright direct subsidy. " Such subsidies," they reported; " have heretofore found no place in our governmental policy, but it seems likely that they will become necessary, if we are to embark upon a program which has for its objective the adequate preparedness of this country for air defense in case of war." [9]

Looking to the European nations, the board added:

The present reported feverish activity for the development of " Commercial Aeronautics " of certain nations already saddled with enormous debts under the guise of developing a new and highly lauded system of transportation, is, as a matter of fact, nothing more than a new race for supremacy in aeronautics.[10]

Direct subsidy met stiff resistance in this country, however. In every instance investigators found it inefficient, costly, and unreliable. Commercial ships built according to military standards were uneconomical for air-line use. The enormous cost of passenger and mail transportation in Europe showed itself in every breakdown of operation statistics. Air lines there did not even follow the best routes, since the system was designated more with an eye to military advantage than to commercial efficiency. There were government restrictions as to equipment, personnel, and even the number of miles to be flown. Few experts in this country cared to recommend a similar procedure, and they were right. The American system produced the finest aircraft in the world. French lines, run on subsidy, brought a later degeneracy to the whole industry.

Yet those who opposed direct subsidy admitted the military value of air transportation. Captain Edward V. Rickenbacker, America's most famous war ace, later president of Eastern Airlines, battled the subsidy lobby at this time, but he did not deny the necessity of training pilots in peacetime. He estimated that each air-line pilot was worth about ninety thousand dollars to the government. The basic value of a man flying the air lines in peacetime is equiva-

lent to eighty-five-per-cent efficiency in wartime, Captain
Rickenbacker told the Lampert Committee in 1925,[11] and
there were others who felt the same way.

Now, if the one big argument for government aid to the
air lines is summed up by the word *defense,* then why
should not the War Department, rather than the postoffice,
make the appropriations? The answer is that the Postoffice
Department was the one agent that could supply the necessary nutrition to the infant industry without stunting its
growth by poisonous military restrictions. If this country
could build up air transportation without military control,
it might develop a system valuable both to commerce and
to defense. Proper use of mail payments to private operators might be the answer.

A plan of this sort was suggested in 1919 by a group
of military and civil aviation leaders who had studied
European conditions. They reported to Secretary of War
Newton D. Baker that the United States needed air transportation both for defense and as a means of rapid communication in a country of great distances. The committee
recommended the establishment of routes and fields at government expense; technical training of pilots by the government; a meteorological service; federal and international regulation of aviation; low-cost insurance; and (last
and most significant) subsidy in the form of air mail, or
the maintenance of private lines until they became profitable.[12]

Later Howard E. Coffin gave more substance to this plea
when he spoke before a special House committee on the
eve of the passage of the first Air Mail Act. He said:

I am not prepared to give you gentlemen any very profound
discussion of these matters, other than I think we have right at
hand the one great agency that no foreign government pos-
sesses, and that is our air mail service. It is a service that is popular; that has great possibilities of expansion and quantity production in this country of unusual distances. It would not mean

a thing in England; it would not mean a thing in France. The overnight train service in Europe will take you almost anywhere you want to go. So that we have here the only great thing that they have not. They have money. I think we have the thing that is worth in the long run a great deal more than money. Money grants have been made from year to year, and they are uncertain because the peoples of the countries are not going to continue to bear taxation necessary for such appropriations unless they are productive of some tangible achievement, and unless, as I have said, we get aviation home to the individual citizen and benefit his private, selfish affairs. The air mail service that we have does that very thing. Why not use it? It is the most wonderful air service in the world at the present time, even with the equipment it is using, which is mostly . . . obsolete. Why not use this vehicle that has already accomplished results, rather than grope around too far looking for something else to do for the moment? The other things will come in time.[13]

Coffin, vice president of Hudson Motor Car Company and former chairman of the wartime Aircraft Production Board, was one of the influential leaders who saw in air-mail subsidy both an answer to the problem of defense and an opportunity to develop commercial aviation.

As a matter of fact, American air transportation had already been given a kind of subsidy, even before the lines were organized, for the lighted airway was ready and waiting for the use of the private operator. The government provided these airways, and since they were invaluable to the private operator, and quite beyond his own means, they may be considered as equivalent to a subsidy. Some such subsidy has accompanied every pioneering enterprise. General Braddock, hewing a road through the wilderness at government expense, was an instrument of subsidization. He was providing a highway for the Conestoga wagon, a road that the trader could never have made for himself. The railroads, so bitter because of government aid to bus and air-line companies, spread to every corner of the country only because they were given countless acres of land as a subsidy. As one air-line pioneer told a Congressional investigating committee, even the manufacturer of passenger automobiles has been heavily subsidized by the government, for how many cars would Henry Ford have sold without the network of highways built at government expense? [14]

Air-mail payments are not in themselves a " subsidy." If a government pays the common carriers for mail service, such payments are no more a " subsidy " than the buying of army blankets or any other commodity. When payments are greater than postal income, however, and when such payments are in excess of fair compensation, air mail becomes a form of subsidy, but it is a fallacy to think of all air mail as subsidy. Only the payments beyond actual cost and fair profit constitute subsidy, and if the defense ingredient is added, " subsidy " becomes well-nigh indefinable. Yet this troublesome word has been a nub of contention all through the history of private operation of the air lines, and time after time it led to misunderstanding and recrimination. (For more on subsidies see Chapter 18.)

The fact that the postoffice very nearly made expenses on its air-mail service in 1924 did much to mollify the anti-subsidy leaders. Subsequent events also proved that there were many more who objected to the *term* " subsidy " than to the *practice* properly sugar-coated. Air-mail payments were not direct subsidy as practiced in Europe, in any case, and such payments were to decrease as the public learned to use the new transportation system. Air-mail " subsidy " turned out to contain very little of the " anæsthetic to initiative " that Captain Rickenbacker so much feared.[15]

And so by 1925 the stage was set for another act in the unfolding drama of the air lines. Air lines were to be handed over to private operators. The railroads were ready to see the government retire as a competitor for mail loads. Business men saw a new frontier of investment. Army officers were agreed that private operators could continue to be the training agencies for defense flyers. Critics of bureaucracy looked for important developments in commercial aviation with the transference of operations to private management. The chief of the air mail himself admitted that private carriers could probably fly the air mail cheaper and more efficiently than the government.[16] With all this weight behind it, the movement to hand over air lines to the private operators gained momentum.

Law and Order in the Airways

On February 2, 1925, Congress passed HR 7064, better known as the Kelly Bill (see Appendix I). Sponsored by Representative Clyde Kelly, " father of the air-mail laws," the purpose of the act is described in the title: " An Act to encourage commercial aviation and to authorize the postmaster general to contract for the mail service." [1] But the point that interested private business was that operators were to be paid up to four fifths of the postal revenue.

The first Air Mail Act (Kelly Law) was the " go " signal for commercial aviation. The Postmaster General reported that within two months after the passage of the bill, he had received more than five thousand inquiries from tentative air-line operators.[2] The government was not interested in turning over transportation of the mails to irresponsible agents, however, and from the beginning it was evident that capital was to play an increasingly important part in the development of the air lines. Air transportation was to be a " long haul " financially. Even with a valuable mail contract it would take an operator many months to write off expensive equipment. That is the rea-

94

son Big Business eventually crowded out the independent promoter.

This was a sad turn of events, in a way. The pioneer operator was a colorful figure — a World War flyer, perhaps, who liked planes and adventure. He risked his life and blazed the trail, but he was not likely to be a very good business man. Seldom did he have access to abundant capital. He was therefore doomed when aviation required high financial stakes. In his place there appeared a new breed: Wall Streeters, who had done most of their flying from swivel chairs; financial promoters, more skillful at spotting capital than in finding landing fields on lonely mountain tops; efficiency experts, intent upon cutting costs rather than reducing the flying time between cities. Something went out of aviation when the business man stepped in, but it was a necessary change. There could be no stabilization until sanity replaced daring as the principal ingredient of air-line operation. It took years to eradicate the World War influence, but the process was already apparent shortly after the government relinquished the airways.

Private capital was available for commercial aviation development just as soon as air lines gave promise of producing some profit, but another obstacle had to be overcome before air transportation could progress in the United States. Not until there was adequate regulation could there be sufficient stability to appeal to the more conservative investor. Business men are usually allergic to government interference, but such was not the case with air-line promoters when the Kelly Bill became law in 1925. Other transportation systems had bucked regulation and some of the hottest fights in our legislative history had been between the railroads and the government, but airline operators howled long and loudly for the government to lead them out of chaos. The fact is that air lines transcend all boundaries and could not exist without rigid control by the federal authority.

There was regulation, of a sort, long before 1925. The arbiter in many disputes during the era of the birdman was the Aero Club of America. The organization forced pilots to adhere to the simple rules of that day, but its power came not from law, but because the club carried over the prestige it had gained as the final authority at flying meets.

The first attempt at legislation was in 1911, when Simeon Eben Baldwin, Chief Justice of the Connecticut Supreme Court of Errors, tried to pass a bill forbidding unlicensed pilots from flying beyond designated fields. The Baldwin Bill also provided for a system of registration, airplane identification marking, and bonding for damages.[3] The bill failed to pass, but when Justice Baldwin became Governor of Connecticut, he forced through a state law in 1912 that included most of the clauses written into his previous bill. Connecticut, from which came many aviation leaders, was thus the first state to take official recognition of air travel.

A few other states were about to consider aviation laws, but the war deflected their interest. Not until 1919 was air legislation brought up again. In February 1919 the National Advisory Committee on Aeronautics submitted a bill to Congress, but although approved by the President, it never got past the committee because of the pressure of post-war business. In the following year other measures were proposed, but for one reason or another nothing came of them.

During this time the " gypsy flyers " were barnstorming the country in their rickety ships. Although they were keeping alive the public's interest in flying, they were a menace to safety, unless properly regulated. In 1924, gypsy flyers were held accountable for two out of three fatal crashes.[4]

In the next four years many bills were written to bring order into the industry, but they were either too lenient or too stringent to win sufficient backing. Nevertheless, these bills served to keep up interest in aeronautical legislation, and by 1925 a definite trend could be noted in their structure. For it became clear that commercial aviation must be kept separate from military development, and it was apparent that no law could cover both branches. It was also generally accepted that the Department of Commerce was the agency in which to vest administrative powers.

All this time Congress had at hand a bill that, with a few changes, became the constitution of the aviation industry in 1926. The Wadsworth-Winslow Bill was initiated by Senator (later Representative) James W. Wadsworth of New York, on January 26, 1922.[5] It was sponsored in the House by Samuel E. Winslow, chairman of the Committee on Interstate and Foreign Commerce, who made numerous changes after conferring with officials of the Department of Commerce.[6] Because of a congested calendar, however, the bill failed of a vote before Congress adjourned. In the first session of the 68th Congress, Senator Wadsworth again introduced his bill, but after going through the same routine, it died on the House calendar in January 1925. Modeled after the British Air Navigation Act of 1920, the Wadsworth-Winslow Bill was an important influence in later legislation.

The 69th Congress picked up the pieces and put them together again. This time the sponsor was Senator Hiram Bingham of Connecticut, an enthusiastic backer of aviation development. Senator Bingham's bill passed the Senate on December 16, 1925 and was referred to Schuyler Merritt, of the House subcommittee on commerce. Merritt, also from Connecticut, had worked with Colonel Winslow on the parent bill.[7] Representative James S. Parker of New York added a few amendments, but the Merritt-Parker Bill did not differ materially from the Wadsworth-Winslow measure. The National Advisory Com-

mittee for Aeronautics scored the Bingham Bill because
it provided for federal establishment and operation of airports, which the NACA believed should be controlled, like
seaports, by local authorities, aided by the government. It
was feared that federal ownership of airports would stifle
local initiative and would lead to pork-barrel abuses.
The Merritt-Parker Bill, on the other hand, was criticized because it regulated both inter- and intra-state aviation. The NACA feared that regulation of intrastate flying might be unconstitutional, and there was some danger
that such a law might stifle private flying, as in Europe.
The influential advisory group reported that, much as it
wanted an air law, it would rather see the bills fail than
go through as written.[8] Accordingly the legislators re-
drafted their measures, and on May 20, 1926 Congress
passed the Bingham-Parker-Merritt Bill.

The Air Commerce Act of 1926 turned out to be an excellent piece of law-making. " It is the legislative corner-
stone for the development of commercial aviation in
America," reported the National Advisory Council for
Aeronautics.[9]

A number of factors hastened its passage after the long
delay in Congress. Transference of the air mail to private
operation early in 1925 emphasized the need for an air
law. There were also a number of surveys at this time that
provided valuable information for both the public and the
lawmakers. These surveys were conducted as a result
of the bitter denunciation of our air services by such
critics as the irascible General William (Billy) Mitchell.
The so-called Lampert Committee, for example, appointed
by the House on March 24, 1924, heard more than a hundred and fifty witnesses tell about the aeronautical problems of the country.[10]

The most important investigating group was the President's Aircraft Board, better known as the Morrow Board.[11]

The Morrow Board had access to all the data gathered by the Lampert Committee. In addition, it called ninety-nine other witnesses for hearings that lasted from September 17 to the middle of October 1925. More than any other agency the Morrow Board was responsible for starting commercial aviation on the right road. Members of the board were respected and influential,[12] and the board was largely responsible for starting the momentum that pushed over the Air Commerce Act of 1926. Among other things proposed by the board, and later carried out by legislation, were the creation of a Bureau of Air Commerce in the Department of Commerce, and the extension of air-mail service by private contract.[13] President Coolidge placed great faith in the board, and he followed its recommendations in his annual message to Congress.[14]

On September 23, 1925 Secretary of Commerce Herbert Hoover outlined a plan for organization of the proposed Bureau of Aeronautics. Hoover suggested that all the various divisions in his department be extended to aid air commerce, rather than establish a new agency for the sole purpose of regulating civil aviation. For example, the Lighthouse Service, with all its experience in maintaining beacons along the seaways, could do the same for the lighted airways, under a special division created for that purpose. Where no adequate agencies existed, new divisions would be created, but the Hoover idea was to utilize the vast experience of his department, and the plan met with the approval of most aviation experts. Eight months later, when the Wadsworth-Parker-Merritt Bill became the Air Commerce Act of 1926, Hoover's outline was followed almost to the letter.[15]

The new Bureau of Aeronautics got off to a bad start. It was given an appropriation of only $550,000, and the Budget Bureau failed to provide inspectors with the necessary traveling expenses. From the first day, the aeronautics branch was swamped with the work of licensing all pilots and planes in the country. The air-commerce regulations nominally were in effect after December 31, 1926, but not until the late spring of 1927 were they fully enforced.

A chief for the new bureau was appointed by President Coolidge in August 1926. He was William P. MacCracken, a thirty-seven-year-old alumnus of the University of Chicago Law School, who had served two years with the Army Air Service during the war. At the time of his appointment MacCracken was secretary to the American Bar Association and was a governor of the National Aeronautics Association. He had been a member of the committee that made a world survey of aviation after the war, and he had written several reports for the law journals on the need for aviation legislation. To take the $7,500 government position, he had to give up his law practice and his position as counsel for one of the new air lines. MacCracken's title was Assistant Secretary of Commerce for Aeronautics. Serving him as a kind of general manager was Major Clarence Young, who later succeeded MacCracken as chief of the bureau. Major Young had served eighteen months as a war flyer and had been shot down and made prisoner on the Italian-Austrian front in 1918. At the time of his appointment he was Commander of the 313th Observation Squadron, Air Corps Reserve. As head of the regulations division, Major Young carried out an extensive program of licensing, identification, and inspection. It was also his duty to enforce the air traffic rules, which he himself had to write, in accordance with provisions of the Air Commerce Act. The aviation industry approved these appointments and looked to MacCracken and Young " to put American business into the air." [16]

Under MacCracken the aeronautics branch of the Department of Commerce was split into several sections. The Division of Air Regulation had charge of inspection, registration, and the examination of airmen seeking interstate licenses. It also sent experts out to investigate all accidents and to make constructive reports as to the cause of crashes. The Airways Division, under the Bureau of Lighthouses, had charge of the extension, construction, and maintenance of the lighted airways, which by June 1927 aggregated about four thousand miles. Under this division was the important Weather Service, which gathered meteorological data and issued reports twice a day. The 1928 review of the Department of Commerce listed forty-two "upper air" weather stations and two hundred meteorologists, who gathered information broadcast over nineteen radio stations.

One of the most important sections was the Airways Mapping Division, since charts are as necessary to the airman as they are to the seaman. The map-makers started by issuing "strip" charts of only the most important airways, but eventually they mapped every mile of the country. An Aeronautical Research Division tested new types of planes and engines, and issued certificates for their manufacture only after government experts were certain that the public was reasonably protected. Data from all these divisions were made available through the Division of Air Information, which issued periodic reports and bulletins for the use of pilots and operators.

Events leading up to the passage of legislation lack the drama and adventure that have been made so important a part of aviation history, but no single phase was more vital to progress in the air than development of government control and regulation. Without the services rendered by the aeronautics branch of the Department of Commerce, air transportation would have been delayed indefinitely. After 1926 commercial flying began to approach the reliability its pioneers had envisioned. In 1926 there was only one fatality on the transcontinental, or "Columbia," mail route, and the record was spotless through the first half of 1927.

The stabilization and sanity brought to commercial aviation by the Air Commerce Act, coupled with the transference of air-mail routes to private operators, were directly responsible for the air-transportation system that now began to evolve.

The Seeds of Empire

ONE morning in September 1925 a group of men filed into the outer office of Postmaster General Harry S. New in the old Postoffice Building across from the Raleigh Hotel in Washington. They had gathered to bid on air-mail routes, as authorized by the Kelly Act eight months before. Postmaster General New had refrained from advertising for bids until he was reasonably certain that the Air Commerce Bill would be enacted, but now he was ready to go ahead.

The Postoffice Department did not intend to hand over all of its routes at one time. Instead, private operators were to begin with " feeder lines," connecting cities in the hinterland with the transcontinental route. Not until these operators had obtained sufficient experience were they to be offered a chance to bid on the main, or " Columbia," line.

Mr. New was aware that the transference of air-mail routes to private operation was an epochal event in the history of civil aviation, and he was determined that the achievements of his department should not be nullified by incompetent private management. For this reason, irresponsible business men were not welcome as bidders that morning. Under the conditions of the advertisement, only those promoters who could provide equipment and a modicum of operating experience were entitled to bid.

The Postoffice Department had advertised eight routes, but only five contracts were awarded when postal officials opened the bids on October 7, 1925. The five original private air-mail contractors were Colonial Air Lines, Robertson Aircraft Corporation, National Air Transport, Western Air Express, and Varney Speed Lines (Walter T. Varney). Three of the eight contracts were withheld because bidders failed to meet the specifications of the advertisement. National Air Transport had offered to carry mail from Chicago to the Twin Cities, but the bid was defective, and the route later went to another operator. General Airways System, Incorporated, failed to win the Chicago-Birmingham route because the Postmaster General was not satisfied with the financial responsibility of the company. The eighth route, from Seattle to Los Angeles, was taken over very shortly by Pacific Air Transport. The seeds of the great air-transportation systems were sown at this time. Colonial Air Lines became one of the nuclei for American Airlines, the biggest and most prosperous of the modern trunk routes. National Air Transport, Varney Lines, and Pacific Air Transport are part of the vast United Air Lines system. Western Air Express eventually became part of Transcontinental & Western Air, Inc., the central airway from New York to Los Angeles.

Contract Air Mail Route Number One (CAM–1) was won by Colonial Air Lines, but the honor of carrying the first domestic air mail by private contract went to the holder of CAM–6 and CAM–7 (awarded two weeks later), who was none other than Henry Ford, at that time the world's largest manufacturer of motor cars. Ford's pioneering in air mail was of great significance, and his part in the air-mail drama is worth reviewing. Governor Ralph W. Cram of Iowa, an officer of the National Aeronautical Association, hailed 1925 as the most momentous year in American aeronautics because of the inauguration of night mail between New York and Chicago; the organization of powerful National Air Transport; *and the entry of Henry Ford into aviation.*[1]

Ford got into the picture late in 1923 when he came to the rescue of the noted inventor William Bushnell Stout. Stout had been experimenting with an all-metal monoplane employing an enormously thick wing to gain amazing efficiency without the use of external bracing wires. The internally braced wing is commonplace today, but in 1924 it was a radical departure from orthodox plane design. Stout designed these ships for transport service, but he did not have sufficient capital to finance a factory. Accordingly, he wrote a hundred prominent industrialists, saying: " I should like a thousand dollars — and I can only promise you one thing; you'll never see it again." [2] Unlike most crackpot letters, this one was backed by the reputation of a man who had made a name for himself as an inventor. Stout collected about twenty thousand dollars, and the amount was sufficient for him to organize Stout Metal Airplane Company. Edsel Ford contributed a thousand dollars to the enterprise, and he argued his father into putting in an equal amount. A year later, when Stout's new ship had proved its worth, the Fords bought out Stout, retaining the aeronautical engineer as director of the factory.

The ship produced by Stout at Dearborn, Michigan, somewhat resembled the German Junkers, with its thick wings, corrugated metal body, and commodious cabin. The first ships were powered with a single Liberty motor, but later they were designed for three Wright Whirlwind aircooled, radial engines. The Ford Tri-Motor (as it was called after the Fords bought out Stout) was an excellent ship. Many of these kidney-splitting old tumbrils were still grinding through the air fifteen years later. They were replaced, not because they wore out, but because they were uneconomical in comparison with later designs. Yet as late as 1938 most of the pipe reaching the Barco oil fields of Colombia was hauled in Ford Tri-Motors.

Ford was so impressed with this excellent ship that he decided to get into commercial aviation. On April 3, 1925 the automobile-manufacturer began an air service out of Detroit to Chicago and Cleveland. Ford Air Transport at first carried company freight exclusively, but it operated with the regularity and reliability of a public carrier. Apparently Ford was training personnel in readiness for his bid on an air line, as authorized by the Kelly Act, passed two months previously. When Ford won his mail contracts in October 1925, he was ready to begin service months ahead of rivals. It took a few weeks to arrange schedules, but on February 15, 1926 a Ford Air Transport monoplane flew over Detroit bound for Cleveland with the first air mail to be carried within the United States under private contract.

Ford was also the first to combine an air-mail route with a passenger service on a year-in, year-out schedule. Day after day the tri-motors roared over the two routes, Detroit to Chicago, and Detroit to Cleveland. The line lost money from the start, but Ford Air Transport, and its successor, Stout Air Services, did not suffer a single passenger fatality from 1926 until the route was taken over by United Air Lines in 1929. Ford eventually liquidated his air line and factory because they lost so much money, but by that time his influence had already had an effect. For the public knew Ford as an able and hard-headed business man, and the future air traveler reasoned that if Ford was backing an air line, there must be something to the business after all. The Ford influence was entirely psychological, but it was none the less valuable.

By 1926 twelve air-mail routes had been awarded by the Postoffice Department. Colonial Air Lines, which won CAM-1, New York to Boston, started in 1923 as the Bee

Line, Incorporated, a charter service out of Naugatuck, Connecticut. The company, like many another of that period, had a difficult time financially, but with the pending Kelly Bill holding out the lure of mail pay, promoters found more capital and reorganized as Colonial Air Lines. After it won a mail contract, the line became Colonial Air Transport (CAT). By 1925 CAT was a "strong" line. The chairman of the board was John H. Trumbull, one-time Governor of Connecticut, and president of Trumbull Electric Manufacturing Company. Other officers and directors were W. Irving Bullard, vice president of the Boston Chamber of Commerce, who was elected president of CAT; Harris Wittemore, of Connecticut Bond & Share; Sherman M. Fairchild, of Fairchild Aerial Camera; Juan T. Trippe, most important figure in the far-reaching Pan American Airways System; Talbot O. Freeman; William A. Rockefeller, and Cornelius Vanderbilt Whitney. CAT began carrying the mail over CAM–1 on June 18, 1926.

Robertson Aircraft Corporation, winner of CAM–2, Chicago to St. Louis, was founded by the brothers Frank and William Robertson, wartime flyers. The Robertsons obtained financial support in their home city, St. Louis. One of the pilots hired by the Robertsons was a slim, slow-smiling young man named Charles A. Lindbergh. With fourteen Liberty De Havilands and two Curtiss "Orioles" (open biplanes), the Robertsons began operations on April 15, 1926.

The most impressive of the new air lines was National Air Transport (NAT). Organized immediately after the passage of the Kelly Bill, NAT was capitalized at $10,500,-000. Moving spirits in the company were Howard E. Coffin, vice president of the Hudson Automobile Company, whose name has figured prominently in aviation since his appointment to the wartime Aircraft Production Board; Colonel Paul Henderson, "father of the night mail," who resigned as Second Assistant Postmaster General to become general manager; and C. M. Keys, Wall Street editor and airplane-motor manufacturer. NAT's list of directors included such prominent leaders as Philip Wrigley, Lester Armour, Charles L. Lawrance (who perfected the American radial engine), William A. Rockefeller, Jeremiah Milbank (president of Allis-Chalmers), C. T. Ludington (who organized his own line out of Philadelphia), W. J. Austin (Cleveland contractor), C. F. Kettering (General Motors), and inventor John Hays Hammond.[3] NAT began operations May 12, 1926 with ten Curtiss "Carrier Pigeons," especially built for the mail service, a Liberty De Haviland, a Travel-Air monoplane, an "Aerial Mercury" (similar to the Carrier Pigeons), and a Ford Tri-Motor.

Western Air Express (WAE) was the only one of the first five lines to show immediate profits. Organized in July 1925 by a colorful old racing driver, Harris M. ("Pop") Hanshue, WAE was backed by Harry Chandler, publisher of the Los Angeles *Times,* and some lesser-known west-coast capitalists. The company began carrying mail on April 17, 1926, over CAM–4, Los Angeles to the "Columbia" line connection at Salt Lake City. The movie colony contributed heavily to the mail loads, and since most families in Los Angeles had ties with the East, WAE ships carried about five hundred pounds of mail every trip. Each night when the big Douglases returned to their home bases, they had earned for WAE a profit of about $1,140, and with the ideal conditions of desert flying, maintenance costs were reduced to the minimum.

Varney Air Lines (at one time called Varney Speed Lines) operated over a much more dangerous terrain. CAM–5 cut across the mountains and wilderness from Elko, Nevada, to Pasco, Washington. The line was organized by Walter T. Varney, operator of a flying school at San Mateo and an airplane taxi service in the San Francisco Bay region. Varney had been flying since 1916, and he was proud of the fact that his planes had traveled more than a million miles without a fatality. Undoubtedly this record impressed Postmaster General New at the time the air-mail routes were put up for bidding. On April 6, 1926 Leon D. Cuddeback, chief pilot, took off from Elko with the first load of mail to go over CAM–5. The Varney line was thus the first of the five original contract winners to begin service.

Throughout the summer of 1926 other operators began mail service, as the postoffice approved additional routes. On September 15, 1926 Verne C. Gorst, west-coast bus-line operator, who had been flying seaplanes since 1912, began mail service between Los Angeles and Seattle over his Pacific Air Transport system, known to the Postoffice Department as CAM–8.

One of the most troublesome of the new lines was CAM–9, Chicago to Twin Cities. In 1920 Assistant Postmaster General Otto Praeger had started service over this route as one of the feeder lines to the newly established transcontinental airway. The western terminal when service began, on September 1, 1920, was a wooden hangar on what is now the Minneapolis Wold-Chamberlain Field, which was then called Speedway Field. The Twin Cities route was a difficult line to operate. Four pilots crashed to their deaths and eight planes were demolished in less than nine months. When Otto Praeger was succeeded by Colonel Shaughnessy, the new Assistant Postmaster General in charge of air mail shut down the feeder line from Chicago to the Twin Cities. Not until the passage of the Kelly Bill was any further attempt made to re-establish it.

When the Postoffice Department began parceling out feeder lines in 1925–6, however, the Chicago-Twin Cities route was ninth on the list. It was awarded to Charles Dickinson, who had made his fortune in the seed business and who spent it on airplanes. Dickinson helped Matty Laird build famous commercial and racing ships at Wichita. He was an inveterate flyer and Dickinson's luxurious whiskers were a familiar sight wherever airmen gathered. The operator of CAM–9 looked more like Santa Claus than an aviator, and the resemblance did not stop there.

Dickinson started operations on June 7, 1926, with three Laird biplanes, equipped with Curtiss OX–5 motors; a Laird "Swallow," Whirlwind-powered, and a mongrel cabin ship. The weather was bad that first day, but Elmer Patridge volunteered to fly the first mail load out of Minneapolis. Just south of the city the pilot lost control of his ship (it was the rebuilt cabin "crate"), and the plane went into a spin. Patridge was killed, and the plane was destroyed. It was an omen of what was to come.

For within three months Dickinson had lost all his equipment except the Whirlwind Laird. All but one of his pilots had quit. In August 1926 Dickinson threw in the towel and gave the Postoffice Department the required forty-five days' notice. On October 1 he withdrew as an airmail operator.

During the forty-five days that Dickinson was winding up his affairs, Colonel L. H. Brittin, vice president of the St. Paul Association (Chamber of Commerce) tried to find backers who would help him continue air-mail service to Chicago. Colonel Brittin finally corralled some stray capital in Detroit and organized Northwest Airways, Incorporated. The officers were Harold H. Emmons of Detroit, president; Colonel Brittin, vice president and general manager; Frank Blair, of the Detroit Union Trust Company, treasurer; and William B. Stout, the inventor, secretary.

The first pilots hired by Northwest Airways were David L. Behncke, later the active leader of the powerful Air Line Pilots Association; Charles W. ("Speed") Holman, the famous racer, who crashed to his death in 1931 at the Omaha air meet; Chester Jacobson; and Robert Radoll. Northwest Airways was the only bidder when CAM–9 was readvertised after Dickinson's dismal failure, and on October 1, the day that the first contract was terminated,

Northwest Airways started service. With three new Stinson Detroiter monoplanes, powered by the reliable Wright Whirlwinds, Northwest Airways broke the jinx of CAM–9. The lighted airway was not yet completed, and so the operators did not provide night service, but their caution was rewarded, for the heretofore dangerous route became one of the safest in the entire country.

Florida Airways Corporation won CAM–10, Atlanta to Jacksonville. Organized by Major Reed M. Chambers and John Harding, veteran distance flyers, the company was opened for business on April 1, 1926, although mail did not fly over the full route until September. Florida Airways did not live long, but it set a remarkable record while it lasted. It completed more than ninety per cent of its flights, and it won the gratitude of thousands by bringing in vital medicines after all other transportation systems had been halted by the disastrous Florida hurricane of September 1926.

The shortest and most profitable route was awarded to Clifford Ball, former Hudson-Essex dealer of McKeesport, Pennsylvania. Ball got into aviation through the back door. He was not a flyer, but he had helped to build Bettis Field, southwest of Pittsburgh, and eventually he owned controlling interest in the property. Some of the taxi flyers using Bettis Field as a base could not pay their rents, and through an exchange of notes Ball acquired seven planes. It occurred to Ball that with a field and planes he was in a position to bid upon some of the air-mail routes advertised by the Postoffice Department. Without quite knowing how it had happened, the erstwhile automobile salesman found himself to be an important air-line operator when he began service on April 21, 1927.[4] For CAM–11, between Cleveland and Pittsburgh, was one of the few new lines to make money. It actually showed higher earnings on its investment than Pop Hanshue's Western Air Express. Ball operated his line until 1930 and then sold out at an excel-

lent price to the group that eventually formed Pennsylvania-Central Airlines.

The last mail route awarded during this first year of
private operation was CAM–12, running up from Pueblo,
Colorado, to meet the " Columbia " line at Cheyenne.
Western Air Express submitted the successful bid and began operations in the last week of 1926. These twelve routes
completed the air-mail system, as the map for January 1927
indicates.

Air mail brought in so much more revenue than did passengers that few of the contractors bothered to install seats
in their planes. Indeed, most of the mail planes were inadequate for passenger service. In an emergency a passenger
might be stuffed up forward with the mail sacks, but air
transportation was too expensive and uncomfortable for
the ordinary traveler. One veteran air-line manager recalls
charging a newly married couple a thousand dollars for a
five-hundred-mile wedding trip with the air mail. Later, it
cost two hundred dollars to fly from Chicago to New York.
There were, however, one or two serious attempts to establish passenger lines independent of government help in
the form of mail payments.

During the Philadelphia Sesquicentennial Exposition of
1926, Thomas E. Mitten, who had made money in street
railways, launched an air line called Philadelphia Rapid
Transit Air Service. Operating Fokker tri-motors on a
regular schedule between Washington and Philadelphia,
the Mitten line just about balanced expenses with a fare
of fifteen dollars. Philadelphia Rapid Transit was entirely
dependent upon the exposition for the bulk of its traffic,
and when the world's fair closed, the air line disappeared.
The line was too short to test the possibilities of air transportation, but it was ably managed by a traffic expert, and
Mitten's statistics were of great interest to other air-line
executives contemplating passenger service.

At about the same time Stout Air Services began carrying

passengers between Detroit and Grand Rapids, Michigan. Operated by the ubiquitous William B. Stout, designer of the famous transport ship, the line was admittedly only an experiment. Its operating record was not encouraging. Fewer than a hundred and fifty passengers a month patronized the Grand Rapids airway, and after a short time service was discontinued. The only significance of the Philadelphia and Grand Rapids ventures was that they indicated the growing interest in the possibility of passenger service, independent of mail payments.

In the summer of 1927 Western Air Express became an experimental laboratory for a study of air passenger traffic under a Daniel Guggenheim Fund grant.[5] Western Air Express was selected by the trustees because it operated under ideal flying conditions and had already made an attempt to augment mail with passenger traffic. The fund provided WAE with the most modern passenger planes obtainable, and this " model air line " at once refuted the argument that passenger traffic was a liability. Within two years WAE paid back to the Guggenheim Fund the full amount of the equipment loan, and it made the payment solely from earnings of its increasingly popular passenger service.[6]

A few other lines toted passengers occasionally. Pacific Air Transport carried 1,252 passengers between Seattle and Los Angeles the year after Boeing took over the line, and Ryan Airlines, a non-mail service, carried more than 5,000 persons in a year of operation between San Diego and the Pacific Air Transport terminus at Los Angeles. Colonial Air Transport was even more enterprising, for in April 1927 it broke all precedent by inaugurating the first night passenger service between New York and Boston.

By and large, however, air passenger service was the domain of the operator who turned to human freight when he was unable to win a mail contract. Such operators were known as " Independents," and they appeared in all sections of the country after 1926. Despite overwhelming evidence to the contrary, many of them believed they could still make a living as passenger-carriers. Many more stuck it out, with their second-hand equipment, believing that if they could establish an equity, they might one day convince the Postoffice Department that they were worthy of carrying the mail. Typical of such operations was the line started by Jack Frye and Paul Richter, who later rose to become president and vice president, respectively, of the great Transcontinental & Western air system.

Jack Frye learned to fly during the war. One day late in 1918 a stocky young man arrived in Los Angeles from Colorado to learn aviation from the ground up. Frye, who was giving private flying lessons, accepted the greenhorn, and in a short time the new pupil was soloing over the California orange groves. The fledgling was Paul Richter, and he learned the flying business so readily that before long he was one of the original "Thirteen Black Cats," Hollywood stunt flyers.[7] Frye, Richter, and W. A. Hamilton (later a well-known aircraft-builder, but at that time foreman of the Duesenberg automobile factory in Los Angeles) bought a wartime Jenny and organized a barnstorming and taxi company. They fared a little better than most gypsy flyers of that day, and the next year they organized Aero Corporation of California, which was far less impressive to look upon than to read about. Aero Corporation accomplished its purpose when it was awarded the agency for the Eaglerock biplane, then a popular training and commercial ship. In the first year the partners sold sixty of these planes, at a profit of about five hundred dollars each.

Encouraged by this success, the partners solicited, and won, the agency for the American Fokker monoplane, which was just beginning to edge out the surplus war equipment in the transport business. Because they had a chance to buy a demonstrator at cost, the three young aviation "executives" decided to start an air line with their one

transport ship. The new enterprise was known as Standard
Air Lines. It was exclusively a passenger line, but it was
surprisingly successful, despite the meager equipment.
Day after day the single-engined Fokker " Universal "
thundered across the desert. Its passengers were the movie
people who had hide-outs in Arizona, and they were enthusiastic patrons of Standard Air Lines. During the week-
end rush the operators piled in pay loads, until the Fokker
groaned with the weight. Air regulations were still enforced only haphazardly, and sometimes the plane took off
from the Phoenix field with extra passengers in the pilot's
" office " and luggage jammed in every available cranny.
The high altitude of the Arizona airports made take-offs
precarious, especially when every seat was filled and the
gasoline tanks were loaded for the long hop across the
desert. Often the straining transport reached the end of
the runway before it would lift in the thin air. " I used to
just kind of *wish* myself off the ground," says Richter.[8]

Sometimes on the long grind between Phoenix and Los
Angeles the pilot would be tapped on the shoulder by an
anxious passenger urgently demanding a comfort stop.
There were no conveniences on those early transports, but
in such cases the pilot accommodatingly headed for a place
marked on the air-line folder as " Desert City." Desert City
was nothing more than a gasoline pump and two outhouses
owned by a man named Ragsdale, but at least twice a week
Mayor Ragsdale entertained the guests of the thunderbird
at Desert City. It was a worthy municipality, passengers
agreed, and the operators began to value it, too, as a " gas
jump " when full tanks would have made take-offs dangerous at Phoenix.

That was air-transport operation in the period up to
1928. During this time all the emphasis was upon air-mail
development. Not until a new administration and additional legislation provided an incentive did air travel become important in the United States. The forgotten man

of American aviation was the Independent, with his frayed cuffs and his second-hand equipment. Unsung and unwanted, he was ignored by both the public and the bureaucrats. The amazing thing is that he could exist at all during the long lean years.

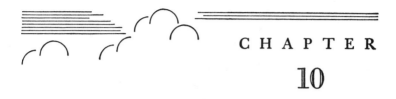

CHAPTER

10

The Wings Grow Stronger

Despite liberal payments by the Postoffice Department, few of the air-mail carriers made much money in their first year of operation. Average income in the second half of 1926 was 42.9 cents a mile, but operating costs were from 50 to 85 cents a mile.[1] One way for the lines to cut those costs was to abolish the tallying system authorized by the Air Mail Act of 1925. Under this law, operators received four fifths of the mail revenue, but as each letter varied as to postage, every piece of mail had to be counted each time the mail sacks were transferred to another line. Tallying each stamp to determine revenue was slow and expensive, and the operators asked for a more efficient means of computing mail payments.

On June 3, 1926 Congress passed an amendment to the Contract Air Mail (Kelly) Act of 1925. The old law was modified to make weight, rather than postal revenue, the basis of payments. This meant that operators no longer were delayed by the necessity of tallying each letter. Over a period of months, mail clerks had discovered that invariably forty letters weighed a pound. Operators therefore argued that it would be simpler just to weigh the mail sacks to determine payments. The new air-mail law (actually only an amendment to the old) acceded to this proposal.

The new rate was three dollars a pound for the first thousand miles of transportation and thirty cents a pound for each additional hundred miles. Although payments to the mail contractors varied according to the various bids, the new rate was kept proportionally the same for each operator by taking the pound rate and multiplying it by a fraction, " the numerator of which is the percentum of revenues derived from air mail to which the contractor was previously entitled under the contract, and the denominator of which is 80." [2] Perhaps the pound rate gave the operators a shade more than before, but the postoffice gained, too, since the postal rate was to be ten cents an ounce for each zone, and since few letters weighed an ounce. When the confusing zoning system was abolished on February 1, 1927, to be replaced by a straight postal rate of ten cents for a half ounce, the postoffice began to lose heavily (see chart on mail revenue, page 129. Figures are from 1929 on, but they indicate the trend started at this time) .

The revision of the postal rates preceded by only a few months the Postoffice Department's decision to turn over the remaining air-mail routes to operators. The air-mail flyer had been a credit to the traditions of the postal service, and his courage received international recognition on the eve of the new era of private operation of the routes, for the Harmon Trophy of 1926 went to an air-mail pilot, " on the theory that consistent flying is more meritorious than spectacular performance." [3] The decision of the award was made by the American section of the International League of Aviators, of which Clifford B. Harmon, early birdman, and New York real-estate man, was president. The 1926 Harmon Trophy went to Shirley J. Short, who from July 1923 to November 1926 flew 2,169 hours, in all kinds of weather, almost half of the time at night, without a single serious mishap. This was a record without equal in any

country in the world, but there were other air-mail pilots
with log books almost as impressive.

The transcontinental, or Columbia, line was to be broken
up into two sections. The government did not believe that
any operator had sufficient resources or experience to assume the responsibility of coast-to-coast service, and the air-
line executives themselves did not care to expand too fast
into strange territory. Accordingly, advertisements called
for two bids: one on the route from New York to Chicago,
and the other from Chicago to San Francisco.

Up in Seattle, where he had a factory, William E. Boeing made a decision. Boeing had been watching the feeder-
line operations. He knew the risks of air transportation, but
he saw that the right kind of operation could be profitable.
Pop Hanshue's Western Air Express was an example of
what a well-managed line could do, for with the passage of
the air-mail amendment, WAE was making a fortune out
of mail payments. Furthermore, Boeing reasoned, an air
line might be a splendid outlet for the products of his
airplane factory.

When the bids were opened on January 15, 1927, the
aviation industry received a jolt. For Boeing and his old
partner, Edward Hubbard, had offered to carry the mail
across the country from San Francisco to Chicago for only
$2.89 a pound ($1.50 for the first thousand miles and 15
cents for each additional hundred miles). In later years
when the air lines were overwhelmed by a hostile government, the transcontinental line was accused of overcharg-
ing for its services, but in 1927 any operator would have
exclaimed that Boeing's bid was simply ridiculous. It was
just half the maximum payment advertised by the postoffice. In comparison, William B. Stout's bid appeared to
be an attempt at skyway robbery. Stout had bid $5.09 for
the same route ($2.64 for the first thousand miles and 26.4
cents for each additional hundred miles), but Stout was
bidding for profits, not for a manufacturing outlet, since he

no longer owned an aircraft factory. Experts predicted that Boeing Air Transport could not last on such meager payments. Yet the Boeing bid became the basic contract upon which the great United Air Lines was to grow.

There was no doubt as to the award, of course. Boeing had the experience, equipment, and financial stability, and he had offered to carry mail more than half-way across the country for the same amount of money paid by the post-office to the operators of the Boston and New York route. If he wished to squander his fortune, that was his concern, but rival operators protested bitterly that Boeing was out to wreck the whole airway system; that he could not operate safely on such an income; and that he was letting his factory bear the brunt of the cost. Nevertheless, Boeing won the line, which was designated CAM–18.

Boeing himself said that between the time he signed the air-mail contract (later sublet by Boeing and Hubbard to Boeing Air Transport) in February, and the start of the new service in July, he designed, built, and put into operation twenty-five planes of a new type especially adapted for air-mail carriage.[4] One of his former engineers maintains that this is a slight exaggeration and that the new Boeing mail planes were already built at the time the contract was signed. The important thing is that less than five months after Boeing won the transcontinental award, his pilots were crossing the continent in ships that had never even been fully tested. This is a marvelous achievement of production; all the more so because the machines were successful from the very first day. Known as the Boeing 40 Mail Planes, they were single-motored biplanes with a cabin for two passengers up forward by the mail pit, but the pilot remained out in the open, where he could gauge by contact the force of wind and rain. In two years these planes traveled more than two million miles before they were replaced by more efficient equipment.

The eastern end of the transcontinental line was awarded

only after a battle. National Air Transport, well financed and well managed, had been operating successfully as a feeder between Chicago and Dallas-Fort Worth. When bids were advertised for the New York to Chicago section of the transcontinental, NAT thought this would tie in very well with its existing route. Colonel Paul Henderson, general manager of the company, thereupon submitted a bid of $1.24 and was awarded the contract on April 2. The contract was withheld, however, pending a hearing on the protests of a rival; for it appears that NAT was not the lowest bidder.

The unexpected threat to National Air Transport was the bid of North American Airways. NAA was a Cleveland company organized by the government air-mail pilots who feared for their jobs when the well-established NAT line bid on the route. The company was organized barely in time to put in its bid. NAA offered to carry the mail at $1.23 a pound, which was one cent under the NAT bid. The Postoffice Department, in awarding the contract to NAT, maintained that the Kelly Act, and past decisions of the Comptroller General, accorded some discretion to the Postmaster General when bids were approximately the same. Comptroller General John R. McCarl agreed that the Postmaster General was not necessarily bound to give the award to the lowest bidder, but McCarl insisted that the Postoffice Department must give reasons for any departure from the usual procedure. Postmaster General New pointed to the law, which provided that contracts were to be awarded to the lowest *responsible* bidder, with emphasis on the " responsible." The Postmaster General argued that the record of NAT showed it to be the more responsible company. Colonel Henderson added that the North American Airways bid was illegal because $100,000 of its capitalization was subscribed by federal employees (the air-mail pilots). Colonel Henderson no doubt was referring to the Act of March 4, 1909,[5] which was a measure passed to forbid postal executives from engaging in private business, but North American Airways got an opinion from Charles Evans Hughes to the effect that the law did not preclude mail flyers from bidding, since they were obviously not executives. McCarl was finally convinced, however, that NAT was the more responsible bidder, and he did not protest further the Postoffice Department's award.

Decision to give the route to NAT probably was to the best interests of the public, since NAT was well established and able to absorb the financial shocks that any new line must experience. If there had been any great difference in the bids, North American Airways might have had a better case, since it had flying experience and apparently satisfactory backing. It was September before the troubles were settled, but by the end of that month National Air Transport was flying regularly between New York and Chicago.

Aviation was all ready for a boom in 1927, and the spark that set it off was the flight of Charles Augustus Lindbergh on May 20, 1927, which was the first anniversary of the Air Commerce Act. Lindbergh took off from Roosevelt Field and landed 33 hours, 30 minutes later at Le Bourget Airport, Paris. His ship, the Ryan-Whirlwind *Spirit of St. Louis,* became a symbol for American youth. It is still the most popular exhibit at the National Museum, where it hangs from the ceiling just inside the main entrance.

The furore caused by the Lindbergh flight puzzles the aviation student. Lindbergh was not the first to cross the Atlantic Ocean. The first crossing was made by the United States Navy's giant seaplane *NC-4* in May 1919. In the following month John Alcock, a Canadian, and A. W. Brown, an American, flew non-stop from Newfoundland to Ireland in a Vickers-Vimy bomber, and the dirigible *R-34* made a crossing in July. It is true that Lindbergh fired the imagination by flying alone and without official aid, and he had the kind of personality that appeals to the public, but the adulation of Lindbergh can be explained only by pointing out that the public was ready for an air hero in 1927, whereas the earlier flyers were ahead of their time. Everything considered, the Alcock-Brown flight is more impressive than Lindbergh's. Nevertheless, the "Lone Eagle's" exploit galvanized aviation into a frenzy of activity.

The extent of the resulting boom may be realized by comparing the number of applications for pilot licenses. For the fiscal year ending June 1927, a period that is almost entirely "pre-Lindbergh," there were only 1,800 applications filed with the Aeronautics Branch of the Department of Commerce. Over a corresponding period after the Lindbergh flight, there were 5,500 such applications. In the same period the number of licensed planes increased from 1,100 to 4,700, while the applications for mechanics' licenses jumped from 1,600 in 1926 to more than 5,000 in 1927.[6] The Lindbergh flight proved nothing that engineers did not already know, but psychologically the effect of that ocean crossing was enormous. Many authorities deny that Lindbergh's flight had anything to do with the aviation boom. These experts say the industry had been building up to it for years, and that it would have come, with or without the "Lone Eagle." This is probably true, but there seems to be little doubt that the flight started the big aviation explosion of 1928–9.

It has appeared that the private operators found little difficulty in capitalizing their small lines. This is true, but community and civic pride rather than convictions of sound business more often kept the small lines going during 1925, 1926, and part of 1927. Gradually the reduction in the postal rates, the great improvement in equipment, and the belief that the air lines might repeat the story of the railroads began to encourage investors. After the Lindbergh flight and the consequent advertising of aviation by other adventurous airmen, air-line stocks boomed. Most of these investments were highly speculative, but the public gobbled up air stocks as fast as new issues appeared. Sometimes the speculator had no idea of what he was buying. Stock of Seaboard Air Line, for example, enjoyed an unprecedented price rise about this time. Officials seeking the reason for this sudden boom discovered that many purchasers of Seaboard Air Line stock thought they were buying their way into the aviation industry. Seaboard Air Line was not an airway, however. It was, and is, an east-coast railroad.

As a result of the demand for aviation stock a few investors reaped enormous profits. In December 1926, for example, Charles W. Deeds, son of Colonel E. A. Deeds, bought 90 shares of the new Pratt & Whitney (aircraft engines) stock. He paid 20 cents a share, or $18. Later young Deeds bought 110 additional shares, and by July 1927 he owned 200 shares, which had cost him only $40. In November 1928 he got a stock dividend of 79 for 1, which raised his holdings to 16,000 shares of stock. When the successful engine company was absorbed by merger with United Aircraft & Transport Corporation, Deeds, now treasurer of Pratt & Whitney, traded his stock for 34,720 shares of United Aircraft. Had Deeds sold his stock at this time, his $40 investment would have returned him $3,367,840.[7]

This is not the place to discuss the ethics of such transactions. If the Deeds case appears to be an indictment of the aviation industry, there are also answers to the charges. Had anyone bought Ford stock in the early days of the motor car, he would have reaped similar profits. But the above example does indicate the expansion of the aviation industry in the later twenties. All this frenzied speculation was to be thoroughly aired five years later, when depression and a change of administration brought on a Senate investigation.

In 1928 Representative Kelly sponsored a second amendment to his original Contract Air Mail Act of 1925 and Congress passed the modified law on May 17. It provided for a reduction of the postal rate to five cents an ounce (instead of ten cents a half ounce). Up to this time, mail loads did not average more than two hundred pounds a trip, except over such "heavy" routes as between New York and Chicago, or Los Angeles and Salt Lake City. The 1926 law had substituted the pound rate for the old postal revenue rate as the basis of payments to air-mail operators, so that operators depended now upon volume of mail, not upon the amount of postage. A reduction in postal rates decreased air-mail revenue, but it increased the volume of air mail. The 1928 law, therefore, was a boon to the air-mail lines, although the gain was at the expense of the government. If this amendment was passed for the purpose of aiding the air lines, the effectiveness of the measure is evident in the chart on page 164, showing mail payments year by year. Compensation to carriers rose from 22.6 cents an airplane mile prior to July 1, 1926, to 73.6 cents a mile for the second half of 1927.[8] This brought mail payments to just a little less than the average operating cost. By the end of 1928, however, payments were up to 92 cents a mile, and by the end of 1929 the government was paying the operators $1.09 a mile for carrying the mail.[9] Some routes, which had been awarded contracts on maximum bids, actually received more for carrying mail than the government received in postal revenue.

The temptation must be obvious. If the air line was paid more than the actual postage, why could not the operator make a profit by getting all his friends to send packages by air mail? Several lines did put on private air-mail publicity campaigns, to their great profit. It was popularly supposed at this time that certain operators kept heavy parcels, notably of telephone books, on the plane, mailing them back and forth on each trip. The postage was considerable, but as the government paid by weight, and as this payment greatly exceeded the cost of stamps, these heavy parcels returned a neat profit to the operator on every trip. Later investigations disclosed that one air-line executive ordered all spare parts and replacements shipped by air mail, and a writer tells of another air line which stayed within the letter of the law by sending Christmas cards that were a shade under the ounce limit for minimum air-mail postage. As the line was remunerated on a per-pound basis, the profit on such a card, properly padded with blank paper, was about nine cents for each card, " a nice combination of good will to man and business sense." [10]

Not all the lines permitted such abuses, of course, and indeed in many cases the operator was in no position to gain by padding his mail sacks. For if he had won his contract in competition with other bidders, his remuneration was likely to be far less than payments to contractors who had won on maximum bids. At one extreme of the payment scale was Western Air Express, one of the five original contractors. Its payments on the profitable run between Los Angeles and Salt Lake City amounted to $3.17 cents a mile, whereas the Chicago-Atlanta line received only 15 cents a mile. Ford, until he suspended operation in 1929, received only 4 cents a mile for his Detroit-Cleveland mail service. There was greed at the head of the table, but many another operator wasted away on the few crumbs of air-mail payments that came his way.

The reduction of postal rates in accordance with the second amendment of the Air Mail Act was of far-reaching consequence, but another important section of the 1928 law was also significant. This clause provided that contractors who had operated routes satisfactorily for two years or more might surrender their old contracts for air-mail " route certificates." [11] Route certificates were, in effect, a kind of franchise entitling the holder to the exclusive operation of such routes for a period of ten years from the date of the original contract.

This provision, on the whole, should have been accepted joyfully by the operators. Certificate-holders might have a measure of security they had never known before. They could plan ahead without the haunting fear of losing the route to a lower bidder. No air-line executive cared to purchase expensive equipment to be paid for over a period of years if the line itself was to be threatened by an outside bidder periodically. If the government seemed to be granting the air lines a kind of monopoly, it was also protecting experienced operators from unfair competition. Under the old system an irresponsible bidder who was unfamiliar with the risks might deprive a veteran carrier of a route that had been pioneered and developed at great expense and sacrifice. An interloper might underbid for the sole purpose of taking away a route for later exploitation. The postoffice was expected to award bids only to responsible operators, but there was always a threat hanging over the head of the air-line executive that some day he might lose his route.

But if the operator gained a measure of stability by his certificate, he paid for security with much of his old independence. He held his franchise during good behavior, and he thereupon depended more and more upon the goodwill of the Postoffice Department. The amendment also provided that the Postmaster General might reduce payments periodically by *negotiation*. In no case was compensation to exceed that provided under the original contract. Such negotiation placed even more power in the hands of the Postmaster General.

The amendment said that the Postmaster General *might* issue a certificate. It did not *require* him to do so. Nor did it force operators to exchange their contracts for a franchise. Because negotiations for a certificate could only result in lower payments (the law clearly expected the postmaster to reduce payments periodically), air-line executives believed the advantages of the certificate did not compensate for the risk of reduced payments. No operator was in a hurry, therefore, to exchange his contract.

Had payments been reduced along with postal rates, air lines might not have had to face trial five years later. The five-cent air-mail rate became effective August 1, 1928. The result was a ninety-five-per-cent increase in air-mail traffic. This just about doubled air-line income, with almost no additional expense to the operators. But the revenue to the government dropped alarmingly (see the table on page 129 for figures from 1929 on). The new rate brought in postal revenues of about $4,250,546.90 in the remaining eleven months of the fiscal year. But payments to operators in this period amounted to $11,169, 015.13. The loss to the government was nearly $7,000,000, which still does not include air-mail ground expense, such as getting mail to and from airports. In other words, the air lines were now only about forty per cent self-supporting.[12]

Postmaster General New could have remedied this situation, had he cared to. Under the 1928 amendment he was authorized to reduce payments when postal rates were cut. He deliberately maintained the old payments under reduced postal rates in order to determine what effect volume would have upon stabilizing the growing air lines. Possibly the approaching elections also had something to do with failure to balance postal revenues and payments. The experiment was to have lasted only six months, but the Postmaster General was so near the end of his term of office by that time that he left the unpleasant task of cutting payments to his successor.

The year 1929 marks the beginning of another stage in aviation development, for the air lines, unlike the railroads, reached the merger period early. From 1925, when private capital first developed the airways, until 1929, most of the lines were small, scattered, and disintegrated. National Air Transport was strongly backed and the route traversed an extensive territory, but the route from New York bent at right angles at Chicago, so that there was really no continuous service. Boeing Air Transport came closest to being a

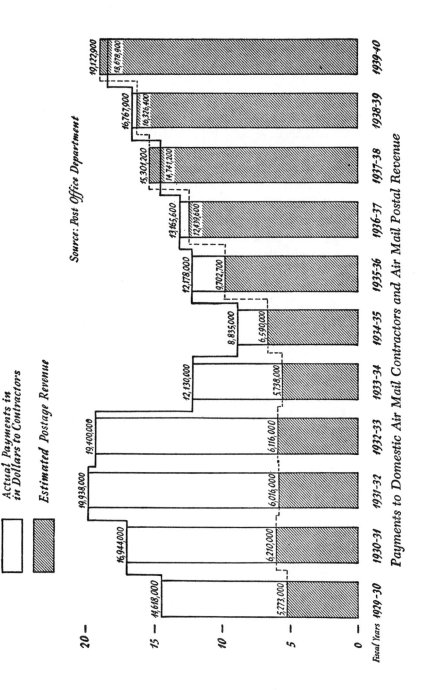

Source: Post Office Department

Actual Payments in
in Dollars to Contractors

Estimated Postage Revenue

Payments to Domestic Air Mail Contractors and Air Mail Postal Revenue

" system " because of its length (Chicago to San Francisco) and because its traffic was " through " — that is, unified. Perhaps even the east- and west-coast lines might have claimed the status of airway systems. On the whole, however, air lines at this time were sectional and incomplete. In 1929 these straggling lines began to weave themselves into the modern air-line pattern. The year saw the beginning of a great merger movement. The holding company appeared, forcing out " the little fellow " ruthlessly and tying the loose ends of the inefficient industry into a network of routes covering the entire country.

There was a good and a bad side to this. As one aviation expert put it: ". . . practically all [these Independent] companies have one thing in common — they lack sound management . . . above all else, then, mergers of the right sort mean the acquisition of capable management." [13] Big, rich corporations could afford to risk the " long haul " profits in opening up a new airway. Many of these companies carried over the needed experience from allied industry, such as the railroads. On the other hand, many an Independent operator who had risked his life and fortune in building up his equity now found himself squeezed by the air-line octopus. In 1929 were heard the first rumblings of the coming storm.

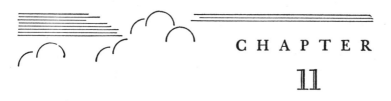

CHAPTER

11

The Urge to Merge

THE " LINDBERGH BOOM " had aircraft-manufacturers believing that at last the public was ready to become a customer. For a time it did appear as though private airplanes
might supersede military aircraft as the backlog of the industry, and in 1929 there were more than twice as many
builders of " sport " planes as there were makers of motor
cars. Stocks reflected this optimism. Wright Aeronautical,
listed at around 20 between 1922 and 1925, sold for 80 after
the Lindbergh flight, and although some of this rise may be
attributed to the Army and Navy Five-Year Plan of 1926,
military orders had petered out by 1929, when Wright
stock reached a high of $300 a share.[1] Only unreasonable
optimism can explain the boom in aviation stocks. In 1929,
investors poured nearly $400,000,000 into manufacturing
plants alone, and this did not include speculation in airports, hangars, and accessories.[2] To justify this investment,
manufacturers should have sold about 25,000 private and
commercial planes, yet in 1929, the peak year of production, airplane-builders disposed of only 3,500 units.[3] It is
amazing that the day of reckoning did not come sooner. As
it was, the crash in aviation stocks preceded the general

market collapse by about four months. It came when manufacturers suddenly realized that the public was more vocal than active in its enthusiasm.

The blame for the collapse in aviation stocks may be placed directly upon overpromotion of an industry which the public did not need. As long as the industry progressed slowly, there was some profit, but, as Colonel Henderson once remarked, aviation was diseased by too much money. It developed safely up to 1928, but when the promoters "found that there was blood in the beast," [4] they were attracted by the scent of possible profits through speculation. These aggressive gentlemen collected capital for lines across territories that could not possibly support an air-transportation system. They started flying and sales services in districts already saturated with such agencies. They ordered planes and motors, and the manufacturers expanded to meet the demand — only to find that there was no demand.

One or two individuals read the signs and predicted that the flying frenzy would wear itself out. These men believed that the industry had one alternative, and that was to sell the public service, not planes. Air transportation was still new. The time was ripe for founding dynasties, as in the railroad age of the previous century. And air transportation now had the encouragement of the Postoffice Department, which was willing to hand out fat mail contracts to the right kind of operator. It was in this atmosphere that aviation entered its next important phase — the merger period.

First of the great air-transportation companies to emerge was United Air Lines, which was organized in December 1928. Until it was dismembered after the air-mail "scandals" of 1933 and 1934, United was a kind of air-line family. One member was National Air Transport, which spanned the mountains and fertile plains from New York to Chicago and then turned sharply south into Kansas, Oklahoma, and Texas. Another member was Boeing Air Transport, stretching from Chicago to San Francisco. Little brother was Varney Air Lines, by this time based at Salt Lake City instead of Elko, and branching up through Washington to reach Seattle and Spokane. Finally, there was Pacific Air Transport, bought by William Boeing from Verne Gorst soon after PAT won a mail contract in 1926 for the route between San Diego and Seattle.

United Aircraft was the creature of Frederick B. Rentschler and William E. Boeing.

When Fred Rentschler got out of Princeton in 1909, he went to work for his father in Hooven, Owens, Rentschler & Company, makers of stationary engines at Hamilton, Ohio. Intelligent engine-inspectors were at a premium during the war, and young Fred was lured to near-by Dayton to check motors, and soon was sent to the Wright-Martin plant at New Brunswick, New Jersey, at that time feverishly engaged in turning out Hispano-Suiza aircraft motors for the French. Rentschler liked the aviation business, and he developed into an able executive. After the war he helped to liquidate Wright-Martin, and he later became first president of Wright Aeronautical Corporation. There he and George J. Mead began to hatch their Great Plan.

Mead had worked with Charles L. Lawrance in the development of the famed Wright " Whirlwind " radial engine, which had set a new standard of performance. Lindbergh's *Spirit of St. Louis* was Whirlwind-powered. So were most of the other transoceanic planes of that period. The Wright engine was without doubt the most reliable and rugged motor the country had ever seen, but it developed only about 200 horsepower. Mead believed he could build a more powerful motor. Military designers were ignoring the air-cooled radial because it did not produce the horse-

power of existing water-cooled engines. Standard military
motors in 1924 were the Curtiss D–12 and, to a lesser extent, the Packard. These motors developed twice the horsepower of the radials, but they were heavy, expensive, and
of limited life span. Mead was sure that he could build a
radial more powerful for its weight than any engine then
manufactured. The engineer had no money to finance a
factory, but he talked over his plans with the young president of Wright. Rentschler was getting restless as president
of Wright, because he believed the bankers were assuming
too much control. And, loving motors as he did, he yearned
for his own company. By 1924 he was so sure of what he
wanted to do that he resigned from Wright Aeronautical
Corporation and devoted himself to organizing his own
company. In the spring of 1925, navy officials assured
Mead and Rentschler that the government would give
every encouragement to the producers of a light, powerful
aircraft motor. There was no commitment on the part of
the navy, but there was a tacit understanding that the government would help defray experimentation costs by ordering a few engines for trial service, providing such motors
lived up to specifications on the test block.

Rentschler scurried around trying to find capital and
factory space for his new company. He had good business
connections, through his family and because of his experiences in the aviation industry. The Rentschlers were
neighbors and friends of President Collins of the Niles-
Bement-Pond Company, makers of precision tools, of
which Colonel E. A. Deeds was a director. A subsidiary
of this prosperous organization was Pratt & Whitney, a
small tool-making factory at Hartford, Connecticut. Pratt
& Whitney lay idle after the war, and it was this factory
that Rentschler took over in 1925. Someone undoubtedly
smoothed the way for the incorporation of the new aircraft
plant. Rentschler denies that Colonel Deeds had anything
to do with its organization,[5] as others have maintained, but

someone may have suggested the Hartford possibilities, for Rentschler later said:

" It came to my attention that the Niles-Bement-Pond Company had surplus plants on hand and also a considerable amount of cash, neither of which could be immediately used in its own business." [6]

At any rate, Pratt & Whitney Aircraft Company was incorporated in July 1925. It was only a " paper " company at first, in compliance with a contract between Niles-Bement-Pond, Rentschler, and Mead. The two young promoters bought a few shares of stock at twenty cents a share, but they put very little capital into the new venture. Niles-Bement-Pond was the heavy investor. From the wealthy parent company Rentschler and Mead received $250,000 in cash and the old Pratt & Whitney building at Hartford. This was sufficient capitalization for starting experiments on the new motor, and a month later Rentschler, Mead, and Donald L. Brown became the first employees of Pratt & Whitney Aircraft Company. Brown had been associated with Mead and Rentschler in the Wright company and later became president of Pratt & Whitney. In the early days, however, Rentschler was president, Mead chief engineer, and Brown factory superintendent. Pratt & Whitney opened its doors on August 1, 1925, and began to turn out the first of its famous engines. Known as the " Wasp," the new motor passed its endurance tests in March 1926.

It was an instantaneous success. The navy promptly ordered six for rigorous testing, and before long the Wasp engine almost entirely replaced the older, water-cooled motors on planes designed for the U. S. Navy. The Curtiss D–12 cost the government well over $9,000, with all experimentation written off. The first Wasps were 410-horsepower engines and were sold to the navy for $8,500, which included $1,700 for experimentation charges. Once the company went into mass production, the same type of engine sold for only $6,000. Furthermore, it had more horse-power per pound than any motor designed up to that time, and, to top it all, it had an apparently unlimited life.

As soon as the experimental period was over and the navy had approved the Wasp, Niles-Bement-Pond advanced half a million more dollars to finance actual production. In exchange, the parent company took $750,000 of Pratt & Whitney preferred stock, which covered both advances. By the end of the year Pratt & Whitney was working busily to fill its orders. The navy was so impressed with the Wasp performance that it placed an order for two hundred of the nine-cylinder radials. Shipments rose in value from $57,000 in 1926 to $15,898,000 in 1929.[7] With military orders as a backlog, Pratt & Whitney mushroomed into an organization with a payroll exceeding a million dollars a month. Even during the darkest days of the depression Pratt & Whitney expanded. Niles-Bement-Pond made such a handsome profit out of its investment that critics began to carp. On the other hand, Niles-Bement-Pond speculated with about a million dollars before it made a cent of profit.

One of Fred Rentschler's good friends was William E. Boeing, who had used part of his lumber fortune to start an airplane factory at Seattle. Boeing had been buying Wright motors for his Seattle factory, and he liked to do business with ebullient Fred Rentschler. They continued to meet after Rentschler left Wright to form his own company. About a year after Boeing won his air-mail contract for the air line between Chicago and San Francisco, he and Rentschler talked over the possibility of a merger. A party to these conversations, which were of the club-soda type, was Chance Vought, former auto racer, and builder of military planes. Boeing was enthusiastic about the Pratt & Whitney motor, which he was now using on his own ships. Why not merge the engine and airplane factories?

The plan appeared to be sound. Boeing needed efficient,

economical motors, since maintenance costs were the difference between profit and loss on the long mail run from Chicago to San Francisco. Rentschler, sure of his military backlog of orders, saw commercial aviation as a field for further expansion. Under such conditions, merger was inevitable. Boeing and Rentschler included Vought in their negotiations, and in October 1928 the three pooled resources.

Through his holding company, Boeing Airplane & Transport Corporation, Boeing first bought up the Vought factory. Pratt & Whitney paid its way into the organization by an exchange of stock involving 800,000 shares of a new super holding company incorporated as United Aircraft & Transport Corporation. Needing propellers for its motors and planes, United Aircraft bought up Hamilton Propeller Company, and when patent rights on metal blades became a matter of litigation, United Aircraft added Standard Steel Propeller. Less important companies added to the United Aircraft list were factories producing light commercial biplanes (Stearman), large amphibian transports (Sikorsky), and military trainers (Northrup), but the mainstay of United Aircraft was still Pratt & Whitney.

In the lush boom times of 1928 and early 1929, with a virtual monopoly of transcontinental air mail, United Aircraft garnered profits from the very first year. The merger had raised air transportation to the status of Big Business. Yet the executives were not satisfied.

United Air Lines, the airway unit of the holding company, was getting too big for its boots. It was the longest airway in the country, but its eastern terminus was at Chicago, eight hundred miles from the Atlantic seaboard. Before United Air Lines could become a great system, it had to span the country, connecting great cities with a unified service. Accordingly, Fred Rentschler began a drive to capture New York for his company.

The fly in the ointment was National Air Transport, one

of the strongest air lines in the country, and already firmly entrenched in New York. National Air Transport was part of a vast aviation empire that rivaled United Aircraft in power and extent. Clement Melville Keys, head of Curtiss Aeroplane & Motor Company, was czar of the National Air Transport dominions, and since the " Curtiss-Keys " group of aircraft companies was a competitor of United Aircraft in every aspect of aviation, it was inconceivable that Keys would let Rentschler into the NAT stronghold without a fight. United Air Lines needed New York in the same way that E. H. Harriman had needed it in the great days of railroading. The man who blocked Harriman's dream of railroad empire was James J. Hill, and it was Hill's protégé, C. M. Keys, who now threatened to check Rentschler's fulfillment of desire. The notorious Harriman-Hill feud at the turn of the century thus had an echo in the fight between Rentschler and Keys for control of the strategic Chicago and New York airway.

Actually, the fight was overrated by the press. National Air Transport did sell out under pressure, but it was less a defeat for Keys than a common-sense acknowledgment of the facts. United Air Lines *could* have avoided the hotly contested National Air Transport route by coming into New York by way of Buffalo. Keys was later frank in admitting that he saw the handwriting on the wall long before United took away the New York-Chicago run.[8]

Rentschler started the skirmishing by buying Stout Air Services, non-mail-carrying successor to the old Ford line, and the safest air line in the country. This brought United east of Chicago as far as Cleveland, which was definitely in National Air Transport's private bailiwick. At this point, brash Mr. Rentschler approached Earle H. Reynolds, Chicago banker, president of National Air Transport, and the largest individual stockholder in the air line. Rentschler suggested that United buy out NAT. A " through " route (coast-to-coast) would benefit both lines, Rentschler pointed out, and the merger could be worked out on approximately a dollar-for-dollar basis, since both companies were heavily backed and inventoried. Reynolds was willing to listen to this siren song and took the matter up with his directors. They received the news calmly enough, but the more C. M. Keys and Counselor Cuthell thought about it, the madder they got. The fight was on.

Unfortunately for Keys, he owned very little of National Air Transport, since his connection with it was indirect, via a holding company. Reynolds, the banker, held the strings to NAT, and it was Reynolds that Rentschler worked on during the ensuing weeks. Fred Rentschler's brother, Gordon, was vice president of the National City Bank of New York. Agents of National City met with Reynolds, and when the smoke cleared away, Reynolds had capitulated to the United group.

Reynolds's sell-out weakened Keys's hold on National Air Transport, but before United Air Lines could claim complete victory, it had to buy up a controlling interest in the open market. When United began buying, NAT stock was selling for $15 a share. Word of the big deal got around and in no time at all NAT had zoomed to $30 a share, even in a depressed market. It was an expensive war, but Rentschler was gaining ground. Keys saw the danger and called signals for a trick play that almost won him the game. The big new holding company of the " Curtiss-Keys " group was North American Aviation Company, backed by the influential Bancamerica-Blair Corporation. North American Aviation became one of the three great aviation " trusts " (the other two being United Aircraft and the Aviation Corporation), and Keys proposed an affiliation with this company. His plan was to issue thirty thousand shares of NAT stock in order to purchase an equal amount of North American Aviation. As Keys was top dog in North American Aviation, the exchange of stock would have given him such a preponderance of voting certificates in NAT that

Rentschler could never hope to build up more than a strong minority interest. It was a clever scheme, but there was just one trouble with it — it didn't work. When Fred Rentschler learned of this proposal he brought up his big guns.

"The air between the coasts is not big enough to be divided," he cried in best Robber Baron form,[9] although he maintained later that he meant only that the transcontinental line could not be split, as Keys intended.[10]

Rentschler's counter-attack was an injunction against the North American Aviation and National Air Transport stock exchange. While the injunction was in force, NAT stock dropped from its artificial high. Soon the United group had picked up enough stock and proxy votes to ensure control, when directors met for the annual meeting in Wilmington. At that time it was agreed that NAT should enter the United camp.

United Air Lines now added the Varney line, which branched off the transcontinental system at Salt Lake City to tap the Pacific Northwest. Varney was one of the first five mail contractors, and when the original four-year contracts expired in November 1929, United apparently made a dicker with the operators. A competitor was threatening the Varney territory, and when the bids were submitted, this line offered to carry the mail at the low rate of 74 cents a mile (the average for the United States was $1.09). Varney Lines, which had never made much profit from air mail, was for some reason so desirous of winning back its old route that it bid only 9 cents a mile, which could not have returned sufficient revenue to pay for the gasoline. But Varney then turned around and sold out at an excellent price to United Air Lines, and when, by a law passed early in 1930, the air lines exchanged contracts for negotiated certificates, the Varney mail rates were restored to the old level.

That was about the end of United's expansion. After

1929 it was mainly concerned with improving equipment and schedules. The line consolidated its services, standardized on Boeing planes, powered by Pratt & Whitney engines, and cut down on unnecessary duplication. By 1930 it was earning $1.24 a share, while the rival Curtiss-Wright system, which had put its chips on the private flying market, collapsed in the first days of the depression.

United's victory in the battle for National Air Transport was far more important to the Rentschler group than the loss was to C. M. Keys, for NAT was only one of many strings in Keys's bow. He had been an editor of the *Wall Street Journal* and had worked with Walter Hines Page on the old *World's Work;* Keys was also an important aviation promoter. He got into the manufacturing end of the industry during the war and eventually won control of Curtiss Aeroplane & Motor Company, one of the most important aircraft factories of the war period. In the booming twenties Keys absorbed a number of aviation enterprises into a holding company, of which Curtiss Aeroplane was the keystone. A rival of Curtiss Aeroplane was Wright Aeronautical Corporation (whose first president had been Rentschler) under the ægis of Richard F. Hoyt, of Hayden, Stone & Company. Keys brought the two groups together into an organization known as Curtiss-Wright Corporation, which was a strange association of names, since the Wrights and Glenn H. Curtiss had fought for years over patent rights. Curtiss-Wright began buying up lesser companies, and by 1929 it owned twenty-nine subsidiaries and was affiliated with eighteen other aviation companies. Eventually it came into the orbit of a new investment company which Keys had started in 1928.

The new company was North American Aviation Company, backed by General Motors (which gained full control in 1933), Hayden, Stone & Company, and Bancamerica-Blair. North American Aviation was organized for the specific purpose of buying up aviation properties of all types.[11] Before long it owned or controlled instrument companies, aircraft factories, engine plants, and important air lines. North American Aviation bought the important Eastern Air Transport system, which operated down the Atlantic coast, and it believed for a while that it owned National Air Transport, until United took it away.

The most important air-line property in the North American Aviation fold was Transcontinental Air Transport (TAT), which became the central cross-country mail and passenger route. TAT was organized even before the North American Aviation Company was incorporated, but the operators spent a year surveying the route, and the line became part of the vast holding company before it actually began service on July 4, 1929. Included in its list of backers were such important names as Henry Breckenridge, Woodrow Wilson's Assistant Secretary of War; J. Cheever Cowdin, vice president of Bancamerica-Blair; Colonel Paul Henderson, former Assistant Postmaster General; W. B. Mayo, general manager of the Ford Company; Earle Reynolds, president of NAT and of the Chicago People's Bank; W. H. Vanderbilt; and J. L. Maddux, president of Maddux Air Lines, the west-coast company which soon merged with TAT.

Most famous name on the TAT roster was that of America's Public Hero Number One, Colonel Charles A. Lindbergh. Lindbergh's popularity after his transatlantic flight and his odyssey through the Americas were of great commercial value. Any company that could link its name with his was assured of public interest and confidence. Lindbergh apparently realized his responsibility, for he was careful to identify himself with companies which he believed were worthy of public support. Because TAT was experimenting with a new type of air-transportation service, Colonel Lindbergh announced his affiliation with the line in 1929.

Lindbergh's motives were unassailable, and his identification with air transportation was of inestimable benefit to the young industry. But the colonel profited, too. Such was the public adulation of the unassuming aviator that it was taken for granted that he lived independent of money, like a god. This was not the case. His remuneration for his services to TAT is indicated in a letter written to him by Keys:

Carrying out the memorandum of agreement, I have tied up for your account 25,000 shares of stock of the Transcontinental Air Transport, Inc., at $10 per share and will deliver to you a check of the Transcontinental Air Transport, Inc., for $250,000 cash upon your request.

In order that all the records shall be clear for income tax purposes, please consult Colonel Breckenridge and see if he agrees with the following procedure:

1. I will deliver to you a check for $250,000 cash together with a brief memorandum showing exactly what it is for, which memorandum Mr. Cuthell and Colonel Breckenridge should prepare.

2. I will deliver to you certificates for 25,000 shares of stock and receive back either the Transcontinental Air Transport check endorsed, or your personal check, according as Colonel Breckenridge and Mr. Cuthell may advise.

3. This will complete the first part of our trade and leave you with the stock in your possession. I suggest that you do not put very much of this stock in your own name because when you sell it — and I hope that you will sell part of it on the first favorable opportunity — either the delivery of the stock in your own name, or the transfer of it on the books would excite a lot of attention, which is quite unnecessary. Colonel Breckenridge will no doubt agree to this advice.[12]

TAT thereupon became known as "The Lindbergh Line," an advertising slogan worth every cent that was paid the flyer.

Before United Aircraft captured National Air Transport as the eastern leg of the United Air Line system, NAT and TAT were both members of the same family, yet they appeared to be competitive, since both reached westward out

of New York. If they were not competitive, why was not
TAT more logically developed as an extension of NAT?
The reason for the two divisions was that each line was
operated as a specialized air-transportation service. TAT
was strictly a passenger service. NAT was exclusively a
mail-carrier. Flying profitable mail cargoes between the
two largest cities in the country, NAT had no desire to
undertake troublesome passenger transportation. Whenever NAT was asked about adding air travel to its mail
service, officers replied that the dangerous Allegheny section made passenger traffic not feasible.

TAT made a special study of air-travel problems. It
called railroad experts to its board of management so that
the air line might have wise counsel on traffic matters.
D. M. Sheaffer, former chief of passenger transportation for
the Pennsylvania Railroad, became chairman of TAT's
executive committee, and the railroad had a substantial
financial interest in the line.

Dependence upon railroads was even more tangible than
the tapping of railroad personnel and capital. The air line
also needed railroad facilities, for TAT was developed as
an *air-rail* service. Over the dangerous mountains TAT
routed its transcontinental passengers in Pullmans of the
Pennsylvania Railroad. Leaving New York at night, the
traveler disembarked next morning at Columbus, Ohio.
TAT passengers were transferred from train to plane at
a special station erected on the edge of the Columbus airport. Here a Ford tri-motor waited to whisk patrons across
the safe flying country of the Middle West. At Waynoka,
Oklahoma, passengers took to the Santa Fe railroad for the
night trip to Clovis, New Mexico, where another plane
waited to complete the trip to Los Angeles. This new system had many advantages. It was safer than other forms of
air travel, and equipment set a new standard in comfort.
Above all, it provided a degree of reliability that the air
lines had never known before. Other air-line executives

could argue that their services saved the business man hours of travel time. They could point with pride to their safety records. But until they could guarantee the maintenance of schedules, they had difficulty in selling air transportation. A traveler lost valuable hours crossing the country by train instead of by plane, but at least he knew he could keep an appointment. He *might* keep his appointment by using the air liner, thereby gaining a day, but if the plane were grounded by weather, as often happened, the exasperated traveler could only vow that thereafter he'd stick to the good old train. TAT's new system remedied this defect of air travel to a large extent.

Air-rail service was still too slow, however. If it took forty-eight hours to reach Los Angeles from New York over the TAT route, there was no great advantage in the service. A fast train was safer, cheaper, and not very much slower. Moreover, air-rail service was too expensive for its value. Average passenger fare per air-mile in 1929 was twelve cents. In the Southwest, fares were lower; but TAT charged sixteen cents a mile, and still lost money. Such travel appealed only to the luxury group. TAT recognized this and catered to such patrons. Travelers received expensive gold pens as "souvenirs." They ate from gold plates. At the airport tear-shaped "aero-cars" waited to carry them to the hotel district.

This all took place in the pre-depression days, of course, but even in those halcyon times TAT could not fill its planes. Seldom did more than two passengers disembark from the Pullmans. The airport railroad stations, which were made to accommodate hundreds of passengers, were still standing a decade later, forlorn monuments to a system that did not succeed. When the depression came, sixteen-cents-a-mile transportation was doomed.

The TAT experiment was a commendable effort, but the results were discouraging. In the first eighteen months the line lost $2,750,000. Operators learned again the bitter lesson that no air line could exist without the financial help of a government air-mail contract. Sadly TAT officials admitted that a service devoted exclusively to passengers was hopeless, at least until the public learned the advantages of air travel. Just as certain were the experts that air-rail service, for all its merits, was a failure.

CHAPTER

12

E Pluribus American

W HILE Transcontinental Air Transport was learning to its sorrow that passenger traffic did not pay, another line was working its haphazard way across the southern tier of states. Known eventually as American Airways, it was the operating subsidiary of a corporation so vast and ramified that it would be impossible to enumerate the component parts on this page. This unwieldy organization was Aviation Corporation (AVCO), parent of the equally complex American Airways.

The line had more roots than a banyan tree, but it started as a mere sprig in the summer of 1927, when John Paul Riddle and T. Higbee Embry organized a flying service at Cincinnati. When the Postoffice Department advertised for bids on a route from their home city to Chicago, the partners put in a bid and won the contract. Embry-Riddle Service began carrying mail over CAM–24 on December 17, 1927, anniversary of the Wright flight.

Until it began carrying mail, the Embry-Riddle enterprise was capitalized at only $10,000, all of which was supplied by the two partners, or their friends. The mail contract made it necessary to seek more capital for the purchase of additional equipment, and the two promoters collected about $90,000 in Cincinnati. Even that was insufficient, however, and it was while the partners were trying to solve their financial problems that American Airways was born.

The Embry-Riddle company was agency for the popular Fairchild monoplane, and when the partners required more capital, a rival of the Fairchild company offered to advance the money if they would take over the rival agency in place of the Fairchild franchise. Directors of Fairchild Aviation Corporation heard about this and made Embry-Riddle a counter-offer. They suggested that Fairchild organize a new subsidiary, with a capitalization of from $500,000 to $1,000,000, which would underwrite such small enterprises as the Cincinnati air line until such time as the financing of these operations attracted the interest of the banks. The suggestion met with such approval that in March 1929 Aviation Corporation appeared with an authorized capital, far greater than originally planned, of 2,000,000 shares which it proposed to sell at $20 a share.

The president of the new company was Graham B. Grosvenor, head of the Fairchild company and former vice president of Otis Elevator. Among the directors were W. A. Harriman, G. M. Pynchon, and Robert Lehman (investment bankers) ; David K. E. Bruce, son-in-law of Andrew Mellon; Robert Dollar, the west-coast shipper; Harry S. New, former Postmaster General; George R. Hann, prominent Pittsburgh aviation promoter; and General Mason M. Patrick, United States Air Services, retired. The stock issue was underwritten by the banks at $17.50 a share, and then was disposed of in a twinkling to the public at the list price. AVCO thus had a working capital of $35,000,000 almost at once. Now the tail began to wag the dog, for Fairchild became the subsidiary of AVCO.

AVCO went out to buy up more than Embry-Riddle (which, as events turned out, was one of the companies AVCO had difficulty in winning over) . Within a short time the new holding company owned control of air lines all over the country. For convenience in describing the development of American Airways, the AVCO empire may be divided, roughly, into five principalities. These were Colonial Air Transport, Universal Aviation Corporation, Southern Air Transport, Embry-Riddle Services, and a group of miscellaneous enterprises with no relationship to any air-line system.

In a previous chapter Colonial Air Transport was traced from its beginning as the Bee Line in Naugatuck, Connecticut, through a series of mergers, to the formation of the Colonial system, under the management of General John F. O'Ryan and associates. Colonial won CAM–1 between Boston and New York, and soon other Colonial enterprises began to appear. Colonial Western Airways won CAM–20, Albany to Buffalo. Canadian Colonial Airways, connecting with Colonial Western at Albany, started carrying mail from New York to Montreal under a foreign air-mail contract (FAM–1). There were in addition Colonial flying schools, Colonial flying fields, and Colonial taxi services. The holding company for all these scattered interests was Colonial Airways Corporation, organized in 1929, at about the time that Aviation Corporation appeared on the scene.

AVCO directors looked at Colonial Airways Corporation and found it good. They invited Colonial stockholders to exchange holdings with AVCO, and soon Colonial and all its subsidiaries were controlled by the lusty Aviation Corporation.

In like manner, the southern territory became a fief of AVCO. The holder of CAM–22 and CAM–21 out of Dallas and Fort Worth to San Antonio and Galveston, respectively, was Texas Air Transport. Texas Air was the property of Temple Bowen, a tough-minded bus-operator, who was to cause AVCO plenty of trouble before he returned to his original business. In 1928 Bowen gave up air transportation, only temporarily, when he sold Texas Air to a company that became known as Southern Air Transport.

Southern Air Transport was the hobby and by-product of A. P. Barrett, a Tennessean who branched out into the transportation business after an unsuccessful career as a politician.[1] Barrett acquired sufficient capital to buy an air line by a series of business manipulations that had nothing at all to do with planes or transportation. He heard that Ranger Gas Company of Ranger, Texas, was for sale, and without knowing much about the community he put in a bid. Much to his surprise, he was the only bidder. Unfortunately, Barrett had no money, having lost everything in a disastrous oil venture. He went to Ranger, however, and convinced the receivers that he could make good on his bid, if given a little time. They granted the request, and Barrett soon made the necessary down payment by collecting outstanding debts of the company.[2] When he finally gained full control of Ranger Gas, he expanded it into the Texas-Louisiana Power Company, with properties in Louisiana, Oklahoma, Kentucky, New Mexico, and Texas. In 1928 he sold out to General Water Works & Electric Corporation, and with part of the profit he bought and merged three bus lines. Barrett liked the transportation business, and he saw aviation as the bus line of the future. In October 1928 he bought Texas Air Transport from Bowen, and soon expanded it into a system he called Southern Air Transport. Soon SAT had become the most important system south of Mason and Dixon's line, and before long it was absorbing other groups of air lines.

One of these lines was Gulf Coast Airways (originally St. Tamany-Gulf Coast), which carried mail over CAM–29, New Orleans to Houston, and CAM–23, Atlanta to New Orleans. Gulf Coast needed more capital for its expanded mail service, and it therefore formed a holding company, Gulf Air Lines, to raise money, as did the Colonial group.

In February 1929 Southern Air Transport stockholders exchanged shares with Gulf Air Lines and its subsidiaries. Shortly after this reorganization Southern Air Transport, in turn, was invited to come into the AVCO family, with Barrett as vice president of the controlling company.

Aviation Corporation directors preferred to buy up " ready made " systems, but sometimes they bought single airways and operated them independently. Such a company was Interstate Airlines, which AVCO picked up in 1929, about a year after Interstate won its bid on CAM–30, Chicago to Atlanta. AVCO even organized its own lines, as in the case of Alaskan Airways, which was rivaled not by other air lines, but by the old reliable dog teams. Most of AVCO's growth was by absorption of systems, however.

One of the biggest airway systems was Universal Aviation Corporation, operating in the Chicago, St. Louis, and Kansas City area. An important unit in the Universal system was Robertson Aircraft Corporation, organized by Major William B. and F. H. Robertson in February 1921, and one of the first five private mail-carriers. The capital stock of Robertson Aircraft originally was only $15,000, representing a Curtiss biplane and an extra 90-horsepower OX–5 motor. Between 1921 and 1926 the Robertsons appear to have prospered, for soon after the company received the award for CAM–2, between St. Louis and Chicago, it had a book value of about $200,000. In the midst of the Lindbergh boom of 1928, Major Robertson and C. M. Keys organized Curtiss-Robertson Airplane and Manufacturing Corporation, makers of the famous Curtiss " Robin " cabin plane. Robertson thereupon gave up the air-transportation business to devote all his time to making planes, and CAM–2 was purchased by a St. Louis group. When the private-plane boom collapsed, Major Robertson returned to the air-transportation field by starting up another line, of which more will be said later. The original Robertson line continued to expand after the brothers left

it. The new operators won CAM–28, which extended the
line to Kansas City and Omaha. By 1929 the airway between Kansas City and Chicago was known as one of the
better enterprises, and it was at this time that it merged
with Universal.

Another Universal acquisition was Braniff Air Lines,
started by Paul Braniff in May 1928, and financed by an
elder brother, Tom E. Braniff, wealthy Oklahoma insurance man. The Braniff line, with no mail contract, carried
passengers at very low fares between Kansas City, Dallas
and Fort Worth. The Braniffs lost money from the start,
and when Universal made an offer in 1929, they sold out.
In 1930 the Braniffs returned to air transportation with a
new and stronger line, which had no connection with the
old company.

Universal Aviation Corporation, which was to bind
these companies together, was organized in Delaware on
July 30, 1928, on the skeleton of Continental Air Lines,
formed the year before to carry mail over CAM–16, Cleveland to Louisville. Continental became " Universal " in
September, when the line received its charter. The new
company issued 245,000 shares, which were bought up
mostly by a syndicate of St. Louis, Chicago, and Minneapolis bankers for $2,300,000, or a little less than $10 a
share. The company began acquiring stock in other aviation enterprises, paying partly in cash and partly with stock
in Universal. Here the threads became almost too tangled
to unravel. For example, Northern Air Lines, organized
in 1928, issued 900 shares of stock to Northern Aeronautics,
a flying service, keeping only ten shares, valued at $1,000,
for itself. In return it received a transfer to its books of
$72,000 in " accounts receivable " from Universal, which
had been given originally to Northern Aeronautics in return for the assumption by that company of the obligation
to repay certain advances amounting to $98,000 made by
individuals. Northern Aeronautics, in turn, issued its 5,000

shares of no-par stock to Universal in exchange for stock in this company, plus 1,000 shares of another flying service, Mid-Plane Sales & Transit Company. It would take an expert accountant to follow such a maze, and this is only one of a dozen similar examples — used here merely to show the complexity of the Universal system.

Late in 1929, Universal directors accepted an invitation to exchange stock with Aviation Corporation, and AVCO ended up with a ninety-five-per-cent controlling interest in Universal. All this financial lucubration started with Embry-Riddle, which had gained its needed capital through its own holding company, Embry-Riddle Aviation Corporation. This was a strictly financial company, which purchased the operating company by means of an exchange of stock and an indeterminate amount of cash. As a subscriber to the holding company's stock issue, AVCO had an interest in the Embry-Riddle line, but it was a long time before the bigger company obtained full control.

In the meantime AVCO had been buying up airports, engine plants, airplane factories, flying services, and instrument companies, until it is doubtful if any officer in Aviation Corporation could have even named the affiliate companies. There were now more than eighty little systems revolving around the great central body. Each little galaxy had its orbit, but frequently they clashed, as when mail and non-mail subsidiaries competed for passengers over the same route. There wasn't even a standard system of bookkeeping, so that the directors themselves did not know whether or not AVCO's operating companies were making money. To simplify the operation of the clumsy organization, directors agreed to form a new company, which would acquire from the old transportation enterprises all the stock which they, in turn, owned in subsidiary lines. The new super holding company was organized late in 1929, and it received its charter on January 25, 1930. This new subsidiary of Aviation Corporation was American Airways.

Its capital was 40,000 shares of preferred stock with a par of $100, and 10,000 shares of no-par common.

At this time Aviation Corporation owned a controlling interest in three subsidiary holding companies: Colonial Airways Corporation, Southern Air Transport, and Universal Aviation Corporation. It had a substantial, although not controlling, interest in Embry-Riddle Aviation Corporation. Finally, it owned directly (not through a subsidiary) all the stock in Interstate Airlines and Alaskan Airways, which were independently operated. The plan was for each of the subsidiary holding companies to sell to the newly formed American Airways all the stocks in their operating subsidiaries, in return for common stock in American Airways. Each company was to receive a block of the 10,000 common shares of American Airways according to the proportionate ratio of its tangible assets to the value of all the combining subsidiaries. In other words, if all of the component parts of the Universal system were worth forty-two per cent of all the equity in American Airways, then it would receive 4,200 shares to distribute to its stockholders, proportionate to their holdings in Universal.

To furnish capital for the new company, AVCO directors proposed that each subsidiary holding company buy a proportional share of a block of 10,000 shares of the $100 preferred stock. This would furnish about a million dollars. The purchase of preferred stock was to be in proportion to the amount of common stock assigned to each subsidiary holding company. All of the subsidiary operating companies accepted this proposal with the exception of Embry-Riddle Aviation Corporation. Accordingly, American Airways issued its 10,000 shares of no-par common to the subsidiary holding companies. Colonial Airways Corporation received 2,226 shares; Southern Air Transport, 2,074; Universal Aviation Corporation, 4,288; and Aviation Corporation, 1,025. In return, American Airways acquired all the stocks of the operating subsidiaries. Embry-Riddle Aviation, which was offered the last 387 of the 10,000 shares, apparently believed the price to be too low. It therefore continued to control its own operating company until 1932, when the 270-mile route became part of the American Airways empire.

Eventually, the subsidiary holding companies disappeared entirely, leaving AVCO as sole stockholder of American Airways. This simplified the corporate structure of AVCO's airway system, but physically American Airways was still a mess. It rambled all over the country — from nowhere to nowhere — and it had no direct entry into New York except from the north. It was the most roundabout way to reach the west coast, and it was losing money at a terrific rate. How the line developed from this sorry state into the most profitable, and one of the safest, in the country, is a story best told in describing a later phase.

American Airways was the third of the great air systems to be formed during this very important period. Cutting across the northern part of the country was United Air Lines, carrying all the transcontinental mail over the route pioneered by the government. Across the central tier of states, Transcontinental Air Transport connected New York, Pittsburgh, St. Louis, Kansas City, and Los Angeles. Still farther south, reaching clear down to the Mexican border, was sprawling American Airways. All of these companies were to change in the next few years — United least; American most. Through 1929 they played the game their own way, but in that year a new figure emerges — a player who not only called all the signals, but who carried the ball much of the time. His emergence marks the beginning of a stormy period in commercial aviation.

Top Sergeant Brown

Swept in with the Hoover administration on March 4, 1929 was a man whose personality and power were to make him the dominant figure in commercial aviation. He was Walter Folger Brown, Toledo attorney and politician. President Harding had picked him in 1921 to serve as chairman of the Joint Congressional Committee on Re-organization of the Executive Departments, and President Coolidge had reappointed him to the post. Brown had long been active in Republican politics. He had worked faithfully for such leaders as Mark Hanna, William Howard Taft, Theodore Roosevelt, and Hiram Johnson, but the man Brown admired most was Coolidge's Secretary of Commerce, Herbert Hoover. Brown left the chairmanship of his committee to become an assistant secretary under Hoover, and it was Brown who " talked Hoover " to political leaders, thereby starting the California engineer on the road to the White House. After Hoover's election in 1928, Brown was rewarded with the portfolio of the Post-office Department. As Postmaster General and top sergeant of the dominant party, Brown was possibly the most powerful politician in the country. This was the man who became czar of civil aviation.

Brown knew little about flying when he took office, and it was several months before air-line operators were aware of his influence. During this time they bombarded the department with statistics and data, coupled with demands for greater privileges. The Postmaster General began to study aviation problems. Before long he knew more about the subject than anyone in the industry. The more he learned about aviation, the more he was convinced that it was his mission to lead the industry out of anarchy.

Brown realized that the Postoffice Department was the agency best fitted to aid commercial aviation. The Department of Commerce was doing its part by building the lighted airways, which the air lines could not possibly have financed, but only the postoffice could give the payments providing the nice balance of government aid and encouragement to private enterprise. Brown envisioned a system of strongly financed, competitive, transcontinental air lines intersected by an extensive network of feeder routes. Such a system, he reasoned, would stimulate manufacturers to build the safe, fast planes that the country required for public convenience and national defense. There was nothing new in this policy. The Postoffice Department had subscribed to it, more or less, throughout previous administrations. Where Brown departed from the old pattern was in administration of the policy.

Finding mail far more profitable than passengers, operators were putting too much reliance on their government contracts. One can hardly blame them for this attitude. As one expert demonstrated in the early days of air mail, the transcontinental passenger fare would have amounted to $1,003.12, assuming that the traveler weighed 150 pounds and paid a fare corresponding to the per-pound postal rate.[1] Nor was that all of the story. Mail not only brought in about eight times as much as a passenger could pay for a fare, but it also was cheaper to handle. Mail required no elaborate waiting-rooms, stewards, service help, ticket agencies, or ground transportation. And operators were content with small planes, adequate for the purpose, but showing little improvement from year to year. Excellent equipment for passenger service was available, and a few lines gave some encouragement to designers of such planes, but until all the lines began carrying passengers, Brown knew that his dream of a super air service could never materialize.[2]

He took drastic steps to accomplish his purpose. First he asked for a law giving him power to change the old post-office policy. On February 19, 1930 he appeared before the House Committee on the Post Office and Post Roads to recommend passage of the third amendment to the Kelly Bill (Air Mail Act of 1925). This amendment, better known as the McNary-Watres Bill, was sponsored by Republican Senator Charles D. McNary of Oregon, who was to be vice-presidential nominee in 1940; and Republican Representative Laurence H. Watres of Pennsylvania. Actual authors of the measure, however, were Brown and his second assistant, Warren Irving Glover, who had charge of air mail. They were aided by three representatives: [3] Mabel Walker Willebrandt, of prohibition fame, representing Aviation Corporation; William P. MacCracken, former Assistant Secretary of Commerce, representative for Western Air Express; and (somewhat unwillingly) Colonel Paul Henderson, former Second Assistant Postmaster General in charge of air mail, representing National Air Transport.[4]

The main provision of the new amendment was a change in the method of computing mail payments (see Appendix II for the McNary-Watres Bill). Operators were to be paid, not according to the old pound-per-mile rate, but according to the amount of space available for mail. It was outright subsidy, but it was an ingenious method of payment that was to have far-reaching consequences. If operators were to be paid by space, there was every advantage in ordering larger ships from aircraft-manufacturers. If mail did not take up all the space in these new ships, operators might install seats and thus attract a profitable passenger traffic. Human cargo would put a premium on faster, safer, more comfortable ships, but the Postoffice Department was willing to do something about that, too, by giving extra payment to lines willing to use multi-motored cabin planes, two-way radio, and aids to navigation. Manufacturers would be stimulated to produce finer equipment, and as the new airliners established records of reliability, passenger traffic would increase. Gradually fares were to replace mail payments as the mainstay of air-line revenue, until operators eventually were independent of subsidy in any form.

This was the purpose of the McNary-Watres Bill, and most of the promises were fulfilled. In short, it was to air transportation what the Jones-White Act was to the steamship lines. The most important provisions of the bill were:

1. That the space-mile rate was to be substituted for the pound-mile rate; the government to pay for cargo space at the rate of not more than $1.25 a mile, whether or not there was any mail to put into this space; and awards to be made to the " lowest responsible bidder " who had owned an air line operated on a daily schedule of at least 250 miles over a period of six months.

2. That any veteran of two years could exchange his mail contract for a route certificate good for ten years, unless revoked by the Postmaster General for " willful neglect " of postal regulations.

3. That the Postmaster General might *extend or consolidate* routes " when in his judgment the public interest will be promoted thereby." [5]

The proposed law gave Brown dictatorial powers over the air-transportation system, and his motives in sponsor-

ing the bill were at once suspected. To his critics, the Postmaster General explained his views, as follows:

Of course they did not all get the basic thought that was
back of my policy and that caused the arguments, usually. That
thought was this: *that we were not buying peanuts and pencils
and pig iron; we were buying a service that was highly specialized and exceedingly hazardous* [italics mine], and that there
was no sense in taking this government's money and dishing it
out . . . to every little fellow that was flying around the map
and was not going to do anything . . . to develop aviation in
the broad sense. But the thing to do was to spend that money
so that, if possible, we could develop . . . some people who
would compete with each other and bring their aeronautical
industry up to a point where it could finally sustain itself.
Helping some little fellow make good his losses for a few years
and have him no further along than when he started — there
was nothing in that; and those were the matters in my talks
with them that they did not quite get my point. They seemed
. . . to think that I was trying to foster an octopus, whereas
what I was trying to do was to get somebody with a big enough
personnel, with enough management and money back of it to
test this thing out and see whether it was possible to get an air
transport company that could live on its own, then there would
be plenty of competition.[6]

Another clause that Brown tried to include in the proposed amendment asked for power to award contracts without competitive bidding, when the public might thereby
be benefited. If an inexperienced and a veteran operator
both bid on a route, the veteran, knowing the hazards,
might put in a bid that was higher than that of his ignorant
rival. Brown believed that it was for the good of the public
for the Postmaster General to *negotiate* in such cases.
Again, since the certificate clause granted what amounted
to a franchise for ten years, Brown thought that only financially stable operators should be granted mail routes, even
though they were not low bidders.

Representative Clyde Kelly, sponsor of the original air-mail law of 1925, flatly refused to support the Postmaster General on the non-competitive clause. One explanation of this attitude may have been that the Congressman believed that Brown and Glover were slighting him. The McNary-Watres Bill was the first air-mail measure that Kelly had not fostered. Kelly, whose interests were primarily with the railway mail clerks, was not a member of the new subcommittee on air-mail legislation, but he always thought of air-mail legislation as his baby, and he perhaps resented the failure of the Postmaster General to consult with him.[7] If this is true, the Congressman evened the score by forcing the abandonment of the clause providing for contracts without competitive bidding. Yet he acquiesced in the inclusion of the clause requiring 250 miles of flying experience as a qualification for bidding, which of course had about the same effect as negotiation might have had.

Even if the 250-mile clause had been buried with non-competitive bidding, Brown would still have had unusual powers under the third, or extension, clause of the proposed law. If the Postmaster General could " extend " and " consolidate " routes, he could avoid opening new routes to dangerous bidding, by extending the old routes into new territory, or, possibly, by " consolidating " smaller systems, if the public interest was thereby " promoted."

" Do you think that will result in considerable pressure? " he was asked by a critical committeeman during a hearing.

" I am inclined to think," replied the Postmaster General, " that if you passed this bill, you will add about six years to my life. . . . But somebody has got to solve this problem, or we are going to have a collapse of the passenger carrying industry in this country." [8]

Brown may appear to have had little sympathy for the small " Independents " or non-mail operators who had hung on with the hope that the pending legislation would save them from bankruptcy, and when they discovered that the Watres Act was being used against them, these operators were loud in their denunciation of the Postmaster General. Brown apparently had no animosity *per se* for the little operators, but he was not going to favor their cause at the expense of stability. The Postmaster General thought that he had to turn his face from the small operators when he failed to obtain the non-competitive bidding clause. Said he:

> I thought if I had that power of negotiation with these people I could give those that were starving and about to fail a little mail pay, and then by some means I could straighten them out and get them to fly some one or two long, important passenger routes, and find out whether or not a passenger operation with a little mail pay could pay and could be supported, because the air mail operators were refusing to carry passengers. . . .
>
> So I thought that the right fellow to encourage . . . in the passenger business was not the air mail operator, who had refused to do it, but these venturesome, plucky, enterprising fellows who had put their money into it. I wanted to help them if I could, but the bill that was passed made it impossible for me to do it, unless I was willing to fasten a ten year contract on a short line, or a lot of short lines. *That* I could not see the propriety of, because every short line had quit and sold out to somebody else, under the pressure of the economic situation.[9]

In the light of later air legislation, the Watres Act appears crude. Nevertheless, most experts agreed at the time that the law was a step in the right direction. Some of these experts later objected to its application, but the editorials of 1930 indicate that the industry as a whole was enthusiastic about it. Giving an operator $1.25 a mile regardless of how much mail he carried may seem an extravagant use of public money. Actually it was a good investment. After one year of operation under the law, *Aircraft Yearbook,* the bible of the industry, pointed out that the total amount spent by the Postoffice Department during the fourteen years of air-mail service, together with the total amount spent by the Department of Commerce on the building and maintenance of the lighted airways, brought the per-mile cost of our air system to less than one third the amount spent by the government for every mile of motor road constructed under the provisions of the Highway Act of 1921.[10] On the same basis, the airway cost per mile was only about 2.94 per cent of the investment represented in a single mile of railway. Admittedly, the airway did not perform the services of the other systems of transportation. On the other hand, as a defense investment the air line was without a peer.

And the Postmaster General fully intended to reduce payments year by year. No operator expected to obtain the maximum bid of $1.25 a mile, but even that was less than the direct subsidy rate of many European countries.[11] The first rate formula went into effect on May 1, 1930, and mail payments to operators amounted to about 97 cents a mile that year ($1.09 in 1929). The rate was reduced on April 1, 1931; again on October 1, 1931; again on January 1, 1932; and again on November 1, 1932. Payments were then down to about 62 cents a mile. In June 1933 there was a further reduction to meet lower appropriations of a depression-minded Congress, and this rate was hacked down in July of the same year. Payments were by this time less than 54 cents, or about half of what they had been when Brown took office.[12] (See chart, page 164.)

There is little doubt that the mail might have been flown at much less expense. The difference between the actual cost of an air-mail service and the amount actually given to operators might therefore be one basis for determining the amount of subsidy,[13] since almost anyone was willing to agree that the Watres Act did provide for a certain amount of subsidy. The reasons for this extra cost, or subsidy, were

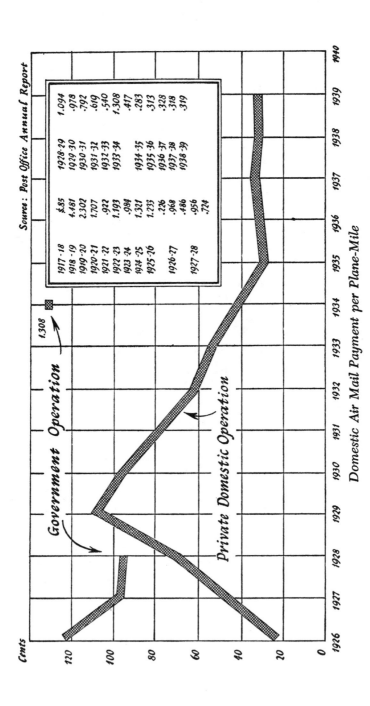

Domestic Air Mail Payment per Plane-Mile

dramatically described by Second Assistant Postmaster Warren Irving Glover, who had charge of air mail. Said Mr. Glover:

I think we must decide if we want an air mail service in this country, and if just an air mail service is desired, I would ask Congress to appropriate three or four million dollars and then we would be ready to give this country just an air mail service which would equal that of any . . . in the world.

The air mail of this country could be carried at a rate a great deal less than it is being carried at the present time . . . but if you want the air mail of this country carried in an open cockpit ship with a young lad of 25 years of age sitting on a parachute, the only human life at stake, then I say that it can be carried at a far less cost to the department than it is now being carried. However, if the Congress is desirous of having the air mail carried as a secondary item and a real invitation extended to the people of the country to fly in properly equipped ships which carry the air mail, then the air mail cannot be carried for much less than the rate at the present time. . . . I have stated before that the postmaster general was very positive that we should surround the flying of passengers with every safety device known; that the government should not fail in any way to give the passenger who flies in the air every ounce of safety possible at its command through the aids offered by the departments of commerce and agriculture and the subventions of the postoffice department.[14]

The consensus of most air-minded persons seemed to be that the country would not be content with an air-mail service " carried in an open-cockpit ship with a young lad of 25 years of age sitting on a parachute." In 1930 there were few who raised their voices in dissent when the government offered to aid air transportation with an air-mail subsidy. The respected National Advisory Committee for Aeronautics reported at that time:

The committee is still of the opinion . . . that air mail service is in effect an experimental laboratory for the development of civil uses of aircraft, and viewing it from this angle alone, believes it worth what it costs over and above the difference between the revenue derived from the excess postage and the cost of carrying, if any.[15]

The depression of 1929 had stunned aviation even more than other industries, since aviation had even further to drop from the heights of the recent " Lindbergh boom." The new air-mail legislation came at the very moment when air transportation was least able to resist the loss of independence that had gone along with postal subsidy. The air lines got their government aid, but with it they got a new boss. On April 29, 1930 Congress approved the McNary-Watres Act. From then until the end of his administration, Walter Folger Brown was dictator of America's air empire.

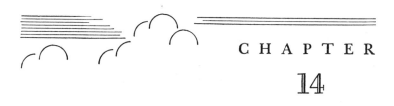

The Shotgun Wedding of TAT and WAE

With the extensive powers granted to him by the Watres Act, Postmaster General Brown was able to construct the co-ordinated airway system so badly needed. United Air Lines carried all the transcontinental air mail in 1930, and it was the Postmaster General's determination that for the good of the country there should be two competitive routes. One was to be a central airway connecting New York, Pittsburgh, St. Louis, Kansas City, and Los Angeles. The other line was to stretch from Atlanta by way of Dallas, Fort Worth, and El Paso to Los Angeles. As Brown's interpretation of federal policy was by this time equivalent to commands, the operators and the Postmaster General at once got down to business.

Two weeks after the McNary-Watres Bill became a law on April 29, 1930, the Postmaster General called a meeting in Washington. Present were representatives from various air lines, and the purpose of the gathering was to work out an agreement as to the distribution of the new air-mail contracts.[1] It was apparent after the first meeting that the operators could not get together without stepping on one another's toes, for, much as they feared Top Sergeant Brown,

they distrusted one another more. Soon they " agreed unan-
imously that the postmaster general should act as umpire in
settling and working out such voluntary rearrangements
as might be necessary, to the end that the . . . transcontinental lines be established." [2] These meetings were what
were to be known later as the " Spoils Conferences."

At least seven companies had expected to bid on sections
of the new routes, but the hopes of the smaller operators
were blasted when the terms of the Watres Act and the in-
decision of the major air-line executives at the Washington
conference placed responsibility for the development of
the airway system upon the Postmaster General. Brown
argued that no transcontinental route could be operated
successfully unless it were under one management. Because few Independent air-line executives had the financial
backing, equipment, or desire to take over a " through "
route, the Postmaster General gave them small consideration. There is little doubt that Brown hoped to give the
southern route to American Airways, and the central airway to a company formed by the merger of Transcontinental Air Transport (TAT) and Western Air Express
(WAE). As usual, Brown had his way.

The Postmaster General did not believe that air-mail
contracts, involving, as they did, the carrying of passengers,
should be subject to competitive bidding, and he was certain that he could avoid the bidding of troublesome Independent operators by resorting to the extension powers
which he believed were granted by Section 7 of the Watres
Act. Thus American Airways might be " extended " from
city to city until it reached the Pacific coast, without once
being threatened by a lower bidder. The Postmaster General " nearly had a stroke of apoplexy," [3] therefore, when
Comptroller General John R. McCarl set a precedent following the petition of Northwest Airways for an extension
to the Chicago and Twin Cities route. Operators had requested, under the terms of the Watres Act, that their line

be stretched on up to Winnipeg. This would have doubled the airway mileage of Northwest Airways, and McCarl held that such an addition was an abuse of the word " extension." On July 24, 1930 the Comptroller General declared that an " extension " might never be longer than the " basic," or original, route. Since McCarl had the power to hold up all contracts which he considered to be illegal, his decision forced the Postmaster General to contemplate some other method for discouraging unwelcome bidders.

Again Brown called upon his brain-trusters and the representatives of the more important lines. During the steaming Washington dog days the " big-league " operators forged a new weapon against luckless Independents. An inkling of what went on in these meetings is disclosed by James G. Woolley, former newspaper man and vice president of Western Air Express (WAE) :

At the time when they got into this thing about stopping this fellow from bidding and that fellow from bidding, which did crop up once or twice in the conferences, I got alarmed about it, and told them I didn't think they could do that. After one of these sessions in the postoffice department, Mr. Mac-Cracken [the Honorable William P. MacCracken, former Assistant Secretary of Commerce for aeronautics] told me to come over to his office, there was going to be a special meeting. As I recall it on that day, Mr. Hanshue [Harris Hanshue, president of Western Air Express, who could not stomach all that was going on] left the . . . postmaster general's consultation room, and went down and got the Pennsylvania to New York. I went over to MacCracken's office and I can name those that were present. . . . I know I and MacCracken and Sheaffer [D. M. Sheaffer, executive chairman of Transcontinental Air Transport (TAT)] and Hann [George R. Hann, of small but essential Pittsburgh Aviation Industries Corporation (PAIC)] and Robbins [Richard W. Robbins, a director of PAIC] and Cuthell [Chester W. Cuthell, counsel for the North American interests] and, I believe, Henderson [Colonel Paul Hender-

son, vice president and general manager of United Air Lines]
. . . all of us were there. . . .

Mr. MacCracken told us that the postmaster general had
told him he had to get some provisions that would stop the
possibility of wildcatters coming in, and he suggested that
maybe if we made them fly a thousand miles of night flying for
six months before, maybe that would stop them. I was getting
to be quite a chronic objector at that time, and they sat down
on me pretty hard, and we had three lawyers in the room, and
they were going to put in some other provision — a man that
had never flown an air mail route — I think they wound up by
merely taking in night flying. I was so damned mad that night
I could not sleep. I went out and got drunk.[4]

The McCarl decision was circumvented, as Woolley suggests, by the night-flying qualifications which were written
into the postoffice advertisement for bids. The notice stipulated that qualified bidders must have flown at night for a
period of at least six months over a route of not less than
250 miles. As only the veteran mail-carriers had operated
on night schedules, this served very well as a bulwark
against "wildcatters." Brown, who was later accused of
inserting the night-flying clause illegally, in order to discriminate against the Independents, argued that as Postmaster General he had every right to prescribe regulations
for the efficient handling of the mail. No one disputed the
right of the postoffice officials to determine the safety characteristics of railway mail cars, Brown pointed out, and the
department would seem to have had the same rights in enforcing a high standard of service on the air lines. Finally,
under the original Air Mail Act, the Postmaster General
was empowered to "make such rules, regulations and orders" as were necessary for carrying out the provisions of
the act.[5]

Regardless of the legality of the advertisement, the night-
flying experience remained as a qualification, when bids
on the two transcontinental lines were called for on August

25, 1930. As predicted, American Airways won the southern route at the maximum rate advertised. Operators dared to submit a high bid because there was no threatening competition. The one rival who might have made trouble had been silenced by Aviation Corporation, parent of American Airways.

A new line, technically not in existence, won the central airway. It was Transcontinental & Western Air, Inc. (TWA), which was the union of Transcontinental Air Transport (the Lindbergh Line) and Western Air Express (WAE). TWA was the type of air line Brown had in mind when he mapped out the federal air-transport system. Western Air Express, which formed the western division, had been so profitably operated by " Pop " Hanshue that it had been one of the few airways ever to pay dividends. The other partner to the merger, Transcontinental Air Transport, had never made money, but it had impressive backing and an experienced personnel. TAT had behind it the great Pennsylvania Railroad, the vast North American Aviation interests, and the underwriting of powerful financiers. Thanks in part to Lindbergh's identification with it, TAT also enjoyed public confidence to an unusual degree. On top of all this, the newly organized TWA could tap the engineering resources of the General Motors group. General Motors was the parent of General Aviation, the company which produced the American Fokker plane in St. Louis. General Motors also owned a large block of Western Air Express stock. When TAT and WAE merged, General Motors became a power in aviation, and when it traded its manufacturing interests to North American Aviation for even more stock in TWA, General Motors took its place with AVCO and United Aircraft as one of the Big Three in air transportation. This did not occur all at once, but the General Motors factor was nevertheless a stabilizing influence at the time of the merger.

Postmaster General Brown was charged with being affili-

ated with Transcontinental Air Transport, and he was accused by his enemies of favoritism in the granting of the
central air-mail route. The basis of the criticism was that
Brown owned 225 shares of Pennsylvania Railroad stock.
Since the railroad held 50,000 shares of TAT, which in
turn owned 47.5 per cent of TWA, it is quite true that
the Postmaster General was " affiliated " with the line that
won the air-mail certificate. On the other hand, if stock in
the central airway had been distributed, the Postmaster
General would have received less than one third of a share
of TWA stock.[6] Even Brown's worst enemies had to admit
that this was not sufficient " affiliation " to justify charges
of favoritism.

Advantageous as the TAT–WAE merger appears, it was
not a happy union. WAE had spurned TAT since 1929.
The two companies operated parallel non-mail, passenger
routes between Los Angeles and Kansas City, and TAT saw
no reason for such ruinous competition. WAE was losing
money on this route, which was exclusively a passenger
operation, but it had been netting about a million dollars
a year on its Los Angeles to Salt Lake City run, and President Hanshue saw no advantage in hitching his line to a
dead horse. Furthermore, Hanshue believed he had as good
a chance as TAT to obtain a contract over at least a part
of the mid-continent route, since he had the experience,
equipment, and backing. Hanshue, therefore, was never
very enthusiastic about merging with TAT.

Hanshue was backed into a corner when the Postmaster
General insisted that the central transcontinental route be
a complete, or " through," airway. Hanshue was a western
operator who had no desire to fly east of Kansas City or
St. Louis. He had hoped that Brown would split the route,
with TAT taking the eastern section and WAE operating
the western leg. Had the Postmaster General retained the
extension powers which he thought were his prior to Mc-
Carl's Northwest Airways decision, Brown might have

awarded the mid-continent route to either TAT or WAE and then forced the contractor to sublet the mail to that part of the airway operated by its rival. The McCarl verdict prevented the carrying out of this plan, however.

TAT was a " through," or coast-to-coast, line, unlike WAE, but it, too, was disqualified from bidding on the new route, because of the night-flying clause. TAT was exclusively an air-rail passenger service and had never flown at night. By the terms of the postoffice advertisement, then, TAT was not qualified to bid on the central route. The advertisement did provide that if one line combined with another, the two might submit a joint bid, when one company had the required night-flying experience. Since Western Air Express had been flying night mail regularly, TAT became increasingly insistent in its courtship of WAE. Of course TAT officials knew that the night-flying clause of the postoffice advertisement was only a ruling of the Postmaster General and, as such, was subject to challenge, but TAT could not oppose the requirement without exposing the central route to the dangers of bidding by the Independent operators. The best way out for TAT was to merge with WAE.

The Postmaster General now had both TAT and WAE over the barrel. One may ask why Western Air Express did not drop the costly passenger route between Los Angeles and Kansas City and confine itself to the profitable Salt Lake City air-mail run. It was not mere greed that made Hanshue fight for the cross-country mail contract, but the realization that the proposed central airway threatened to reduce mail volume, and therefore payments, over the Salt Lake route. Up to this time air traffic from Los Angeles went by way of Western Air Express to Salt Lake City and thence east over the United Air Lines system. Most Westerners had affiliations with the East and the mail sacks were heavy. Movie films and the luxury trade of Hollywood also, as I have said, moved east over WAE. After 1931, however, much of this traffic would flow over the more direct central transcontinental route. Hanshue was thus almost forced to merge with TAT to protect his investment, provided he failed to obtain a mail contract over the Kansas City section.

Much against his will, Pop Hanshue met TAT executives in the summer of 1930. At first he agreed to merge only upon an exchange of one share of WAE stock for five of TAT.[7] This rebuke cooled the ardor of TAT for the moment, since, as TAT executives pointed out, the book values of the two lines were nearer three to one, and since their mileage was about the same.

At this point Postmaster General Brown began polishing up his shotgun. " As a result of the discussions with all the interested parties," wrote D. M. Sheaffer, executive chairman of TAT, " it became evident that the award of an air mail contract might [and that *might* is the crux of the matter] be made to the central transcontinental, providing the two companies organized for the operation of the service." [8] The threat of losing that contract (or the lure of getting it) was enough to accomplish what the Postmaster General had wanted all along. Hanshue finally said yes, but he always had about the same attitude toward TAT that a mother might have toward a city slicker with designs on an only daughter. Sour Mr. Hanshue wrote to Sheaffer and Keys of TAT:

Last year, Western Air Express received a total of $2,355,000 in revenue for mail, and a total revenue of $2,950,000, from which the net profit was $963,600. In the meantime we were being assured by the postmaster general that our position of earning in the industry would be maintained and that we would receive mail on the passenger lines, which we had pioneered and flown at a loss of $750,000 during 1929.

At the beginning of 1930, on the strength of assurances of the postmaster general, Western Air Express took over Aero Corporation of California and Standard Air Lines, paying

$1,000,000, round numbers, in stock, for that company, whose most important asset to us was the Standard Air Lines. After this deal was completed, our directors thought we were sitting pretty to secure mail, in accordance with the terms of the Watres Act, on sufficient passenger mileage, to receive the same revenue from mail as we had received previously on the Salt Lake and Denver routes under the pound basis.

The deal for Aero Corporation was barely completed when we were advised by the postmaster general that we must sell the Standard Air Lines to Aviation Corporation (American Airways) and combine our Kansas City and San Francisco divisions with TAT. This did not set well with our directors, and they advised me to " stand pat " and insist on the postoffice department giving us the mail on our portion of the two transcontinentals. However, after several conferences with the postmaster general, I could see that this could not be done without a battle, which might upset temporarily the whole plan and work a hardship on everyone in the industry, so I consented to make an attempt to merge the properties of the TAT and Western Air Express on the central transcontinental on a 50–50 basis.[9]

TAT and WAE eventually went through with the union, but not until a third company, Pittsburgh Aviation Industries Corporation (PAIC), came to live with them. The part of PAIC in the merger has been the subject of much suspicion, because of the important financial and political affiliations of its officers and because its only assets were proclaimed by later critics to be no more than a small amount of equipment and Butler airport, twenty-three miles from Pittsburgh. This criticism was not justified, according to PAIC's organizer, George R. Hann, who said:

Pittsburgh Aviation Industries Corporation was repeatedly referred to in the air mail controversy as having been a small company of inconsequential assets. Such was not the fact, as evidenced by a balance sheet at the beginning of 1930 showing a net worth of more than $1,000,000, including net current assets in excess of $400,000. PAIC's other assets at that time totaled $700,000, and included one of the largest and best equipped airports in the United States.

The company had more than a dozen airplanes and owned substantial overhaul and maintenance equipment. The company's airport held a certificate of the highest rating issued by the Department of Commerce, and was fully lighted for night operations. Its Penn School also held the highest Department of Commerce rating. Although not engaged in passenger operations, PAIC, at the time of the formation of TWA, had behind it the experience of hundreds of thousands of miles of flying.[10]

The 1929 report of the company bears out this statement, but regardless of the importance of PAIC, neither TAT nor WAE had any desire to include the Pittsburgh group in their plans. Yet PAIC had been a party to merger proceedings from the very beginning of the TAT–WAE transaction, and was one of the hand-picked lines represented at the " Spoils Conferences " in Washington. A rival line, with a much more ostentatious transportation program, had received no invitation from the Postmaster General. At once there was suspicion that PAIC was favored because its powerful executives threatened to block the vital TAT–WAE merger unless PAIC were " taken care of." PAIC was accused of driving a hard bargain in getting the transcontinental route " for reason of its influence in the state of Pennsylvania," [11] but there were legitimate reasons for granting PAIC demands.

The moving spirit of PAIC was George Rice Hann, Pittsburgh attorney. In 1928, when the company appeared, aviation was on the crest of the " Lindbergh boom." Cities vied with one another to become leading air centers, just as they had fought years before to outmaneuver one another for railroad service. PAIC was formed for the specific purpose of taking away some of Cleveland's glory, and the Pittsburgh company was really a civic rather than a private enterprise. Early in 1928 Hann had aroused local interest

in aviation by taking a group of Pittsburgh business leaders on a junket to Eastern airports and factories. When
PAIC received its charter, in December 1928, its list of
directors were those citizens who usually backed civic proj-
ects. In Pittsburgh no such list is complete unless it includes
the name of the city's leading family. There is nothing unusual, then, in finding three Mellons listed as directors of PAIC. This was enough to give later critics a basis
for calling PAIC " the Mellon group." Actually the Mellons owned less than five per cent of the stock, and Hann
says he " got down on his knees " to get the Mellons, and
others, to give even that much help to the new company.[12]
R. B. Mellon resigned within a few months of his election
as a director. W. L. Mellon never attended a meeting. The
most active Mellon in PAIC was Richard K., favorite
nephew of Andrew Mellon, former Secretary of the Treasury, and even he attended only 14 of the 61 directors' meetings held over a period of about five years.[13] Finally, the
Mellon stock interest in the resulting TAT–WAE–PAIC
merger amounted to less than half of one per cent.

PAIC squeezed into the TAT–WAE merger because the
Pittsburgh group held " pioneer rights " in Pennsylvania.
TAT, which was to be the eastern section of the mid-
continent route, had never flown across Pennsylvania, since
TAT travelers were transported over the dangerous mountain stretch by the Pennsylvania Railroad. The eastern flying terminus of the Lindbergh Line was Columbus, where
passengers transferred from Pullman to plane.

During TAT's period of air-rail experimentation PAIC
had spent much money in building an organization for the
day when it could start regular service across the state.
Advised by the Department of Commerce that scheduled
passenger service over the mountains was impractical until
the lighted airway, radio stations, and emergency fields
were completed, PAIC concentrated upon adding to its experience by a flying service operating out of Pittsburgh and

the Butler airport. In addition, its influential executives were instrumental in getting a $250,000 airway improvement bill passed by the state legislature.[14] Because of the expense and effort involved in pioneering the Pennsylvania section, which TAT had ignored, PAIC believed it had an equity in the new central route. This might have gone unchallenged had PAIC not had a rival. The rival was Pittsburgh Airways, and its route between New York and Pittsburgh, although premature, according to Department of Commerce standards, might seem to have made it as worthy of consideration as PAIC.

Pittsburgh Airways was organized by James Condon, onetime navy bombing observer, and Theodore Taney, a former gypsy flyer. The air line appeared in 1928 at about the time PAIC was in the process of organizing. Taney and Condon were backed by a few Pittsburghers, the most prominent of whom was Oliver M. Kaufmann, whose family owned one of the city's big department stores, but Pittsburgh Airways did not have the impressive list of directors that PAIC had. It was an active air line, however, not just a potential transportation company. Pittsburgh Airways started the first passenger service over the Alleghenies. The service was haphazard, and without benefit of lighted beacons, but it did appear on the official airway map of 1929.

Pittsburgh Airways was given no consideration at any time during the merger conversations because it was not interested in joining with TAT and WAE. Pittsburgh Airways wanted its own air-mail contract across Pennsylvania. PAIC, on the other hand, was willing to convert its equity in Pennsylvania into shares of stock in the new transcontinental route. Postmaster General Brown, consistent with his policy of favoring " through " routes, therefore *had* to favor PAIC over Pittsburgh Airways.

Later, Pittsburgh Airways made a bold attempt to wrest the central route away from the TAT–WAE–PAIC group, after Condon and Taney were convinced beyond a doubt that it was hopeless to ask for a mail contract across the state. In August 1930 Pittsburgh Airways made an agreement with two other short lines. One of these was United States Airways, operating between Kansas City and Denver. The other was Ohio Transport, which is reported to have carried passengers between Youngstown and Dayton. Pittsburgh Airways, Ohio Transport, and United States Airways agreed to submit a joint bid for the transcontinental route. If successful in their bidding, these three companies were to merge into a new " paper " organization to be called United Avigation Company.

Postmaster General Brown obviously preferred that the TAT–WAE–PAIC group rather than United Avigation operate the transcontinental route. The big combine had the experience, stability, and personnel to build up the kind of air line that he had in mind. Brown was certain that the little Independents comprising United Avigation Company could not possibly carry out such an ambitious venture as the operation of the new transcontinental line, and subsequent events proved that the Postmaster General was correct. As the summer and fall dragged along, Brown began to feel apprehensive, since the failure of TAT and WAE to agree on merger terms only increased the uncertainty of the bidding for the central route, and indirectly affected bidding on the southern airway. Brown demanded that TAT and WAE consummate the merger at once, before too many Independents began to nibble for the contract. PAIC was also getting impatient. President Hann of PAIC telegraphed D. M. Sheaffer of TAT at this time:

We had well attended meeting this afternoon at which I gave all available figures and explained situation and proposed setup. Harris [Harris Hanshue, president of Western Air Express] and you must come across on the basis I argued last Saturday or our committee is going to send several members to see Brown and ask his arbitration. I think your company is making such a jump from terrific losses to seeing daylight that you can well afford in your position in view of all the railroad's friends here in Pittsburgh to settle this matter once and for all by conceding our small demands. It is out of my hands now and I would like you and Harris to come out and try your persuasion with this crowd if you want to get into a good controversy.[15]

Under such pressure the new cross-country route was organized as Transcontinental & Western Air, Inc. Western Air Express took 47.5 per cent of the stock and Transcontinental Air Transport took an equal amount. PAIC, which had demanded ten per cent of the new stock, in exchange for Butler airport and its equity in the state of Pennsylvania, finally agreed to " pipe down " for five per cent of the TWA issue. This appeared to be an inconsequential interest in the new transcontinental route, but since TAT and WAE held equal blocks of stock, the five-per-cent interest was enough for PAIC to enjoy the balance of power, and its own man, Richard W. Robbins, soon became president of the new central airway.

Mr. Robbins's explanation of his rise to the presidency of TWA is as follows:

PAIC never put me in as managing director, or president, of T. & W.A. The suggestion never came from PAIC. The fact is, that along in the Spring of 1931, the new operating company, Transcontinental & Western Air, was losing money hand over fist. My recollection is that losses from October, 1930, through March, 1931, ran around $200,000 a month. Then came the Rockne accident [crash of a TWA liner at Bazaar, Kansas, which killed Knute Rockne, famous Notre Dame football coach] followed by Hanshue's illness [some said, induced by the enforced merger]. During all this period as a director, I had been a severe critic of the management for these losses. One day after a somewhat heated directors' meeting, two of T. & W.A.'s directors, C. E. Wilson, now president of General Motors, and E. R. Breech, now vice president of General Motors . . . invited me to lunch and first broached to me the matter of my becoming managing director of T. & W.A.

. . . Finally, I took the job with some reluctance . . . because it was possible that the corporation would end up in bankruptcy, and I did not want to become prominently identified with a business failure. I insisted upon each director being privately canvassed . . . and only took the job when I had the assurances that I was the unanimous choice of the 15 members. . . . The PAIC people were as surprised as I was, when I was first offered the job.[16]

Robbins is careful to point out that he was not *put* into the presidency by PAIC, but there is no doubt that the Pittsburgher was chosen because the PAIC group held the balance of power between the still antagonistic TAT and WAE members of the board.

When the bids were opened on August 25, 1930, TWA was awarded the central route. At once a howl went up from the rival bidder, which was United Avigation Company. TWA had felt safe enough in submitting a bid of 97.5 per cent of the maximum rate, but United Avigation had bid only 64 per cent of the maximum.

On October 9, 1930 Comptroller General McCarl wrote to Brown, pointing out that the TWA award was illegal. The Postmaster General was ready with an answer. TWA's attorneys, William P. MacCracken and Chester W. Cuthell, had already examined the bid of United Avigation in the office of Chase Gove, Mr. Glover's assistant.[17] They conferred next day with Brown. On October 23 the Postmaster General answered McCarl by saying that United Avigation was disqualified from bidding because the company had had no night-flying experience, as stipulated in the advertisement. Brown also indicated that there was really no such company as United Avigation, since final details of the merger as well as financial backing hinged on a successful bid.[18]

McCarl replied on December 16. He pointed out that the night-flying requirements were illegal, inasmuch as there was no such provision in the Watres Act. The comptroller also disagreed with Brown as to the responsibility of the low bidder. Brown had indicated that, in his opinion, United Avigation was not the lowest *responsible* bidder. McCarl held that the various companies merged into United Avigation had good records and responsible backers. He reiterated that he would block the TWA award until the Postmaster General could show cause why United Avigation should not be awarded the contract.

Brown replied on December 29. Again he called attention to the loose organization of United Avigation. The company did not even own its own subsidiaries, he said. He quoted from a memorandum submitted by the low bidder, in which it was stated that United Avigation would consummate the merger of independent companies only after it had received a contract. This, Brown argued, disqualified it as a bidder, for, under the terms of the advertisement, how could the company be " the responsible bidder " when it was not technically in existence? TWA wasn't much more than an agreement, either, but, as Brown pointed out, United Avigation expected to carry mail only over those sections of the route with which its various operators were familiar. If it won the whole route, it planned to sublet the western end to WAE. This not only was bad faith, Brown insisted, but it was impractical, since Western Air Express would not have agreed to carry mail at the rate United Avigation had bid. (Even on its higher bid TWA lost more than a million dollars the first year.) Lastly, not only would the low bidder have been forced to default almost at the beginning, but, as Brown maintained, its assets were actually only promises to pay.[19]

Comptroller General McCarl may not have been convinced by these arguments, but he was forced to acquiesce in the TWA award because United Avigation suddenly ceased to press charges. The low bidder had the backing of Representative Kelly, who had advised United Avigation to fight the TWA award and who had pointed out the illegality of the night-flying clause. With Kelly as an ally, the United Avigation executives might have continued to press their claims. They lost out when N. A. Letson, president of United States Airways, one of the three companies forming United Avigation, suddenly dropped the fight. Letson had been offered a windfall from another direction.

In the midst of the Brown-McCarl correspondence, a press release from Second Assistant Postmaster General Glover announced that American Airways had won the air-mail contract between Kansas City and Denver, which was the route of Letson's United States Airways. That American Airways had no night-flying experience over this route seemed to make no difference to the Postoffice Department, although, in spirit at least, the award was in violation of the advertisement disqualifying other bidders (American Airways had flown the required 250 miles on other night routes, and therefore technically was qualified). American Airways received the route under the extension powers of the Watres Act. Instead of flying the route itself, however, it was forced to sublet the mail contract to Letson at a cost to the government of $4.98 a pound — the highest rate in the entire United States. United States Airways profited much more under this arrangement than it could hope to have earned with the low bid of United Avigation. Without Letson's backing the United Avigation merger collapsed. Had it not been for Letson's defection, United Avigation would surely have fought its case through to a finish, says Stewart Dunn of Pittsburgh, who was attorney for the company.[20]

Even the President of the United States became involved in the award of the mail contract to Transcontinental & Western Air. In 1928 a young alumnus of Stanford and Harvard universities was hired by Western Air Express as a radio engineer. He was Herbert Clark Hoover, Jr., son of the President. Hoover was a lad of considerable talent. At twenty-six he headed the non-profit, co-operative Aeronautical Radio, Incorporated, serving the air lines as Radio Corporation serves shipping, or as Marconi serves the British merchant marine. When Western Air Express and Transcontinental Air Transport merged, young Hoover became chief radio engineer for the new Transcontinental & Western Air company. It was charged that Hoover, Jr., owed his position to his connections. This may or may not be true. The fact is he was an able engineer. He had already won a Guggenheim fellowship for his contributions to the science of aeronautical radio, and his work with TWA was recognized by the industry. He might have done even more had his job not been stopped by a long convalescence in a tuberculosis sanatorium.

When TWA won the mail contract over the low bid of United Avigation, the suspicion arose that Brown was favoring the line employing the son of his chief. There were those who thought TWA had hired young Hoover primarily for this purpose, although the young man had been working for WAE long before the passage of the Watres Act. Yet the very presence of Hoover, Jr., in Washington was enough to set tongues wagging.[21]

The Baltimore *Sun* was first to remark about the connection of President Hoover and the TWA merger. Hoover was hurt by this implied criticism and he called upon postal officials for an explanation. Unfortunately, the men who knew most about the details were not in Washington. Brown was on his vacation in Nova Scotia; Glover was attending conventions in Texas and Louisiana. First Assistant Postmaster General Arch Coleman, who was left in charge of the department, knew nothing of the air-mail situation, but he gave the President all the information available. Hoover turned over all the material to John Lord O'Brian, assistant to the Attorney General, and O'Brian gave hurried counsel to the exasperated chief executive.[22] O'Brian said that, in his opinion, Hoover, Jr., should resign at once from TWA. The attorney also recommended that the central route be put up for bidding again. This may have been simply a curbstone judgment to pacify the President, since neither Coleman nor O'Brian professed to know much about aviation, but the exchange of notes was later used as damaging evidence in a drastic investigation by the Senate.

On the other hand, O'Brian made it clear to Coleman that he suspected the whole TWA deal of being anything but a bona fide business transaction, and again he advocated the readvertisement of bids for the central route.[23] When Glover was informed of this, he pooh-poohed the whole thing. He wrote to his assistant, Chase Gove, who had been keeping track of the Washington negotiations:

Believe we can work out the Avigation bid. Halliburton [Erle Halliburton, whose merger with American Airways hinged on the successful bidding of TWA] is going after Letson, and even Letson stockholders do not approve of this action.

Do not know what you have told the P.M.G. [Brown], but there is no use recommending the award be made to the high bidder and then getting cold feet and saying you and Earl [Earl Wadsworth, superintendent of mail] agree that we should throw out all bids. We had better stick together, or we'll hang together.[24]

Behind all the intrigue loomed the figure of Top Sergeant Brown, giving the orders that were making commercial aviation into a disciplined and efficient industry. Even the transportation men, who hated the Postmaster General, did not dispute the fact that Brown was accomplishing wonders. Eastern Air Transport's tough Captain Thomas Doe said: " I absolutely believe that Postmaster General Brown did the thing he thought best for the aviation industry. . . . I think that if you will read the testimony given before the Black committee you will find that he knew everything about this air mail business — about the schedules and everything else. I think he knew more about it than anybody in the industry." [25]

The United Avigation challenge and the correspondence between the Comptroller and the Postmaster General delayed the merger of TAT and WAE for many months. Not until February 13, 1931 were final details worked out. Despite the cries of the ignored Independents, Brown probably did the wise thing when he awarded the bid to the strong combination rather than to United Avigation or to any other group.

But even in the TWA household there was not universal joy. Harris Hanshue of WAE did not attempt to hide his bitterness. After the merger papers had been signed, old " Pop " Hanshue was sitting disconsolately with fellow officials in a New York hotel suite. TAT executives were hoping that the new transcontinental line would standardize on Curtiss Condor planes, since TAT was affiliated with the Curtiss-Keys, North American group, makers of the ship. Condors were huge biplanes, powered at that time by twin Curtiss Conqueror engines. The Condor was a reliable and luxurious ship, famous for its quietness. It was also a notoriously poor climber. Pilots had trouble " goosing " it over the Alleghenies, and there was some doubt as to whether it would be able to clear the Rockies. Someone asked " Pop " how long it would be before he placed his order for Condors over the WAE division of the central route.

" Oh, not for a long, long time," mumbled Hanshue.

" But, Mr. Hanshue," wailed the questioner, " they'll be out of the factory in six months."

" I wasn't thinking of that," answered the disgruntled Hanshue. " I was thinking of what a hell of a long time it's going to take to tunnel through those goddam mountains." [26]

CHAPTER

15

Mr. Gadfly Halliburton

T HERE was only one bid for the southern transcontinental
line and it was submitted by the newly organized American
Airways. Aviation Corporation (AVCO) had completed
the first phase of its growth in 1930, with the acquisition
of a dozen or more airways. In January 1930 Frederic G.
Coburn succeeded Grosvenor as president of the corporation. Coburn was an executive of Sanderson & Porter, the
engineering company in charge of the air-line operations
of AVCO, and his promotion to the presidency of the corporation was coincident with the formation of American
Airways, AVCO's vast operating subsidiary. Coburn at once
began the task of consolidating his sprawling air empire.
He lopped off many unprofitable lines, and under his direction American Airways began to take more definite form.
There was a new spirit of unity in the organization. When
the Postmaster General called for bids on the new southern
route, American was ready to make an offer.

Thanks to the night-flying qualification inserted in the
postoffice advertisements for bids, American Airways had
the field to itself. There were other lines willing to bid on
the new route, but they were prevented from qualifying be-

cause they lacked night-flying experience. One of these lines was Delta Air Service, which cut through the deep South from Birmingham to Dallas. The operator of the Delta line was C. E. Woolman, who had managed airways since 1925.

When Congress was debating the Watres Act, Woolman and the directors of Eastern Air Transport agreed upon a plan for a co-ordinated bid on a southern route. Eastern Air Transport, a subsidiary of North American Aviation, operated two lines from New York to the South. One fork of EAT was the coastal airway to Florida. The other branched off at Richmond to reach Atlanta, where it was to connect with Delta Air Service, extended from Birmingham. EAT hoped to win a mail contract between Atlanta and New Orleans under the extension powers of the Postmaster General. Since Delta had a " pioneer equity " in this section, the plan was for EAT to sublet the contract to Delta, but when the decision of Comptroller General McCarl in the Northwest Airways case upset the Postmaster General's plans for granting extensions, EAT had no more use for Delta. Woolman then set his heart on capturing that part of the proposed southern transcontinental mail route which he had already been flying, but when the advertisement for bids appeared, he was dismayed to find that he was disqualified for lack of night-flying experience. Delta had veteran pilots, excellent equipment, a pioneer equity in its route, and a good operating record, yet, abandoned as it was by EAT and the Postmaster General, the little line was forced to sell out to the new American Airways (although it reappeared four years later as booming Delta Air Lines). Queried in 1940 as to his version of the 1930 squeeze play, Woolman answered:

Replying to your letter of the 22d, will state that this is rather an old sore, but will give you a brief outline of what happened. . . .

As you know, we were forced to sell the line at about fifty cents on the dollar, following which, we continued our dusting operations, extending them into Mexico and Florida for winter operations and keeping our organization together.

. . . You asked if we really would have bid on the Southern transcontinental back in 1930 and, in reply, will state that our chief contention at that time was that we should be permitted to bid on the route which we had pioneered. Most assuredly we would have entered a bid [had the night-flying clause not been inserted in the advertisement].[1]

Questioned by Senator Hugo Black in a later investigation, Postmaster General Brown defended his action as follows:

He [Woolman] could have bid when the thing was put up for bidding. He could have made a combination with somebody that could qualify under the night flying clause, if he wanted to. There were plenty of them, but he did not want to fly from Birmingham to Los Angeles. He wanted to fly where he was flying, and I was determined to have an operation all the way from Atlanta to Los Angeles because I knew from what we had discovered that a short line could not pay the expense of maintaining a ground force. . . . They all had to quit. I don't mean quit; they had to sell out.[2]

Senator Black, in the drawl that could so infuriate his opponents, resented the Postmaster General's implication that an air line out of Birmingham was relatively unimportant. The Senator was himself from Birmingham. If the Postmaster General was attempting to operate the air lines as the railroads were operated, Senator Black did not understand why air mail to the west coast could not be carried by one line to a metropolitan center for trans-shipment over another route. The railroads did that; why not the air lines? Brown answered:

Oh, yes; the railroad operation is a pretty steady, dependable operation as to time, but . . . we never had any luck of consequence in getting an air mail operator to wait for another one. A plane comes in two hours late, because of a head wind, and the operator, who is to take the mail and passengers next, has had to keep his people waiting. They want to get to their destinations and go to dinner or have a party or something or other, and the pressure on the fellow who has the independent line to start is so great that we could not get along well.

That was one reason I wanted this unified service from coast to coast . . . because I foresaw the time when there would be practically a nonstop operation from coast to coast, and it could not be broken between lines midway or any place.[3]

The Postmaster General may have kept troublesome Independents from bidding on the southern route, but there was one operator too clever for even shrewd Mr. Brown. He was Erle P. Halliburton, a hard-boiled Oklahoman who was as colorful as his famous cousin, Richard Halliburton, author and traveler, lost on a Chinese junk a decade later. Erle Halliburton had made money in oil and invested it in air lines. He was the controlling stockholder in a bustling little airway called Southwest Air Fast Express, better known as SAFEway. SAFEway operated out of Tulsa into Texas, Kansas, and Missouri. Halliburton was one of the first to experiment with an exclusive passenger service offering fares at railroad rates. In a country of easy money, vast distances, and excellent flying terrain, SAFEway was fairly successful. It is true that it lost money, but it came so close to breaking even that only an air-mail contract was needed to make the line profitable. Halliburton was even willing to carry the mail at one fourth the prevailing rate. With excellent equipment and a fine maintenance record, SAFEway appeared to be one of the few lines eligible to bid on the southern route.

Halliburton had already attempted to obtain a mail contract. In 1929 he had teamed up with William P. Mc-Adoo, Woodrow Wilson's Secretary of the Treasury. Mc-Adoo headed a " paper " air line called Southern Skylines, Incorporated, which was designed to be the western leg of Halliburton's proposed transcontinental line, but Republican Top Sergeant Brown had scant regard for Democratic

Wheel-horse McAdoo or for Mr. Halliburton, and the proposed airway received no consideration in the Postoffice Department.

Halliburton received his first rebuff in November 1929, five months before the passage of the Watres Act. Hearings were being held at this time before the Inter-Departmental Committee, which was a group of War, Postoffice, and Commerce Department officials attempting to overcome departmental jealousies in the development of American aviation. The committee discussed three possible routes for the southern airway. One of the suggested routes was from St. Louis to Los Angeles by way of Oklahoma City, Tulsa, Dallas and Fort Worth, and El Paso. Another route was mapped from Atlanta through Shreveport, Dallas and Fort Worth, and El Paso to Los Angeles. The third proposal was a route from New Orleans through Houston and San Antonio to connect with some point on another transcontinental line. No mention was made of possible air lines east of these terminals.[4] The supposition was that eastern lines would be extended to meet the eastern terminals of the southern route.

On November 21, Halliburton upset the apple-cart by offering to carry the mail *all the way* across the country. SAFEway and its affiliate, Southern Skylines, would carry, not only special air mail, but first-class mail as well, from New York to Los Angeles — and for payment that would have toppled the whole air-mail rate structure. At this time air mail was still being carried at the per-pound rate, since the space-mile basis was not used until the passage of the Watres Act in April 1930. Halliburton agreed to carry the mail the three thousand miles for $2.10 a pound, whereas, he pointed out, it cost the government $8.77 to fly a pound of mail to Los Angeles from Washington in 1929 and $5.77 per pound by way of the Chicago, Omaha, and Salt Lake route.[5]

Postmaster General Brown believed that Independents

like Halliburton would ruin plans for a sound, strongly
knit air service, and the Oklahoma operator was snubbed
wherever he turned. Of course he was not asked to the
" Spoils Conferences " in May and June, when the air system was discussed by the key operators. Halliburton was
furious at this slight, but he invited himself anyway,
through William B. Mayo of the Ford Company, who had
gone to Washington as the representative of Ford.

Mayo was builder of the Ford tri-motor monoplane.
Halliburton had just ordered $600,000 worth of this equip-
ment, and he hinted that he would buy more if he obtained
a contract. With this as a lever, Halliburton called Mayo
and demanded an invitation to the aviation conferences.
Mayo went directly to President Hoover, and the next day
Halliburton was on his way to Washington, not as a welcome delegate to the meetings, but because Mayo " was
interested in the successful operation of my company." [6]

From then on, Halliburton was an utter nuisance to the
Postmaster General. The Oklahoman wanted a mail contract, and he didn't care what part of the country he was
allotted. When the bids were advertised, he even tried to
line up with L. H. Brittin, of Northwest Airways, but was
snubbed when, according to testimony, he learned that
Northwest would lose its chance for a certificate and extensions if it combined with SAFEway. [7]

By now Halliburton was upsetting all the schemes and
calculations of the department, for his threatened underbidding had the whole industry in a turmoil. He was
flitting like a banshee through the corridors of the old
Postoffice Building. Once or twice Assistant Postmaster
General Glover all but had him ejected bodily. Halliburton only continued his heckling. He made accusations
of an embarrassing nature. He wrote indignant letters to
influential political leaders.

" I will ruin you, if it is the last act of my life," Mr.

Glover is charged with saying. "You have tried to buck this thing all the way through, and you are not going to do it." [8]

Brown was once asked if he had tried to silence Mr. Gadfly Halliburton.

"Oh, Halliburton is the sort of fellow most anybody would like to quiet," sighed the exasperated Postmaster General. [9]

Brown and the big operators were relieved when the Postoffice Department advertised for bids, for they believed that the clause requiring six months of night flying would surely disqualify Halliburton. To their dismay, they found they were not yet rid of their pest. Canny Mr. Halliburton was not tricked by the night-flying clause. Looking up the McNary-Watres Act, he found no such disqualifying provision. Then he donned his war paint. He threatened action in the United States courts. He wrote letters to powerful politicians. To Patrick J. Hurley, Secretary of War, Halliburton transcribed his charges, pointing to the illegality of the postoffice advertisements requiring night flying, and adding:

Why the Transcontinental Air Transport, which prostituted the names of Lindbergh and Earhart to the general public and then expected the taxpayers to pay for this prostitution should be favored by the postmaster general is beyond my understanding of all that is just [referring to the award of the central route].

If these contracts are awarded, as above outlined, I am quite certain it cannot help but result in an investigation of the postoffice department, and due to the connection of Herbert Hoover Jr., with Western Air Express and the part which they will play in connection with the operation, I am sure it will result in serious criticism of Mr. Hoover himself, and for that reason, as well as for personal reasons, I am passing this information on to you for whatever purpose you may care to use it. [10]

Halliburton was now a serious menace to the development of the airway system as mapped by the Postmaster General and the major air-line executives. Something had to be done with him. Something *was* done with him. American Airways bought him out for $1,400,000, although Halliburton's hard assets at that time did not exceed $800,000 in his own generous estimate, and in spite of the fact that he had already lost a million dollars.[11]

The details of this transaction were unusual. American Airways, through a subsidiary, was to bid jointly with Halliburton for the southern route. If the bid was successful, American was to have a 120-day option to purchase SAFEway at the agreed figure of $1,400,000. If the option was not taken up in this period, however, Halliburton reserved the right to buy American Airways for his own transcontinental airway.[12]

There was a close connection between this transaction and the awarding of the central transcontinental route. It will be recalled that Transcontinental Air Transport and Western Air Express had agreed to merge, somewhat unwillingly, for the purpose of bidding on the central route. The merged company was to be known as Transcontinental & Western Air (TWA), and there was an agreement between TWA and American Airways that if both lines got the routes they were seeking, Transcontinental & Western Air was to pay American Airways $284,500 in cash for " an interest in the hangar and some property in Tulsa," [13] and, in addition, would buy twenty thousand shares of Western Air Express stock owned by American Airways. TWA was to pay $1,115,500 for this stock. The total amount that American Airways would thereby receive from TWA was $1,400,000, which was exactly the amount American had agreed to pay troublesome Mr. Halliburton.

Now it becomes plain why there was so much consternation when United Avigation underbid TWA for the central transcontinental route. It completely demolished the entire air-line structure, as planned by the air-line and postoffice executives. No wonder the Postmaster General fought so hard to keep United Avigation from taking away the TWA award!

The key figure in the United Avigation group, as cited in Chapter XIV, was N. A. Letson, president of United States Airways. Through the dreary winter, while Comptroller General McCarl insisted upon the consideration of United Avigation as a bidder for the central route, various forces, including Erle Halliburton, were working upon Mr. Letson. The upshot of it was that American Airways won a mail contract over the United States Airways route from Kansas City to Denver. American Airways received this route under the extension powers granted to the Postmaster General by the Watres Act, but the significance is that American Airways immediately sublet the route to United States Airways at the full rate. Letson at once ceased his clamoring for the central route. Without Letson and his United States Airways, United Avigation collapsed like a punctured balloon.

The train of circumstances went like this: United Avigation ceased its opposition to the TWA award of the central airway. TWA thereupon won its coveted transcontinental air-mail contract. It accordingly paid American Airways $1,400,000 for the stock of Western Air Express and the " interest in a hangar at Tulsa." American Airways took the money and paid Mr. Halliburton his price. This left American Airways as the only bidder for the southern route.

The agreement between American Airways and TWA has been interpreted in many ways. The mildest charge is that the two lines were guilty of " collusion." The strongest accusation was that American Airways threatened to bid against TWA on the central route unless TWA handed over enough cash so that American Airways could pay

Halliburton his hush money. Such critics overlook one important fact. Postmaster General Brown *insisted that the transcontinental routes be competitive.* American Airways therefore *had* to sell its holdings in Western Air Express, which was to become part of a competitive system. American Airways could name its own price because it was vital to Western Air Express and Transcontinental Air Transport to merge, in order to qualify as air-mail bidders. The Postmaster General contended that "collusion" would have existed only if American Airways had retained an interest in its rival transcontinental line. But in either case it was a strange business procedure.

Bids for the two new transcontinental routes were called for August 25, 1930. That was a Monday. On Saturday, Halliburton and officials representing American Airways, Western Air Express, and Transcontinental Air Transport met to confirm their unusual agreement. If they were acting in collusion, which implies conspiracy, they behaved strangely when they met in Assistant Postmaster General Glover's drab office Monday morning. For the fact is that these officials distrusted each other to such an extent that it would have been impossible for them to submerge their own interests for any group action. William P. MacCracken of TWA and President F. G. Coburn of American Airways were so suspicious of each other that they came to the meeting with their pockets crammed with bids on each other's lines, just in case anyone made a false step.[14]

Fortunately for all those present, plans worked out according to schedule. American Airways, unopposed by any competitor, got the southern route at the maximum rate. Transcontinental & Western Air won the central award. Halliburton received his pay-off. And Postmaster General Brown got the answer to his prayer for a great air-line system. Everyone was happy except the little Independents, who wondered what the country was coming to, with Washington bureaucracy what it was.

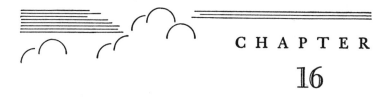

CHAPTER

16

The Reach Exceeds the Grasp

By the spring of 1931, air lines were reaching most of the population centers of the United States. Spanning the country were three great transcontinental systems. The oldest and most profitable was United Air Lines, operating over the old government route between New York and San Francisco, via Chicago and Omaha. To the south were Transcontinental & Western Air, and American Airways. Northwest Airways, across the northern tier of states, was well on the way to becoming a fourth cross-country route.

Three important routes cut the country transversely. The east coast was the exclusive territory of Eastern Air Transport, affiliated with Transcontinental & Western Airways through the parent North American Aviation Company. United Air Lines operated the old Pacific Air Transport service down the west coast, and another important transverse route branched off from the main line at Chicago and followed the old National Air Transport Airway into Texas. In addition there were numerous Independent lines, some of them rather extensive, growing rank as morning-glory vines. Only a few were making much profit, but

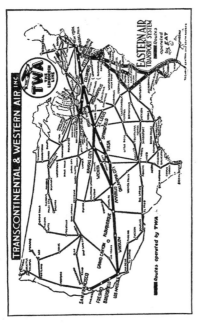

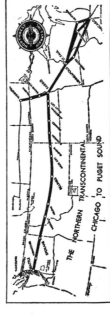

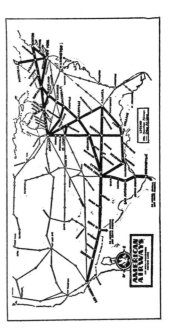

Trunk Air Lines of the United States as they appeared at the end of Postmaster Brown's administration.

with the exception of American Airways the air lines were now entering upon a period of stabilization.

The depression was beginning to pinch Aviation Corporation, parent of American Airways. In its first three years of operation AVCO was said to have squandered $38,-000,000.[1] By 1931 it was necessary to retrench. President Frederick G. Coburn of Aviation Corporation realized this, but before he could effect the necessary economies, he was ousted. Coburn was an engineer and operations expert. He had been appointed president for the sole purpose of bringing order to the clumsy American Airways system. This he had accomplished to a large extent, but it was left for another to bring about the financial reforms, and the man chosen for the task was Lamotte T. Cohû, president of Air Investors, Inc., underwriters of Aviation Corporation stock. In March 1932 popular President Coburn called his office staff together and with tears in his eyes announced his resignation.[2] Cohû at once took charge. One of his first duties was to investigate the crash of an American Airways plane near San Bernardino, California. Among the victims was Albert Coburn, twenty-one years old, son of the man Cohû had just replaced.

Competing with American Airways in the Chicago and west-coast areas were two small, non-mail-carrying lines called, respectively, Century Air Lines and Century Pacific Lines. Both were owned by E. L. Cord, whose phenomenal rise as an automobile salesman had carried him to the top of the Auburn automobile company. Cord believed that the operations of the air lines were extravagant beyond all reason. He saw no necessity, for example, of paying pilots the standard seven thousand dollars a year when there were hundreds of able flyers in those depression days who were only too glad to work for half that amount. Fortunately for the pilots, they were afforded some protection from employers such as Cord. Many airmen had joined a new union, organized by the American Federation of

Labor, known as the Air Line Pilots Association. It was headed by David L. Behncke, former Northwest Airways pilot. When Cord announced drastic pay cuts at the end of 1931, the association objected. In February 1932 the union declared the first air-line strike since the army pilots had walked out in 1919.

Cord believed he could carry the mail at half the prevailing rate, providing he could effect such economies as the wage reduction. His air-mail offer was being considered by the postoffice officials when the strike occurred. Cord apparently did not know that both the Postoffice Department and the Department of Commerce were opposed to his high-handed methods. The Department of Commerce, for example, cared more for safety than for economy, and it did not propose to license airmen whose morale had been shattered by ruthless employers. Postmaster General Brown, for his part, admittedly cared less about carrying mail cheaply than he did about building up a sound airway system. As a result, Cord did not stand a chance of obtaining mail contracts for his lines, yet by a strange turn of events he changed defeat into victory.

Failing to win a contract, Cord offered his unprofitable lines to Aviation Corporation. Because American Airways was only too glad to be rid of an undercutting competitor, Cord was able to sell the Century properties for 140,000 shares of American Airways stock, which was sufficient interest to make him a director of Aviation Corporation.

The more Cord saw of AVCO, the more his blood boiled. He was appalled at the losses incurred by the clumsy organization, and he determined to do something about the matter. His chance came when Aviation Corporation tried to buy certain assets of North American Aviation in exchange for American Airways stock. Cord feared that his own power would be lessened by admitting this big new stockholder, and so he obtained a temporary injunction restraining AVCO from completing the North American transaction until stockholders could decide the issue. Pending final disposition of the case, Cord waged an intensive campaign to expose the extravagance of the administration. Eventually this developed into a battle for control of American Airways.

Cord bought full-page advertisements in the New York newspapers to carry his message to stockholders. William Green, president of the American Federation of Labor, furnished ammunition to the opposition by blasting at Cord for his attitude in the Century strike. In the following weeks charges were hurled back and forth. It was the most savage fight since the Rentschler-Keys feud, and the charges made by both factions were the first rumblings of the storm that was soon to break over the heads of all the operators. For if the accusations were only one tenth true, aviation was badly in need of a house-cleaning, many believed. In the end Cord emerged with control of American Airways and AVCO, and at once he began his own house-cleaning.

President Cohû, of Aviation Corporation, was forced to walk the plank, but since the proxy battle had increased the value of his Air Investors holdings, he escaped, not without profit. Later he found a place for himself as general manager of thriving Northrup Aircraft, Incorporated, builders of military planes. Cord replaced Cohû with Major Lester D. Seymour, former vice president of United Aircraft, noted for his aversion to riding in airplanes. Seymour detached American Airways from Aviation Corporation, moved the general offices to Chicago, split the line into convenient sections, and began to build up a respectable system.

While this was going on, Postmaster General Brown was putting the finishing touches on his airway map. He had won most of his major objectives by February 1931, when Transcontinental & Western Air became the third cross-country route, but there was still a little mopping up to be done. At this point Brown called up the extension clause of the Watres Act, which he had been holding more or less in reserve since the adverse ruling of Comptroller General McCarl in July 1930. But once the new routes were established, the clause again became an important weapon, since "basic" routes were now sufficiently long to permit almost any kind of extension.

Brown did not stint in his use of the extension clause, and before leaving office, he added almost nine thousand miles to the airway system in this way [3] (see chart, Appendix IV). Sometimes neither the Postmaster General nor the operator desired this extra mileage. United Air Lines, for example, had to take over the unprofitable route from Omaha to Watertown, South Dakota. At the time of this extension the Watertown route was being flown by three small lines, each with its lobbyists yapping for postal appropriations. Apparently the Postmaster General was afraid to give a mail contract to one of these lines for fear of angering the various political proponents, including Senator Norbeck and Representative Christopherson.[4] Brown brought peace to the Dakota airways by turning down all the small operators involved. Instead, he forced United Air Lines to take it over. United executives cursed the day they had ever heard of Postmaster General Brown, but, as usual, they knuckled under.

Many of these later extensions were ruinous to the Independent competitor. A mail-carrier could invariably drive away a non-mail-carrier. Occasionally, however, some Independent would fight back viciously. Such a one was Temple Bowen.

Temple Bowen was the southwestern bus-line operator who sold Texas Air Transport in 1928 and started up a rival air line two weeks later. His new venture finally put him in competition with United Air Lines, which operated a branch to the Southwest from its main line at Chicago. Also competing with Bowen was American Airways, now operating Bowen's old line.

Bowen computed his operating costs at 22.74 cents a mile; a figure so low, in comparison with those of other operations, that he was on the verge of making a profit.[5] Accordingly, Bowen offered to carry mail between Dallas and Louisville at the ridiculously low rate of 25 cents a mile. He was furious when American Airways was " extended " from Louisville to Dallas, and Bowen didn't feel any better when he learned that the interloper was receiving more than twice as much (53 cents a mile) for carrying the mail as he had offered to bid.[6]

There was another side to the story, of course. Bowen had discredited himself with the Postoffice Department when he sold his Texas lines to a company that became a subsidiary of American Airways. The purchase price was $175,000, which was more than the equipment was worth, but which the purchaser was willing to pay because there was the possibility of winning a mail contract in an exclusive territory. Within two weeks, however, Bowen was back with his new company, operating over the old route in competition with the route that soon became part of American Airways. Bowen had bought new, fast, single-engined Lockheed " Vega " monoplanes. With lower maintenance costs, Bowen reduced passenger fares to railroad levels. This was fine for Texas traffic, but the Postmaster General and the operators of American Airways called the Bowen maneuvers " highly unethical," and, anyway, Brown had no intention of permitting operators to use mail contracts for speculative purposes.

Operators such as Bowen, who had been bucking what they maintained was an unfair combination of the government and Big Business, saw things differently. An air line sold out to a rich rival. It used the profit to buy the superior equipment that would enable it to compete with the financially stronger line. And why shouldn't it win a mail contract if it had a better service? Was the private transaction of buying and selling air lines any business of the government? Who was the Postmaster General to talk about ethics when he extended rival lines at much higher mail rates, and without even a chance for bidding?

Bowen's wrath knew no bounds when American Airways, by a series of extensions, was wafted all the way from Nashville to Fort Worth, over territory Bowen considered his, and at double the rate he had offered to bid. That was not all. The postoffice sent out pamphlets by franked mail pointing to the advantages of air travel on American Airways' ships. Even letters were stamped at the postoffice: " Fly with the Air Mail," which, Bowen charged, was the rankest kind of free advertising. In retaliation Bowen painted signs on his new planes reading: " Fly Past the Air Mail," which was no idle boast, since the fast little Lockheeds could literally fly circles around the lumbering Fords and Fokkers.[7] American Airways responded by refusing to wait even one minute for Bowen planes at connecting points. This meant that Bowen pilots had to overtake the transcontinental transports, which was easy enough. It was only the financial pace that was too swift for Bowen. Although he stuck it out until 1934, American Airways and the depression were too strong, and he gave up flying to go back to his bus lines.

There were other instances in which the word " extension " was stretched to the limit. Even after its merger with Transcontinental Air Transport, Western Air Express had retained its identity in a feeder route from Pueblo, Colorado, to the United Air Line division point at Cheyenne, Wyoming. Executives of Western Air Express knew that they could increase the effectiveness of their operations by extending their service to meet the central and southern transcontinental systems at El Paso, Texas. The simplest solution to the problem seemed to be an extension of Western Air Express from Pueblo south to El Paso, but the McCarl ruling in the Northwest Airways case constrained the Postmaster General not to grant extensions longer than the " basic " route, and the new extensions would have tripled the original mileage of Western Air Express.

There were alternative solutions, however. One was to put the Pueblo and El Paso section up for regular bidding, which would have opened up to competitors the area that Western Air Express claimed as its private preserve. The other way was much simpler. Brown merely forced American Airways to extend an off-line service north from El Paso, and then sublet the mail contract *at the full rate* to Western Air Express.[8] Because American Airways was a long route, it could absorb such extensions without violating the McCarl ruling. American Airways executives certainly had no enthusiasm for this extension, but because the Postmaster General was in a position to aid or hinder the line on other fronts, there was nothing to do but comply.

That was only one of many peculiar extensions. Under the Watres Act the Postmaster General had the power to consolidate lines " for the public interest." Using this power, Brown consolidated the Cleveland-Louisville airway and Colonial Western, operating between Cleveland and Albany. Both lines were taken over by Aviation Corporation, and the routes were folded into the American Airways empire to form a right of way from Albany to the south. Brown soon granted the line an extension to Nashville, and then to Memphis. Eventually this section of American Airways reached all the way to Dallas and Fort Worth, without once being threatened by competitive bidding.

An even broader interpretation of the word " extension " is disclosed in the much discussed Memphis case. Here the extensions were *at right angles to, and in the middle of,* an existing route, which is a most curious use of the word " extension." This method very effectively got rid of another troublesome competitor.

It will be recalled that the brothers Frank and Major William Robertson were operators of one of the first five private air-mail routes, CAM–2, St. Louis to Chicago. In 1928 the Robertsons sold their line and mail contracts to Steifel & Nicholas Company of St. Louis, which later turned the route over to Aviation Corporation. The price was $300,000 which netted the Robertsons a considerable profit.[9] As the original investment in the line had been about $30,000, the Robertson brothers appeared to have made a good thing out of their venture.

The brothers got out of the air-line business and set up shop at Lambert Field, near St. Louis, as airplane-manufacturers. With C. M. Keys, of the Curtiss-Keys group, holding fifty per cent of the stock, the plant was incorporated as Curtiss-Robertson Company, makers of the Curtiss " Robin " monoplanes. The Robin was a good ship. In August 1930 Dale Jackson and Forest O'Brien set an endurance record of 647 hours of uninterrupted flight in one, and it was in a nine-year-old Robin that Douglas " Wrong-Way " Corrigan flew the Atlantic in 1938. Soon there was disagreement among the executives, however, and when the depression wiped out civil flying, the Robertson brothers withdrew to organize Robertson Airplane Service Company. In April 1930 they began an air passenger service from St. Louis to New Orleans, operating on a daily schedule, with single-engine Ryan monoplanes, of the type that Lindbergh had popularized by his transatlantic flight.

The Robertson brothers had every reason to believe that they would obtain a mail contract over the new route. The Mississippi Valley had been strangely neglected by air-line operators. It was good flying country and connected important trade centers. Yet until the Robertsons attempted it, there was no through service to New Orleans. Major

William B. Robertson says he had every assurance that Postmaster General Brown and his assistant, W. Irving Glover, would encourage the venture.[10] Unfortunately, the Robertsons ran foul of American Airways, which maintained that, while it was not operating over the Robertson route as yet, it had bought the "pioneer rights" when the Robertsons sold their original line in 1928. Soon the Robertsons were being received very coolly in Washington.

In fact, they never did get a contract. According to the testimony of Major Robertson, "a Mr. Sacks, connected with some Republican organization in Missouri," offered to get such a contract from Postmaster General, and Republican Party Leader, Brown, if, in turn, the Robertsons would agree to join up with the Wedell-Williams line.[11] For this service, says the major, Sacks asked five per cent of the gross — a fee which the Robertsons believed to be little short of a holdup.

"Mr. Sacks" was William Sacks, St. Louis attorney and Republican state committeeman for Missouri. He had been instrumental in swinging the Missouri delegates to Hoover in the 1928 convention,[12] and, Major Robertson intimates, because of Sacks's importance to Party Leader Brown, he might easily have been able to obtain the Robertson contract.

There were other reasons why the Postmaster General might have been prevailed upon to grant a contract to the Robertsons. There was, for example, the little matter of Wedell-Williams Air Service Corporation. Wedell-Williams was a passenger line operating between New Orleans, Shreveport, and Dallas and Fort Worth, with another leg from New Orleans to Houston, via Beaumont, Texas. The operators of the line were James ("Jimmy") Wedell, a racing pilot who later crashed in one of his own planes, and Harry P. Williams, a wealthy lumberman, better known as the husband of Marguerite Clarke, the screen actress. Williams was a relative of Ernest Lee Jahncke, Republican boss of New Orleans and onetime Assistant Secretary of the Navy. Wedell-Williams Corporation was exerting pressure upon the Postmaster General in Washington, and had the Robertsons been willing to merge, the new company might have won a contract.

If there seems to be evidence of political skulduggery, there is also evidence that Postmaster General Brown acted in good faith in the Robertson affair. His worst enemies were unable to disclose any dishonesty during later protracted Senate hearings, but there is another good reason why Brown might have had no intention of granting the Robertsons a contract that might appear to have been theirs rightfully. Brown had not forgiven the Robertsons for their $300,000 sell-out of CAM–2 and their later return to the old stand. Time and again the Postmaster General had cracked down on such operators, for he was determined that there should be no speculation in air-mail contracts. Lastly, Sacks himself testified that, instead of his going to the Robertsons with the suggestion of winning a contract at the price of a five-per-cent fee, the Robertsons had come to Sacks.[13]

The Robertsons killed any chances they might have had by their delay in merging with Wedell-Williams. Telegrams exhibited later indicated that the Robertsons were considering the merger only as a last resort. P. D. C. Ball, owner of the St. Louis Browns, and a Robertson backer, was getting impatient, however, and he insisted that the merger of Robertson with Wedell-Williams take place at once. Postmaster General Brown by this time was ready to wash his hands of the dallying Robertsons, and he issued an ultimatum giving them just ten days to join up with Wedell-Williams. Spurred by this threat, the Robertsons and Wedell-Williams came to an agreement whereby the Robertsons were to hold fifty-one per cent of the stock. It took so long to arrange the details, however, that the deadline passed. By the time the Robertsons and their new partners were ready to talk business, the mail contract had already been awarded to American Airways.

For American Airways maintained all along that the Robertsons had ceded the route by the sale of CAM–2 in 1928, and despite the time lapse and the fact that CAM–2 was miles from the disputed area, American expected to take over the airway between St. Louis and New Orleans. Doubtless the Postmaster General would have preferred to give American Airways the valley route, but the situation now became embarrassing. The Robertsons were experienced and successful operators, whereas American had never flown a mile of the new route, and the only way to freeze out Robertson was by an extension of American Airways. Yet how could the Postmaster General extend a line that did not even touch the disputed territory?

Brown solved the problem neatly, although by so doing he gave an entirely new meaning to the word " extension." The southern transcontinental route from Atlanta to Dallas crossed the river at Jackson, Mississippi. Brown simply " extended " American Airways by two right-angle branches, one going south to New Orleans and the other north to Memphis. There was still a missing link between Memphis and St. Louis, but the Postmaster General plugged the gap by extending American Airways' route between Chicago and St. Louis south to the Tennessee metropolis. The Robertsons were hoist with their own petard, since American Airways now brought the mail all the way into Chicago from New Orleans over the very route the Robertsons had relinquished in 1928. The Robertsons hung on for twenty-two months, but eventually they were forced out of business. Frank died of tuberculosis. Major William Robertson kept his line going until the contracts were put up for rebidding in 1934. Then, although he had operated efficiently and without a casualty, he lost out to another company, which underbid him by one cent. He retired from air-line operation and devoted himself to conducting a flying school in St. Louis.

Another Independent operator who learned to dislike Postmaster General Brown was Alfred Frank, whose little National Parks Airways wandered from Salt Lake City up into Montana. As the sole operator in Montana, Frank believed it only reasonable that he be granted an extension of about two hundred miles to reach Missoula and Billings. The Postoffice Department refused to grant the extension, but not long after that, Northwest Airways, which had never flown a mile into Montana, was granted an extension all the way from Mandan, North Dakota, to Billings. This was more than twice the mileage Frank had requested, and it was given to a line that had no pioneer rights in Montana.

When Northwest Airways began service between Chicago and the Twin Cities in 1926, it was a very modest enterprise. Solely by extensions, it had developed into what finally amounted to a fourth transcontinental system. After Comptroller General McCarl ruled against the extension of Northwest Airways up to Winnipeg in 1930, L. H. Brittin, eccentric vice president, thought up a new interpretation for " extension." He pointed out that his line had several unprofitable routes, which the Postoffice Department had foisted upon it. The airways from Chicago to Madison and to Green Bay were examples of such wasteful operation. Northwest asked that it be permitted to drop these routes and *to replace the mileage with an equal extension westward.* This method of hacking off a segment in one area and grafting it to another route may appear a little unorthodox, but the bitterest critics of the Postmaster General did not object. Comptroller General McCarl approved the Northwest Airways maneuvers, and the New Deal administration, which tried to discredit Republican Leader Brown, used the same tactics later on. The fact is that the Postmaster General had every right to extend lines in this way, under the consolidation clause of the Watres Act.

Brown was only consistent when he favored Northwest Airways over little National Parks Airways. The Northwest enterprise was the kind of line Brown liked. It had the solid backing of Chicago, Detroit, and Twin Cities capitalists, who owned 55 per cent of the stock. Aviation Corporation and Transcontinental & Western Air each owned about 22.5 per cent, off and on, and there was no attempt on the part of the Postmaster General to prevent such interlocking airline ownership, as in the American Airways-TWA-Halliburton deal, since Northwest Airways was not a competitor of TWA or Aviation Corporation. Both the Republican administration and the New Dealers, who followed, favored Northwest Airways over Al Frank. For one thing, Northwest was developing into a valuable northern transcontinental route, and it ran " from somewhere to somewhere," as the Postmaster General demanded of an air line. With Chicago as one terminus and Seattle as another, Northwest Airways was potentially a valuable airway system. All this is true enough, but it didn't make Al Frank feel any better.

November 1932 arrived and the New Deal tide washed away the Hoover administration and Walter Folger Brown. The Postmaster General's work was about done, but he added a few more flourishes before his successor took over the department. Transcontinental & Western Air was extended from Columbus to Chicago, and from Los Angeles to San Francisco, much to the annoyance of United Air Lines, whose hunting grounds were thereby invaded. Northwest Airways got its extension to Billings in the very last hours of the Hoover administration. Al Frank never forgave this perfidy, and he and Colonel Paul Henderson, of United Air Lines, later had their revenge.

Postmaster General Brown could look upon his handiwork with a great deal of satisfaction. He had cracked a few heads together, but he had brought order to a chaotic industry. When Brown left office in March 1933, there were 34 air-mail routes operating 27,062 miles of airway.[14] Sleek, three-mile-a-minute luxury liners had taken the place of the lumbering tri-motor transports. Passenger traffic was increasing at the rate of 500,000 a year, in spite of the depression. The young lad of twenty-five was no longer alone in his plane; for beside him was a co-pilot, and in the spacious cabin a dozen travelers lounged in reclining chairs.

Railroads had never progressed at this rate. The first railroad passenger service was established in England in 1828, but not until 1845 were travelers carried regularly at night.[15] In 1933, air lines in this country carried forty-two times as many passengers as all British railroads had transported in 1841, more than thirteen years after the beginning of railroad passenger service. Furthermore, the air lines were on the road to becoming self-sufficient. It is true that every line depended upon government payments, but these had been reduced continuously during the Brown administration. It had cost the Postoffice Department $1.10 a mile to fly the mail in 1929.[16] By 1933 these payments were down to 54 cents a mile,[17] and the year 1940 was set as the time when mail would be carried at cost and the air lines would be truly independent.

Despite this impressive record, commercial aviation went into a tail spin shortly after the Democrats succeeded to power. For the New Deal undertook to chastise the airline operators for their ruthless conquest of the airways. The charges, as summed up by Postmaster General James A. Farley, were:

1. That the air-mail appropriations were expended " for the benefit of a few favored corporations," which used the funds " as the basis of wild stock promotions, resulting in profits of tens of millions of dollars to promoters, who invested little or no cash."

2. That the five original air-mail contracts, due to expire November 7, 1929, were extended illegally by the Postmaster General and his assistant, Warren Irving Glover, to enable these favored lines to escape competitive bidding until the passage of the Watres Act could enable the Postmaster General to provide for them.

3. That the Postmaster General handed out almost 15,000 miles of airway by extension, without the required competitive bidding on almost 9,000 of those miles.

4. That the airway system of the United States was mapped out in a series of " spoils conferences," held in Washington during May and June 1930, to which only certain favored operators were invited.

5. That postoffice and air-line executives had destroyed certain incriminating evidence, which, in the case of the postoffice officials, was illegal.

6. That the southern route (American Airways) was bid on by only one line after a " prearranged " deal with an unwanted rival (Erle Halliburton).

7. That the central transcontinental route went to the high bidder " without justification " at a pecuniary loss to the government of more than two and one half million dollars.

8. That from July 1930 through December 1933, air-mail contractors were paid more than $78,000,000, although actual service rendered amounted to only about 40 per cent of that amount.

9. That because the air-mail contracts were obtained by collusion, they were held illegally, and that it was the duty of the administrative officers to disqualify such contractors for a period of five years.[18]

Before the New Deal was a year old, the air-mail situation had developed into a " scandal." Retribution was effected by cancellation of the all-important air-mail contracts. It was a Cadmean victory, however, for the marvelous air-line system, built with such pride, was so nearly wrecked that it took four years to repair the damage.

The Black Committee

THERE had been an investigation of the air-mail contract awards in the closing days of the Hoover administration, when Chairman James M. Mead, of the House Postoffice Committee, had probed into the conduct of the Postoffice Department. The Mead Committee took page after page of revealing testimony and perhaps prepared the way for what was to come, but the final report of the Republican-dominated legislators exonerated the GOP's leading politico, Postmaster General Walter Folger Brown. New Dealers lost no time in again stirring up the mail stew, however, and this time Brown found himself in hot water. The Independent operators, whom the Republican Postmaster General had treated so ruthlessly, were now the fair-haired boys of the succeeding administration, or so they thought, and they gloated as they saw the tumbril rolled out for Hoover's hard-boiled hetman.

Ammunition for the attack on Brown had been accumulating over a period of several years. In the summer of 1931 Fulton Lewis, later a popular radio commentator over Washington's station WOL, began the first serious exposé of the Postoffice Department. Lewis was then a Hearst reporter, fresh from the University of Virginia, and he was assigned to cover the Departments of Agriculture and Commerce. One day he met his friend William Briggs, who had recently joined the staff of Ludington Lines, a non-mail, passenger service operating between New York, Philadelphia, and Washington. Briggs told Lewis that the Postoffice Department had just rejected Ludington's bid to carry mail between Washington and New York at the low rate of 25 cents a mile.[1] Lewis was sympathetic, but he was only casually interested until he happened to see a Postoffice Department handout, in which it was announced that Eastern Air Transport had been awarded the route *on a bid of 89 cents a mile.* Since the postoffice had but recently rejected the Ludington offer, Lewis was puzzled by the apparent extravagance of postal officials. He began to use his spare time to burrow into the postoffice files, and the deeper he dug into the dreary galleries of the old building, the more his excitement mounted. Soon he believed he had enough evidence to hang former Postmaster General Brown.

Lewis had no reason to feel remorse over any misfortune that might befall Walter Folger Brown, for the reporter had married the daughter of Brown's political rival, Colonel Claudius Huston, chairman of the Republican National Committee. When Herbert Hoover was Secretary of Commerce, two of his most loyal henchmen were Brown and Huston, and after the 1928 election Hoover rewarded his two assistant secretaries by appointing Brown Postmaster General and Huston as party boss. In the spring of 1930 Huston was criticized for using party funds unwisely, and he was replaced as Republican chairman by Simeon D. Fess, Ohio Senator. Whether or not Brown had anything to do with Huston's discomfiture is conjectural, but Huston had no great love for the Postmaster General, and it is possible that this attitude carried over to his son-in-law, Lewis. On the other hand, it is unfair to assume that Lewis built his case against Brown solely out of revenge, for any reporter worth his salt would have delighted in uncovering the rich lode of news that Lewis was mining in the recesses of the postoffice galleries. Lewis was no ordinary reporter, as his subsequent career made clear, and he was sure that he had another Teapot Dome scandal within his eager grasp. His immediate superiors thought so too, and they told him to spend all his time tracking down the air-mail contracts story. Soon the reporter was interviewing officials and operators all over the country, and he amassed so much information that he was ready to " break " his story early in 1932. Because his disclosures were so sensational, he was advised to send his material to his chief, William Randolph Hearst, for a final check. Expecting to be congratulated for his scoop, Lewis waited week after week for the " go " signal from San Simeon. Believing his material might somehow have gone astray, the reporter queried the publisher again. He was never answered.

Possibly the fact that Arthur Brisbane, the great Hearst editor, was a friend of Brown's may have had something to do with the silence, although Brown later denied that he asked Brisbane, or anyone else, to intercede with the Sage of San Simeon.[2] Brisbane knew through his editors what was going on in Washington, however, and he might have put in a word without telling anyone. At any rate, the Hearst press, which usually delighted in " breaking " such " scandals," ignored the Lewis story, although the reporter was to have his Great Moment a year later, when he aided the Senate investigation of the air-mail contracts.

The award of the air-mail contract to Eastern Air Transport on a bid of 89 cents, after Ludington had been turned down on a 25-cent offer, appears to be inexcusable at first glance, but the story that started Lewis on his private investigation has another side to it.

Ludington Lines was incorporated originally as New York, Philadelphia & Washington Airway Corporation, which was an inappropriate title, inasmuch as the line did not even touch the states in which these cities are located. Terminals were respectively Newark, New Jersey; Camden, New Jersey; and Hoover Airport, on the Virginia side of the Potomac River. The line soon took the name of its principal backers, the wealthy and socially prominent Philadelphians Charles Townsend Ludington, then in his early thirties, and a younger brother, Nicholas. Townsend Ludington had organized the company that built Camden Airport, and he was also a director in several other aviation enterprises. Active management of the line was in the hands of a former West Point football star and Olympic athlete, Eugene (" Gene ") Vidal, later director of the Bureau of Air Commerce.

Vidal had started out with the old Transcontinental Air Transport, when that line was exclusively a passenger-carrier. TAT's air-rail experiment was such a costly failure that stockholders demanded somebody's scalp, and Vidal was discharged from TAT as a kind of sacrifice to the outraged. Certainly the losses of TAT were not directly attributable to Vidal, but he was thrown to the wolves, and with him went Paul F. (" Dog ") Collins, veteran war pilot, who later headed Northeast Airways, successor to the Boston-Maine line. Vidal and Collins apparently were ejected from TAT because they maintained that air lines could make a profit from passenger traffic. They were still talking this way when they met the Ludingtons, and before long they had convinced the Philadelphia patricians that there were profits in air transportation.

Vidal and Collins had what appeared to be a sound plan. At that time about 96,000 travelers shuttled every week between New York and Philadelphia; 79,000 between New York and Washington. Many of them were in a hurry and were willing to pay for fast service, as the railroads had already discovered. Ludington Lines could provide that speed, and, what is more, the operators proposed to carry passengers on tickets that would cost little more than the train fare. Finally, Ludington promised a new type of airline service, for planes were to leave terminals " every hour on the hour." [3]

Ludington began service in September 1930, using the stations of the Pennsylvania Railroad for the sale of tickets and the pickup of passengers. To be self-sustaining, Ludington had to effect every known economy. Equipment consisted of tri-motor Stinson monoplanes, able enough to perform well on the short run, and costing only about $24,000, or about half as much as the Ford transports, then standard equipment on several of the major lines. To save gasoline, pilots taxied to the starting line on only one motor. The ships took off on high-test aviation fuel, but once aloft, they buzzed along on regular automobile gasoline, costing from three to four cents a gallon less.

These economies were effective. At the end of the first year Ludington showed a net profit of $8,073. Operators of other carrier services would have sneered at such a small margin on the large investment, but the Ludingtons were elated, for it was the first time in the history of commercial aviation that an air line had *not* lost money without calling on the government for assistance in the form of mail contracts.

If the line could show a profit from passenger revenue alone, what a harvest it might reap with a little mail pay! Long before the first year was up, Vidal began his campaign to obtain a mail franchise. He had proved his point about passenger traffic; now it was time to show stockholders a few dividends. Vidal had every reason to believe that he could win a contract. The recently passed Watres Act provided for competitive bidding, and Ludington needed such a small increase in revenue that no rival could possibly meet its low bid. Yet as Briggs told Fulton Lewis in the summer of 1931, Ludington had lost, hands down.

The reason was that Ludington did not fit into the picture of the American air-line system, as sketched by the Postoffice Department. The line that did fit into the picture was Eastern Air Transport, one of the " big boys " in aviation. Pioneered by Harold Pitcairn (Pitcairn Aviation, Inc.) in 1926, the line followed the Atlantic seaboard from New York to Richmond. The line then split into two antennæ — one feeling its way to Miami; the other crossing the mountains to Atlanta. Pitcairn received an air-mail contract in February 1927, and by 1928 the special Pitcairn " Mailwing " biplanes were establishing enviable reputations for reliability. The flow of mail to and from Florida tourists counteracted the usual winter slump, and because the territory was the exclusive domain of one operator, Pitcairn had been able to put in a maximum bid. The result was that this airway has always been one of the more valuable air-transportation properties.

Harold Pitcairn was much more interested in building autogiros than in becoming an air-line tycoon, and on July 10, 1929 he sold his air line to the booming young North American Aviation Company. The new owners changed the name of the line to Eastern Air Transport in January 1930, and Eastern began to expand. It was one of the first lines to begin scheduled passenger service, in August 1930. It was one of the safest routes in the world and operated for ten years without a fatality. Finally, it pioneered in equipment adapted for passenger comfort. EAT started with Fords and Fokkers, but because of the affiliation with the Curtiss group, which was also a subsidiary of North American Aviation, it soon standardized on big twin-motored Curtiss " Condors." The Condor was a cumbersome biplane transport, but it was one of the most comfortable of the passenger ships. Comfort was an important point in the air-line program of EAT's president, Captain Thomas B. Doe. The Condor was the first transport designed so that passengers could converse in ordinary tones. Condors were slow, but very reliable. When the Curtiss " Conqueror " engines were replaced with "Whirlwinds" and "Cyclones," they were the equal of any transport available up to the end of 1932. All this equipment and experimentation cost money, but by 1931 EAT was ready to reap the reward of its pioneering.

This was the line that won the mail contract between New York and Washington on a bid more than three times that of Ludington's. Furthermore, with a mail contract as a backlog of revenue, EAT soon forced the Ludingtons to retire as operators. Here was a situation made to order for the critics of Postmaster General Brown. A courageous little company, ably managed, and safely operated as a new standard of air-line convenience, is frozen out by Big Business — and with taxpayers paying the bill, to the extent of more than three times the minimum bid. In spite of this, the Postmaster General probably did the wise thing in awarding the contract to Eastern Air Transport.

The trouble with the Ludington Line was that it operated over only about two hundred miles of airway, and it just was not adequate to meet the demands of the Post-office Department. As Brown once remarked, he was not buying peanuts and pig iron — he was buying a great air service,[4] and 25-cent bids did not sway him from his course.

Brown knew that a series of short lines across the country was an inefficient way of building the great system he had in mind. Numerous studies of transportation supported his contention. Hearings on the Transportation Act of 1920, when the railroads were handed back to private owners after the war, hinted that unification of the carriers was to be encouraged.[5] The report of the Coolidge National Transportation Committee, and later the findings of Joseph B. Eastman, federal co-ordinator of transportation, also stressed the need of unity.[6] And there was an even better reason why Brown could not give Ludington a mail contract: it would have been just as expensive in the long run.

Ludington was willing to carry mail for only 25 cents a mile because of its heavy passenger traffic between the nation's largest city and the capital. Not only was this populous territory ideal for a passenger service, but it was over excellent flying terrain, which added to the economy of air transportation. Had this same mileage been across the Sierras, or over the lonely plains, or through the rugged Appalachian country, the cost of air transportation would have been far greater than Ludington could have faced. Ludington was conducting an operation under the most ideal conditions. No air-line executive cared to pioneer the hinterland at great risk and at great financial loss if he had to meet the competition of rivals flying over only populous and profitable sections.

Had Ludington been able or willing to expand into the kind of air line Brown knew this country needed, the company would have seen its operating charges soar out of sight. Vidal ran the line for about 35 cents a mile. Yet United Air Lines, famed for its excellent management, could not meet operating expenses unless it earned more than twice that. United required three ships for every transcontinental trip. Five pilots, paid an average of $7,200 a year, and five co-pilots, earning about $2,700 a year, manned these planes. Added to the flying costs were the salaries of the five stewardesses, and all together the total *air* costs for United amounted to about 23.5 cents a mile.[7]

United's ground costs were even higher, since it took from six to eight groundlings to keep one pilot in the air. Two thirds of the cost of getting an air liner to its destination could be chalked up to office and maintenance work. Ships had to be conditioned for the long flights, and engines had to be rebuilt as they accumulated hours of flying time in their logs. Frequent inspection of instruments and controls also raised maintenance costs. And even more costly was the practice of writing ships off the books every three years — not because they were worn out, but simply to meet the competition of other major airway systems. It is not surprising, then, that United's ground costs amounted to 33 cents for every mile of flight.

The combined charges for ground maintenance, air costs, administration, and advertising brought United's total operating costs up to 72 cents a mile. That was the best a well-managed, experienced, low-bidding line could do, and that figure did not include such items as the building up of necessary reserves, and the profit that any private enterprise is supposed to enjoy. Eastern Air Transport's costs were comparable to those of United, and it was not, as yet, in a position to carry as much mail. Looked at in this light, the EAT bid of 89 cents does not appear out of line.

Ludington could afford to carry mail for 25 cents a mile because the shorter air line was freed of many expenses and responsibilities forced upon the major operators. Had Ludington agreed to expand into a trunk system, it would have found its passenger revenue cut so alarmingly, as it stretched farther and farther from the big cities, that low mail payments would no longer have netted profit. At the same time, expenses would have mounted. Instead of four small fields, the larger line would have needed seventeen (comparing Ludington with United) ; and instead of three small ships to provide hourly service between near-by points, Ludington would have required eighteen or twenty merely to maintain three trips a day across the country.

Ludington escaped many of the other problems of the big operator. It did not use co-pilots, because the flights were of such short duration that there was no danger of fatigue. There was no need of expensive radio, since the ships were out of touch with officials only a few minutes between cities. There was no need of a weather service, because pilots kept each other posted as to conditions ahead, and in any case terminals were so close together that pilots could usually reach their destinations before weather grounded them.

All this has been put down as an example of why Brown appeared to discriminate against the " little fellows." If the Postmaster General had used mail subsidy to aid such lines as Ludington, he could never have fashioned his great airway system. Giving a short line a contract merely because it was low bidder would have been futile and expensive. It would have discouraged operators from pioneering across the barren lands. It would have resulted in a jumbled, disconnected system that, in the long run, would have cost the taxpayer far more than he would have saved by helping operators unwilling to fly less profitable routes. The Postmaster General suffered for his methods, but when all the facts are known, he appears in a better light.

Ludington Lines went to Eastern Air Transport in February 1933. Unable to meet the competition of the subsidized lines, Vidal and Collins had to give up. Eastern Air Transport might have taken over the Ludington route without paying a cent for it, but as Hainer Hinshaw, airline lobbyist, once testified, the Postmaster General's order for the Independents to sell was equally a command for the " big boys " to buy, and in many cases the " little fellows " jacked up their prices so high that sometimes forced retirement was not only painless, but a pleasure.[8] There is some indication that Brown told EAT's Captain Doe that there would be no contract forthcoming until the big line did right by Ludington.[9]

Under these circumstances, Ludington disappeared. Perhaps it was just as well. The little air line had been depending upon the station facilities of the Pennsylvania Railroad, but since EAT was affiliated with the railroad (via Transcontinental Air Transport, which was part of Transcontinental & Western Air, which was under the wing of North American Aviation, which owned EAT) ,

Ludington was faced with the loss of air terminals, and on its narrow margin of profit it could not build its own.

It was the Ludington case that started Fulton Lewis on his investigation, but as the months rolled by and Hearst refused to reply to his employee, the Hoover administration dragged along to its unhappy end. Anyone in the aviation business could have predicted that the New Dealers would do a thorough job of house-cleaning, particularly in the domain of Postmaster General Brown. Already the Independent operators whom Brown had brought to the brink of ruin were whispering to New Deal legislators, eager to hear all there was to know about Republican malfeasance. Even the trade journals had hoisted storm warnings for all air-line executives to see.[10]

The attack began the month before the new administration took command, when senators authorized an inquisition to be conducted by the Special Committee on Investigation of the Air Mail and Ocean Mail Contracts. Called the "Black Committee," after its chairman, soft-spoken Senator Hugo L. Black of Alabama, the committee was a group of three Democrats and two Republicans. The Democrats were Senator Black, Senator William H. King of Utah, and Senator Patrick A. McCarran of Nevada, who later initiated important aviation legislation. The Republican members were Senator Wallace H. White of Maine, and Senator Warren R. Austin of Vermont. As special investigator for the committee, the Senate appointed A. G. Patterson. These were the men who constituted the tribunal hearing air-mail complaints, but the inquisition actually was Senator Black's show, and the mild-appearing Southerner with the sensitive jaw and the thin, sandy hair soon made himself a scourge to the big operators. When Senator Black became a Supreme Court justice, in 1937, the most vociferous critics of the appointment were those who had felt his lash during the air-mail investigation. To Senator Black, however, the hearings and resulting drastic action by the Postoffice Department and President of the United States were all part of a righteous crusade against the injustices of a previous administration.[11]

Strangely enough, the original purpose of the Black Committee was not to investigate the air-mail situation at all, but to put an end to the long controversy over the *ocean* mail contracts. Air-mail legislation was due for revision, but the original plan was for a separate hearing on this aspect of the postal service. It was only by chance that air mail was lumped with the scrutiny of steamship subsidies, and the air-mail " scandals " developed about like this:

Postmaster General Brown had promised to aid John B. (Jack) Kohler, who operated a line between Milwaukee and Grand Rapids, across Lake Michigan. The Kohler airway was the small type of operation that Brown usually ignored in his plans, but Kohler had played ball with the Postmaster General, and Brown was in a position to help the operator retire gracefully. E. L. Cord, who owned American Airways, had bought Trans-America Airlines, which connected with Kohler at Grand Rapids and carried traffic to Detroit. The plan was for Trans-America to take over Kohler, but Cord offered Kohler only a " scrap price," and so the Postmaster General resorted to other tactics. In the last days of his administration Brown got Northwest Airways to take over Kohler, and then to sublet the route to the original operator much to the displeasure of Northwest executives, who finally agreed, only because they did not care to see Cord squeezing into their territory. To soften the blow, the Postmaster General granted Northwest's petition for permission to drop its unprofitable Wisconsin branches and to add the mileage of these canceled routes to its main line.

This was the deal that brought Northwest Airways to Billings, much to the disgust of Alfred Frank, whose National Parks Airways had enjoyed a virtual monopoly of the territory. Also outraged was Colonel Paul Henderson

of United Air Line, since Northwest Airways not only
paralleled the pioneering United main line, but also threatened to drain away mail and passenger traffic from the
Pacific Northwest, which United served by the old Varney
system out of Salt Lake City. Al Frank and Senator King
were friends and fellow residents of Salt Lake City, and the
air-line operator took his troubles to the legislator. Senator
King was impressed by Frank's story, and when he heard
that Colonel Henderson was involved, he called United's
general manager to Washington for a conference. The colonel had so much more to add that Senator King, who had
been named as one of the committeemen to hear the pending ocean-mail testimony, asked the Senate to include air
mail in the investigation. Colonel Henderson later said that
he saw the danger to the transportation industry and that
he tried to dissuade Senator King from the proposed probe
of air-mail subsidies, but Senator King was not to be side-
tracked.[12] Instead of being given a separate hearing, air
mail was thrown in with the noisome shipping mess. Senator King, who had started all the excitement, thereupon
retired to the wings and was virtually forgotten during the
long inquisition.

Soon the committee's investigator, Patterson, heard of
the Fulton Lewis dossier on air-mail contracts, and he took
Senator Black with him to study the evidence which the
reporter had gathered at his home. Patterson and the Senator were elated by what they saw and they demanded the
material for use in the pending air-mail hearing. Lewis replied that he could not release his evidence until he heard
from his employer, William Randolph Hearst, who had
ignored Lewis up to this time. Lewis again telegraphed San
Simeon for advice, but again there was only silence from
that direction. Senator Black now took a hand in the proceedings. He himself wired Hearst for permission to use the
Lewis material, and after more delay Hearst very reluc-
tantly gave his consent. The newspaper-publisher had frus-

trated a great scoop, but Lewis had his recognition when he sat at Senator Black's right hand during part of the hearings. It was observed that witnesses frequently squirmed uncomfortably following a conversation between the reporter and the chairman, for there is no doubt that Lewis knew where the operators were most vulnerable.

The hearings of the Black Committee began in Room 312 of the Senate Office Building on Tuesday, September 28, 1933. The opening act of the drama was dull. Senators Austin and White, minority party members, did not even make an appearance. All the fall, while Ferdinand Pecora played to a full house in an adjoining room, where he was conducting a banking and currency probe, the Black Committee performed before an apathetic audience. The ocean-mail subsidies were " old stuff," and the testimony had been heard so many times that the press had lost interest. Not until October did Chairman Black get to the air-mail situation. Then things began to pick up. One morning Interstate Commerce investigators seized the files of air-line executives all over the country. So quickly did these falcons descend that many a piece of memoranda, better burned, found its way to Room 312 of the Senate Office Building. Suddenly the Black Committee had become front-page news.

CHAPTER

18

Washington Opera Bouffe

SEIZURE of private correspondence brought many note-worthy witnesses to Room 312 in the Senate Office Building. One was William P. MacCracken, Jr., who had been instrumental in lifting commercial aviation out of the wood-and-linen period of operation following the war. With the American Bar Association behind him, Mac-Cracken had labored diligently on legislation leading to the Air Commerce Act of 1926. He had won the respect of the industry, as the first Assistant Secretary of Commerce to be given the task of administering the regulations provided by the 1926 law. In recognition of his ability, he was appointed to the venerated National Advisory Committee for Aeronautics upon his resignation from the Commerce Department a year or so later. It was an open secret that MacCracken was co-author of the McNary-Watres Bill of 1930. When the Black Committee began calling witnesses, MacCracken was the Washington representative for several important aviation companies, including Western Air Express, Pan American Airways, Goodyear Zeppelin, Ludington Lines, and Northwest Airways.

MacCracken stepped into the air-mail mess when he

refused to give Investigator Patterson access to certain files, on the plea that attorneys were bound by the ethics of their profession not to reveal confidential matters without the consent of the client. Senators White and Austin, the Black Committee's Republican minority, subscribed to this thesis at first, but the other members maintained all along that MacCracken was not entitled to legal privilege, since they held that his relationship with his clients was not as an attorney, but as a lobbyist.

MacCracken obtained waivers from most of his clients, but Chairman Black discovered that three air-line officials had retrieved certain of their papers *after* the investigating committee had served MacCracken with a subpoena to appear with all available records.[1] The three air-line officials involved were Harris Hanshue, president of Western Air Express; his assistant, Gilbert Givven; and Colonel L. H. Brittin, of Northwest Airways. MacCracken gave certain papers from the Western Air Express file to Givven in response to a long-distance telephone call from Hanshue. Hanshue asked that he have a chance to examine one or two papers before he gave his consent to their being turned over to the Senate Committee. MacCracken exacted a promise that the papers would be returned intact at once, but apparently the wires were tapped, for the committee appeared to know all about this conversation, and the upshot was that Hanshue turned them back to the committee upon request.

In like manner Colonel Brittin looked over his files, although MacCracken did not know about this until later. Colonel Brittin, a notorious penny-pincher, had long made free use of MacCracken's office space and secretarial service. At the time of the air-mail scandals the colonel was having a little domestic trouble, and he had no intention of flaunting his private affairs before the unsympathetic senators. Eventually all of these papers were made available to the Senate inquisitors, since all the clients waived their

privileges, but before the last waiver came in, Senator
Black became impatient and secured from the Senate a
warrant for the arrest of MacCracken on a charge of contempt of Senate. Explaining what happened then, Mac-
Cracken says:

While Chesley Jurney, the Senate Sergeant-at-Arms, was on
his way to my office to serve this warrant, the final waiver [Colo-
nel Brittin's] came in, with the result that all my files were then
turned over to the Senate Committee, and while I was placed
under arrest by the formal reading of the warrant, I was not
taken under custody. The warrant was served on Friday and
was returnable on Monday. Both Frank Hogan [MacCracken's
attorney] and I reported on Monday to Jurney, and were by
him escorted to seats in the Senate gallery. Senator Black then
explained to the Senate what had happened and on his motion,
the files were turned over to the committee and I was discharged from arrest. Then a motion was made that Brittin,
Hanshue, Givven, Lee [MacCracken's law partner] and myself
be taken into custody by the Sergeant-at-Arms and brought before the bar of the Senate to show cause why we should not be
punished for contempt. This motion was withdrawn and a
brief recess taken in order to prepare a written motion. When
the written motion was submitted, Lee and myself were not included. After the motion was adopted, Senator LaFollette [of
Wisconsin] got up and said that while he had no objection to
the action that had been taken, he wanted to call attention
to the fact that my name was not included. Thereupon Senator
Black moved to reconsider . . . amending it to include my
name, which was done. The four of us were served with citations to appear before the Senate on Friday of that week for
trial. Instead of appearing for trial, I sent up by Frank Hogan
a formal written protest denying the jurisdiction of the Senate
to punish me, once they had received all the files. My failure to
appear on Friday resulted in the issuance of a second warrant,
and the game of " hide and seek " between Jurney and myself.[2]

The " game of hide and seek " was one of the amusing
interludes in the Senate investigation and gave the Senate

Committee the publicity it needed. For Attorney Hogan, legal crutch for Edward L. Doheny and the Riggs National Bank, was an experienced jouster with the government, and Hogan advised MacCracken to keep out of sight until after the Senate adjourned on Saturday noon. All Saturday morning Sergeant-at-Arms Jurney hunted Mac-Cracken, intent upon serving the second warrant, but when the clock struck twelve and the Senate recessed, Officer Jurney closed up for the week, leaving the warrant in the Senate safe. Immediately MacCracken came out of hiding. Saturday evening he presented himself at Jurney's home and demanded that he be arrested. A few minutes later two of Attorney Hogan's assistants arrived, and in Jurney's presence MacCracken swore to a petition for a writ of habeas corpus (temporary release).

There were good reasons for all this maneuvering. Mac-Cracken believed that he had been unfairly treated by the majority block of the Senate Committee. By hiding until the Senate adjourned and then obtaining a writ from the District of Columbia Supreme Court, MacCracken could bring the case to the attention of the civil courts, thereby removing himself from the jurisdiction of the Senate Committee. The plan was to stay out of sight until the Black Committee went home for the week end, then to appear before Jurney for arrest, and finally, to obtain a writ of habeas corpus, which would be heard by the civil court the first thing Monday morning. Once discharged by this court, MacCracken would be troubled no more.

There was an unexpected hitch to this plan. MacCracken gave himself up to Jurney Saturday evening, but the Sergeant-at-Arms refused to take the accused into custody for the reason that the arrest warrant was at that moment far away in the Senate safe. MacCracken argued that formal service of a warrant was unnecessary, and that by voluntarily surrendering he had *ipso facto* waived the need of a warrant. When Jurney still refused to arrest MacCracken,

the air-line representative camped on the doorstep of the
Sergeant-at-Arms and insisted that he was Jurney's prisoner. All Saturday night and Sunday morning MacCracken
stuck close to Jurney. For refusal to serve the warrant put
MacCracken in an embarrassing position. The District of
Columbia court had granted a habeas corpus on the assumption that the accused was an unwilling prisoner. Unless MacCracken were under arrest by the time the court
was in session Monday morning, he might be cited for contempt of court, and, what was much worse, his case would
be thrown back to the Senate Committee.

Then began a curious game of hide and seek, with Jurney, the Senate's arresting officer, endeavoring to escape
from his prisoner, while MacCracken clung like a tick to
the Sergeant-at-Arms. Sunday afternoon Jurney evolved
a plan for escaping from his prisoner, since Jurney, too,
had a problem. For if MacCracken remained a " prisoner,"
or if he could force Jurney to produce the arrest warrant
the first thing Monday morning, he would level the last
obstacle for a hearing on the habeas corpus writ before the
civil court, and the Senate would have to relinquish Mac-
Cracken. If Jurney could get away from MacCracken, however, until the court dismissed the writ of habeas corpus,
the Sergeant-at-Arms might then pick up his prisoner and
return him to the Senate Committee. This was why Jurney
and MacCracken played tag all day Sunday. Late Sunday
afternoon Jurney left the Senate Office Building with Mac-
Cracken still trailing him closely. A car drove up to the
curb. MacCracken recognized it as the district attorney's.
Without warning, Jurney leaped on the running board.
The vehicle picked up speed and left MacCracken standing disconsolately on the sidewalk. Officer Jurney had successfully escaped from his prisoner.

That was the last of Jurney until Monday morning.
When court convened, MacCracken appeared for his hearing on the writ of habeas corpus. Jurney, who had kept out

of sight up to this point, now popped up in the witness chair to swear that MacCracken had never been under arrest, since the warrant was not served. MacCracken maintained that he had waived the warrant and was a prisoner, but the court ruled in favor of Jurney. Since MacCracken was not under arrest, the court held that he had obtained the habeas corpus " improvidently," and he was fined one hundred dollars for contempt of court. The writ was of course dismissed. At once Jurney produced his warrant and marched MacCracken to the Senate Office Building, where the Black Committee waited. There MacCracken and Colonel Brittin were sentenced to ten days' imprisonment for contempt of Senate. The two fought the verdict, contending that the upper House had only coercive, not punitive, powers,[3] but eventually they served their sentences.

The above incident is described out of all proportion to its real significance, and perhaps it is unfair to devote the same space to it as to MacCracken's very important contributions. The story serves admirably, however, to show why the Black Committee began to appear as front-page news all over the country. With publicity beating pitilessly on many a big name, the public began to think of the air-mail situation as a " scandal." This attitude was nourished daily, while air-line executives squirmed under the questioning of suave and deadly Chairman Black.

There was the case of Frederick B. Rentschler, kingpin of United Aircraft & Transport, holding company for United Air Lines and the Pratt & Whitney engine company. Here was a fine example of profiteering at the expense of the taxpayer, said the critics. Rentschler's 1,375 shares of Pratt & Whitney had cost him only $275 in July 1925, when the famed Pratt & Whitney " Wasp " motor was still only a problem on the drafting board. In December 1926 he sold 110 shares of this stock to C. W. Deeds, the thirty-year-old son of Colonel E. A. Deeds, director of the company that had advanced the capital and factory space for the manufacture of the aircraft motor. That left Rentschler with 1,265 shares, which had cost him only $253.

In November 1928 Pratt & Whitney paid a stock dividend of 79 for one, which left Rentschler with 101,200 shares. A little later United Aircraft & Transport Corporation absorbed Pratt & Whitney in a merger that involved another exchange of stock, and Rentschler emerged with 219,604 shares in the holding company. In 1933, just before the air-mail " scandals," when United Aircraft was quoted at around 97, the paper profit on the original investment of $253 amounted to more than $21,000,000. Had profits been computed as of May 1929, when stocks were still unaffected by the depression, Rentschler's little investment would have returned him a profit of more than $35,000,-000. Even in the dark days of 1934, when United's stock dropped to from $30 to $35, Rentschler's shares were worth about $7,000,000.[4]

In addition to stock, Rentschler received a salary of $100,000 in 1929 from United Aircraft and a bonus of $143,000 from Pratt & Whitney — an income for that year of $243,000, exclusive of stock. Between 1927 and 1933 he was said to have pocketed more than $1,500,000 in salaries and bonuses alone.[5] The Black Committee made it appear as though the chairman of United Aircraft had extracted all this money from the taxpayer, via mail payments to United Air Lines.

Strangely enough, Rentschler did not act at all like a pirate when the Senate Committee called him as a witness. He admitted his vast profits, but instead of hanging his head in shame, he was able to look his accusers squarely in the eyes. Certainly the bonus was excessive, he admitted later, but there was a reason. The Pratt & Whitney motors were phenomenally successful, and lest Messrs. Rentschler, Mead, et al., be lured away by competitors, Niles-Bement-Pond, the original backers, had a contract stipulating payment of a percentage of earnings. This contract continued in force after the United Aircraft merger. Niles-Bement-Pond apparently looked upon it as a kind of retainer. It was far more than it should have been because no one knew that the Pratt & Whitney engine would earn such profits, but the high " bonus " was not the fault of Rentschler.

The $100,000 salary, presumably derived from the air line but actually paid by United Aircraft, the holding company, was also exorbitant, but United, as the only trans-continental mail line of that day, was making money. If United Air Lines made money, again that was not entirely the fault of Rentschler. The situation is explained by Colonel Paul Henderson, general manager of United Air Lines at one time, but no great admirer of Rentschler. Queried by Chairman Black as to whether " it was fair to the people of the United States to make [*sic*] such a mail business that in one year a company will make a million dollars profit off of a $750 [*sic*] investment," Colonel Henderson replied:

When the Boeing company [predecessor of United Air Lines] secured its contract from the government, there was no knowledge on anybody's part whether there would be ten pounds of mail or 10,000 pounds of mail to be carried between San Francisco and New York each day, except the knowledge of how much mail was then moving on the government line, and it was a very small amount of mail. The contract was for four years. It is true that shortly after, the Boeing company took a contract and at a fixed rate of $3 a pound, and it is true that shortly after the Boeing company started to operate, the weight of the mail to be transported increased substantially. The reason it increased was because the government lowered the rate charged to the public. It is true that for the first two years of that contract neither the government, nor the Boeing company, had any control over the revenue which the Boeing company received [because the lines were bound by *contract*], and it is also true that at that time, it was a very handsome revenue.

. . . Then my point is this, sir: at the end of two years the postmaster general could have reduced Boeing's rates by asking them to surrender their contract [and to reduce payments] to any amount that they saw fit, and notwithstanding that the Boeing company's representatives were here urging that the rates be reduced and that they be given, in lieu of their contract, a route certificate for the first two years of satisfactory service.[6] This was never done until — the date I have forgotten [7] — but there was a period of much longer than a year . . . during which the government paid the Boeing company $1.50 a pound for carrying the mail, when it might, had the government wished to exercise its right . . . have paid any sum [the government] cared to fix. Had that happened, the Boeing company's profits during the four-year period could have been as low as the government wished them to be.[8]

Now I will directly answer your question. Of course I do not approve of making a million dollars of a $750 investment, but I do believe that there were very unusual circumstances here. The Boeing company, in taking the contract, had no knowledge of how much air mail they were going to carry. They bid lower than anyone else. The other companies were furious at the low rate bid by Boeing. . . . For two years, the government, under the existing law, could not lower their rate. Neither could the Boeing company lower it. At the end of two years, Boeing, and all of their people, did the best they could to get the government to reduce rates [in exchange for a route certificate].[9]

In perspective, Rentschler appears to have made too much money, but it was not gouged out of the taxpayer and the profits were not derived from speculation, but rather from successful operation of a first-class manufacturing plant. Pratt & Whitney backers risked more than a million dollars before they received one cent in return, and the government, United Aircraft's best customer, saved thousands of dollars annually on the cheaper, better motor. Lastly, the engine company supplied much-needed competition in the radial-engine field.

The United Aircraft companies were not the only ones accused of profiteering at the expense of the public. The New Deal's Postmaster General James A. Farley charged that most of the big lines had been paid air-mail subsidies out of all proportion to the services rendered. According to the Farley bill of complaint, American Airways, which should have been paid $3,338,673 for carrying mail over the southern route, actually received payments of $5,308,-958 during the administration of Postmaster General Brown. Similarly, Transcontinental & Western Air, which won the central route on what Farley called an illegal bid, was accused of squeezing five million dollars more from the government than a rival bidder had asked. All together, Farley charged, the air lines had cheated the government out of $46,800,000 between July 1930 and January 1934.[10]

No wonder the word " subsidy " began to be used interchangeably with " graft," " waste," and " collusion." Farley had preponderant opinion behind him when he made his sensational charges in February 1934, yet there is nothing inherently wrong in postal subsidies, and even if the Postmaster General could prove that the air lines received payments far above mail revenue, that still did not mean that subsidy was " bad." If the mere support of a service at public expense is wrong, then the American public suffers at many hands. There is a newspaper " subsidy," for example, whereby publishers send their products through the mails at great expense to the public. Cost of this service has been estimated to be as high as six million dollars a year,[11] while the total value of parcel post, and other below-cost services, has been set at more than $36,000,000 annually.[12] Indirectly, these subsidies benefit private individuals, but few object to the vast expenditures, for the taxpayer believes that he is the gainer. It is not the amount of money involved that makes a subsidy right or wrong, therefore. It is only a question of how the money is used.

Various experts have attempted to estimate the actual subsidy paid to the air lines during Brown's administration of the Postoffice Department. These estimates vary from the high of Postmaster General Farley to the lows mentioned by the operators at each air-mail appropriation hearing. In his *Economics of Air Mail Transportation* Paul T. David has attempted to show the actual subsidy paid to the air lines while the Watres Act was in force.[13] His table in Appendix III indicates that the air-mail subsidy between 1931 and 1933 amounted to $34,506,435. Many of the operators dispute David's figures, but the table provides a logical basis for argument and appears to be reasonable.

Granted that there was an air-mail subsidy, it remains to be seen whether it was justified. Even had the New Dealers admitted the fairness of the mail payments, they would still have gone baying after Walter Folger Brown. For there was evidence that the executives of the major air lines had met secretly, like thieves in the night, to divide up the air-mail contracts. If the evil of subsidies is dependent upon whose pocket is lined, then it is important to know whether or not the air-line operators were guilty of collusion.

CHAPTER

19

The "Spoils Conferences"

I AM convinced," wrote Postmaster General Farley to Senator Black in February 1934, following the Senate investigation of the air-mail contracts, " that before any of these contracts were awarded, those interested held meetings for the purpose of dividing territory and contracts among themselves . . . resulting in . . . the practical elimination of competitive bidding." [1] The meetings to which the New Deal Postmaster General referred were held intermittently between May 15 and June 4, 1930, and although little notice was taken of them at the time, they were used as damaging evidence against the big operators during the Senate hearings.

On the afternoon of May 15, 1930, just two weeks after the passage of the McNary-Watres Act, a Mr. Thomas H. McKee arrived in Washington as the representative of Wedell-Williams Air Service Corporation, which was losing money flying passengers between scattered points in Louisiana and Texas. McKee had come to the capital with the idea of winning an air-mail contract to ease the financial strain, as provided by the new air-mail law. Neither Postmaster General Brown nor his assistant, W. Irving Glover, would see the man from the South, however, and McKee was about to give up his quest when he learned from a friend in the Department of Commerce that a number of major operators were gathering for " mysterious meetings " in the old Postoffice Building. McKee hastened over to see what was going on, but was denied admittance to the inner sanctum. It was only by posing as a " big shot " in the industry that McKee forced his way into the conference chamber.

Seated around a table were the traditional " fifteen men in a smoke-filled room." [2] Most of them were important airline executives, and the leader appeared to be William P. MacCracken, Jr., Western Air Express representative, and co-author of the Watres Act. From the hostile glances directed his way, McKee concluded that he was not exactly welcome, but he demanded of MacCracken that he be told the purpose of the gathering.

" Mr. McKee," MacCracken is said to have replied, " we have been authorized to draw up this new air mail picture for the country." [3]

Thereupon McKee was told in so many words to get out and to stay out. Furious at the treatment he had received, McKee called on Earl Wadsworth, superintendent of air mail, who had written courteously to him at various times. According to testimony, Wadsworth pointed out that the Postoffice Department was not interested in giving mail contracts to lines " under 700 miles in length," [4] although the limit in the Watres Act was clearly placed at 250 miles. This meant that the Big Boys were to be favored at the expense of the short lines, and since it had been proved that no line could exist without mail payments, it appeared as though the group in the smoky room were relegating the Independent operators to bankruptcy and oblivion.

McKee hustled around to see Ernest Lee Jahncke, Assistant Secretary of the Navy and Republican boss of McKee's home town, New Orleans. Jahncke asked McKee to write a letter stating his grievances, and this note was then forwarded to Postmaster General Brown, with whom Jahncke had political associations. Exhibited in the Senate investigation of 1933–4, the letter seems mild enough coming from one in McKee's state of perturbation, but it so enraged Brown that he threatened to have nothing more to do with the Wedell-Williams line until McKee apologized for his effrontery.[5]

The meetings described by McKee were the so-called " Spoils Conferences," and as portrayed during the Black Committee hearings they made the major air lines appear as monopolies of the worst type. What was even worse was the part that the Postmaster General had played in abetting the conspiracy. Critics had one word to sum up the situation. " Collusion," they called it.

Webster defines collusion as the " act of colluding; deceit; fraud . . . implies playing into another's hands for fraud or deceit." Collusion also connotes furtiveness and connivance, also chargeable to the Spoils Conferences. Whether or not the contracts were awarded fraudulently remains to be seen, but this much is certain — that Postmaster General Brown called together only a chosen few, and that when the last wisp of cigar smoke cleared away, the Big Three (United Aircraft, Aviation Corporation, and the North American-General Motors group) emerged *with all but two of the twenty air-mail contracts.*

Actually, there was no collusion at all, if the word implies a concert of action, since the operators failed completely to reach any kind of agreement. Suspicious, jealous of each other, and only too willing to stab a rival, the conferees got exactly nowhere in working out their own problems. In desperation they turned to Top Sergeant Brown, whom they all feared and hated, but who appeared to be the only person capable of settling their disputes. The Postmaster General was now in an excellent position to push through his plan for an airway empire, and with the ten-year certificates as a kind of truncheon, he was able to make the operators do many things that they would have resisted otherwise, and for which they were held accountable by Chairman Black.

Many of the operators accused of dividing up the airway system even rebelled at the Spoils Conferences. Harris Hanshue, of Western Air Express, left the meetings in disgust. Colonel Paul Henderson, of United Air Lines, objected to the legality of the proceedings and was reassured only after North American Aviation's counsel, Chester W. Cuthell, replied: " I quite agree with you; if we were holding this meeting across the street in the Raleigh Hotel, it would be an improper meeting; but because we are holding it at the invitation of a member of the cabinet, and in the office of the Postoffice Department, it is perfectly all right." [6]

Responsibility for the " Spoils Conferences " must rest on Postmaster General Brown, and it is no more fair to accuse the operators of " collusion " and illegality than it would be to penalize a football team for obeying the referee. If the operators had worked out things happily during those Washington meetings, why did President F. G. Coburn of American Airways and W. P. MacCracken of United confront each other when the bids were opened shortly after, ready at the drop of an inflection to bid on each other's stakes should either show the slightest sign of a double cross?

Referring to that day, Chairman Black asked: " You were still nervous and fearful that something might happen? "

" Yes, sir," replied Coburn.

" In spite of all the qualifications which had been added? "

" Yes, sir. I was nervous as a witch." [7]

But if there was no collusion, why did the operators meet so secretly? McKee testified that he found out about the

mysterious conferences only by accident, and the clan-
destine nature of the gathering was given much publicity
in 1934. Actually, the Spoils Conferences were known to
everyone who kept his eyes open. Superintendent Wadsworth kept detailed minutes of the meetings. The Postoffice Department publicity bureau issued daily releases.
From *the very first meeting* the press reported on the conference, although interest was so slight that little space was
devoted to details.

" Mr. Brown is known to have in mind the consolidation
of various routes so as to cover the country with an air service," reported the New York *Times,* adding: " He asked
the airmen to prepare him a map showing in detail the
various routes they would recommend." [8]

Even the *purpose* of the meetings was known three years
before Senator Black made his sensational disclosures regarding the " secret " meetings. The authoritative trade
journal *Aero Digest* described the conferences in its issue
of June 5, 1930,[9] and the widely read *Aviation* reported:

Again and again . . . there have been repeated conferences
between practically all the air mail carriers in Washington, discussing " consolidation of routes." Obviously, the object is, by
the use of this clause, and the use of the clause giving the postmaster general the right to issue ten-year certificates, to avoid
as much as possible, competitive bidding, which is unsettling to
the business, and to a certain degree at least, uneconomical.[10]

Postmaster General Farley and his advisers called the
" Spoils Conferences " illegal, regardless of collusion or
secrecy, but even Farley knew that there was nothing
wrong in bringing together the operators, for in June 1933
he himself held a conference to discuss rearrangement of
the postal routes. What Brown's successor objected to was
the way the Republican Postmaster General had dictated
orders to the industry. Yet the Watres Act (see Appendix
II) clearly gave the Postmaster General the right to con-

solidate lines and extend routes in the public interest. The argument before the Black Committee therefore boiled down to whether or not Brown had acted for the public interest. If Postoffice Solicitor Karl Crowley, Farley's legal counsel, could not prove the " Spoils Conferences " to be collusive, he would appear to have no grounds for challenging the legality of the meetings. And denying Brown's powers under the Watres Act put Farley in a tight spot in defending the conference of operators called by the New Deal Postmaster General in 1933. Querying Crowley about the legality of the meetings, Senator Austin of the Black Committee asked:

So both the present postmaster general and the comptroller general and the solicitor, being yourself, agree that there is a law which was in existence after the enactment of the Kelly-Watres [McNary-Watres] Act that gave this arbitrary power to the postmaster general?

SOLICITOR GENERAL CROWLEY: Gave him the power, yes. . . . I would not call it arbitrary, as you have defined it.

AUSTIN: But he certainly had the power.

CROWLEY: Gave him the power when the public interest required it.

AUSTIN: Now, then, who, under that act, was to decide whether the public interest required it?

CROWLEY: Why, the postmaster general, of course. It was his duty to decide it.

AUSTIN: Do you adhere to the principle enunciated by Postmaster General Farley and former Postmaster General Brown, that it is an obligation of the office that the cabinet officer in charge of that department must follow his own judgment and discretion under these laws?

CROWLEY: It is my opinion that he must act in the public interest and that the public welfare must require it; that he cannot act in collusion nor in conspiracy with the people who are to benefit by these contracts — in this instance, these extensions, as certainly the evidence shows was done.

AUSTIN: Well, I did not ask you that. I was asking you about the power of the postmaster general and his duty under the power. He should follow his own diagnosis of the case, should he not?

CROWLEY: Yes . . . but as the Supreme Court has many times said, an administrative officer must exercise honesty and common sense.

AUSTIN: Let us assume that generally men do, and that Republicans, as well as Democrats, can be brought within that assumption.

CROWLEY: I am sure so.

AUSTIN: Now if a postmaster general acts under section seven and calls together the operators holding these certificates and consults with them regarding a curtailment of their service, the cutting out of cities that shall be served, the reduction of pay that they shall receive; is that collusive and fraudulent?

CROWLEY: I assume you refer to the conference of Mr. Howes [in 1933].

AUSTIN: It does not make any difference, does it? If it does, we might just as well finish this hearing, for it is the law I am dealing with, and acts under the law.

CROWLEY: Senator, there could be no collusion or fraud in such a conference as the one that was called here, made necessary in the reduction of appropriations. Why, Chairman Mead, chairman of the postoffice committee at the House, was present at that particular meeting, and there was no agreement made there, and no agreement was made as a result of that meeting.

AUSTIN: Exactly. You could not justly charge a meeting of Democrats with collusion, although it came as a result of an invitation of the Democratic postmaster general, and although it was attended by all those who had contracts under the government, could you?

CROWLEY: I have never known them being charged with that.

AUSTIN: They are not charged with that by me, you understand?

CROWLEY: Yes, sir.

AUSTIN: And the submission by them of such different plans to the postmaster general is not collusive, is it not, or fraudulent?

CROWLEY: It certainly was not. Of course it was not.[11]

Testimony on the " Spoils Conferences " was damaging to the major air lines, but almost as harmful was the evidence marshaled by the Black Committee to show that Postmaster General Brown had acted illegally in extending the original mail contracts. The first five air-mail contracts had been let for a period of four years, when the private operators took over the air lines in 1925. These five routes should have been put up for rebidding after November 7, 1929, but as the deadline approached, Brown ordered Assistant Postmaster General Glover to extend the contracts for six months. When Farley charged his predecessor with collusion in 1934, he added:

I am satisfied that the extension of these contracts for said period of six months was illegal. There was no attempt whatever to readvertise said routes or to reaward them, or emergency requiring them to be let without competitive bidding, and the course pursued was part of the conspiracy to divide the airways among the favored companies.[12]

Undoubtedly Brown favored the Big Boys by granting the contract extensions, but whether this action was illegal, or even unethical, is another matter. The policy of the Postoffice Department had always been to protect the " pioneer equities " of the veteran operators. The Postmaster General knew that the pending McNary-Watres Bill would give him the necessary powers of negotiation to ensure such protection, and he was sure the measure would be approved within a few months. The only alternative to extending the contracts was to put them up for rebidding. This might have permitted some upstart to take away a route built up slowly and painfully by a veteran operator who knew the difficulties of air-line operation and had based his bid accordingly. It was for the best interests of the public, Brown believed, that he ordered the extensions.

If Brown discriminated against the Independents by acknowledging the " pioneer equities " of the major lines, his judgment was backed by able legislators, for the pending McNary-Watres Bill clearly recognized the rights of the veteran operators. Furthermore, the six-month extension saved the government money, since otherwise the Postmaster General would have had to award contracts on the old costly, per-pound basis. Solicitor Crowley maintained that Brown's action was illegal, regardless of saving and precedent, but the fact is that the Republican Postmaster General even had the law behind him. The Postal Laws and Regulations state specifically that " in all cases of regular contracts, the contract may, *in the discretion of the Postmaster General,* be continued in force beyond its express terms for a period not exceeding six months, until a new contract with the same, or other contractor shall be made by the Postmaster General." [13] Farley apparently was ignorant of any such law, or at least it so appears from the following:

SENATOR AUSTIN: Now, Mr. Farley, did your counsel [Crowley] call your attention to this authority and tell you that a postmaster general had this authority, which I am about to read; namely, Paragraph 2, Section 1808, of the Postal Laws and Regulations . . . ?

FARLEY: Nothing specific of that nature was called to my attention, but, I repeat, this letter [enumerating the charges against Brown] was prepared with all the facts . . . and I was thoroughly advised as to its legality.

AUSTIN: Were you advised in connection with the judgment you were about to sign, and did sign, saying these extensions for six months were illegal; that there was a basic law that gave expressly the discretion to do that very thing?

FARLEY: I am not familiar with that section of the law referred to, Senator.

AUSTIN: That is plain enough for any layman to understand, is it not?

FARLEY: Sure it is; but I repeat, every move that I made was made upon the advice of Mr. Crowley and the Attorney General.[14]

Ten years after the Black Committee hearings it is easy to say that the charges against Brown and the operators were not justified and that the New Deal unfairly persecuted the preceding administrators, but in 1933 Farley, Black, Crowley, and the others sounded very convincing when they shouted their charges of graft, profiteering, collusion, and outright lawlessness. After the sad ending of the Hoover administration, a vast section of the public was ready to believe anything evil about the Republicans. One of the avowed purposes of the New Deal was to " turn the rascals out," and many of the shrewd politicians looked upon air mail as an excellent whipping-boy.

The New Dealers were certain of the justification of their crusade and they did not hesitate to exact dreadful punishment of the air lines. So quick and so drastic was the retribution that the air lines faced bankruptcy and utter ruin. For on February 9, 1934 President Roosevelt ordered the cancellation of all the air-mail contracts. Without the food of government payments the old operators were doomed to slow death.

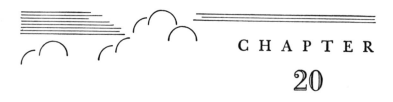

CHAPTER

20

Death and the Army Take Over

At two o'clock on Wednesday morning, February 7, 1934, Solicitor Karl Crowley of the Postoffice Department completed plans for the cancellation of the air-mail contracts. All he needed now was the consent of his superiors before executing the order that would bring the previous Republican administration to book for its conduct in awarding the air-mail routes. On Thursday, Crowley and Farley, with the Postmaster General's two assistants, Harllee Branch and William W. Howes, went to see President Roosevelt before proceeding with their plans. The Chief Executive respected the judgment of his Postmaster General, who in turn placed great faith in Crowley's advice as to the justification for the cancellation proposal.

The President listened to his political strategists, but before approving the cancellation order, he asked that Attorney General Homer Cummings look over the evidence, most of which had been obtained from the Black Committee hearings. Cummings studied the huge pile of material that evening. Since he could not possibly have digested it all in the short time it was in his possession, he too must

have depended upon Crowley's judgment, for by ten o'clock
Friday morning he believed he had read enough to justify
the proposed action against the air lines. Authority for
cancellation of contracts was provided by either (1) the
postal laws, granting the Postmaster General punitive powers when conspiracy was apparent, as in the Star Route
Frauds, or (2) the Independent Offices Act of June 1933,
better known as the Economy Bill, which authorized cancellation of contracts, but only after a full hearing and a
sixty-day notice.

At two p.m. of the same day (Friday), the President
summoned General Benjamin D. Foulois, veteran army
pilot and chief of the air corps. The general was asked if
his boys were capable of taking back the air-mail service
that they had relinquished in 1918. General Foulois, glad
of the opportunity to show off his air force, which was
badly in need of appropriations and government encouragement, said yes.[1] That was all the assurance the President
needed to complete the cancellation sequence.[2] At four
p.m., Friday, February 9, 1934, the following order was
issued from the Executive Mansion:

Whereas by an order of the Postmaster General of the United
States, all domestic mail contracts for carrying the mails have
been annulled; and

Whereas the public interest requires that air mail continue
to be afforded and the cancellation of said contracts has created
an emergency in this respect;

Now, therefore, I, Franklin D. Roosevelt, President of the
United States under and by virtue of the authority in me
vested, do hereby order and direct that the Postmaster General,
Secretary of War, and Secretary of Commerce, together with
other officers of their respective departments, cooperate to the
end that necessary air mail service be afforded.

It is further ordered and directed that the Secretary of War
place at the disposal of the Postmaster General such airplanes,
landing fields, pilots, and other employees and equipment of
the Army of the United States needed or required for the trans-

portation of mail during the present emergency over routes and schedules prescribed by the Postmaster General.

Franklin D. Roosevelt

The White House, February 9, 1934
No. 6591.[3]

Without further warning, the operators (culpable and blameless alike) were ordered to complete their last mail trips on February 19, 1934. That gave the operators just ten days to prepare for the blow. Since the air-line executives were forbidden to sue the government for an impartial trial, they turned for justice to the highest of all authorities, Public Opinion. On the very last day before the army took over the mails, the public was given a graphic example of what the air lines had accomplished up to the moment of cancellation.

At nine o'clock on the night of February 18, mechanics at Union Air Terminal, Los Angeles, made a final check on a new type of transport plane. Rushed to completion for this particular trip by workmen at the near-by Douglas factory, the ship was the first of a series to be ordered by Transcontinental & Western Air and Eastern Air Transport. It was known to the trade as the " DC–2," and its two Wright " Cyclone " engines were capable of pushing it through the air with fourteen passengers at a speed of nearly two hundred miles an hour. On the day it rolled out of the Douglas shops, the new plane made obsolete all other air-transport equipment in this country or any other.

At nine fifty the big ship rumbled up to the loading ramp. There were excited cries of farewell. Up in the pilot's office Jack Frye, TWA executive and veteran flyer, checked over the instruments. The co-pilot was Captain E. V. Rickenbacker, recently named as vice president of Eastern Air Transport. At exactly ten p.m. Frye signaled the ground crew, and the Douglas lifted gently from the runway. Frye banked and began the steep climb toward Tejon Pass. He was heading for Newark, three thousand miles away, and jammed into the bow cargo pit was the last load of mail to be carried under private contract.

The flight was a defiant answer to the critics of the air lines. It was a final gesture, meant to show what courage and American ingenuity had accomplished. Down from the Great Lakes a blizzard was sweeping, threatening to cut all communication across the Middle West. Cold and snowdrifts halted earthbound travelers through the Rockies. Above the darkened countryside the silvery skyliner roared eastward, aided rather than hindered by the gale.

"You must reach Newark by four p.m. or you won't find it," the weather experts had told Frye and Captain Rickenbacker.[4]

According to the flight plan, that left only a fifteen-minute margin, since available data indicated that the Douglas should arrive at its destination about three forty-five. The ship crossed the Rockies in the clear at 14,000 feet. There were snow flurries during the refueling at Kansas City, and farther on, Missouri lay under a blanket of white, but it was smooth riding at more than a mile above the frozen earth, and with the robot pilot guiding the ship, the navigators checked performance. The plane was ahead of schedule, but as it began the long glide for the Columbus airport, the ceiling of visibility was less than 1,000 feet. Fifteen minutes after the ship left the Ohio capital, the snow closed in completely, blotting out familiar runways and hangars.

The plane crossed the " hell stretch " of the Alleghenies at 16,000 feet. Snow began to swirl thickly, but at 19,500 feet the ship broke through the cloud layer into brilliant sunshine. Below, the storm gained in momentum and the mercury dropped to twenty-two degrees below zero. Inside the spacious cabin it was warm and snug, however, and a tail wind pushed the ship along at 230 miles an hour. Soon the travelers were leaving the storm behind, and shortly before noon they alighted at Newark, more than three hours ahead of schedule. The new plane had set a transcontinental flying record of thirteen hours and four minutes. That was racing-plane performance. Stronger than any argument the operators might have made before the Black Committee was this feat of transportation.

Next day the army began flying the mail, but not until 16,000 of the 27,000 miles of postal routes had been lopped away. General Foulois had told the President three days earlier that his men were ready. Executive officers believed the army pilots could learn the routes " in three or four days," and the general testified that his men had enough night-flying experience to justify the continuance of full service.[5] Immediately after the issuance of the cancellation order, the army put out a call for transport pilots. Experienced commercial crews were offered the chance to continue under army management, but as army pay was only about half that paid by the air lines, few of the old mail pilots accepted. A hand-picked staff of 200 officers and 324 enlisted men was thereupon assigned to air-mail duty. Equipment consisted of 148 battle planes and a few heavy bombers for use on the main lines. There was no provision at all for passengers.

Officials were confident that the army pilots could make as good a showing as they had in 1918, when they carried the first scheduled mail. They learned to their sorrow that they had made a fearful mistake. For immediately army pilots began dropping out of the sky like acorns. The toll at the end of the first week was:

> Five pilots dead
> Six critically injured
> Eight planes washed out
> Property damage of about $300,000.

Had the army been carrying passengers with the mail, the death toll would have been even more alarming. Yet the military ships were flying only sixty per cent of the old routes on reduced schedules. On the other hand, the army record was not so bad as it appears to be on paper. That first week was one of vicious gales and blinding snowstorms. Even the experienced operators, who continued with curtailed passenger service, fared badly during the winter's worst period of bad weather. A United Air Lines transport plowed into the slopes of Parley's Canyon while crossing the Wasatch Mountains during a blizzard, and when rescuers from Salt Lake City reached the scene, they found eight bodies strewn across the snow. Army officers might have reduced the toll by grounding planes during this dangerous period, but they were so intent upon making a good beginning that they ordered flights which private operators would surely have canceled. Nor were all the victims that first week actually flying on mail schedules. Second Lieutenants Edwin D. White and Jean D. Grenier, first to die, crashed three days before the army began substituting for the operators, and although the young airmen were engaged in carrying out air-mail orders, it may be unfair to list them as victims of the army interim.

Even so, the army record was disillusioning, since the military pilots were woefully unprepared for their tasks. Battle planes were not equipped or designed for flying the air lanes, but even with transport ships and the best of navigational aids, there would have been trouble. The interim of air-mail operation did not prove that the military pilots were incompetent, but it did indicate that it was dangerous to fly the airways on regular schedule without proper training. Air-line pilots spent years learning the business, and they traveled thousands of miles as co-pilots, memorizing a particular section of the route, before they were entrusted with sole responsibility for carrying passengers and the United States mail. Yet the army pilots were expected to fly the airways safely after only a week of training.

Government officials and army flyers appeared to believe that because military pilots were successful in 1918, they could duplicate their feats in 1934. There was a vast difference between air-line operation and the mere maintenance of a route across two hundred miles of excellent flying terrain, however, and the private operators knew this. Their warnings were taken as only the croakings of resentful pessimists, but there were neutral observers who might have been heeded. Will Rogers, humorist and experienced air traveler, wrote:

. . . You are going to lose some fine boys in these army flyers, who are marvelously trained in their line, but not in night cross-country flying in rain and snow.

I trust an air line, for I know that the pilot has flown that course hundreds of times. He knows it in the dark. Neither could the mail pilots do the army flyer's stunts and their close formation flying.

I do wish they would prosecute the crooks, but . . . I hope they don't stop every industry where they find crookedness at the top.[6]

By the second week in March the mounting toll of army crashes appalled the nation. President Roosevelt, who knew that the best way to handle a red-hot poker is to drop it, ordered curtailment of air-mail service until his Postmaster General could devise a plan for returning the service to the private operators. While Farley drew up new contracts, the army was to carry the mail only by day, and only when weather conditions were such as to warrant cross-country flying. Abandonment of night mail service counteracted the advantages of air transportation, yet despite restricted flying, army pilots kept right on crashing. Four more were added to the list during this time, and the administration found that the cancellation of contracts, which was to have discredited the previous officials, had become a terrible boomerang. On March 10 President Roosevelt announced that air mail would be returned to private contractors just as soon as possible. In the meantime he ordered the abandonment of all air-mail service.

Then for the first time since 1921 the United States was without an aerial post.[7] All mail planes were grounded for one week while mechanics installed better equipment. Business men who had come to depend upon quick inter-coastal communication fumed at the delay. Fortunately, they still had one way of sending letters across the country by air. The private lines had continued to fly on schedule with passengers, and operators also retained the air-express service which they had built up through the years. Suddenly the express loads began to increase in bulk and weight, and after March 10 air-express volume went up 120 per cent. The explanation was that business men were shipping bundles of letters across the country by air express and then mailing them to their destinations. This was a violation of the postal rules, apparently, but it was done on a large scale, as the statistics indicated.

After a week of inactivity the army flyers began mail service again. Orders were to complete schedules only during the day and only under ideal weather conditions. Mail flowed only along the main routes, and only the best pilots manned the improved ships. In spite of such precautions the death toll immediately rose again. By April, twelve airmen had crashed, and sixty-six had made forced landings. Public opinion, slow to crystallize at the time of the cancellation order, now turned against the administration, and when Colonel Charles A. Lindbergh placed the blame upon the New Dealers, the President discovered that he had made a colossal mistake.[8] For a time the nation's two most popular heroes, Lindbergh and Roosevelt, were pitted against each other. Colonel Lindbergh was at once accused of being the tool of the air-line operators who employed him, but he was too well liked at that time to be brushed aside lightly, and as the weeks dragged by, more and more of the public sided with him.

The army also revealed that the private operators were

not at all the leeches that they had been made out to be in
the Black Committee hearings, for when the War Department submitted an accounting of its air-mail costs, as required by law, the public learned something about the expenses of air-mail service. Reporting on the army's audit
for the period, the New York *Herald Tribune* aviation expert, C. B. Allen, wrote:

. . . Most significant revelations, ignoring for the moment
the sacrifice of human life involved in the fiasco, are that the
total cost of the experiment is set at $3,767,355.22 and that the
average cost a mile of flying the mail under army auspices was
$2.21. The latter figure compares with the $0.54 a mile average
paid the former air mail operators during the fiscal year 1933.
. . . It might be added that immediately prior to this wholesale cancellation of contracts, the average rate had been reduced
to $0.426 a mile and that the postmaster general possessed al-
most unlimited power to enforce further reductions under the
existing Watres Act.
Other interesting figures from the cost table appended to the
postmaster general's accounting of disbursements due to the air
mail's military interlude show that the average pound-mile payment during this period was 8½ mills — the major air lines having clamored for years for the opportunity to fly the mail at 2
mills a pound-mile.
The average hourly cost of operating the various types of military planes used in the mail service is given as $255.50, whereas
the postoffice department on numerous occasions has become
indignant over commercial operators' insistence that it cost
them anywhere from $125 down to $75 an hour to fly their modern, multi-motored air liners carrying passengers, mail, and
express.[9]

In rebuttal, it is only fair to point out that army transportation of the mail was an emergency service; that a permanent government organization might have reduced expenses; and that more efficient equipment and experienced
personnel might very well have resulted in a much better
record. It must also be pointed out that the army mail serv-

ice had the worst possible publicity. The bulk of the nation's press was against the New Deal, and the army fiasco provided a convenient stake at which to burn the President. Granting all this, one must conclude that the army failed to measure up to expectations. No one blamed General Foulois, who suffered, nevertheless, since he had been begging all along for more funds to improve his neglected air corps. That the President was misled by the general's optimism is evident, but knowing the predicament of the veteran army airman, it is easy to sympathize with him.

The New Deal had made its first major blunder, but it, too, was not entirely to blame. Indeed, it is difficult to place the blame for the blow that knocked the air lines groggy for nearly four years. There were, however, at least five candidates for the role of villain in the air-line drama.

CHAPTER

21

Who Is the Villain?

STRANGELY enough, the air-line operators had been taken completely off guard by the order canceling mail contracts. Many expected the new administration to make changes in the mail laws, and it was pretty generally known that some of the executives were in for trouble following the Black Committee hearings, but only a few leaders who had kept their ears to the ground heard the rumble of approaching disaster. To the industry as a whole, the cancellations were as sudden and as devastating as an earthquake. Yet cancellation talk was in the air months before the President took his drastic step.

The ascendancy of the New Deal had been the signal for the Independents to rise in rebellion against the domination of the big operators. Owners of small lines demanded revenge for the treatment they had received during the term of Postmaster General Brown, and many of them were fully justified in believing that they had been discriminated against. The leader of the Independent insurgents was Tom E. Braniff, president of Braniff Airways, most potent of the non-mail-carrying air lines.

Tom Braniff did not take easily to being kicked around

by Washington officials. He had been beating his way to the top ever since he arrived in Oklahoma City as a sixteen-year-old fortune-hunter back in 1900. Tom grew with the city. By 1917 he owned his own insurance, farm-loan, and real-estate company. Soon he was doing an annual business of seven million dollars and had built the largest office building in the city.[1]

Tom Braniff got into aviation somewhat against his better judgment. A younger brother, Paul, was bitten by the flying bug following the Lindbergh flight of 1927, and soon the Braniffs owned a Stinson " Detroiter," which was the first cabin plane in that section of the country. Tom bought the ship and Paul flew it on company business. Since there was not enough traveling to keep the trim monoplane busy, Paul conceived the idea of beginning a passenger service between Oklahoma City and Tulsa, 116 miles to the northeast. Tom eventually allowed himself to be argued into the venture, and Braniff Airways was born. Three times a day Paul ferried what passengers he could find between the two cities. Later the brothers expanded into Kansas and Missouri. They lost money steadily, and when Universal Aviation Corporation offered to relieve him of the financial responsibility, Tom Braniff sold out, in November 1929. The elder brother had put up all the money and he was glad to get out of aviation so easily, but when the McNary-Watres Bill gave promise of mail subsidies, Tom was ready to try again.

On November 3, 1930 the Braniffs began another air-line operation, this time between Oklahoma City and Wichita Falls, Texas. Early in 1931 they extended the line to Kansas City. Unfortunately for them, their line competed with the Chicago-Dallas section of United Air Lines and with that part of American Airways formed by the old Universal system. Since the larger air lines held mail contracts already, the Postmaster General refused to give Braniff Airways any help in the form of mail payments, and the Oklahomans became all-out antagonists of Walter Folger Brown and the whole Postoffice Department.

Tom became the dominant personality in an organization known as the Independent Scheduled Air Transport Operator's Association, made up exclusively of non-subsidized passenger-carriers out to get mail payments at whatever cost. The members of the association were Bowen Air Lines, operating between San Antonio and Kansas City; Hanford Tri-State Air Lines, working out of Sioux City; Rapid Air Transport, Omaha; Intercity Air Lines of Boston; Reed Air Lines, Lawton, Oklahoma; and Wyoming Air Service, flying between Denver and Billings.[2] The association had a representative in Washington, who was also the agent for the Braniffs. He was William I. Denning, an attorney and former representative of Robertson Airplane Service. Denning kept Tom Braniff posted on the Washington situation, and from the correspondence exhibited in the Senate hearings, there is a hint as to the part played by the Independents in the cancellation drama.

On April 29, 1933, long before the Black Committee had been splashed all over the front page, the Senate Investigating Committee had sent out elaborate questionnaires to all air-line executives. These were returned by the end of June and should have warned the operators of what to expect. At about the same time Postmaster General Farley called his own meeting of the operators to discuss reduction of mail payments and services. Although appropriations had been slashed twenty-five per cent, everyone knew that was only the beginning. On top of all this, the Comptroller General was threatening to force the cancellation of routes that had been established by Brown without competitive bidding (not because they were illegal, but to help in balancing the budget). If such extensions were canceled, there was a possibility that the Postoffice Department might put them up for rebidding at a very much lower scale of payments. The Independent operators saw this as a fine opportunity to muscle back into the air-mail service. Such payments would not bring fat profits, but they would tide the small lines over the bleak days ahead and might give them a permanent place on the airway map. There was nothing to lose and a great deal to gain by encouraging cancellation of the air-mail route extensions. Accordingly, the Independents began to exert pressure in Washington. Both the Independent operators and the new administration had common cause against Brown and the major air-line executives, or so it appeared in 1933. What the Independents wanted most was action by their allies before the small lines were forced into bankruptcy. All through this period, then, the struggling Independents heckled the government to take the drastic action culminating in the cancellation of the contracts. Certainly they hastened the process. This is evident in the following letter sent by Denning to Tom Braniff on May 15, 1933, nine months before the President signed his White House order:

DEAR MR. BRANIFF:

Thanks for the information contained in your letter of May 12 regarding the attitude of Mr. Howes [William W. Howes, Assistant Postmaster General under James A. Farley].

I confidently believe that the Comptroller General will shortly tell Mr. Farley that he may cancel practically all extensions made by the former postmaster general. However, it would be up to Mr. Farley to take action. In view of the necessity of reducing the expenditures to conform with the appropriations, I have no doubt but what many of the extensions will be canceled, but it remains to be developed whether an advertisement for bids will be issued for service to take the place of any canceled extension.

I think the independent operators should continue to lay their cases before the postmaster general and show the necessity for early action in their behalf.

The independent operators may rest assured that those operators holding mail contracts are leaving no stone unturned in their efforts to continue the existing status quo.

I shall advise you as soon as the provision authorizing the President to cancel contracts becomes a law.

Cordially yours,

(signed) *W. I. Denning*[3]

That the Independent air-line operators foresaw the coming air-mail "scandals" and were prepared to make the most of them is indicated by another letter from Denning to Braniff, written on June 26, 1933.[4] It is evident from this note that men like Braniff were following every move in Washington and knew just how the cancellations would come about. Furthermore, the Independents, not the big-league operators, were by now the fair-haired boys of the Postoffice Department.

"All of the data on Braniff Airways has been turned over to Mr. Cisler [superintendent of air mail]," wrote Denning in the same communication, "and he is going over it with a view to seeing what, if anything, can be done."

To which Braniff replied:

Apparently there will be little, if any, new territory covered by air mail contracts and a good many of the existing ones will be canceled. That leaves the situation where we might just as well *evidence our interest in routes which we would regard as the most desirable and on which we are prepared to finance and equip an operation* [italics added]. If existing contracts are not to be canceled, the mail in excess of the amount contracted for should at least be turned over to other operators who are willing to carry it at a saving to the government.

. . . I would appreciate your discussing this matter with Mr. Cisler and if you think it desirable to do so also arrange a conference with Mr. Howes. The time for decision on the part of the Post Office Department is close at hand, and I trust that this letter arrives at an opportune time.[5]

It would be impossible to determine exactly how much the Independent operators had to do with the collapse of the airway system in 1934. Many of the key figures in the transportation industry blamed the Independent for being the direct cause of the cancellations. Others maintain that operators like Braniff had only a minor part in the air-mail showdown. In either case, it is not fair to assume that the Independent was motivated by sheer jealousy and spiteful-ness, as many charge, because the small operator had every reason to be resentful of the way he had been treated, and he believed sincerely that the cancellations righted a great wrong. Nor is it fair to charge that the Roosevelt administration acted solely for revenge, since there were many Republicans who believed that the aviation industry needed a shaking up, following the Black in-vestigation.

A large proportion of those injured by the cancellation order blamed Postmaster General Farley for the black days that followed disruption of the air-mail service. As the car-toon facing page 257 indicates, Farley was even held respon-sible for the deaths of the twelve army flyers. As chief of the Postoffice Department, Farley " took the rap " for the cancellation order, but it is clear, in perspective, that Far-ley not only was ignorant of the situation, but was actually hostile to the Senate investigation that culminated in the White House order of February 9. On February 14 Post-master General Farley wrote his lengthy letter to Senator Black, summing up his reasons for canceling the air-mail contracts. The charges were strong and positive (see end of Chapter 16), yet on February 2 he had made no such accusations when he appeared before the Black Committee. Something had occurred to change his mind between Feb-ruary 2 and February 8, when postal officials were ready to recommend to the President that the contracts be an-nulled. What happened to turn Farley against the mail operators? Did he find new evidence after leaving the Sen-ate hearing? Or was he simply advised during the interim to authorize the cancellations?

When Postmaster General Brown left office in March

1933, he was accused of having burned some of his correspondence in the department furnace. Brown denied he had destroyed any official papers, and neither the Black Committee nor private investigators could ever prove that he had burned any evidence against himself. A box full of papers did follow Brown to New York, however, and he returned these just at the time the cancellation storm was about to break. It was assumed that Farley must have found pay dirt in the missing files, but if so, he was very unconvincing in telling about it,[6] nor did the recovered papers produce any damaging evidence before the Black Committee, although Farley surely would have given the investigators access to any of the files.

It is much more likely that Farley reached his decision between February 2 and February 8 solely upon the advice of his counselors. They had gone into the evidence and were convinced that here was an opportunity to administer a *coup de grâce* to the beaten Republicans. Farley himself appeared to have not the faintest notion of what the air-mail scandals were all about. He didn't even know upon what grounds he had ordered the cancellations.[7] Again and again on the witness stand Farley told inquisitors that he had come to a decision " because of the facts," [8] but when asked for these facts, he could only refer to the advice of his counsel. The following testimony is only one of a dozen or more examples of how Farley and Senator Austin of the Black Committee swung around this circle. Queried as to his reasons for the cancellation order, Farley replied:

Well; I will answer it this way, Senator, that with all the facts before us we felt the law had been violated and that the contracts were not in order, and I got the legal advice that I felt I should have, being a layman, and, upon their advice, I annulled the contracts.

Austin: I don't think you understand my question, or you would not answer it that way. You have admitted that you know that there are two methods of procedure under this Watres Act, and all I am asking you is which method you understood they were attempting to operate under, regardless of whether they did legally or illegally.

FARLEY: I was not concerned with what method they were legally operating under.

AUSTIN: I see. You would pass judgment, then, regardless of which feature of the act they were operating under?

FARLEY: I will answer it by saying, with the facts before me, as I have repeated, on more than one occasion, with the advice given me by counsel, I acted as I did.

AUSTIN: You don't respond to the question. As a matter of fact, I judge from your answers — and if this is not fair, I want you to say so — I judge from your answers, that you did not consider which one of these two methods these gentlemen were attempting to work under.

FARLEY: We considered all the facts, Senator, and were guided accordingly.

AUSTIN: All right. Well, you cannot answer the question intelligently.

SENATOR MCCARRAN: Not the way you want it.

AUSTIN: No, nor any way. I am perfectly willing, Mr. Farley, to have you answer the question any way you wish.

FARLEY: I am perfectly willing to let my answer stand.

AUSTIN: If you assume these people [members of the " Spoils Conference "] met together by invitation of the postmaster general, similar to the invitation that your office issued to them afterward, to consider the equities that pioneers ought to have considered in judging whether extensions should be made to them or not, then the fact of meeting together would not be regarded by you as an illegal thing, would it?

FARLEY: I don't think I should answer any questions as to what happened prior to my going into office, Senator Austin, in all justice to Senator — General Brown.

AUSTIN: You have done so. You canceled all these contracts, and, in your letter of February 14, you stated why.

FARLEY: Yes, sir.

AUSTIN: And I am examining you to find out, if I can whether it makes any difference to you, or not, whether the law authorized the contractors to get together and to talk over equities with the postmaster general. That is what I am after. Do you consider such meetings as collusive?

FARLEY: I would consider any meeting collusive where a crowd of men met in a room and discussed — where contracts for mail lines were allotted to this, that, and the other fellow.

AUSTIN: Did you have an idea air lines were allotted in this case?

FARLEY: I will answer your question by giving the answer I have given on more than one occasion here — that I acted upon the facts presented, after due legal advice.[9]

That Farley not only was ignorant of the air-mail situation, but was unsympathetic to the whole investigation is indicated by a conversation Brown described in the Black Committee hearing. When former Postmaster General Brown brought back the missing papers, which he had found stored in his New York apartment, he delivered them personally to his successor. According to Brown, he and Farley had a pleasant chat in the Postmaster General's office. Describing that dialogue, Brown told the committee:

He [Farley] said, " What do you want me to do? " And I said, " Nothing." I said, " After you think — after you have thought this over [the return of the missing letters] you may think I am entitled to a letter acknowledging the receipt of this correspondence, and if you do, I will be glad to have it." He reached for the button that used to be on the desk to call a stenographer and said, " I will do it now." I said, " Now Mr. Postmaster General, this is a matter of some importance, and I would rather you would not write the letter until after you have given it consideration and perhaps talked to your advisors about it." He said, " *Well, I haven't any sympathy with these investigations.*" And I said, " Well I knew you were too good a sportsman to hit a political opponent below the belt." And he said, " Or anybody else." Then I said, " Well, some of your inspectors who have been assigned to the Black Committee have been a little rough; they were a little rough with Jim Maher."

McCarran: Who is Jim Maher?

Brown: He is a stenographer in the postoffice department, or was. Then he said, " I had to give these inspectors to the Senate Committee, didn't I? " I said, " Certainly not. I never assigned any inspectors to a senate committee. We always had enough work for them to do in the department." And he said, " I guess that is so . . . but I think these were assigned when I was away." . . . Then I asked him, I said to him that I could not understand what this investigation was all about, that in the little contacts I had had with Senator Black, I had always treated him with every courtesy and I could not understand it and would like to know if he knew the reason. He made an answer about it and then added, " But don't repeat that." That is why I felt I ought not to repeat it.[10]

Eventually the committee forced Brown to repeat the confidential statement, and the former Postmaster General testified that Farley had called Chairman Black of the Senate Investigation Committee " a publicity hound — but don't tell anybody I said so, because I have to get along with him." [11]

" Genial Jim " Farley may have disliked acid Senator Hugo Black, but would he have communicated such opinions to a political rival? He might have. Farley denied the statement about Black, but that does not refute Brown's testimony. No politician is branded a liar for denying private statements later made public, and the two Postmasters General might very naturally have exchanged confidences, just as rival football coaches might discuss their teams in terms of " the trade." The internal evidence indicates that Farley had little use for Black, although he speaks well enough of the Alabama Senator in his autobiography,[12] but a well-known Washington newspaper columnist, whose reliability is much respected, has this to say about Farley's dig at Black:

. . . As you note, Farley called Black a publicity hound. While the quotation came from a third party, it was understood to be correct at the time by most of us in Washington, and Farley's denial was taken as a "diplomatic denial."

I was in Europe during the row over the Black appointment to the Court, and I have no first-hand knowledge of what Farley's attitude was. However, Farley's whole personal inclination is against the tactics which Black used in his Senate investigation. Furthermore, he looks at everything from the point of view of party harmony, and therefore could safely be regarded as unsympathetic to this appointment [Black to the Supreme Court].

With Farley I think it should always be remembered that he is controlled by two lines of feeling which often conflict. First, he considers himself as a lieutenant of the President, and therefore obligated much as an attorney to carry out the wishes of his chief. He obtained a special dispensation during the purge. Otherwise he has done what he could to line up the votes whenever the President wanted it, regardless of his own personal views as to the wisdom of the matter in hand. Second, as Democratic Chairman and as a lifelong party worker, he wants above all to have party harmony, and instinctively is against anything which will create division. As long as a politician plays ball with the organization, Farley doesn't ask any more questions.

So far as my contact and observation go, Farley is an absolute square shooter, and I think this is the judgment of everyone in Washington.[13]

It was probably with reluctance, then, that Farley went through with the cancellation plans. Once committed, he was willing to bear the brunt of criticism and vilification. Failure to take the blame would have deflected odium to the Chief Executive, to whom Farley was intensely loyal ("if the day ever comes when his orders and directions can't be carried out . . . I shall not be around"),[14] but as time went on, many of those operators who leveled their sharpest attacks at the Postmaster General admitted that they had accused the wrong man.

Who, then, *is* the villain of the cancellation farce? Was it the Independent, with his schemes and his undercover attempt to edge into the air-mail service? Perhaps — partly — but who can blame him? He had been forced out of potentially lucrative territories. He had seen the little enterprise that had taken his hard-earned money slowly strangled by competition with more powerful rivals. He had been cast aside as unfit and unworthy — he who had builded a service on courage and initiative while others waited to reap the rewards. What had the Independent done except to fight back? Surely that did not make him the villain of the piece.

Was the villain Solicitor Karl Crowley of the Postoffice Department, who undoubtedly advised Farley on the cancellation of contracts? Crowley is described by his enemies as the fanatical type of New Dealer more concerned with smearing Republican predecessors than with guarding the air-mail service, but with the testimony of the Black Committee and the charges of the Independents before him, Crowley might very well have felt justifiable resentment against Top Sergeant Brown and the favored operators.

Could publicity-wise Senator Hugo Black, sniffing the glories of another Teapot Dome exposé, have been the villain? Possibly, but even the Republicans had investigated air mail and had found it wanton, and there is no doubt that a jolt was due for the operators. There was widespread criticism of the *methods* used by Inquisitor Black and his committee, but if the industry needed an airing, it is hardly fair to hiss the Senator as the villain.

Or was the bad actor the air-line operator, greedy for profit, wasteful, arrogant, heedless of the public's interests? Granted that there were such operators, most of the executives were not of that stripe, and even so, with air transportation so strictly supervised by the government, no line could have lasted long without the approval of Washington officials.

That leaves only Postmaster General Walter Folger Brown, with his dictatorial methods and his obsession to build an airway system according to his own terms. He may be the villain, but those who had to bow to his inexorable will might well ponder the philosophy running through the following soliloquy. Postmaster Brown explained:

". . . I could think of no other way to make the industry self-sustaining; make it economically independent; than to compel the air mail contractor to get some revenue from the public. Almost all of them were refusing to carry passengers and were depending wholly upon the Post Office department and we were getting nowhere in the development of airplanes. They were just using little, light, open-cockpit ships to move mail, with very great dependability, but no progress in a broad sense was being made in the art.

" I believed that it was my duty to force them, if I could under the law, to get revenue from non-postal sources, and the obvious one was passengers; and after we could get the people flying themselves . . . we thought then they would send their freight . . . by planes, and the purpose of it was altogether to help develop an industry that could live without a subsidy — that could live on its own. . . . I think I will have to give .you the picture . . . if you will bear with me for a minute.

" NAT [National Air Transport] had the best mail operation in the country . . . but they were not carrying a passenger, and they told me they did not intend to carry any passengers. After considerable pressure, they finally agreed they would carry some passengers from Cleveland west, but Colonel Henderson, who was the contact man for the organization . . . said that it was not safe to fly passengers from New York to Cleveland — that around Bellefonte, Pennsylvania, the Allegheny mountains were jumbled up together, and the result was that it was a graveyard of aviators . . .

" Colonel Lindbergh was the technical adviser of TAT [Transcontinental Air Transport]. He had set up that flying operation for them. They did not fly across the Allegheny mountains; they went across in a Pennsylvania Railroad train from New York to Columbus, Ohio, and from there they took a plane and flew on to Waynoka, Oklahoma. . . .

" It was apparent that TAT did not believe it was good practice at that time to fly the Allegheny mountains from New York to Pittsburgh. . . . I could not justify an air mail contract from New York over that central transcontinental route that was being served by TAT with the Pennsylvania railroad and the Santa Fe railroad, because it took 48 hours to get from coast to coast. I was convinced that we ought to be able to get from coast to coast in practically a quarter of that time, when we got the art developed. . . . But I had either to surrender my passenger ideas or force the carrying of passengers across the continent. It seemed to me that the best way to get United Aircraft [United Air Lines, merged with NAT to form, at that time, the only coast-to-coast route] to do it was to get somebody else to do it first. So I set up the advertisement. . . . I felt very keenly the responsibility of forcing the carrying of passengers. I was not a technical man myself and Colonel Lindbergh came to see me and we talked it over. . . . I knew that Pan American [Pan American Airways, operating in the Caribbean and South America] had just started to fly over the Andes mountains at an altitude of 15,000 feet, hopping across from Santiago to Montevideo, and I did not think I was wrong about it. I thought NAT was reluctant to do it because they did not want the responsibility of the passengers; they did not want the danger of personal injury suits . . . they did not want to buy insurance against it; they did not want to invest money in passenger transport planes.

" At any rate, I decided to take the responsibility and I used the power in the Watres Act, wrote it into the advertisement, to compel the carrying of passengers. We, of course, expected a continuous operation as soon as the thing could be worked out.

" It was utterly impossible to fly from coast to coast in a continuous operation without flying partly in darkness. . . . So we thought it was best to prepare a regulation, as we had the right to do under the law, for the guidance of our department, and the language upon which I relied was this . . . THE HEAD OF EACH DEPARTMENT IS AUTHORIZED TO PRESCRIBE REGULATIONS NOT INCONSISTENT WITH LAW FOR THE GOVERNMENT OF HIS DEPARTMENT, THE CONDUCT OF ITS OFFICERS AND CLERKS, THE DISTRIBUTION AND PERFORMANCE OF ITS BUSINESS. We provided under that grant of authority a regulation that in bidding on air-passenger operations over a route that was 2,000 miles long there should be six months experience on the part of the bidder in night flying over a route. . . .

" The time came for starting service on T&WA, and I was invited to go out on the first flight. It was a very bitter cold day; a terrific wind. Colonel Lindbergh came down to the airport at Newark bundled up in a leather coat. Miss Earhart [Amelia Earhart Putnam, the late famous aviatrix] went along. The colonel did not go. He saw us off, and in a big Ford [trimotor monoplane] we started off on that first trip with passengers over the mountains.

" We came into the airport at Camden. I think the wind was blowing around 50 or 60 miles an hour out of the northwest, and the pilot miscalculated his speed as he got ready to set the plane down on the field. He was coming so fast that he was sure he could not stop, and so, when he was a few hundred yards away from the station . . . instead of setting the plane down, he gave it the gun — I mean he opened his throttles — and started to try to get up again. Of course he did not try to lift the plane at once until he had gathered sufficient speed. . . . We saw the plane going as fast as it could, going directly for the building on the field, and I wondered whether I had been premature in the passenger operation. Just as he got to the building he pulled the stick back and lifted the ship over the building, and some of us are just getting over it now. He circled the field and came in easily the next time. . . .

" Some more passengers got aboard and we started on to Harrisburg. There we had better luck in getting in, and Governor Fisher and some of the other face cards came down to welcome us. We made some speeches and everybody was happy, and then we went on to Pittsburgh.

". . . I left the plane at Columbus, because we had gotten over the mountains and over the part that seemed to me hazardous. The plane went on and the passengers that were in it had their breakfasts in New York and their dinners in Kansas City. . . .

" Well, soon after that we had a flight on the line from Atlanta west, and I went down on that. We got into some fog near

Richmond and the plane was forced down and we had . . . to get on a train to go down to Atlanta. I wondered again whether I was a little too enterprising. We got to Atlanta, though, and started west for Dallas, and at some point or other, one of the planes . . . that was going along with us, a Ford, in taking off . . . had knocked off one of the wheels on the undercarriage. So when the plane came in it had only one wheel in front and the little wheel behind. We watched the boys set that plane down, thinking they would probably kill everybody . . . but they put the passengers over on the side where the wheel was . . . and put them in belts, and he brought that plane in on the two wheels like a bicycle, until she lost all of her air and then she tipped over and took this leg down that had no wheel on it, and the thing spun around like this and nobody was hurt. But it impressed me a little just the same.

"On that trip I got a telegram from Colonel Henderson, which I found in a sport coat of mine. . . . Let's see if I can find it here.

HON. WALTER F. BROWN,

CARE POSTMASTER, ATLANTA, GA.

FOLLOWING MY CONVERSATION WITH YOU YESTER-
DAY, I HAVE HAD A DETAILED DISCUSSION WITH
MR. WADSWORTH [in charge of air-mail maintenance]
AND DECIDED THAT N.A.T. WILL START DAYLIGHT
PASSENGER SERVICE NEW YORK TO CHICAGO WITH
TRIMOTOR PLANES ON OCTOBER 20. AM DOING THIS
SO THAT N.A.T.'S POLICY MAY BE WHOLLY CONSIST-
ENT WITH YOUR EXPRESSED DESIRES. HOPE YOU
HAVE ENJOYED YOUR FLIGHT TO ATLANTA.

" *Well, we were beginning to get our way, forcing NAT to fly.* . . . Then we went down on a flight that Eastern Air Transport was making from Washington to Jacksonville, and we got down to Florence. . . . The airport there had very thick sand and a little bit of grass on top, and this big Condor plane had 18 passengers in it. . . . The plane got stuck in the sand and we had to call on the people who were down to greet us to help get the plane out of the sand and upon the grass. When the pilot started off and opened his throttles we were going straight at a high tension power line. We went over it, but we did not clear it by six inches. It gave us quite a thrill.

" I had a speech that I was making and telling people how safe it was to fly, trying to get them to patronize these lines, because if the patronage did not come, obviously my whole effort was a failure. So I had a speech that I had developed with some care, telling them how safe it was, how beautiful and swift and clean it was. I had made that speech on numerous occasions.

" We got down at Savannah. We were at the very beautiful club . . . having a luncheon . . . sponsored by the Chamber of Commerce. We had finished our lunch and I was getting ready to unlimber my safety speech when Mr. Keys [the famous air promoter] who was along with Mrs. Keys, was called away from the table. He came back in a minute or two, just as the presiding officer . . . had started to introduce me, and he whispered in my ear, ' T&WA have just had a terrible accident. A plane out in Kansas is completely washed out and Knute Rockne was aboard.' I said ' What in the world am I going to say? What happened? . . .' He said, ' We don't know a thing about it.'

" Just then I heard the toastmaster say. ' The postmaster general will now address you.' I did not know what to do, so I made my speech just as usual. . . . I did not tell a soul. I did not tell Mrs. Brown about the accident. I did not tell Mr. Glover, who was in charge of the air mail. The only people who knew about it were Mr. Keys and myself. All the people saw us go out to the airport and we took off for Jacksonville.

". . . I speak of these things just to let you know what the responsibility is of a man in ordering service in which you are [charged] with the lives of your fellow citizens. I can understand the feeling of the officer who ordered the army boys out the other day in the storm. I can understand the feeling of responsibility that he had. *There never was an air mail pilot [killed] while I was there, or an accident occurred that was not a personal grief to me.*

" I used to sit on the little veranda of my apartment at the Shoreham and see the pilot lift his plane up at night from Washington Airport on his way off alone to Pittsburgh, over the mountains, knowing there was only one lighted airport between Washington and Greensburg, and wondering whether he was going to make it.

" Because of that responsibility, because of the reluctance of these other people to fly passengers, I did everything I could think of to make the operation safe. I thought experience in night flying was essential. I do not mean merely on the part of the pilots, for I would not think that was over 50 per cent, but upon the operations managements. No traveller who is experienced will ever forget the first time he landed at night. When you are up in the sky it is all right as long as you are up, but when the time comes to come down at night, with the ground foggy in the hollows and the confusion of the lights and the long shadows and with no way of determining your distances, with obstructions that are supposed to have lights on them and usually have, but may not have, you are very glad to know there is a man down at that airport talking to your pilot; telling him which way the wind is blowing . . . and that no one is coming into the field at that time . . . that there are no muddy spots on the field; and that the necessary precautions are there in case anything fails. In fact, you would be miserable if all those preparations had not been made.

" That is why I put [the night-flying clause] into the advertisement and took responsibility for it . . . because one major disaster at that time . . . would have ruined the whole thing I was trying to do." [15]

Here is no hard-boiled martinet, giving orders for the sheer love of dictating. This is a man with a vision. That he was unpopular is undeniable, but no one could ever show that Postmaster General Brown had acted other than for the public interest. It was years before he was cleared of complicity in what the critics called a diabolical conspiracy, but Brown's vindication came seven years later. On July 14, 1941 Commissioner Richard H. Akers, of the

U. S. Court of Claims, stated unequivocally that there was no fraud or collusion in Brown's administration. In 115 pages of closely packed information, Commissioner Akers comes to the inevitable conclusion that there actually are no villains in the cancellation drama. The Senate Committee findings set the stage for a " shootin' " climax. The denouement was a flop.

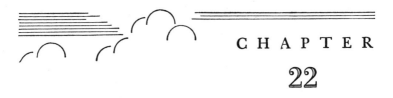

CHAPTER

22

Invitation to a Crap Game

"POSTMASTER GENERAL FARLEY has extended an open invitation to all the crapshooters of the vintage of 1929," growled one air-line president when plans were announced for the return of air mail to private contractors.

Had the operators played their cards right, they might have skinned enough out of the Postmaster General to more than offset the losses of the cancellation period. The embarrassed administration was ready to eat humble pie, following the disastrous army interlude, and the air lines might easily have emerged with more favorable mail contracts. If the air lines had been the " trust " described in the Black Committee hearings, all this might have taken place. Instead, there was the same old dissension that had characterized air-line meetings in the days of the " Spoils Conferences."

So desperate were the operators for mail payments that they played right into the hand of the harried Postmaster General. Farley had no difficulty in whipping the airways into line. He was even able to save face for the administration by insisting that no line could win a contract if it had been represented at the " Spoils Conference." Even when reorganized, such companies were to be ineligible for mail payments until they were purged of all executives who had met with Walter Folger Brown.

Under such qualifications, forty-five operators gathered in Superintendent Cisler's office shortly after noon on April 20, 1934. They had come to see the Postmaster General open their bids, and the tension was almost unbearable. Farley, accompanied by his assistants, Howes, Branch, and Crowley, arrived late, obviously embarrassed, and pushed his way through the unfriendly group to the conference table. Someone had utilized a table model of a zooming Boeing transport for a hat-rack, and, appropriately, even the two clocks in the room did not agree.

Packed into the dingy office was every type of air-line entrepreneur. Some were Independents, heretofore treated like poor relations. Others had appeared there many times, although they now represented different companies with oddly familiar names. All air lines were disqualified from bidding on new contracts if they were tainted by the " Spoils Conferences," but no one failed to recognize American Air-lines as the old American Airways; or Eastern Air Lines, sprung from the ashes of Eastern Air Transport. Trans-continental & Western Air had merely added an " Inc." to its name, while United Air Lines had changed not at all, since the original contract had been awarded to United's subsidiaries.

The first bid opened was that of General Airlines, successor to Western Air Express. General won the Cheyenne-Denver-Pueblo route on a bid of 39 cents (one of the highest awarded that day) , and the assembled operators must have thought that things were not so bad after all. Trans-continental & Western Air won the Newark to Los Angeles route back, but only on a bid of 24 cents, which all present knew was meager payment for the service. A big surprise was the Eastern Air Lines bid of only 19 cents a mile for the routes between Chicago and Atlanta and between Newark and New Orleans, and there was another gasp when the airway between Chicago and New Orleans went to an interloper, Pacific Seaboard Airlines, on a bid of $17\frac{1}{2}$ cents. Pacific Seaboard wrested the territory from Major William Robertson, an experienced operator who had been flying the Mississippi Valley route for twenty-two months without an accident. Major Robertson lost to a rival who had never flown a plane beyond eye-range of the Pacific Ocean, and it did not make the veteran St. Louis promoter feel any better when he found that he was underbid by only half a cent a mile.

The new contracts were to be effective for three months only, or until new legislation replaced the McNary-Watres Act. This explains why many of the operators were willing to submit such low bids. Their object was to *get* a contract, no matter what the remuneration, and then to hang on with the hope that new laws would provide for higher payments. Only a few of the representatives had dared to bid anywhere near the maximum of 45 cents a mile, and even that was nine cents below the average payment of 1933.

One thing that kept the operators milling like a school of frightened herring was fear of E. L. Cord, who had recently won control of Aviation Corporation and American Airways. Cord was the one operator who benefited by the cancellations. He had gained control of rambling American Airways after the " Spoils Conferences " and hence was eligible to bid in April without restrictions. It was well known that he had contributed heavily to the Roosevelt campaign fund, so he had many friends in Washington. His Century Air Lines, still technically alive, could absorb the AVCO empire, if American Airways had to suffer too greatly for past sins. Cord had the world by the tail, and his worried rivals wondered what he was going to do. Would he pyramid American Airways as he had Auburn Motors? Was he planning to become the dominant figure in commercial aviation? No operator knew, and until Cord made a move, it was safer to bid low. Incidentally, Cord fooled all his rivals by hedging. Apparently he reasoned that there was no sense in losing money on the temporary contracts, as long as the routes were to be readvertised with the passage of new air-mail laws. Cord thereupon bid only for his old main line. Had competitors known that, they might have bid higher, but they were fearful of the risk. On the whole, the laugh was on Cord, since later legislation " froze " the routes, as of April 1934. Nevertheless, Cord emerged with a much simplified and more efficient air-line system, soon to develop into the biggest and most prosperous in the world.

Postmaster General Farley opened more bids on April 27. All together he awarded fifteen. Veteran operators were United, TWA, Eastern, General (Western Air) , and American. Newcomers were Pacific Seaboard, Central Airlines, Braniff, and Wyoming Air Service. Independents cried that there was still discrimination, since the advertisement called for multi-motor equipment on certain routes. Only those lines already in possession of big planes could bid on such routes, of course, since it was impossible to get delivery of new ships within the thirty-day interim before service was to begin. Even so, some of the Independents got their feet in the door. Braniff took the Chicago-Texas route from United, and Hanford Tri-State temporarily snatched the Chicago-Pembina airway from Northwest Airways. Alfred Frank got back his run between Salt Lake City and Great Falls, and a new company, Northern Air Transport, underbid Northwest for the Seattle-Fargo route, although it later was disqualified in favor of the pioneering line.

The army relinquished the mail routes the first week in May. After an ignominious beginning, it had performed its tasks creditably and it ended its chapter of air-mail history in a burst of glory. Using new Curtiss attack planes and Martin bombers, army mail pilots brought the last cargo from San Francisco to Newark in fourteen hours and eight minutes. It was not a record, but it meant flying at more than 190 miles an hour, which even the critics had to admit was impressive.

On May 8, United Air Lines and Transcontinental & Western carried the first mail authorized under the new contracts. TWA began again as dramatically as it had dropped mail service. Carrying the first load out of Los Angeles in his new Northrup " Gamma," Vice President Frye brought the mail into Newark just eleven and a half hours later. It was a new transcontinental record and an apt gesture to show that the air lines were off again under full power.

Operators were back where they had started, but they had learned some valuable lessons between February 19 and May 8. Hidden abuses were now cut away like cancerous tissue. An industry that had tended to overpromote itself was now chastened. Speculative operators were squeezed out, since there was no longer much hope for quick profits. Shoestring companies, whose proprietors had disrupted agreements by their willingness to wreck the rate structure were silenced, and it was noteworthy that only a few of the rebels were willing or able to carry mail on the terms they had once demanded. Furthermore, negotiation rather than competition was recognized as the more effective way of stabilizing the industry — a trend that retired Postmaster General Brown must have noted with a faintly superior smile. Lastly, the air-mail " scandals " emphasized the need for effective legislation providing the necessary control without hampering restrictions.

Since 1926 the air lines had been operating under two sets of laws. Air-mail legislation, such as the Kelly and Watres Acts, governed the vital payments, without which no operator could exist. Because these payments gave the Postmaster General enormous powers, enabling him to exert a preponderant influence in the shaping of the airway system, much space has been devoted to the administration of these laws. Equally important, however, was the legislation affecting the actual operation of the air lines. Since shortly after the passage of the Air Commerce Act of 1926, a bureau of the Department of Commerce had regulated commercial aviation almost as though it were a public utility. The bureau built and maintained the lighted airways, without which there could have been no air-line system. It licensed aircraft and pilots, in the interests of public safety. It prescribed traffic rules for both the private flyer and the transport pilot. The aeronautics branch has never received credit for its part in the development of the air lines, since its part was seldom spectacular, but wise administration by able officials had a large share in making the air lines of the United States the envy of other nations.

As time went on, the aeronautics branch outgrew its usefulness, and the Air Commerce Act of 1926 began to show signs of wear. When the Democrats took over in 1933, the nominal director of the bureau was Eugene L. Vidal, the former manager of Ludington Lines. Gene Vidal had fared so badly at the hands of Postmaster General Brown and the Republican administration that there was a certain poetic justice in his appointment to the position. There was more honor than power in the bureau directorship at this time, however, for Vidal succeeded to the post at a time when the aeronautics branch of the Department of Commerce was beginning to creak in the joints. The air-mail cancellations indirectly affected the bureau, since many influential business leaders had been injured by the New Deal administration, and they made the bureau the target of their brickbats. For some unknown reason, the Bureau of Air Commerce, as it came to be known, was split into three bodies, each with a separate head. Vidal was director in name only. He had all the responsibilities that go with the title, but few of the powers. Unhappy Mr. Vidal took all the blame for mistakes, but he had to share credit with his two colleagues, J. Carroll Cone and Rex Martin. There was a notable lack of team work, and the industry suffered as a result.

Resentment flared into the open after the crash of a sky-liner near Kirksville, Missouri, on May 6, 1935. Among the victims was Senator Bronson Cutting of New Mexico, one of the most popular leaders of the upper house. It is a tradition of the Senate to authorize an investigation in such cases, and Dr. Royal S. Copeland of New York was appointed chairman of a board of inquiry. Senator Copeland diagnosed the ills of the industry as due, in part at least, to inefficiency in the aeronautics branch of the Department of Commerce. The bureau was accused of wasting time and money in a futile effort to develop a " flivver plane " for the masses. Administrators of the Air Commerce Act were charged with political favoritism, incompetence, and carelessness. Vidal himself did not fare so badly. The committee rebuked him mildly and reported that he appeared to be " lacking in iron," but since Vidal was hardly in the position to enforce orders, perhaps even this accusation was unfair. The point is that as early as 1934, aviation leaders knew that there would have to be reorganization of the regulatory body. Already legislators were working on new air-mail laws. Logical procedure would have been to combine with them all other air-line regulation, but it took four years of sweat and trouble before the lawmakers came around to this point of view.

After the air-mail contract cancellations, legislators were bombarded with suggestions as they attacked the problems of commercial aviation. The House alone received more than forty aviation bills between February 19, when the army took over the mail routes, and March 10, when the President announced his air-line reorganization plans.[1] Only one of these measures had the approval of the Chief Executive. It was sponsored by Senators Hugo L. Black and Kenneth McKellar of Tennessee, chairman of the Senate

Postoffice Committee. Since the President's nod of approval was equivalent to a command at a time when Congress was acceding to most of his wishes, the Black-McKellar Bill should have slid through the legislative machine easily enough, but it met a serious challenge in a measure proposed on March 26 by Senator Patrick A. McCarran of Nevada. Senator McCarran had been a member of the Black Committee and had learned much about aviation during the protracted hearings. He was the first legislator to propose that all civil aviation be controlled by one authority having quasi-administrative power similar to that of the Interstate Commerce Commission. Senator McCarran's bill was voted down 46 to 26, but it is significant that the plan outlined by the Nevadan at this time was the basis of the law hailed enthusiastically four years later.

While these bills were debated in Congress, Postmaster General Farley awarded the three-month contracts that returned air-mail transportation to private operators. Actually the contracts were effective only about a month, for on June 12, 1934 Congress passed the Black-McKellar Bill. Called " The Air Mail Act of 1934," the measure repealed all antecedent legislation, including the Watres Act, and made the carriers subject to three divisions of the federal government. The Postoffice Department was to award contracts and was to determine routes and schedules. Delegated to the Interstate Commerce Commission was the duty of fixing rates and payments. The Bureau of Air Commerce was to continue its regulation of the airways and the licensing of pilots and machines. The new law also authorized the Postoffice Department to charge only six cents an ounce for air-mail letters. It had cost eight cents to send messages by plane since July 1932, but careful studies indicated that the lower rate would actually bring in more revenue, and the record of the next seven years verified the reports of the rate experts.[2]

Those operators who had stayed away from the April

bidding, not caring to lose money on the temporary contracts, were jolted out of their complacency by the terms of the Black-McKellar Act. The new law provided for the continuation of the temporary contracts, much to the relief of the lucky operators, always fearful of the Cord type of expansionist. Moreover, there was some relief from the financial strain, inasmuch as the Interstate Commerce Commission began at once to revise rates upward. Mail routes were limited to a total of 29,000 miles, to prevent extension abuses, and there were to be no mergers or transfers of contracts without the approval of the Postmaster General. Air lines were ordered to separate themselves from manufacturing affiliates, and as an antidote for the unwarranted salaries and bonuses that had scandalized the Black Committee, executives were limited to incomes of not more than $17,-500. Even this very condensed version of the 1934 law hints at its complexity, but there was one more clause more important than all the others.

Apparently the legislators recognized both the temporary nature of the Black-McKellar Bill and the confusion of the industry, for the act authorized the creation of a Federal Aviation Commission to work out a more effective aviation policy. To the groggy air lines, this was the first ray of hope since the lights went out on February 9. Otherwise the Black-McKellar Bill was greeted without enthusiasm. The division of responsibility between the Interstate Commerce Commission and the Postoffice and Commerce Departments was confusing to both the operators and the government officials. A clause that provided for year-by-year bidding discouraged executives from investing heavily in equipment, since the future was too uncertain to warrant much of an expenditure — especially with such meager income.

By the middle of summer, things were so black that two of the bigger air lines were on the point of suspending operations. All the lines were losing money. United Air Lines was $854,000 in the red at the end of the first quarter of

1934.[3] The North American group (Transcontinental &
Western Air and Eastern Air Lines) lost $405,000 in the
same period.[4] American Airlines did a little better, but
would have lost more had it not reduced schedules. The
lines had already been hit hard by the depression, but the
cancellation of the contracts had raised many more bruises.
United Air Lines stock dropped from 35 just before the
cancellation order to 14, when the army took over the mail
routes. North American Aviation, listed at 8, dropped to
$2\frac{5}{8}$; while Aviation Corporation plunged from 10 to 4 in
the same period.[5] Many factors besides the cancellations
affected the operators, of course. With the depression becoming more acute daily, fewer salesmen and business executives needed speedy transportation, which was the one
service the air lines could provide that justified higher fares.
The Black Committee hearings had been the worst kind of
publicity, and the army's disastrous interim of operation
had shaken the faith of potential passengers. Passage of the
National Recovery Act (the NRA), regulating hours,
wages, and trade practices, came at the very moment when
commercial aviation was least able to bear the added bur-
den. Lastly, it cost the air lines thousands of dollars to re-
organize as prescribed by law.

Splitting air lines from aircraft companies necessitated
expensive auditing, and there were legal fees that ran into
five figures. Indirectly the reorganization of the air lines
and affiliate factories was even more costly, since the operators now had to buy equipment on the open market. With
no mail payments during the period of army operation,
with no stability provided by the new law, and with no hope
of immediate profits, commercial aviation appeared to be
heading for a dead-stick crash.

Despairingly the operators clutched at one straw — the
provision in the 1934 law for a thorough study of the problems. Appointed by President Roosevelt immediately after
the passage of the Air Mail Act of 1934, the Federal Avia-

tion Commission was charged with submitting a full report on air transportation by February 1, 1935. The chairman was Clark Howell, publisher of the Atlanta *Constitution,* who answered a call from Washington in the dead of night and at once gave up all other duties to concentrate on his task. Howell was assisted by an able advisory committee, consisting of Jerome C. Hunsaker, famed engineer and teacher, but at that time president of Goodyear Zeppelin; Franklin K. Lane, son of Woodrow Wilson's Secretary of State, and a former war bird; Edward Pearson Warner, editor of *Aviation,* and also a noted scholar; Albert J. Berres, an expert of personnel problems; and J. Carroll Cone, lured away from the Bureau of Aeronautics to serve as secretary of the commission.

Late in January 1935 the " Howell Commission " submitted 102 recommendations to the President. Many of these suggestions were already written into a bill proposed on January 22 by Senator McCarran. Eight days later Representative Clarence Lea presented a similar bill to the House. Such immediate response indicates that the commission had done its work well. The indefatigable Howell had even gone to Europe at his own expense to see if he could learn anything of value in the leading air lines of the Old World.

Recommendations of the Federal Aviation Commission were incorporated point for point in the legislation that was to follow. The most significant clause was the suggestion to create a separate administrative body to regulate commercial aviation as the Interstate Commerce Commission supervised the railroads. This was merely Senator McCarran's old plan, rejected by Congress six months before.

The commission deserves credit for diagnosing the ills of the industry, but the administration also merits praise, for the President was very evidently making a sincere effort to clean up a messy situation. He had appointed experts who were known to oppose some of the New Deal policies, and eventually they had their way. Not at first, though. The Howell Commission proposed a *separate* controlling authority for aviation. The President leaned toward regulation by the Interstate Commerce Commission. Aviation experts pointed out that the ICC was already too overloaded with work to take on additional burdens, and the operators argued that the ICC, closely identified with the railroads, would not give the proper attention to a rival transportation system. The President disagreed at first. He maintained that the ICC had the experience and organization for more efficient regulation of the air lines, and he insisted that the operators be under the surveillance of the administrative branch of the government, so that they could never again " act up."

On June 7, 1935 the President asked that Congress follow his plan. Three days later Senator McCarran acceded to his chief's demands by introducing a new bill, incorporating many of the recommendations of the Howell Commission, but providing for regulation by the Interstate Commerce Commission. The subcommittee on commerce held extended hearings and called in expert witnesses. Commissioner Joseph B. Eastman of the ICC liked the McCarran Bill, but officials in the Postoffice and Commerce Departments objected to the measure.[6] Senator McCarran rewrote the bill to meet these objections, and on July 29 he reintroduced the measure. Had it passed, commercial aviation might have been spared more trouble, but before the bill was brought to a vote, Congress adjourned.

In the meantime Congress passed an amendment to the Air Mail Act of 1934. Sponsored by James M. Mead, chairman of the House Postoffice Committee, the new law was passed on August 14, 1935.[7] It provided for a slight increase in airway mileage and made contracts effective for three years instead of one, thereby giving the operators much more stability. In accordance with recent labor rulings, wage-earners were specifically authorized to organize and were granted wages and hours privileges. On the other hand, the Black-McKellar-Mead Law made it virtually a crime for an air-line operator to make any money. The Interstate Commerce Commission was ordered to investigate air-line income to determine whether or not there were any " unreasonable " profits. As all the lines were obviously losing money, operators viewed this clause as only another bothersome restriction. The ICC was also to investigate expenditures of operators with a view to detecting purchases from individuals on the postoffice black list. There was also a curious clause defining airways of more than 750 miles as " primary " routes. No company was eligible to operate more than one primary, with two exceptions. They were the two coastal routes of United Air Lines (between Seattle and San Diego) and Eastern Air Lines (between New York and Miami) . Another rule prohibited any company from offering any kind of " off line " service to any city not on the main route but reached by any other air-mail carrier. This was to prevent cutthroat competition, but it led to some rather amusing problems later on. Finally, the law prohibited rebates, passes, and discriminatory rates.

While this was going on, the operators set themselves to the task of repairing the damage suffered at the hands of Messrs. Roosevelt, Farley, Black, Crowley, et al.

CHAPTER

23

Head Winds and Ceiling Zero

Previous to the cancellation order, American Airways was a rambling and disintegrated system. More than seventy per cent of its revenue was air-mail subsidy, but even so, it had lost money. It is true that Aviation Corporation made $596,000 in 1933, but not from its air-line subsidiary. AVCO profited solely from stock manipulation. AVCO's operating company actually lost $160,000 that year, despite the fact that it received about a third of all air-mail appropriations for doing only about ten per cent of the transportation.[1] With the reletting of contracts, the company was reorganized as American Airlines. It broke away from AVCO by purchasing from the parent company all the equipment of American Airways, and there was a reshuffle of personnel.

The new president of the line was C. R. Smith, the drawling young Southerner who had come up from Texas Air Transport to the vice-presidency under Cohû. Smith was an operations man, one of the best in the industry. He was believed to be anti-Cord during the battle for control of American Airways and should have been fired when Cord and Lucius Manning won the AVCO empire. For a time he was banished to the southern division, but he accomplished such wonders there that Cord, who was willing to put business above personal feelings, brought Smith back to be the big boss when Major Lester D. Seymour, American's non-flying president, resigned, following the cancellation period.

E. L. Cord soon fled to England — ostensibly to escape kidnappers, but actually to avoid questioning by the Securities and Exchange Commission, his enemies charged. Whatever the reason, Cord retired as active head of American Airlines, although he remained the largest stockholder (with nineteen per cent of the stock in 1940).

Smith was left with a free hand to build up the clumsy air line — which he did admirably over the next six years. The very month that American won back its mail contract (May 1934), he placed an order for big, all-metal Douglas Sleeper Planes (DST's), which gave his line the finest equipment in the world. The sleeper ships were similar in appearance to the DC–2's, already five years ahead of any other commercial plane, but they were bigger, faster, and more efficient. It took courage to buy such equipment in the face of mounting deficits, but business began to increase as the gleaming Douglases lured traffic over the southern route. American Airlines eventually soared into an atmosphere of profit and tranquillity, but in doing so it again came under the sign of Aviation Corporation.

It is getting ahead of the story, perhaps, but inasmuch as the laws of 1934 were designed to prevent just what happened, it might be appropriate to tell how AVCO got back into the air lines. By 1937, American Airlines needed about $2,000,000 to buy more equipment. It was beginning to show a profit by that time, but the banks were still fearful of the aviation industry, and so American turned to the Reconstruction Finance Corporation for help. The RFC was entitled to make such loans, but it hesitated in this case because American still owed $3,415,000 to Aviation Corporation for equipment it had purchased from the old American Airways. The RFC insisted that the line fund this debt before applying for a loan. American refinanced by issuing $3,650,000 in debentures, due in 1941, and now converted into common stock. Aviation Corporation acquired these debentures, so that technically AVCO might, in a showdown, have been able to recapture its old subsidiary.

American received more route extensions and more mail pay than any other air line during Brown's administration of the Postoffice Department, while United Air Lines, its biggest rival, added only the few miles it was forced to accept against its will. United profited not at all by the " Spoils Conferences," since, as its general manager pointed out, " we were not searching for any new service. We were simply hoping to retain what we had." [2] Yet United was made to suffer, while American profited from reorganization.

United Air Lines, unlike American Airways, was closely bound to several manufacturing affiliates, all controlled by a super holding company, United Aircraft & Transport Corporation. When United Aircraft was forced to split up by the terms of the Black-McKellar-Mead laws, United Air Lines & Transport, a new company, bought up all the air lines formerly operated by United Aircraft.[3] Another holding company, United Aircraft Corporation, succeeded to control of the Eastern manufacturing units, including Pratt & Whitney Aircraft (motors), Chance Vought Corporation (navy planes), Sikorsky Aviation Corporation (seaplanes), and Hamilton-Standard Propeller. The third division of United consisted of the Western manufacturing units, controlled by Boeing Airplane Company of Seattle, and including Stearman Aircraft Company (training and small commercial ships), of Wichita. On August 31, 1934 the old United Aircraft & Transport Corporation was dissolved, and the divisions began to function independently.

United Air Lines still carried the bulk of the transconti-

nental air mail after 1934, but it was losing traffic to the
other cross-country lines, which were now serious competitors. It also lost its route between Chicago, Dallas and Fort
Worth to Braniff. In addition United lost more of its personnel than any other line, following the cancellations. The
new president, W. A. Patterson, was almost unknown to
the industry prior to 1934, but he was soon giving a good
account of himself in tending to the wounds of the battered
company.

Transcontinental & Western Air was also closely tied up
with manufacturing units, through its affiliations with
North American Aviation and the General Motors group.
Wright Aeronautical Corporation (engines) and Fokker
Aircraft used TWA as an outlet in the same way that Boeing and Pratt & Whitney used United, but the ties were a
little less strong in the case of TWA, since there were signs
of disintegration even before the cancellations. General
Motors got into the picture by buying up the stock of the
old Fokker plant. The plan was to build the American
Fokker for use on the air lines of this country. The Fokker
was an excellent ship for its day, but inasmuch as other
lines already had affiliations with manufacturing companies, General Aviation (the aircraft subsidiary of General
Motors) was assured of an outlet when directors authorized the purchase of fifty thousand shares of Western Air
Express stock. The merger of Transcontinental Air Transport and Western Air Express put General Motors and
North American Aviation in joint control of Transcontinental & Western Air.

General Motors did not fit its new role. There was much
unpleasant publicity following the Rockne crash in March
1931, and the American Fokker was discredited by the Bureau of Air Commerce. The order for periodic inspection
of Fokker wings turned operators away from this popular
ship, since it was too difficult to get inside the plywood
covering. General Motors retreated from the manufactur-

ing field. In April 1933 it completed virtual liquidation of General Aviation by trading control of the manufacturing subsidiary for more stock in TWA. General Motors at the time of the cancellations therefore controlled what it had long shared — the central air-mail and passenger route. After the Presidential order of February 9, 1934, General Motors retreated even further from its unfortunate aviation foray. In 1935 it sold the controlling interest in TWA to Lehman Brothers and the Atlas Corporation.

Richard W. Robbins, the capable and popular president of TWA since the merger of the central transcontinental routes, had to resign from the company in accordance with the terms of the Air Mail Act of 1934. TWA directors soon chose as president Jack Frye, former vice president in charge of operations, and Paul Richter stepped into Frye's old office. Frye and Richter had grown with TWA since their little one-plane Standard Air Lines, operating between Los Angeles and Phoenix, had been absorbed by Western Air Express in 1930. When Western Air Express became part of TWA in 1931, Frye and Richter not only remained, but went on up the ladder. In 1939 Lehman Brothers disposed of its TWA holdings. The largest block of stock (ultimately about thirty per cent) went to Howard Hughes, who had gained most of his wealth from royalties on an oil-drilling patent that had become his property. Frye and Richter held about six per cent of the stock after the Lehman sale. This was enough to give the three working control of the central route.

TWA became known as " the airman's air line." Hughes was a racer and round-the-world flyer. Richter was a former Hollywood stunt pilot. President Frye had broken the transcontinental plane record both before and after the cancellation period. Frye and Richter kept up their transport licenses by piloting air liners at regular intervals. TWA was a pioneer in high-altitude or " overweather " flying. It was the first domestic air line to take delivery of the superb

four-engined Boeing " Stratoliners." TWA's engineers developed radio aids to avigation and perfected de-icing
equipment, which were important contributions to safe
flying. Never a big money-maker, the line was so efficiently
operated that it became a kind of school for would-be pilots
and maintenance men.

Eastern Air Lines, which dominated the Atlantic coast,
was one of the few lines that did not split from its parent
company, following the Air Mail Act of 1934. Until March
1938 it was affiliated with TWA, through North American
Aviation. In spite of this apparent flouting of the law, the
company won back its old contracts. Captain Thomas B.
Doe, forced to resign by the terms of the Farley contracts,
was soon succeeded by Captain E. V. Rickenbacker, who
had joined Eastern Air Lines as vice president after the
breakup of General Aviation. Eastern Air Lines recovered
sooner than did its associates. It suffered less from winter
slump than the other lines, thanks to the Florida tourist
trade, and traffic was heavy between New York, Washington, and the booming Southern cities inadequately served
by railroads. Rickenbacker saved money for the line by
leasing equipment from other operators during the winter,
ordinarily a slack season, but Eastern's busiest period. This
gave the line the lowest maintenance charges in the industry, and with no threat of competition, the line enjoyed
high mail and passenger revenue.

Several other lines emerged at this time as important carriers. One was Braniff Airways, which had won United's
old Chicago-Texas route. Another was Pennsylvania-Central Airlines (PCA). This was a fusion of Pennsylvania
Air Lines (PAL) and Central Airlines. It took over the
route pioneered by Clifford Ball, one of the earliest of the
private contractors. Ball flew between Pittsburgh and
Cleveland. In 1930 he sold his route for $137,000. The pur-
chaser was a new company called Pennsylvania Air Lines,
which was a subsidiary of Pittsburgh Aviation Industries

Corporation — the same PAIC that became one of the parties to the merger of Western Air Express and Transcontinental Air Transport. Under Major H. S. Martin, former PAIC head, Pennsylvania Air Lines was extended to Washington, and then to Detroit. With the cancellation of the air-mail contracts in 1934, Pennsylvania Air Lines fell on evil days. It lost its contracts to an underbidding company called Central Airlines.

Central Airlines was really the continuation of the old Pittsburgh Airways, which had fought PAIC for the pioneer rights in the state of Pennsylvania and had been one of the three little companies whose low bid for the central transcontinental air-mail route was rejected after much debate. Pittsburgh Airways was driven into bankruptcy and disappeared, but it popped up again (or at least the same promoters did) when the new air-mail contracts were put up for bidding. Central Airlines, successor to Pittsburgh Airways, was formed by James (Jim) Condon, who, with Theodore Taney, had once operated Pittsburgh Airways. Condon was financed by the wealthy sons of a Greensburg, Pennsylvania, coal operator. They were John Coulter and his brother, Richard, who crashed to his death in 1937. The Coulters put up about $300,000, and when bids were opened, the new Central Airlines was awarded Pennsylvania Air Lines' old Detroit-Washington route. All that Pennsylvania Air Lines got out of the redistribution of contracts was the Milwaukee-Detroit route, which it purchased from previous holders.

Then for two years the two lines fought each other. Pennsylvania Air Lines continued to operate between Washington and Milwaukee, but mail from Milwaukee had to be transferred to rival Central transports at Detroit. Neither line prospered. Central had the mail, but it was not popular as a passenger-carrier. PAL had built up a fine passenger clientele, but it could not make money without a mail contract. Competition was disastrous, for each line tried to undercut fares. Had Central Airlines found the capital, it might have won out. There is some evidence that it was being encouraged by the American Airlines and Cord crowd, for Sigmund Janas, later identified as a Cord man, took over active control of Central Airlines at this time.

The president of Pennsylvania Air Lines after the cancellation period was C. Bedell Monro, son of a Pittsburgh glass-manufacturer, and a former instructor of English at the University of Pittsburgh. Monro had flown with a brother-in-law after the war, and in 1927 he and F. R. Crawford, later a PAL executive, formed Mo-Craw Airplane & Advertising Company, which " did not represent much except enthusiasm." [4] The two bought an old OX–5 Waco for $3,500, " sight unseen," from a Norfolk dealer. The ship crashed on the take-off, and the boys learned later that the former owner had paid only $800 for it. That was the first lesson the partners had in air-line operation. " It was a cheap lesson," quiet, handsome Mr. Monro recalls. [5]

When the rebidding on the contracts required reorganization of the old lines, Monro and Crawford took over the new Pennsylvania Air Lines & Transport Company, Inc. All during the disastrous competition with Central Airlines, Monro tried to buy out his rival. Condon and Janas, perhaps with the encouragement of the Cord interests, always jacked up the price beyond reach of struggling PAL, and in addition, the Air Mail Act of 1934 specifically prevented the merging of parallel routes.

The turning-point came in 1936, when a spring flood interrupted all communication in the Pittsburgh area. Pennsylvania Air Lines won favorable publicity at that time, and in September 1936 the Postoffice Department approved a merger of the two rivals. A new company, Pennsylvania-Central Airlines, was incorporated in Delaware late that month. Final details were worked out on October

22, and on November 1, 1936 the new line began carrying mail and passengers between Washington and Milwaukee. Central Airlines was paid $600,000 for its equity, and the Coulter brothers also got 35,000 shares of stock in the new air line, which gave them a voice in the direction. Service was soon extended to Norfolk, Chicago, and Sault Ste. Marie, Michigan.

Other new lines appearing after the air-mail cancellations were Chicago & Southern Air Lines, Delta Air Lines, Continental Air Lines, Inland Air Lines, Mid-Continent Airlines, National Airlines, and Northeast Airlines. Chicago & Southern was the new and more appropriate name for Pacific Seaboard Air Lines, which had transferred its operations from the west coast after winning the Mississippi Valley contract route. Delta was the re-emergence of an old line that had been a potential bidder for the southern transcontinental route when Postmaster General Brown was building his airway system. Squeezed out by more powerful competitors, Delta had maintained itself as crop-dusting and taxi service. It returned to the transportation business under the aggressive leadership of the same C. E. Woolman who had fought for air mail in 1930, and soon it was booming along as operator of a mail and passenger route from Charleston, South Carolina, to Dallas and Fort Worth, via Atlanta, Birmingham, Jackson, and Shreveport.

Inland Air Lines succeeded Wyoming Air Service on the Cheyenne-Billings run, with another branch up into the Black Hills, and thence east to Rapid City and Pierre. Continental was successor to the operation between El Paso and Denver. Mid-Continent was only Hanford-Tri-State lines dolled up with new equipment as a feeder line running out of Tulsa in two branches to Twin Cities and Minot, North Dakota. National Airlines became a competitor of Eastern Air Lines in the Florida territory, while Northeast Airlines much later succeeded the Boston &

Maine and Central Vermont operations in the New England states. (For thumbnail histories of various American air lines, see Appendix IV.)

These changes in the airway map took place slowly and only through travail. After 1934 the air lines began to gain strength, but they still were fighting for recovery as late as the spring of 1938. Few were making money. Morale was bad, and was not improved when the lines went through a period of terrible accidents between 1935 and 1937. Not until it could operate under a fair and workable charter could the industry hope to reach maturity. How commercial aviation won this magna charta is described in the following chapter.

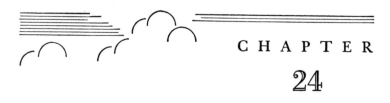

CHAPTER

24

Back to "Normalcy"

THE AIR lines began a long convalescence after the stroke
of 1934, but there could be no complete cure as long as
quacks prescribed the medicine. What commercial aviation
needed most was peace and quiet. Between 1934 and 1938
all it got was rough treatment. Yet throughout this trying
period friends were working patiently to find effective rem-
edies.

Senator Pat McCarran, Representative Clarence Lea,
and members of the Federal Aviation Commission had
been saying all along that the air lines would recover as
soon as a responsible practitioner was given full charge
of the patient. With the charges of the Black Committee
still ringing through the land, there was a tendency to let
the air lines suffer for their sins, however, and the recom-
mendation for putting air transportation in the hands of an
authority was therefore ignored. Senator McCarran's modified plan, which failed of a vote before the 74th Congress
adjourned, was reintroduced as a bill during the first week
of the next legislative session. This time the measure was
divided into two sections. One part was written to provide

for the regulation of air transportation economically, while
the other was devoted to safety rules. Representative Lea
brought up a similar bill in the House. The Lea Bill gave
the Chief Executive more control than Senator McCarran
was willing to grant,[1] but the two lawmakers had long since
ironed out most of their other differences.

Senator McCarran was ill at this time, however, and the
upper house delayed action on the measure until its sponsor
was present to defend his views. The lower house was so
preoccupied with relief legislation that it, too, shelved proposed aviation measures for future consideration. Interdepartmental jealousies also acted as a drag. The Postoffice,
Commerce, and War Departments, as well as a number of
lesser agencies, had stakes in civil aviation, and there was
a general suspicion that the McCarran-Lea Bill would take
away cherished prerogatives. To smooth ruffled sensibili-
ties, the President appointed a committee of assistant secretaries from each of the departments, bureaus, and commissions having anything to do with commercial aviation.
This committee held hearings during the hot summer after-
noons of 1937. Representative Lea worked with the group,
answering questions intelligently and easily, and eventually the jealous officials worked out their differences.

The President all this time had clung to his faith in the
Interstate Commerce Commission as the body best fitted
to control civil aviation. Without the President's approval,
the McCarran-Lea Bill had no chance. It was James Roosevelt, son and confidential secretary to the President, who
effected reconciliation between the Chief Executive and
the legislators.[2] " Jimmy " had attended the hearings of
the Interdepartmental Committee as his father's scout, and
he understood the desperate need for a new aviation charter. He had learned that legislative leaders, department
heads, air-line operators, and editors agreed as to the funda-
mentals of such a law, and knowing this, Jimmy was pecul-
iarly fitted to act as mediator between the White House

and the group working for a separate aviation authority. Apparently he performed his part capably, for late in the summer of 1937 the President called Senator McCarran and Representative Lea to the Executive Mansion. There he informed them that he had changed his mind about the aviation situation and had come to the conclusion that the two legislators were right.[3] He added that he was now willing to approve the main provisions of the original McCarran Bill, which Congress had turned down in 1934.

The old bill, and its counterpart three years later, were modeled after the time-tested Interstate Commerce Act, and, as Senator McCarran later explained, they followed the bus and railroad bill paragraph by paragraph.

After their White House conference Senator McCarran and Representative Lea dusted off their old bills. There were a few changes to be made and some differences to adjust, but since the two lawmakers had been mulling over aviation problems together for nearly four years, there was not much to thresh out. The Lea plan still gave the President more power than Senator McCarran was willing to concede, but the Senate bill counterbalanced extreme centralization of authority, and President Roosevelt was willing to compromise.

On June 23, 1938 the President signed the McCarran-Lea Bill, and civil aviation was given a new constitution. Known as the Civil Aeronautics Act, it was the most important piece of air legislation ever passed by Congress. To the debilitated industry it was a magic tonic. Air-line executives settled back with relief. Colonel E. S. Gorrell, who represented the operators as head of the Air Transport Association, called the law " a wise and considered measure." [4] Equally enthusiastic was David L. Behncke of the Air Line Pilots Association, who pronounced the act " fair " and " sound." [5] One editor wrote:

The tumult and the shouting has died. The dust is beginning to settle again on Capitol Hill. And departing, the 75th Congress has left behind it at least one very definite footprint in the sands of time; the Civil Aeronautics Act of 1938. . . . Congress has done its job.[6]

The Civil Aeronautics Act, like the Air Commerce Act of 1926, was passed under the commerce clause of the Federal Constitution. Its distinctive feature was the establishment of the office of Administrator. Even the legislative sponsors apparently did not plan on such a happy solution to their problem, for it was not until March 10, 1938 that the Administrator was even mentioned in either the House or the Senate draft of the bill.[7] On that day the Committee on Interstate and Foreign Commerce began hearings on the House measure. Witnesses were Representative Lea, members of the President's Interdepartmental Committee, and Clinton Hester, counsel for the Treasury Department, who was called in to advise on technical matters pertaining to legal limitations of the proposed law. Hester argued that the President had executive power granted by the Constitution, and that since the new aeronautics Authority was to be executive in nature, it was only right that the President assume responsibility for controlling these executive functions. Hester pointed out that the proposed aviation board, or Authority, was unique, in that it was to be an agency having great powers ordinarily vested only in the Chief Executive. The Lea Bill did give the President such " general direction " over the Authority, which was interpreted as the right to review decisions of the agency. Legislators feared, however, that such a proposal would run counter to the troublesome decision of the Supreme Court in *Humphreys Executor vs. United States,* in which the Court had held that regulatory bodies were beyond the overt control of the President.[8] Subcommittee members objected to that part of the Lea Bill which held that " the exercise and performance of powers and duties of the Authority, which are not subject to review of the courts, shall be subject to the general direction of the President." [9]

Hester maintained that this was inserted only to protect the Constitutional right of the President, and to keep the Authority from being bound by the Humphreys decision, which would have placed the aeronautics board outside the executive division of the government.

Representative Alfred L. Bulwinkle first suggested the plan finally accepted by the lawmakers. He recommended that the President delegate his powers to an agent, or "Administrator," who could be recalled at any time by the Chief Executive. This would give the President some influence in the execution of regulations laid down by the Authority without violating the Humphreys dictum.

The Civil Aeronautics Authority was to consist of an administrator and a board of five members, who were to receive $12,000 a year for their services. Not more than three of the board could be members of the same political party. None was to have any financial interest in any aviation enterprise. The board would hear complaints, determine rates, and formulate broad policies for a more efficient airway system. Appointed for a six-year term, no member of the board could be dismissed except for cause. Its decisions were to be the law of civil aviation, and findings of fact, if supported by evidence, were not reversible by the courts. Co-operating with the Administrator and Authority, but not directly affiliated, was the three-man Air Safety Board, appointed by the President and subject to recall at any time. The safety board was to investigate accidents and to publish reports on the cause and prevention of airplane crashes. Members received $7,500 a year.

On August 22, 1938 the Authority took over the airway personnel and property of the Postoffice Department, the Interstate Commerce Commission, and the Bureau of Air Commerce. Since the new agency had broken away from all department affiliations and had no building of its own (headquarters were in the new Commerce Building), offices and bureaus were scattered all over the city. Vacant offices, lofts, and out-of-the-way buildings were occupied by the harried Authority, but despite the apparent confusion the agency performed well from the start. An Air Carrier Economic Regulation Division took over control of the air lines. It issued certificates of convenience as an effective check against unnecessary competition. It forbade operators to open up, or abandon, routes without the approval of the Authority. The board enforced strict compliance with existing labor legislation. Passes, discriminatory rates, and fluctuating tariffs were forbidden in order to prevent ills that had beset the railroad and bus lines at one time or another. The Authority tossed overboard the old conception of competition, thereby coming back to the policy advocated by Postmaster General Brown, eight years before.

The mail policy of the Authority was patterned after the Railway Mail Service Pay Act, by which the Postmaster General retained such rights as enforcing the rules and regulations for transporting the posts, but the old contract mail system was abolished in favor of negotiated, non-competitive certificates.

There was still some danger of friction between the Civil Aeronautics Authority and the Postoffice Department. The Authority issued certificates, without which no line could operate, but the postoffice paid the freight and determined schedules. Thus two lines serving the same city might be approved as carriers, but the Postmaster General could still favor one or the other by arranging schedules to his liking. That meant that operators must continue to play ball with the Postoffice Department officials, but the CAA now fixed mail rates, and this acted as a check upon inordinate discrimination.

The Authority had the power to examine accounts at any time and to investigate mergers, interlocking directorships, pools, federal loans, and interline agreements. Operators had to submit monthly and annual reports on their activities, and to publish an annual list of stockholders who owned more than a five-per-cent interest in the companies.

The safety regulations provided in the new law were the revised rules of the superseded Bureau of Air Commerce.

The Civil Aeronautics Act was effective after August 22, but the Authority began to function long before that. Members of the board began to arrive in Washington by the middle of July, and on August 8, 1938 they were sworn in by Judge Harold M. Stephens of the District Court of Appeals. Next day the board held its first meeting.

The industry was not impressed by the caliber of the Presidential appointees. "The . . . talent in the Civil Aeronautics Authority sloshes about like a gallon of gas in an empty tank," said an editorial in *Aviation*.[10] Suspicions were largely unfounded, however, although understandable after four years of disillusionment.

Clinton M. Hester was appointed the first Administrator. The forty-three-year-old former Treasury Department counsel was believed to be "close to the White House," but aviation men credited him with perfecting the highly technical licensing clauses of the Lea Bill, and they were reconciled to his membership on the board.

Picked as chairman of the CAA was Edward J. Noble, president of Life Savers, Incorporated, makers of a mint candy drop. Because Noble flew an autogiro, he was recognized as a member of the flying fraternity and his appointment was passed as "acceptable." Critics pointed out, however, that his experience was not commensurate with his position.

Vice chairman of the CAA was Harllee Branch, former Washington newspaper correspondent, who had been executive assistant to Postmaster General Farley and then Second Assistant Postmaster General in charge of air mail. Branch was a strong Democrat, but even the pro-Republican press admitted that he was an able member of the new board.

Other members of the CAA were Oswald Ryan, George

G. Mason, Jr., and Robert M. Hinckley. Ryan was an Indiana Representative in Congress, who had fought overseas, and who had been counsel for the Federal Power and Immigration commissions. He was listed as one of the two Republican members of the CAA, but he was known to be sympathetic to the New Deal. According to the trade journals, " his aeronautical experience, if any, has so far defied detection," [11] but that criticism was made in the early days of the CAA. Mason was more acceptable to the industry than any other member, for he was politically independent and he was familiar with aviation problems through his position as an executive of Pan American Airways. Unfortunately, all his experience was based on Latin-American operations, but at least he could speak the language of the operator. Hinckley was a former member of the Utah state legislature. He had once operated an air service out of Ogden, and he was known as an inveterate air traveler. Since 1931 he had served as Far Western Administrator of the Works Progress Administration. A dozen others might have served aviation as well, or better, the critics believed, and there was a suspicion that politics had entered into the appointment (to put it mildly), but Hinckley proceeded to give a very good account of himself and eventually succeeded to the chairmanship, after Noble became assistant to Secretary of Commerce Harry L. Hopkins.

Under the Air Safety Board, the air lines established an amazing safety record. During the interim before the Civil Aeronautics Authority was returned to the Department of Commerce in 1940, air lines chalked up fifteen months of capacity operation without a fatality (and then two more under the new set-up). The members of the Safety Board were Lieutenant Colonel W. Sumpter Smith, Thomas O. Hardin, and C. B. Allen. Colonel Smith was an airport engineer who had once served in the aviation branch of the Signal Corps. Hardin, formerly a pilot for Texas Air Transport, Southern Air Transport, and American Airways, was vice president of the Air Line Pilots Association and was the active flyer required by law to be a member of the board. The third member was not picked at once. Chairman Noble apparently wanted C. B. Allen, aviation editor of the New York *Herald Tribune,* but the appointment was said to have been held up by the President. Allen was a flyer who understood the problems of the industry, and presumably he was selected by Noble to take over the delicate press relations of the board. His paper had been a consistent critic of the administration, however, and that may have had something to do with the delay in his appointment. He was announced as the third member on August 25.

One of the first snarls the Authority had to untangle as it got down to business was the dispute between Eastern Air Lines and Braniff Airways. Just before the passage of the Civil Aeronautics Act, the Postoffice Department advertised for bids on the routes between Houston and San Antonio, and Houston and Brownsville. The prize for the winner was the Brownsville terminal, giving direct connection with Mexican and Latin-American traffic over the Pan American Airways System and its subsidiaries. Eastern coveted the route, but as the territory was in the Braniff preserve, Eastern could not get into Brownsville because of the " off line " clause in the Air Mail Act of 1935. When the Postoffice Department advertised for bids for the route, Eastern executives believed they had a chance to get a foot in the door. All they had to do was underbid Braniff, and no matter how low the bid, the CAA was certain to make things right when it took over regulation of the air lines. Braniff was equally determined to hold on to its territorial rights, and it put in what it thought was the lowest possible legal bid. Braniff offered to carry the mail over the two routes for $.00001907378 cents a mile, which the operators had computed as exactly $1 a year. Despite this unique offer, Braniff was underbid, for Eastern asked only zero cents a mile for carrying the mail. The Postoffice De-

partment gave the contract to Eastern Air Lines, but only
over the protest of the Braniff executives. The Braniffs
argued that it was illegal for the government to accept
" gratuitous service," which was exactly the term to apply
to Eastern's mail transportation, but the postoffice, knowing the CAA would have to go over the whole thing in a
month anyway, let Eastern continue as the mail-carrier.

When the Civil Aeronautics Authority opened up for
business on August 23, 1938, it found the controversy between Eastern Air Lines and Braniff Airways on its doorstep. The Solomons of the air lines went into a huddle.
Only one disputant could win a route certificate, without
which no line could operate under the new law. Both were
excellent air lines; both had pioneer equities in the territory; both were able to give the public the finest of service.
The CAA acted promptly, and in so doing, it set a precedent. Eastern won the certificate on the basis that lines
already established in territories by previous negotiations
were to stay, unless it could be proved beyond a doubt that
such enfranchisement was inimical to the public interest.

Other problems confronted the new controlling board,
but it proceeded cautiously, and as members warmed to the
task, the Authority began to win the respect of the industry. A new spirit of co-operation dispelled the old distrust
between operators and the government officials. As one
writer expressed it:

The industry actually wrote its own ticket. . . . The Civil
Aeronautics Act has given aviation the most powerful tool we
have ever had for sound and rapid progress on all fronts. The
government has gone well over half way in the matter, and
might rightfully resent any claim from now on that it was
standing in the way of progress. Definitely, the ball has been
passed back to the aviation industry — and on its own terms —
and it is up to us to carry it on a steady march down the field.
But if we fumble — Lord help us! [12]

The Age of the Skyliner

AFTER the passage of the Civil Aeronautics Act of 1938, the most important development in air transportation was the improvement of equipment. While air-line operators worried through the gloomy period between 1934 and 1938, aircraft-designers were preparing the way for the new era. The renaissance of airplane-designing began just before the cancellation of the air-mail contracts, but the greatest advances came later. Strangely enough, the very laws that made the operators writhe in agony were indirectly responsible for some of the progress. Before the cancellation period many air lines were affiliated with aircraft factories. Thus TWA was most likely to use Fokker and General Aviation equipment, because of the relationship with the General Motors group. In the same way Eastern Air Transport chose Curtiss Condors, while United Air Lines standardized on Boeing ships. After the cancellations air lines and factories were split. It cost the operators more to buy equipment on the open market, but the separation of subsidiaries meant that air lines could now have the most efficient equipment without regard to aircraft affiliations.

The result was that aircraft were improved more in this

period than in any similar span since the First World War. This was not so apparent at the time, since interest was distracted by legislative troubles. Not until emphasis shifted was the man in the street aware of the great change that had taken place in air transportation. Outwardly there was little to distinguish the air liner of late 1933 from the 1940 transport. Actually the latter was as far in advance of its predecessor as the steamship *Manhattan* compared with the *Great Western*.

Come out to the airport and see for yourself. There is the air liner — twelve tons of metal fashioned into the graceful hull that makes the transport plane a thing of functional beauty. Watch it as it takes off. Here at the control tower the roar of the two 1,100-horsepower " Twin-Cyclones " is far louder than it is to the twenty-one passengers, lolling comfortably in reclining chairs. In a moment the craft is out of sight. At 180 miles an hour, this is the fastest transportation known to man. Yet, in spite of this speed, the traveler is more likely to reach his destination safely than in his own slow motor car.

The captain of the ship is a member of the Air Line Pilots Association, since 1936 protected by the Railway Labor Act and affiliated with the American Federation of Labor. His is one of the highest paid jobs in the list of organized labor. With a base wage of $3,000 a year (in effect, a kind of " retainer ") he gets extra pay for the hours he is in the air. The Civil Aeronautics Authority limits flying time to a monthly maximum of 85 hours, but pay ranges from a low of $4.20 an hour for piloting slow equipment in the daytime, to $7.50 for guiding one of the big sleeper planes through the night.[1] His income for the year should amount to about $8,500. The U.S. Shipping Board paid its steamship captains only $3,480 a year, and even the skipper of the *Leviathan*, largest U.S. packet, earned only $7,500 while the steamship was in operation.[2] Under such conditions, it is not surprising that air-line personnel is of the very highest type.

Clamped to the ears of the captain, or co-pilot, are a pair of phone receivers, through which filters a peculiar buzz. "Dah-dah," murmur the receivers, indicating that the ship is "on course." Occasionally the wind drifts the big plane off its track. Instantly the ear phones change their note to "dah-dee" or "dee-dah," according to whether the ship has veered to the right or left. As the signal changes, the mechanical "robot" pilot swings the plane back to its proper lane, until "on course" sounds again. Every forty seconds or so there is a break in the signal while the weather data is broadcast. Probably the radio-beacon range number is checked at the same time, as an aid to determining position, although the pilot may determine his position at any time by means of his radio direction-finder.

Darkness has obscured the land, and low clouds have rolled across the moon, but the navigators have no fear. Sixty miles more, and the ship will roll up to the Cleveland airport ramp. The captain takes over the controls from his assistant and drops the nose of the craft slightly for the long glide to the landing field. The glide would be even longer were the speed or altitude greater. The plane drops at the rate of four hundred feet a minute, and motors are scarcely audible now. Their work is nearly over. At eight hundred feet they burst into song again, but only for a moment. Louder and louder comes the "on course" signal through the ear phones. Abruptly the sound ceases. The ship has entered the "cone of silence" above the beacon station. If the night is clear, the passengers may glimpse the top of the Union Station Terminal Tower, backed by the gleam of Lake Erie off to the north, for the cone of silence indicates that the ship is near its destination.

The airport dispatcher is guiding the pilot now. The field is almost clear. Visibility is adequate; the wind mild.

A small commercial ship has been given the green light at the south end of the field, but it will be out of the way by the time the skyliner circles into the wind.

The co-pilot lowers the retractable landing gear. Wing flaps drop and the ship acts as though four-wheel brakes had been applied, although actually it is still plunging on at eighty miles an hour. Back come the throttles. The glide flattens out. At the very moment the inclinometer stops at "level," the throttles are completely closed. Landing wheels brush the runway. The marker lights blur by. Brakes take hold. Already the stewardess is fumbling at the door. The motors cease their muttering and attendants wheel out the movable ramp. Unconcernedly the passengers emerge to go about their separate businesses.

There is no danger or excitement — and very little drama — in this routine arrival, yet in this scene all the elements that are making aviation successful have been mentioned. The history of aviation has its episodes of daring, danger, scandal, ruthlessness, and intrigue. Too often ignored are the minor details that have really made flight what it is today. Postmasters General Walter F. Brown and James A. Farley have had considerable attention paid to them in this book, yet they have had no more influence upon aviation than has Fred E. Weick, for example, whose experiments in engine streamlining helped to change airline loss to profit. Commercial aviation got its long pants when it began to be a sound business. It could not be a sound business until air travel was economical, safe, reliable, comfortable, fast, and popular. It is impossible to mention all those who contributed to improve air service, but in the aggregate they are far more important to this study than the air-mail cancellations, or even the legislation leading up to the passage of the Civil Aeronautics Act.

There was no real technical progress in air transportation until 1926, but since that date, American commercial planes have outdistanced all others. This progress has not been steady. There have been periods of virtual stagnation. At other times the industry was revolutionized within a year's time. Outwardly there seems to be little advance since the year of reorganization following the cancellations. The Douglas ships that were standard after 1936 appear little different from the DC–2's or Boeing 247's of 1934–5, many of which were still giving faithful service six years later; but, passenger traffic figures disclose the rapid growth of aviation.

There has been a steady increase in air traffic of about 19 per cent each year from 1935 to 1939.[3] That in itself is commendable progress, but for 1939 the increase was *42.2 per cent*. March 1940 was 64.2 per cent ahead of March 1939, and there was a 31 per cent improvement the next year. In the first six months of 1941, domestic air lines flew more passenger miles than in *any full year* previous to 1939. Nothing in transportation history can compare with that growth. In 1935 the major lines flew 314,000,000 passenger miles. In five years this shot up to 1,144,163,818 passenger miles. It is dangerous to predict what will happen in aviation, since progress in one five-year period does not ensure the same progress over the next five years, but even war and defense plans in 1941 did not break the upcurve.

There has been a continuous decrease in dependence on mail during these last five years. Air-mail " subsidy " is becoming archaic, since the amount paid to the carrier is half a million dollars less than postal revenue (chart, p. 129). On a few lines, notably Pan American's transatlantic route, the government has made considerable profit on its mail. The percentage of income from mail on the domestic lines had dropped from 38 per cent in 1935 to less than 30 per cent in 1941, and the trend is expected to continue.[4] Mail still represents the difference between profit and loss, but the air lines no longer need fear the cry of " subsidy."

In terms of dollars and cents, air transportation is still a small industry, only acting like Big Business, but it is beginning to amount to something. In the fiscal year 1935 a group of air lines representing 99 per cent of the mail and passenger business had a gross revenue of $22,942,544 and a deficit of $3,322,417. In 1939 these lines grossed $47,319,-892, with a profit of $993,311 — inconsequential, it is true, but a sign of better times to come. The fiscal year ending March 31, 1940 showed a gross of $59,038,463, and a net income of $5,019,490.[5] By the summer of 1941, two of the air lines, American Airlines and Eastern Air Lines, were listed in the fifteen leading passenger-carriers, along with twelve railroads and one bus system. American was tenth on the list; Eastern, fifteenth. Both United Air Lines and TWA were listed in the first twenty-five. Aviation is beginning to pay.

While mail payments have shown relative decreases, passenger fares have also been reduced slightly, although they appeared to be stabilized by 1940 at between 5.11 and 5.15 cents a mile.[6] How, then, has increased revenue come about? Largely by increased traffic and by rather sensational economies.

The role of the designer has been the controlling factor in reconciling high performance (needed to get traffic) with economy (without which the lines could not operate). It has been found that the speed of airplanes is the major inducement to air travel, but this inducement is not sufficient to allow the air lines to ignore rail fares. Air traffic volume may be maintained when fares are from 25 to 50 per cent higher than standard rail fares, but beyond that point there is a limit to potential patronage. If the air lines can make air travel safe enough so that the passenger is willing to pay a little extra for speed, the planes will be filled. And if the operator can cut his costs while still maintaining safety and high performance, he can make money.

Cruising speeds increased from 120 to 190 miles an hour between 1933 and 1941, but of far greater importance is the reduction in operating costs per passenger mile from 7 to

4 cents.[7] Two thirds of the total expense of running an air line is directly affected by design, construction, and performance of planes and motors.[8] It is in this sphere that the greatest progress has been made, and each step in advance has an interrelation with other improvements. As Warner points out, an improvement in design causing operating costs to drop from 4 to 2 cents per passenger mile would also permit reduced fares. This would give rise to more passengers, thereby reducing overhead and again cutting operating costs below 2 cents, while actually increasing income. If costs are considered in terms of seat mile, rather than plane mile, a number of factors will be seen to influence economical operation of an air line. Since fuel and oil are one of the major expenses, a reduction in fuel costs, through utilizing less horsepower to obtain the same speed, obviously is an important factor. Greater speed with less horsepower has been accomplished in recent years.

Again, if traffic will bear it, larger planes providing more seats will also reduce costs, since the fixed charges for personnel and maintenance are about the same for a fourteen-passenger as for a twenty-one-passenger ship. If, at the same time, the speed can be increased so that the same ship can make a trip oftener, or go much farther during the maximum flying time of a pilot, again there is a saving. In fact, if speed can be doubled economically, running costs can be just about halved.[9] Doubling the speed economically, however, means accomplishing the result not by increased horsepower, but by more scientific design. If a plane can fly 10 per cent faster on the same amount of power, there should be a corresponding 5-per-cent reduction in operating costs per seat mile. A 10-per-cent increase in speed merely by increasing horsepower calls for engines of at least 25 per cent greater power, however, and the costs per seat mile go up at least 15 per cent, and probably more, since the added weight of engine and fuel would also decrease the pay load.[10]

In the last decade the speed of planes has risen as much as fifty per cent. This has not been pure gain, however, since some of the speed has been obtained at the expense of horsepower. For example, the early transports only expended about 50 horsepower for each passenger. By the time transport speeds were up around the two hundred mark, as much as 160 horsepower per passenger was common.[11]

This rise in power output was compatible with economy only because of the high " wing loading " of the superliners. Wing loading is the ratio of total weight to wing area. In the little " flivver planes " this factor may be as low as 6.8. In the larger ships, the wing-loading factor may range from 10 to 15. But the wing loading of the modern transport is around 25 and is still increasing. Obviously, the higher the wing loading — that is, the less area presented to the air in proportion to the weight of the ship — the less horsepower is required to drag the plane through the atmosphere. On the other hand, the higher the wing loading, the faster the landing and take-off. Stalling and landing speed of a flivver plane with a 7.5 wing loading is about 35 miles an hour. A military pursuit plane with a wing loading in the upper thirties comes in at around 90 miles an hour. While the slowest landing is not the safest landing, nevertheless there are extreme high speeds beyond which it is dangerous to land passenger planes. The problem of the air-line operator has been to obtain ships with wing loadings high enough to increase speed with no increase in horsepower, while maintaining safe landing speeds and steep climbs. This has been accomplished by engineering developments, so that ships with high wing loadings which a few years ago would have been unable to land on even average-sized fields without overshooting (because of excessive gliding speed) now land easily on small airports. Of the five major developments in the last twenty years, Warner lists increased wing loading first, the years 1925–7 being the key dates for the beginning of the trend.

The second major development overlapped the first, occurring mainly in 1925–6. This was the trend toward multi-motor equipment. Planes with more than one engine are not new. *L'Aérophile* published plans for a twin-motor air transport, not unlike modern skyliners in design, as far back as 1906.[12] Many of the wartime De Havilands were fitted with twin Liberty engines in 1920 to carry increased mail loads. While it would seem that they should have been safer than single-engined ships, they were far from being so. The early multi-motor planes were never able to cruise, much less climb, on only one motor. With two engines, and therefore twice as much danger of engine failure, these ships were more dangerous than single-engined ships.

The first efficient multi-motor planes to appear on the air lines in this country were the Ford and Fokker trimotors. Because they could maintain flight on two engines and had a beneficial psychological effect upon passengers, they were the favorite equipment of the air lines for a time, but they were so uneconomical that they could not have earned their way without government help.

Not until the Boeing 247, an all-metal monoplane, appeared in 1933 did multi-motor equipment become economically advantageous. The Boeing actually could fly on one motor, and because it was safer and more efficient, operators supplanted obsolete planes with the new type of transport. Soon other manufacturers were producing even more remarkable equipment.

Between 1929 and 1931 there was a period of stagnation in the development of air-line equipment. Designers were busy during this time, but operators had neither the incentive, nor the resources to cast out obsolete units. Had the air lines adopted the new engine cowling perfected by Fred E. Weick, under the auspices of the National Advisory Committee for Aeronautics, they might have saved thou-

sands of dollars. Before the invention of the NACA cowl,
radial engines had remained uncovered, so that the cylinders could have the full advantage of cooling air drafts.
The new cowling was a shell that covered motors so as to
reduce engine drag as much as fifty per cent, without inter-
fering with vital air cooling. This was equivalent to increasing speed from six to ten per cent. In many cases this was
the difference between air-line profit and loss. The NACA
cowl made it possible to attach engines directly to the wing,
where motors belong. Theretofore the air disturbance from
the propeller had made it necessary to suspend the power
plant below the wing. Such a design resulted in loss of
power, but it was necessary until the NACA cowl solved the
problem. The change in design brought about savings to
operators of as much as five cents a mile.[18]

In spite of these advantages, operators were slow to adopt
the new cowl. Weick made his experiments in 1927; it was
not until 1933 that the engine shell became standard on
the air lines. By this time the efficiency of the cowl had
been increased even more, following the experiments of
A. L. McClain, F. M. Thomas, and R. B. Beisel, of United
Aircraft's Pratt & Whitney division. The improved cowl
was provided with baffle plates between the engine cylinders. These plates directed the streams of cooling air to the
parts of the motor that most needed cooling. A " skirt " at
the rear of the engine for increasing or decreasing the air
flow through the cylinders, also raised the efficiency of the
design.

The fourth great advance in technical progress overlapped the third, and occurred between 1930 and 1936.
This was the development of the new anti-knock, high-
octane fuel. Gasoline containing tetra-ethyl lead had appeared as early as 1924, but it took ten years to adapt it to
aircraft use. High-octane gas performs several functions.
It reduces the number of gallons of fuel required for a
given flight, thereby increasing the pay load. It gives the

same amount of power on a smaller engine or increases the power of the original motor. Anything that will increase speed without increase of power is money in the pocket of the operator. Warner estimates that the lines could afford to pay one cent more a gallon for every reduction of 1/100 pounds per hour of fuel-consumption.[14] But the greatest contribution of high-octane gas was the increase of horsepower per cylinder from 60 to 130. It has been said that the Douglas DC ships, which revolutionized air transportation after 1934, would not have been able to get off the ground on the ordinary fuels of even six years before. The NACA cowl and high-octane fuel interacted upon each other to the great advantage of the operator.

Other refinements during this fourth period increased the efficiency of air transports. Retractable landing gear, wing flaps, and the controllable pitch propeller were the most important contributions during this time. Getting rid of dragging landing gear was not exactly new. The early transatlantic flyers dropped off their wheels immediately after the take-off, in order to reduce wind resistance. James V. Martin, who was continually in litigation over patents during the twenties, suggested the use of retractable landing gear, and even used it on a military design. Racing planes of 1920 also were fitted with tuck-away wheels, as were all amphibian planes. The transport-designer did not bother with retractable wheels, however, until the middle thirties. The main reason was that at slower speeds the added weight of the retracting device did not compensate for the slight gain in speed. But when the speed of air transport was increased, resistance of the landing gear was enough of a problem to be worth study. The result was the adoption of the retractable gear. First appearing on the Boeing single-engined Monomail of 1929, it was not in general use until 1933. Lockheed (Loughead) used it on his famous Orion ships, but that was two years before the transport operator was willing to put it into regular use.

Wing flaps are also an old story. Originally used by the English in 1914 on an experimental combat ship, they were considered mainly as a form of brake. Flaps are hinged panels at the trailing edges of the wings. By increasing wind resistance during landings, they permit fast ships to land safely in smaller areas. The real use of the flap, however, is not as a brake, but as a means of modifying the wing loading and foil so that fast ships may take off, as well as land, at speeds within control of the ordinary pilot. They appeared to such good advantage on the winning Curtiss Tanager and Handley-Page ships in the Daniel Guggenheim competition in 1929 that designers for the first time took them seriously. Not until 1934 did they meet with general approval, however, and the Douglas of that year was the first liner to make them standard equipment.

One problem of the operators had been the excessive vibration after engine failure. On the old transports, when an engine " cut out," the rush of air against the " dead " propeller made it whirl, in the same way that a windmill is turned by the breeze. Not only did this cause further damage to the engine, but the propeller might whirl so fast as to tear itself from its mount. In addition, the drag of the dead propeller destroyed a certain amount of lift and control. The controllable pitch propeller counteracted these defects. By " feathering " the blades so that they presented a cutting edge to the air, the propeller could be held motionless. In some cases the reduction in drag permitted the other engine not only to hold level flight, but actually to climb with full load near sea level.

The last important technical development of recent times had been the perfection of internally braced wings. The early biplanes were a mass of bracing wires and spars, adding untold drag to the plane. Wartime ships reduced some of this external bracing, but still depended upon wires and struts. At that time such construction had its advantages. External bracing is strong, accessible, and easily adapted to mass production. Furthermore, until speed becomes a premium, the advantages of external bracing compensate for the added drag. Even today, the slower planes stick to this principle. But when speeds get up around two hundred miles an hour, reduction of drag, through smoother design, becomes very important.

Internal bracing is only the perfection of an old idea. John Moisant, the pioneer birdman, flew a ship employing many of the principles of design used today, including all-metal construction, a form of rigid wing bracing, and air-cooled power plant. Anthony Fokker, the Dutch designer, whose war planes swept the skies in 1917–18, was working on the internally braced wing when Germany surrendered. A few of his Fokker D–8's actually saw service. They were high-wing monoplanes with a very thick, strong wing requiring no outside bracing. The German Junkers ships used the same principle. Cantilever or cellular construction was applied to make a thick, tapering, very strong, self-contained wing. A few Junkers were tried out on the mail routes in the early twenties and no doubt gave the necessary impetus for similar development in this country.

The first American designer to take up internal wing bracing was William Bushnell Stout, grandson of David Bushnell, pioneer submarine inventor, whose undersea "Turtle" was used against the British fleet in the Revolutionary War. It was Stout who interested Ford in aviation, as described in Chapter IX, and in the twenties he was the foremost American designer of transport planes. His tri-motor monoplane, which became standard equipment on many air lines, incorporated the internal-bracing principle. It had an enormously thick wing for that day, but neither the Stout plane nor its prototype, the Junkers, was the ultimate in internally braced wing design. In the modern plane the covering is more than a mere surface area. The modern ship is of the "stressed skin" type, meaning that the covering itself contributes to the structural strength of the plane. The Ford-Stout tri-motors were sometimes called "Flying Washboards" because the covering, or skin, was corrugated in the direction of the slip stream (see picture). These corrugated ridges gave lateral rigidity to the wings, but longitudinally the wing was as flimsy as an accordion and had to be braced from within with heavy longerons, or beams, running the length of the wing. The Fokker was more nearly the stressed-skin ship, which was later to supersede all other types in transport design. Fokker used plywood veneer for covering the wings, but the fuselage was still of orthodox construction.

The Lockheed Vega was the first true stressed-skin, cantilever monoplane. The favorite of famous fliers, including Sir Hubert Wilkins and Wiley Post, it was the fastest ship of its day. A few were built for commercial use on one or two lines in the South, and the speed of 160 miles an hour impressed the designers of transport ships. The Vega appeared in 1927. It was not until 1933, however, that all-metal, cantilever, stressed-skin construction was adopted by the transport industry.

One or two other developments should be mentioned in reviewing technical progress. The double rudder has become more and more popular. The big Caproni and Handley-Page bombers used multiple rudders during the First World War. The objective was to provide more control surface without setting up too much stress in one place. Sometimes the designer of multi-motor equipment set his rudders in the slip streams of the outboard engines so that the added pressure increased maneuverability, but the Lockheed Electra, a fast little transport adopted by several lines, notably Northwest Airways, was the first to use the double rudder scientifically. The Electra designers placed the rudders at the very ends of the rear wing, or stabilizer, where they acted like the sides of a sluice. The air, instead of sliding off the edges of the stabilizer, was kept on the control surface. Furthermore, as the rudder projected as far above the stabilizer as below, air pressure against the steering control was balanced so that there was less twist and stress. Unfortunately, the early Electras failed to overcome tail-surface flutter, and after a serious crash early in 1938, the double rudder fell into temporary disrepute.

The last great engineering advance was the conquering of sound. To the pilot the roar of the motors is a reassuring song. To the passenger it is only a pain in the eardrum and a destroyer of conversation. In 1931 Dr. Stephen J. Zand was invited to experiment on the Curtiss Condor, the slow but luxurious biplane transport favored by Eastern Air Transport. Dr. Zand cut sound within the cabin from 115 to 60 decibels. In the layman's language that meant that the cabin, when Dr. Zand was through with his work, filtered in only one fifty-thousandth of the former sound energy. Today transports are as quiet as railroad trains. Many passengers would consider this the most important development of all, and as the attitude of the passenger is important to the operator, the reduction of sound is of more consequence than the technical engineer might admit.

How all these developments have affected air transportation is shown in the following table:

TOTAL COSTS DIRECT AND INDIRECT [15]	COSTS PER MILE IN CENTS	COSTS PER TON MILE
De Haviland 4 (early mail plane)	48.3	161.0
Boeing 40 (single engine, passgr. & mail)	43.6	72.7
Ford Tri-motor	69.3	43.3
Lockheed Vega	38.1	56.5
Boeing 247 (1st modern transpt., 2 motors)	51.9	37.2
Douglas DC–3	68.6	27.4

Note that the much smaller De Haviland was only slightly cheaper to move through the air than the giant DC–3 (48.3 cents a mile as against 68.6), but that the DC–3 carried its load at only about one sixth the cost (27.4 cents, as against 161 cents). Translated into groundling terms, this would mean that if there were two trucks using about the same amount of gas and oil, one (the DC–3) could carry six times as much as the other (De Haviland). Dr. Warner, who compiled this data, assumes that the old De Haviland would be working under the same conditions as the modern plane (high-octane fuel, paraffin oil, etc.), which of course shows up the old equipment to much better advantage.

Since airplane efficiency is so important for profitable air-line operation, no history of commercial aviation would be complete without some mention of how such equipment was developed. There is a tendency to view the various phases of aviation separately. Thus, the student of economics concentrates his attention upon that phase of air-line development. The engineer sees aviation in terms of technological progress. The historian emphasizes political and legislative changes. The military man ignores civil aviation altogether. Actually, all of these aspects are only part of the story of the air lines. The following chapters are concerned with the development of modern equipment and its influence on air travel.

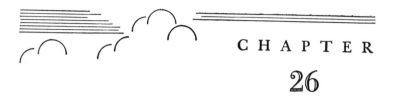

CHAPTER

26

They Made the Sky Ships

Oh, where are the planes of yesterday?
The winds have blown them all away —
Or was it that they did not pay?
Oh, where are the planes of yesterday? [1]

So wrote William B. Stout in 1932, at the time that his tri-motor transport was standard equipment on three of the major air lines. Waggish Designer Stout was one of the first to point out that his own sturdy ship was not the answer to the operator's prayers. " A plane must support itself in the air financially, as well as mechanically," [2] added Stout. For the engineer knew that the equipment of 1932 was expensive to operate, and he was fully aware that air lines could never become prosperous without further help from the designer.

The perfect airplane design would still be useless, however, without sufficient power to pull it through the air, and motors are just as important to air-line development as the planes themselves. Sir George Cayley understood this as far back as 1809, when the pioneer aeronautical engineer was drawing plans for a flying machine. The Cayley wing employed many of the aerodynamic principles in use today, but even had Sir George's craft been capable of flight, it could never have left the ground with the motors available at that time. There are engineers who believe that Henson's aerial carriage of 1843 was aerodynamically sound, and that the scientist might have forestalled the Wrights by sixty years, given the light-weight, internal-combustion engine. Henson had to depend upon steam for power, and although he devised the most efficient engine of his day, he was never able to reduce the ratio to less than thirty pounds per horse-power.[3] That was a remarkably light steam engine, but the power-weight ratio was still too high for heavier-than-air flight. Not until weight was reduced to within four or five times the horsepower did aircraft-builders make machines that could fly.

It is evident, then, why the development of airplane motors is fully as important as progress in wing design. The objective has been to build a motor producing the maximum power with a minimum of weight and fuel-consumption. Since motors dissipate power when they are over-heated, one of the pressing problems of the engineer was the proper cooling of such high-speed power plants. Early aviation motors were water-cooled, but these little engines were superseded almost immediately by lighter, air-cooled motors, with the cylinders set around a hub, like the spokes of a wheel. Such an arrangement of cylinders, as has been said in Chapter I, presented the greatest frontal area to the cooling drafts from the propeller slip stream. These motors were called "radials," and it was an engine of this type that powered Langley's ill-fated "Aerodrome." The Langley engine, designed by Charles M. Manly, was a five-cylinder, air-cooled radial developing 52 horsepower at 950 revolutions a minute. Its power-weight differential was 3.6 pounds per horsepower, and even a quarter of a century later such a ratio was respectable.[4] In 1903 it was amazing.

The First World War brought back into favor the liquid-cooled motor, since, in spite of its greater weight ratio, it was the only engine that could produce the high power necessary for military craft. The return to "normalcy" after 1918 shifted the attention of engineers back to the radial. Air-cooled motors were cheaper and more reliable, and that made them suitable for commercial use. There were no radiators or water pumps to get out of order or to reduce pay load. The radial motor was easy to overhaul, and there was less strain on the shorter crankshaft. Above all, it was long-lived. No one knows how long such motors will last, but they are good for at least four thousand hours, experience has shown. The only drawback has been the limitation of power output. More power means bigger motors, and bigger radials mean greater diameter and greater frontal resistance to the air. At one time seventy horsepower per cylinder was the maximum performance for an air-cooled engine, but by setting the cylinders tandem (in effect, one radial behind another) this performance has been doubled. Even if this were the maximum of power obtainable from radials, commercial operators were not likely to shift to liquid cooling, because the air-cooled motor, with its low maintenance costs, was more perfectly adapted to transportation needs. Since the radial has played such an important part in air-line development, the men who perfected it have an important place in the history of commercial aviation.

Charles Manly made his little motor by hand, and he was not particularly interested in its commercial possibilities. The father of the commercial air-cooled motor in this country was Charles L. Lawrance, who built small, three-cylinder radials for wartime trainers. Lawrance did not *invent* the modern radial (the Anzani engine used by Blériot on his famous flights in 1909 was very similar in appearance to the Lawrance design), but he did popularize the air-cooled motor in the United States. So efficient was his radial that the Wright Aeronautical Corporation bought the manufacturing rights as a protective step after the war. Lawrance became a Wright director. Soon he and his assistants were experimenting on larger and more powerful power plants. The result of this research was the Wright " Whirlwind." It was a Whirlwind that pulled Lindbergh over the seas to Le Bourget in 1927. Whirlwinds carried daring airmen across the Pacific, Arctic, and Indian oceans. By 1928 the Whirlwind had set a record of more than 8,500,000 flying miles without failure.

The only drawback to the Whirlwind was that it could not produce the high power necessary for military use, since radials appeared to be limited to around 250 horsepower. It was with this problem in mind that young Fred Rentschler and George Mead left Wright to produce the famous Pratt & Whitney " Wasp." The Wasp was similar in appearance to the Whirlwind, but it was designed to produce almost twice the horsepower without a proportionate increase in weight. Soon the navy was standardizing on the reliable new radials, and before long the air liners began to appear with perhaps a big Wasp buzzing away on the " nose," and two smaller Whirlwinds attached outboard to the wings.

One reason for the long life of the new radial was the cylinder valve developed by the Thompson Products Company, of Cleveland. Valves were subject to the intense internal heat of the cylinders, and under ordinary circumstances they could not be expected to last more than 25 hours before " running red." At this point they invariably failed completely. The problem was solved by making the valves of tungsten metal, hollowing them out, and filling them partially with a mixture of sodium nitrate and potassium nitrate.[5] The salts absorbed, and carried away, heat, so that valves lasted four and five times as long as before. The life of an air-cooled motor was between 50 and 100 hours in 1916. In 1940, radial motors were nearly immortal, if properly maintained, and crashes because of engine failure were rare.[6]

All this time, designers were engaged in perfecting more efficient planes, but a number of years passed before motor-makers, engineers, instrument-designers, and draftsmen got together to produce the modern transport ship. Not until all the surplus wartime equipment was absorbed or junked did the aeronautical engineer have his chance. Then, very slowly, the air liner began to emerge. The development of the modern transport has been mentioned from time to time in these pages, but at the risk of repetition, and only to emphasize the importance of technical advances within the industry, it may be worth while to point out progress in the design of the skyliner.

The most famous of the early transports were the Fokker, Stout, and Boeing tri-motors. Fokker became a millionaire before he was thirty by building the dreaded fighting craft used by Germany from 1915 to 1918. After the war Fokker built his ships in Holland, but there was little demand for commercial planes in post-war Europe, and in September 1925 he moved to this country. Backed by the General Motors interests, he was soon delivering planes to operators all over the country.

The Fokker was a monoplane with an abnormally thick, internally braced, plywood-covered wing. Pilots said that at excessive speed the Fokker " shed its shingles," but the plane established enviable records for safety and reliability. It was a single-engined Fokker " Universal " that first carried mail over CAM–1. Fokkers flew across the seven seas and many of the air-line operators selected Fokker tri-motor transports as their earliest equipment. Tony Fokker even presaged the day of four-motor transports when, in 1929, he built his gigantic F–32, which was ten years ahead of its time. Not until 1940 did four-motor transports appear on the airways. The F–32 was altogether too large for the traffic of its day, and no operator could have afforded its maintenance. Dour old " Pop " Hanshue summed up the attitude of the operator when he saw the F–32 for the first time while he was being importuned to merge his line with Transcontinental Air Transport. During the merger discussion the big four-motor Fokker transport appeared overhead, filling the air with the thunder of two thousand stampeding horses. All the directors rushed to the window, except " Pop " Hanshue. An official of TAT turned to him.

" Look," shouted the director, pointing to the lumbering craft. " Isn't she marvelous? "

" Hmph," growled " Pop," squinting out of the window. " She's marvelous, all right — and leaking gas at every pore." [7]

Fokker planes went into eclipse after the Knute Rockne crash of 1931. Bureau of Commerce inspectors suspected dry rot in the wooden internal wing construction of the TWA liner. Operators denied this, maintaining that the accident was caused by ice on the wing, but inspectors insisted that henceforth Fokker transports were to be given periodic examination. As the plywood wing covering made such inspection extremely costly, operators began to replace Fokkers with more convenient equipment. That was the end of this excellent ship.

Rival of the Fokker was the Stout all-metal, tri-motor monoplane, later manufactured by Henry Ford. For years, these great " tin geese " wallowed along the air lanes, carrying passengers and mail safely, if noisily and expensively, day in and day out, in fair weather and foul. They defied time, and as late as 1940 there were still Stout-designed ships lugging oil pipe and freight across the jungles of South America. [8]

William B. Stout, designer of the ship, was the Buster Brown of the aircraft industry. Eccentric, a great joker, and unpredictable, he was the delight of his colleagues. After attending the University of Minnesota, Stout wrote aviation copy for the Chicago *Tribune*. He saw his first airplane when Glenn H. Curtiss brought the " June Bug " to St.

Paul for an exhibition in 1910. Then and there Stout made aviation his career. He founded, and edited, the influential *Aerial Age* magazine, leaving this position to build bicycles and automobiles for the Scripps-Booth Motor Company of Detroit. Alvan Macauley hired Stout to take charge of Packard's wartime aeronautical division, but the brilliant young engineer left in 1917 to become technical adviser for Howard Coffin, head of the Aircraft Production Board.

All this time Stout had been dreaming of a super airplane. During the war he experimented with the ubiquitous De Haviland 4, and he reached the conclusion, concurrently with Junkers in Germany, that the spars and bracing wires of wartime planes reduced speed materially and were entirely unnecessary. Using his own funds, he built a strange contraption on the lines of a vampire bat. Its most prominent feature was a thick wing, minus external bracing. C. W. Nash, the automobile-manufacturer, was interested, and he backed Stout to the extent of one 150-horsepower Hispano-Suiza engine. With Lieutenant Jimmy Johnson at the controls, the Bat Wing made a successful flight.

Stout then went to R. L. Stranahan, president of the Champion Spark Plug Company, who helped Stout finance the Stout Engineering Laboratories. In 1921 Stout completed an improved Bat Wing, powered with a 200-horsepower Packard engine, and Bert Acosta, the famous test pilot and long-distance flier, put the ship through its paces. Intending only to taxi it the first time, Acosta was so pleased with the way it handled that he took off. The navy encouraged the inventor with an order for a twin-engined torpedo plane, and in building the ship Stout used metal in place of wood veneer for the first time. Eddie Stinson, who had learned to fly under the tutelage of his sister, Katherine, tested this Navy Bat in 1922. Stinson reported favorably on it, but the navy, instead of letting him complete the tests, sent up one of its own pilots, who crashed. The pilot escaped with a few cuts, but the plane was a wreck. The navy rejected the design and Stout lost his $162,000 investment. It was the " bluest day in my career," Stout said ruefully.[9] Although the navy later partially reimbursed him, Stout was " through with the government."

The Stout Metal Plane Company was organized in 1923 around the plans for a new, internally braced, duralumin monoplane of radical design. It was at this time that Stout wrote his famous dunning letter, asking for a thousand dollars which, he assured the donors, they would never see again.[10]

Stout collected about twenty thousand dollars, which was enough with which to begin production. There followed a long period of discouraging experimentation. The plane slowly took shape, but there was never enough money to meet the four-hundred-dollar monthly payroll regularly. Once Stout was at the end of his rope, unable to raise money enough to pay his men, when he received a check for a thousand dollars from a toy company, as royalty on a little mechanical golfer he had contrived in one of his lighter moments. The unexpected income was enough to meet the payroll.

There were, however, enough rich men interested in aviation, and eventually Stout acquired considerable influential backing. Edsel Ford bought a thousand dollars' worth of stock, and put in another thousand dollars for his father. Other potent members of the Stout corporate family were William B. Mayo (Ford's chief engineer), the Fisher brothers (Fisher Bodies), Walter P. Chrysler, Lawrence Buhl (Buhl aircraft), J. G. Vincent (co-inventor of the Liberty engine), Harold Pitcairn (pioneer air-line operator and builder of autogiros), R. E. Olds, Harvey Firestone, P. W. Litchfield (Goodyear), C. F. Kettering (General Motors), Marshall Field, William E. Scripps, Sidney Waldon (Liberty motor), W. S. Knudsen, Harold

H. Emmons, Alvan Macauley, Gar Wood, Horace E. Dodge, and E. D. Stair (newspaper-publisher).

The first plane to roll from the forms was an all-metal "air sedan" powered by a Curtiss OX–5, 90-horsepower, water-cooled motor. Found to be underpowered, the ship was redesigned for a 150-horsepower Hispano-Suiza (Hisso). It made more than three hundred test flights, mostly at Selfridge Field. Today it is on display at the Ford museum at Dearborn.

Stout's most annoying problem was the power plant. There were only three good motors available for him then. They were the OX–5, which was too light; the Hispano-Suiza, which was difficult to obtain; and the Liberty, which was too big. There were two solutions — either to make the plane small enough for the OX–5, or to adapt it to the Liberty motor. Stout decided upon the latter.

His next ship was the "Air Pullman," a single-engined monoplane of excellent design. In 1924 one of these was sold to the government as a mail plane. The sale resulted from a forced landing while the plane was bringing a party of business men and aviation officials back to Detroit from the Dayton air races. Aboard was Professor E. P. Warner of the Massachusetts Institute of Technology, later editor of *Aviation* and a member of the Civil Aeronautics Authority, but at that time making a survey of equipment for the Postoffice Department. Warner was so impressed by the sturdiness of the ship in withstanding the bumps of the emergency landing that he recommended it for government service.

The redesigning for the Liberty motor made it necessary for Stout to seek financial assistance again. Henry and Edsel Ford and William Mayo were convinced that Stout was on the right track, and they answered Stout's appeal. Ford leased to Stout a large field at Dearborn and then financed a small factory on the site. Here was built the "Air Transport," first ship to carry the mail under private contract after the passage of the Kelly Bill in 1925. Ford bought the first five transports for his new air line between Chicago and Cleveland.

The Cleveland air line was started as a private express service in April, but it was used to transport passengers after July 1, 1925. Later that month, Ford approached Stout with an offer to buy out Stout Metal Plane at two dollars for every dollar invested by stockholders. On July 31 the little factory was closed down for inventory, and when it reopened on August 3, it was under the Ford ownership, with Stout remaining as an officer and adviser. There was no public announcement of this change of administration until a squib appeared in the *Ford News* of August 8.

Only eight of the Liberty " Air Transports " were built, although they were so widely used that there was an impression of quantity production. Ford called the Air Transport " the most highly developed airplane in America," and " the most logical, dependable and safe." [11] That this was no exaggeration is attested by the fact that there was never even a serious injury to a passenger on a Ford ship (the planes became known as " Ford Tri-Motors " after the Ford purchase).

The next development was an eight-place tri-motor, announced for December 1925, but not available until June 1926. The ships were to be powered by the new Wright Whirlwinds. On January 17, Sunday morning, the Dearborn factory was destroyed by fire of mysterious origin, and thirteen motors were lost. Between January and June, when the new tri-motors appeared, all the Ford air-line services were performed by the two Liberty transports which Ford had retained. There were no other ships available as reserves, and so these dependable monoplanes were kept in constant service, one on each of the lines (Detroit-Cleveland and Detroit-Chicago). They were inspected each night, but were flown every day, rain or shine, without rest or favor. One year later they were still in regular use, after nearly 150,000 miles of service without a single fatality and on a 96.6-per-cent perfect schedule. With such a record, it is no wonder that the air-line operator was impressed with the Ford plane.

After the old hangars burned, Ford built a fine new factory near the same site, and work went ahead on the tri-motor. Early in the spring it was tested by Major R. W. Schroeder, then chief test pilot for Ford and later a United Air Lines executive. From then on, the factory produced only tri-motors. At the time, they were the largest commercial airplanes in the United States. Florida Airways, an early, but shortlived line, was the first to standardize on Fords (the Liberty type), but other operators soon placed orders for the tri-motors.

Early in 1928 the Ford 5–AT appeared, powered with three 410-horsepower Pratt & Whitney Wasps. Tested in August, the new ships were soon in regular service on such important lines as National Air Transport, Transcontinental Air Transport, Stout Air Services, Colonial Air Transport, Northwest Airways, and Maddux Air Lines. The Ford monoplane was never produced in typical Ford fashion, however. By October 1929, a year after full production, only 135 were in use. Ford did much to stimulate popular acceptance of commercial aviation, but actually he seems to have belied his utterances as to the possibilities of aircraft. For all his encouragement, he himself would not fly. Not until August 10, 1927 did he ride in a plane, and then only as the guest of Lindbergh for a short hop over Detroit. By 1932 he had had enough of aviation, and the factory ceased manufacturing the solid old " flying washboards," remembered so affectionately by veteran pilots.

With Fokkers disappearing from the airways and Ford out of the picture, other designers now attempted to supply the demands of the air-line operators. Various types of ships made bids for supremacy. For a time General Motors tried to sell a huge tri-motor to affiliated lines, with disastrous financial consequences. The Curtiss Condor was another transport ship popular for a time, especially on the Eastern Air Transport and American Airways lines. United tried to standardize on Boeings, with which manufacturing company it was affiliated through United Aircraft & Transport Company. The Boeing 40, a single-engined biplane, it will be recalled, was the first to carry passengers across the country in an enclosed cabin up among the mail sacks. Later, a huge 24-passenger tri-motor biplane made its appearance on the northern transcontinental route. It was designed to clear the mountains easily, and its performance was a little better than that of the Ford-Stout. No one was ever killed on a Boeing tri-motor, but the ships ate up profits at every trip and were soon supplanted by more economical equipment. They still appear now and then, however. In 1940 one of these Boeings was still to be seen on the tarmac at Chicago, and another was barnstorming the country.

In 1933 appeared the Boeing 247, a graceful, low-wing, metal, bi-motor monoplane. It was fast and comfortable and a strong candidate for supremacy, but before it appeared in great quantity, an even more amazing ship began to scud along the air lanes. This was the Douglas transport, which was to become the standard equipment of the air lines.

Donald Wills Douglas, whose banker father expected him to be an admiral, turned to aviation one afternoon in 1909, when he left his studies at the Naval Academy to see a historic event in near-by Washington. Orville Wright was test-hopping his flimsy craft for the United States Army at Fort Meyer, and one of the fascinated spectators was seventeen-year-old Don Douglas. After three years at Annapolis, Douglas left the navy to go to Massachusetts Institute of Technology. There is an apocryphal story that he was asked to leave the Naval Academy when one of his model airplanes knocked the hat from the dignified cranium of a passing admiral.[12] At any rate, he was finally graduated in 1914 from M.I.T. and became an instructor there in aeronautical engineering at a salary of five hundred dollars a year. He worked on wind tunnels with Commander J. C. Hunsaker, and a year later helped to design the navy's first dirigible at the New Haven plant of Connecticut Aircraft Company.

Glenn Martin, who now had his own factory at Cleveland, heard of the young engineer, and late in 1915 he offered Douglas the position of chief engineer. He was released to aid the Signal Corps as chief designer during the early days of war defense, but as soon as possible he returned to help design the huge and successful Martin bomber.

With all this experience, Douglas was ready to start out on his own in 1920. Aided by David R. Davis, who later developed the advanced "Davis Wing," Douglas started his first mockup (or full-size model) behind a barber shop at Santa Monica. His first product, the Cloudster, was a failure, but soon he was building crack observation planes for the army. In 1924 a squadron of army planes made a round-the-world flight in Douglas ships, and from then on, success was assured. His commercial transport, built for Western Air Express in 1925, on the same general lines as the army observation planes, was one of the most efficient carriers of its day. Within a year or two the factory at Santa Monica was booming. Douglas later received the Collier and Guggenheim awards for his contributions to aviation.

Until 1932 Douglas had the sense to see that Uncle Sam was the only customer who could buy good planes in quantity. Douglas, therefore, built planes only for the military forces, thereby acquiring an aeronautical education " for which the United States government paid me $19,000,-000." [13] He got into the transport business only after the Fokker and Ford monopolies had been broken.

The great Douglas transports of the DC class were conceived when North American Aviation, which owned 89,000 shares of Douglas, made inquiries for a new type of plane. Transcontinental & Western Air, a subsidiary of North American, had been using Fokkers and Fords until 1932, and Harold E. Talbot, Jr., chairman of North American, knew that United Air Lines was about to adopt the new Boeing 247, which would make the thundering trimotors as obsolete as the horse and buggy. In the highly competitive transport business, that was a serious threat. North American was affiliated with Curtiss-Wright, but all that factory could offer was the clumsy Condor, certainly no match for the new Boeings, except, perhaps, in comfort.

With the whole transport business in a turmoil, Douglas shrewdly saw his chance to open up a new outlet for his ships. The DC–1, forerunner of all the DC's, was designed in five days. Douglas had an uncanny ability in picking assistants not only whom he could trust as friends, but who were exceptionally able. One of these was Chief Engineer Arthur E. Raymond, son of the founder of the Raymond-Whitcomb Tours. It is said that young Raymond figured production and performance statistics while on the train east (he never flew) to sell Douglas to TWA. Raymond's plans called for a plane capable of taking off on one of the two engines from even the highest airports on the route, and it was this feature that sold the ships to the operators.

The first plane of this type to be used on an airline was the DC–2, one of the most " researched " planes ever built. Aircraft pilots were called in to give ideas. The mockup was changed a dozen times. By running wings around, instead of through, the cabin, vibration was kept out and noise reduced to that of a Pullman car. The ship changed all standards of airplane operation, and yet there was really nothing new about it. The innovations of the DC's had been tried out before. The novelty of the DC ships was that they incorporated all these new developments in one plane.

The result was a ship capable of cruising at 180 miles an hour, at an economy unheard of up to that time. It was in this ship that Jack Frye broke the transcontinental record with the last load of mail carried under the old private contracts in 1934.

The public welcomed the new craft as it did the streamline trains later built to lure back some of the airway trade. The Boeing company, which had started out to capture the transport field, saw its beautiful and efficient plane outperformed by a rival whose ship was different only in detail. In vain United Air Lines spent two million dollars to "soup up" their slower equipment, but eventually Boeing withdrew from the transport business. The tables were now turned — Boeing began to concentrate on military planes, while Douglas rapidly took over the equipping of all the air lines. As a result, the air lines agreed to end expensive cutthroat competition by standardizing on Douglas. In 1939 Boeing returned as a competitor, with the four-engined "Stratoliner," an adaptation of a bomber design, and a rival of the new DC–4 for overweather flying with large loads. Between 1934 and 1939, however, Douglas planes had the major airways to themselves.

As long as air lines made most of their profits from carrying the posts, efficient, economical equipment was the most important consideration. When passenger traffic increased and began to supersede dwindling mail subsidies as a revenue-producer, safety became an increasingly important factor. Not until the operator could answer reassuringly the query: "How safe is flying?" could he fill his ships with revenue-producing "loads." That was the next problem to solve.

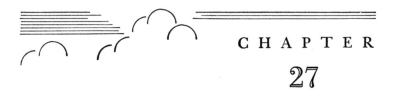

CHAPTER

27

Safety Pays Dividends

THE GREATEST deterrent to air travel has been *fear*. It was fear that rode in the empty seats during the early days of air transportation, when the public took to the airways only for thrills, or because of an emergency. Not until the public accepted the skyliner casually could the operator hope to prosper on passenger traffic. Realization of this brought a note of harmony into the hitherto discordant industry. The cutthroat rivalry of the pre-cancellation days was succeeded by a period of intelligent co-operation. Air-line executives learned a valuable lesson in the early thirties when they discovered that commercial aviation was destined to rise as a system, not as a series of short individual lines. They also learned the value of integration and team work. They found, for example, that a bad crash on any air line affected traffic on all other airways.

The effect of accidents upon passenger traffic is revealed in the records of 1936 and 1937. This was a particularly bad period for the air lines, since there were nine serious crashes. That the morale of the traveler suffered at this time is evidenced by the fact that the passenger miles reported for the first six months of 1937 showed an increase of only

13.9 per cent as compared with the first six months of 1936, whereas the last six months of 1936 were 29.6 per cent better than the corresponding period in 1935. Air travel has always increased year by year, but the rate has been retarded at intervals. Usually these intervals coincide with an increase in traffic fatalities. That is the reason air lines spend vast amounts of money in perfecting the safest possible operation. The investment pays good dividends.

There is an economic limit to safety, however, as Jerome Lederer has pointed out.[1] The pedestrian is well aware that it is safer to cross the street at the traffic light, but if his business is pressing, he may be willing to risk a dash in the middle of the block. In like manner travelers are willing to patronize the more dangerous forms of transportation if the saving in time compensates for the risks. The airplane might be made as safe as the ox cart, but if it thereby became so slow and expensive as to drive busy passengers to the express train and bus, safety would cease to have much value. The problem of the air-line operator has been to cut down risks without materially affecting the one great asset of the plane, which is speed. When air lines struck a balance between speed and safety, they had no trouble selling their services; and when they learned how to perform this service economically, they made money. The operator must see to it that neither safety, speed, nor economy dominates at the expense of the other two.

For example, planes could fly much more cheaply if they did not have to be taken out of service for frequent inspections. They go into the overhaul hangars long before motors need be torn down. While they are in the hangar, they are not earning money, but even more costly to the operator is the maintenance. Aircraft technicians and inspectors are highly skilled artisans, and they receive handsome wages or salaries. Replaced parts eat into the profits — and the oftener a plane undergoes a minor or major overhaul, the slimmer the " nut " (net income) .

Again, profitable pay loads might be increased were the
plane not weighted down with reserve fuel tanks, de-icing
equipment, wing flaps, heavy fire-walls, instruments in duplicate, and extra personnel — all provided to increase the
margin of safety. The operator also sets aside money for
research and experimentation, and he replaces ships long
before they are obsolete, partly for economic reasons, but
also to increase the safety factor.

Soon after soft-spoken C. R. Smith took the helm of
American Airlines, he made himself an abominable nuisance with his interminable office memoranda on air-line
safety. Veterans knew that such fussing was money in the
till. After its unsolved crash of January 1936 (hangar gos-
sip had it that a madman shot the pilot), not a passenger
was killed on an American " Flagship " until October
1941. The company established a legend of safety, and before long the line was carrying one third of all the passenger traffic in the United States.[2] Not all this success was
attributable to safety. Superior equipment, excellent promotion, a brilliant sales campaign, and better schedules all
contributed, but safety was an important factor.

Operators had been talking about safety for many years
without knowing exactly what they meant. There were several lines that had never had an accident up to 1934, including Northwest Airlines (eleven years without a crash),
Pennsylvania-Central (first accident in August 1940), and
Eastern Air Lines (first in 1937); yet flying was a risk at
that period. How much of a risk, the actuary wanted to
know. Measured in passenger miles, the record of the air
lines was impressive, but since the air traveler goes many
miles in a short time, some of the experts were not satisfied
with this criterion. They were much more interested in
how long one might expect to fly before meeting disaster.[3]

One way of determining air travel safety is to compare
scheduled flying with other forms of transportation on a
passenger-hour rather than on a passenger-mile basis. What

the potential passenger wants to know is what chance he has of coming down safely after an hour of air travel, as compared with his chances of alighting safely after one hour on, say, a train. According to figures of the Actuarial Society of America, it was 53 times as dangerous to fly in the mid-thirties as it was to travel the same length of time in a Pullman car.[4] The transport plane was found to be 33 times as dangerous as the day coach and 8 times as hazardous as a trip by private automobile. Based on time rather than miles traveled, the figures are alarming, particularly when it is pointed out that the data refer only to regularly scheduled transportation on United States air lines, the safest in the world.

Year by year, safety records have improved, however. Investigators took detailed notes at the scene of every crash, and the lessons they learned saved other lives. Sometimes the inspectors placed the blame on careless operators and airway technicians. Regarding the crash that killed Senator Bronson Cutting and four others at Atlanta, Missouri (south of Kirksville), on May 6, 1935, inspectors reported that the plane was improperly dispatched from Albuquerque; the pilots violated government regulations; and reserve tanks did not contain the required minimum for forty-five minutes of extra flying.[5] These mistakes resulted in a tightening up of lax supervision, especially after the Civil Aeronautics Authority superseded the Bureau of Air Commerce.

Sometimes the accidents occurred through no fault of the operator, as in a crash on August 3, 1935. Investigators discovered that water had seeped into the airport gasoline tanks after a heavy rain, and a rule went out that henceforth air liners were to be refueled from tank trucks and not from underground storage reservoirs. Equally blameless was Eastern Air Lines on August 10, 1937, when an EAL ship crashed at Daytona Beach, Florida. The pilot of that plane ran into a high-tension wire which an electric company had strung across the field to bring emergency power to a community following a cloudburst. Investigators found that the power company had not given the airport and operators adequate notice.

Occasionally, fatal crashes could be traced to faulty construction. A curious accident due to a minor structural flaw was the crash of a skyliner on the night of February 9, 1937 in San Francisco Bay, two miles from the airport. Spectators saw the big ship circle the field in the twilight as it hovered for the landing. The plane began the usual gentle glide, but instead of flattening out, it continued to drop, until it hit the water and disappeared. Pilot A. R. Thompson and thirteen others were killed in that crash. Investigators found that the pilot and co-pilot had pulled back on the wheel (controlling the angle of descent) so hard that they had bent the wheel post. They had not been able to pull the ship out of the dive because a radio earphone had slipped down between the control column and the seat support. Unable to lift the ship's nose, the navigators had pulled frantically at the jammed control until the crash. While this was a " fluke " accident, unlikely to happen again, the findings of the investigator made the plane-designers eliminate the possibility of repetition.

Careful inspection, improved equipment, and the investigation of all accidents began to cut the toll of casualties, and every year new instruments decreased dependence upon the human element. Yet with the best of equipment, accidents continued to occur. In 1936 and 1937 commercial aviation suffered from a series of confidence-shaking crashes. In one month, from December 15, 1936 to January 15, 1937, there were five accidents. All occurred on well-managed lines. The first of this series occurred on the Western Air Express route between Salt Lake City and Los Angeles. Three days later a Northwest Airlines plane fell eighty miles west of Elk River. On December 19 an Eastern Air Lines plane ran into " soup " (fog) over Camden. Pilot Dick Merrill, transatlantic flyer, brought his ship down on a ridge near Port Jervis, New York, without loss of life, but the makings of a bad crash were there. On December 23 a Braniff liner killed six at Dallas during a test run. Four days later a United Air Lines ship, with twelve passengers aboard, plowed into the mountains near Saugus, California, only twenty miles from the Burbank terminal, and on January 12 Western Air Express suffered its second bad crash in less than a month when it, too, lost a ship near Saugus. Martin Johnson, the famous explorer, lost his life in that accident, although eight others escaped death.

These accidents are described briefly to show the type of crash that was marring the air lines' safety records. Surely equipment could not be blamed for these accidents, since by the end of 1936 all the major lines had standardized upon the superb Douglas planes. Government aids to navigation were not all they might have been, but pilots knew the limitations and acted accordingly. Nor was the operator at fault, for although it is true that he strove to complete as many trips as possible, canceled schedules cost him much less than the loss of the new ships. Some of the trouble was that operators were putting too much emphasis upon speed. This was partly the fault of the Postoffice Department, which was awarding contracts to lines providing the fastest schedules. C. B. Allen, of the New York *Herald Tribune,* and member of the Air Safety Board, suggested that the Bureau of Air Commerce regulate lines so that they could not exceed the bounds of safety by straining men and motors. But the big trouble, according to Allen, was in the personnel. Pilots must be impressed with the need of eternal vigilance, argued this writer, and he pointed out that an " air log," automatically registering course, speed, and performance on a revolving drum, might serve as such a check upon careless flying.[6]

Furthermore, new equipment, which was so necessary for

the efficiency and safety of commercial aviation, paradoxically was the cause of many accidents. It took time for a pilot to learn the idiosyncrasies of a new craft. Douglas ships, for example, were so far in advance of earlier planes that pilots had trouble mastering them. Seldom is new equipment defective, for the government goes to great pains to check new designs, and operators would not think of accepting ships until they had passed the most rigid tests. In spite of all this, new ships still cause trouble.

The death of Nick Mamer may be traced to the use of new equipment. Mamer had pioneered the run between St. Paul and Seattle, which was later taken over by Northwest Airlines. For more than eleven years Northwest flew some 72,000,000 passenger miles over rugged terrain without a single fatality. Mamer himself had flown more than 10,000 hours without trouble. Yet in January 1938 he and nine others were found in the charred wreckage of a new liner near nine-thousand-foot Bridges Peak, just north of Bozeman. Northwest had just purchased new, 225-mile-an-hour Lockheed 14's — the fastest commercial ship then known. They had been thoroughly tested before delivery. Yet as rescuers picked up bodies strewn along the ridge, the Bureau of Air Commerce grounded all Lockheeds for structural weakness.

Lockheed was confronted with the same thing that had ruined Tony Fokker — the blacklisting of equipment by operators. For inspectors found that the new ships were subject to " tail flutter." When wind tore away the H-shaped double rudder, there was nothing for Mamer to do but brace himself for the crash. Incidentally, Northwest Airlines was penalized for the crash by suspension for fifteen days — a very unfair edict of the Bureau of Air Commerce, considering the line's excellent safety record and the fact that the bureau itself had passed upon the fitness of the new planes. At this time the bureau was in its final stage of disintegration, preceding the passage of the Civil

Aeronautics Act. Eventually Northwest won back its patronage, but the Mamer incident was the sort of thing that keeps operators awake nights when they buy new equipment.

On March 26, 1939 eight passengers were killed on a Braniff B-Liner near Oklahoma City. From then until August 31, 1940 the air lines enjoyed seventeen months of record-breaking air transportation, unmarred by even a minor accident. The strange thing is that there were no startling innovations, in either equipment or procedure, during this period. The marvelous safety record was due almost entirely to strict adherence to rules laid down by the new Civil Aeronautics Authority.

For one thing, flight personnel was better and more efficient. This was the era of the scientific flyer — the serious student of avigation. In this connection, the formation of the Air Line Pilots Association has been one of the most stabilizing influences in commercial aviation, for it raised the standards of flight personnel, although the association was once the target of vicious attacks by some of the operators.

The Air Line Pilots Association was organized on April 1, 1931 as the successor to an older organization. Pilots had banded together as early as 1919, when the mail flyers struck against Second Assistant Postmaster General Otto Praeger in answer to his " suicide " orders. Airmen were still too individualistic to join a union, however, and it was some time before there was much progress in actual organization. A group called the Commercial Aircraft Association was formed in Akron in May 1924, but most of the early organizations were shortlived. One of the earliest groups to prescribe standards for commercial airmen was the Professional Pilots Association. Members were required to have had at least four years of experience as commercial pilots; they had to indicate that they had flown carefully all that time; and they had to show some familiarity with transport equipment. More like a society than a union, the group might have become strong had times been more propitious, but not until air-line pilots became more important to the industry could there be an effective union.

The Air Line Pilots Association was formed when E. L. Cord and other operators threatened to lower the status of flying to something only slightly above taxi-driving. Testimony before the Black Committee in 1933 revealed that sometimes pilots received only fifteen dollars a week for their services as transport flyers.[7] Under these circumstances, the Air Line Pilots Association had no difficulty in winning members. The strike against Cord's Century Air Lines indicated the effectiveness of organizing, and in December the group was affiliated with the American Federation of Labor. Since then it has maintained a permanent secretary in Washington, and its president, David L. Behncke, a veteran air-line pilot, is an important figure at almost every hearing on air-line matters. Undoubtedly the Air Line Pilots Association has been a powerful force in promoting safety.

Sound operating policies also affect safety. Following the cancellation period, many lines were on the verge of bankruptcy. On the other hand, equipment was being developed faster than it could be assimilated. Out of sheer necessity, operators decided to end the disastrous competition that was cutting even further into revenues. Co-operation rather than competition became the watchword. Operators agreed not to advertise the safety of any particular line, for experience had shown that when a line advertises itself as safer than any other, the prospective customer does not patronize that line — or any other; he takes the train. Late in 1937, American Airlines advertised: " Is there a low level airway through southern sunshine to California? " The implication, of course, was that a " low level " route was somehow safer. United Air Lines' president, W. A. Patterson, resented this implied slur on such routes as his own, which crossed high mountains and windy plains with just as much safety. A few years before, Patterson's protest would have been to no avail. So correlated were the air lines by 1937, however, that American ceased its new campaign at once.

Again in 1938 the air lines exhibited their growing solidarity. One of the worst hurricanes on record had ripped the New England coast. All communication lines were down. Radio was almost silent. Even the trains stopped, or ran on reduced schedule. During the blow air liners were grounded, of course, but American Airlines, which is the only route between New York and Boston, was ready for business at nine the next morning. Usually American carried about 200 passengers daily on this run. On the two days following the storm, 1,000 patrons fought for seats, and hundreds were turned away. This was in addition to 60,000 pounds of express, consisting mostly of medical supplies, and 57,000 pounds of mail. Unable to meet the demand, American asked the Civil Aeronautics Authority for permission to waive its franchise temporarily, so that it might call in help from other lines. United, Eastern, and TWA responded. The next week was the busiest in the history of the world's aviation. The significant thing, however, is that the lines could pool their interests.

Such solidarity in transport aviation was fostered by the Air Transport Association of America. The ATA is the operators' equivalent of the Air Line Pilots Association. Theoretically the two groups are opposed to each other. A frank pilot would probably say that the ATA was the bosses' club, and that it must be watched with great care. Actually there is a minimum of friction.

The ATA was once part of the Aeronautical Chamber of Commerce, but it broke away in 1936, when the transport industry complained that the central group was putting too much emphasis on manufacturing. Headed by Colonel E. S. Gorrell, a West Pointer, and former president of Marmon and Stutz (automobiles) , ATA does all it can to promote transport flying. It compiles statistics for use by members. It writes joint advertising. It stimulates trade through its Air Traffic Conference. Under the ATA, operators began to effect savings. They standardized on equipment, and in 1936 they agreed to share the expense of developing a new, larger transcontinental transport.

New developments in flight technique also accounted for the splendid record of 1939–40. Pilots spent more and more time learning instrument navigation. The " Link Trainer," a stationary device for simulating conditions of what the layman calls " blind flying," was standard equipment at division points, and the line's chief pilot became one of the key men in the organization, because of his responsibility in picking and training personnel. Kenneth B. Collings, who had been writing an annual report on air-line safety, was able to state in May 1940 that air travel, formerly eight times as dangerous as automobile touring, was only two thirds as hazardous in 1939.[8]

Based on the *passenger-mile* rather than the *passenger-hour* ratio, safety statistics looked even better. Since the reputable National Safety Council believed the former measurement of safety to be more accurate, its statistics make reassuring reading to prospective air travelers.

There was a slump in air-line safety in 1940, following seventeen months of carefree operation, but even so, the operators had reason to be proud. Figures showed that it was somewhat safer to travel by skyliner than by bus or private automobile, while the two-year average of air-line safety statistics compared favorably with that of the railroads. Frank L. Jones, vice president of the Equitable Life Assurance Society of the United States, and an officer in the National Safety Council, said in the summer of 1941 that his company's underwriters were content to use the deaths-per-million-miles statistics as the basis for measuring safety,[9] and since the Equitable is a leader in the insurance business, these figures may be accepted as a criterion.

So encouraging were the statistics that the big insurance companies followed the Equitable in withdrawing restrictions affecting air travel. That the conservative underwriters would put air and rail travel in the same class is testimonial to the progress in air-line safety. The insurance companies withdrew policy restriction immediately after the seventeen-month safety period, but in the fall of 1940 air-line safety again became a matter of grave concern, and any continued drop in the safety norm might bring a return of insurance restrictions.

Transportation Accident Death Rates, 1937–1939 [10]

PASSENGER DEATHS IN:	1939 MILEAGE	1939 DEATHS	DEATH RATE PER 100,000,000 MILES 1939	DEATH RATE PER 100,000,000 MILES AVERAGE 1937–9
Passenger automobiles and buses	436,000,000,000	16,300	3.7	4.1
Railroad passenger trains	22,690,000,000	32	0.14	0.19
Scheduled air transport planes	749,787,000	9	1.2	4.1
Privately operated planes	205,000,000	112	54.6	99.6
ALL DEATHS CONNECTED WITH OPERATION OF:				
Passenger automobiles and buses	436,000,000,000	27,600	6.3	7.2
Railroad passenger trains	22,690,000,000	1,775	7.8	8.8
Scheduled air transport planes	749,787,000	12	1.6	5.5
Privately operated planes	205,000,000	112	54.6	100.0

Transportation Accident Death Rates,
1938–1940

1940			DEATH RATE PER 100,000,000 MILES	
PASSENGER DEATHS IN:	MILEAGE	DEATHS	1940	AVERAGE 1938–40
Passenger automobiles and buses	489,000,000,000	17,300	3.5	3.7
Railroad passenger trains	23,800,000,000	80	0.34	0.28
Scheduled air transport planes	1,147,000,000	35	3.1	2.8
Privately operated planes	250,000,000	237	94.8	86.0
ALL DEATHS CONNECTED WITH OPERATION OF:				
Passenger automobiles and buses	489,000,000,000	29,000	5.9	6.3
Railroad passenger trains	23,800,000,000	2,078	8.7	8.6
Scheduled air transport planes	1,147,000,000	45	3.9	3.7
Privately operated planes	250,000,000	237	94.8	86.4

Eternal vigilance and care are the answer to the safety problem. In 1927, air-line operators believed they were creating a favorable impression when they advertised that it took a ground force of four to maintain one ship in the air. By 1935, there were sixteen employees for every ship aloft, and in 1941, forty groundlings were needed to move a transport from one point to another.[11]

Every trip is as carefully planned as an ocean voyage. The pilot follows a " flight plan," prepared from data compiled by the weather experts and veteran airmen. The flight plan must be followed exactly, and any deviation, except from necessity, calls for elaborate reports to the chief pilot and government authorities.

The ship itself is groomed carefully for every trip. Every three hundred hours it gets a thorough overhaul at one of the shops set up at convenient points. Ships are wheeled into these hangars almost on the minute of the overhaul limit. Off come the propellers, engines, wings, and tail assembly. Jacks raise the mighty fuselage so that the complicated, retracting undercarriage may be plucked away. Surgical hands of master craftsmen reach into the mass of nerve fibers controlling the ship, and out come the radios and instrument panels. Finally even the hull is ripped to pieces, until all the conduits and wires are exposed, like the entrails of a great whale. Every inch of this giant craft is scrutinized.

In the motor-inspection department, skillful mechanics pull apart the powerful engine. Each of the myriad parts is washed in gasoline. Then they start down the line. Parts that are visibly worn are yanked away at once. If nothing appears wrong, the pieces are examined under a microscope. If they still appear to be all right, they are subjected to the magnaflux. This device magnetizes the inspected part. A metallic dust is poured over the surface, and flaws not apparent under the microscope show up at once. Pumps, spark plugs, and ignition system receive just as careful an inspection. Then the parts begin to flow back to the mechanics again, while riggers replace wings and panels.

When the engine is assembled, it is put on a mount and run steadily for twenty-four hours, while an expert checks every possible reaction. Not until then does the crane swing the motor back to the wing nacelle. Rebuilding this plane has been slow and costly. The mere replacing of an obsolete radio, for example, is more expensive than the plane

with which this same operator began service in 1925. But
the air-line executive does not begrudge these bills. He
knows the value of safety. Detection of a flaw during the
three-hundred-hour overhaul means that an engine will
not fail in time of need. And that, in turn, prevents the
crash that is the great bugaboo of commercial aviation.

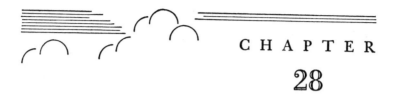

C H A P T E R

28

Peace and War

For a year and a half after the passage of the Civil Aeronautics Act, operators enjoyed the happiest period in the history of air transportation. The excellent safety record and the termination of the terrible depression brought to the airways such a stream of mail and passenger traffic that the air lines began to show respectable profits. There was a new spirit of co-operation and efficiency in the associations of government officials and air-line executives. Best of all, the public began to accept the airliner casually, which was the most hopeful sign that commercial aviation had taken its place beside the railroad and the bus line as an important carrier.

Unfortunately, the Civil Aeronautics Authority regulated the air lines only twenty-two months before the administration began tinkering again with the machinery of control. Following the recommendations of the so-called Brownlow Committee, President Roosevelt announced his " Plan Number Four " for the reorganization of the CAA. He asked for the consolidation of the Authority and the Air Safety Board as a single agency to be known as the Civil Aeronautics Board, under the jurisdiction of the Com-

merce Department. To the air-line operator it appeared
as though civil aviation were again to be thrown into the
political arena. " It is unfortunate," wrote one editor, " that
aviation should be made the guinea pig for academic experimentation, particularly when the experiment may im-
pair the operation of a successful existing agency." [1]

The President went right on with his reorganization plan
despite all criticism. He advanced no good reasons for the
change, although proponents pointed out that there was
some overlapping of duties under the old set-up, and they
maintained that the reorganization would relieve the government of expensive bookkeeping. There was also a hint
that the administration wished to whittle away some of the
prerogatives of the Air Safety Board. Military chieftains
and the Authority itself had run foul of the three-man safety
bureau, and it is significant that the new plan made the
safety board definitely subsidiary to the regulatory body.
Since the air lines had already operated fifteen months under the safety board without a single serious accident,
many aviation experts were for leaving well enough alone,
regardless of expense or duplication. Nevertheless the
President had his way.

Control of civil aviation went back to the Department
of Commerce on June 11, 1940. Senator Pat McCarran and
Representative Clarence Lea, who had worked so hard for
the Civil Aeronautics Act, fought the reorganization measure as best they could. The House did reject Plan Four by
a vote of 232 to 153, but when the President made a personal issue of the proposal, the Representatives fell into
line. The bill passed in the Senate 46 to 34. Both houses
might have put up stronger opposition had the thunder of
war not absorbed the loud protest. On July 1, 1940 the
new Civil Aeronautics Board (CAB) assumed the duties
of the Authority (CAA).

The new plan provided for a quasi-administrative board,
similar to the old Authority, but with an Administrator of

Civil Aeronautics under the direct supervision of an Assistant Secretary of Commerce. The board and the Administrator, when spoken of together, were still technically the Civil Aeronautics Authority, but they were not so closely bound as before. The CAB, like the CAA, prescribed rates, issued certificates of convenience, decreed regulations, and maintained standards of safety. It shared with the Administrator the responsibility for suspending safety certificates.

The independent Air Safety Board was replaced by a Bureau of Air Safety under the wing of the CAB, where it could no longer " needle " the regulatory body into enforcing rules not approved by the controlling board. The safety bureau could only make recommendations, which the CAB could act upon as it saw fit.

There was only a slight change in the personnel of the regulatory agency. Chairman Robert H. Hinckley of the old CAA became Assistant Secretary of Commerce in charge of civil aviation. Harllee Branch replaced him as chairman of the CAB, and Dr. George B. Baker was appointed to fill the vacancy left by Branch's promotion. The director of the new safety bureau was Jerome Lederer, formerly an engineer and adviser for a group of insurance companies. Hester remained as Administrator.

The CAB was under suspicion from the very beginning. Enemies of the New Deal said the reorganization was only another instance of the President's greed for power. Actually there is no evidence that the CAB was one whit less independent than the CAA. Members of the board could be dismissed only for cause. Their terms of office were the same. The dictum of the Humphreys decision placed them beyond the influence of the Chief Executive. True, the safety division suffered some loss of power, but the standards it set were as high as in the days of the Air Safety Board, and field personnel was about the same. The Administrator now had to answer to the Assistant Secretary of

Commerce, who could be influenced by the Chief Executive, but his independence was no less, since the old Administrator served only at the pleasure of the President. Furthermore, Colonel Donald H. Connolly soon succeeded Hester as Administrator, and the colonel was not the type of executive to play around with politics.

The industry was skeptical just the same. There was some overlapping of authority by the board and the Administrator on the matter of safety enforcement, and operators wondered what they would do if they received conflicting orders. A few of the operators who had been pinched before by New Deal manipulations resented the reorganization merely because the President desired it. Other critics were sincere and logical in their condemnation of the change. Wrote one editor:

"Any accidents on the air lines are sure to be laid squarely on the doorsteps of the President and the Senators who approved the plan." [2]

Unfortunately for the CAB, exactly what the industry feared came to pass. After seventeen months of operation without a fatality, during which the railroads had suffered three disastrous wrecks, a Pennsylvania-Central DC–3 crashed on August 31, 1940, near Lovettsville, Virginia. Twenty-five victims, including Senator Ernest Lundeen of Minnesota, lost their lives. It was the worst accident in the history of American aviation. Pennsylvania-Central, which had had a spotless safety record, was exonerated (the crash occurred during a violent storm), but resentment against the CAB flared up, since the reorganization plan had just been made effective.

Within six months there were four transport crashes that took forty-seven lives and cost the operators six million dollars in lost revenue. On Bountiful Peak, fifteen miles from Salt Lake City, a United Air Lines ship crashed in a snowstorm on November 4, killing all ten aboard. The fault was not the air line's, since government observers had failed to report that the radio beam was out of line. Another United " Mainliner " crashed on the edge of the Chicago airport on December 4, killing ten. Faulty piloting appeared to have been the cause. On January 23, 1941 a Transcontinental & Western Air transport, flying on instruments, hooked a wing in a clump of trees. The pilot and one passenger were killed. No one could place the blame. There were four more crashes in the next two months, and the death toll climbed to fifty-four.

The same violent reaction against the administration set in as in the period of army mail operation. At first the operators were as vehement as the opponents of the New Deal, but by the turn of the year they were defending the CAB. It is easy to charge that the President was responsible for the carnage because of his reorganization order, and the opposition in both houses of Congress was quick to strike out with accusations. The upper body was particularly vindictive, since one of its own members had been a victim. Immediately after the Lovettsville crash there was a veritable pæan of " I told you so."

Actually, it is difficult to see how the reorganization of the CAA could have had the slightest effect on the accident record. Safety regulations were even more strictly enforced under the CAB, and personnel was as good or better. Even the air-line spokesmen admitted the injustice of charges against the CAB. Nevertheless the rumor persisted that the reorganization was responsible for the series of horrible crashes.

On February 27, 1941 an Eastern Air Lines ship crashed near Atlanta, killing seven and injuring nine, including Captain E. V. Rickenbacker. Next day Senator Clark of Missouri promised that his committee investigating the death of Senator Lundeen would begin special hearings on the air-transport situation. The Senator charged that there was " confusion " in the regulations. Senator McCarran called the Atlanta crash " legalized murder " resulting from improper enforcement of regulations. Coming from the father of the Civil Aeronautics Act, this was a serious accusation. To many an average citizen it was clear that the reorganization of the CAA was the root of the evil. This is not at all clear to the student, but it *is* clear that Plan Four was a convenient peg upon which to hang the blame.

The eight air-line accidents once again resurrected that old devil Fear. A rumor spread that the famous DC–3's, standard on most important air lines, had bad stalling characteristics. The National Advisory Committee for Aeronautics even investigated the charges, but since the same ship was standard when the air lines established their seventeen-month safety record and were the darlings of all who knew planes, the argument was not valid. Others maintained that aircraft factories were sending so much material to European battle fronts that airliners were being operated too long on defective replacements. There is not the slightest evidence to show that operators had difficulty getting parts, and the fact is that of the eight crashes, only one could be blamed on structural failure (and that was a non-fatal crash near Charleston, West Virginia).

There were three explanations for the series of crashes. They were the law of averages (it was time for at least one crack-up after the perfect record of 1939–40); increased schedules and traffic (more flying means more chance of accident); and the human element. The last is most important. After seventeen months of safe flying, pilots may have relaxed from the required "eternal vigilance." This human failing might be blamed for the Chicago crash, and possibly the St. Louis accident resulted from the same type of carelessness.

The accidents of 1940 and early 1941 might have had the same disastrous effect upon traffic as the crashes of 1936 and 1937. Only the war kept the traffic curve from breaking. By 1941 so many were depending upon the air lines in the defense effort that there was talk of limiting service to those who could prove the necessity for air travel. Ordinary travelers had to get reservations well in advance.

Although it may appear from the accident record that flying was no longer safe in 1941, such was not the case. Based on passenger-mile statistics, air transportation was still safer than riding in one's own motor car. By the spring of 1941, air-line accidents dropped again, and the insurance companies continued to write policies without restrictions. The executive of one of the largest companies said in the summer of 1941 he believed that air transportation would have temporary safety lapses, but that it was destined to be the safest form of modern travel.

Every year the engineer reduces the hazard of flying. Weather, once the great enemy of safe air transportation, was given a stiff body blow with the development of instrument flying. For years pilots have followed radio beams to their destinations, but the radio beam is useless in effecting a "blind" landing when weather shuts out familiar lights or markers. For fifteen years technicians experimented with systems that would permit safe landings in fog or sleet. By 1941 they were well on the way to reaching their goal.

Instrument landing was accomplished by Lieutenant James H. Doolittle in September 1929, when the skillful army pilot actually made landings with only the aid of his radio and altimeter. Directed by the airport assistants, a pilot might make successful blind landings if he could depend upon his altimeter to tell him when to flatten for the actual contact with the ground. The old altimeters were only barometers, reacting to atmospheric pressure, and they were too inaccurate and too slow in registering changes to permit of instrument landings. Later a much more sensitive altimeter was perfected, but already engineers had found another solution to their problem.

On September 16, 1931 M. S. Boggs tested a new system of instrument landing.[3] Perfected in the Bureau of Standards, the Boggs system made it possible for any ship to reach the airport safely, regardless of weather or atmospheric conditions. On the landing field engineers placed a " localizer," which was a radio device emitting a peculiar beam. The beam could be pointed in any direction. For some unknown reason, this strange electrical impulse traveled along the ground a short distance and then bent upward at about the angle a plane would follow in landing. If a pilot could keep on this beam, he could come into any airport without once looking up from his dashboard.

Placed in the maze of gadgets on the plane's dashboard, the blind-flying instrument appeared as a small dial with two pointers. With both pointers at zero the ship was on the landing beam. Deflection up or down or to either side was registered by the needle reacting to lateral or vertical deviation. A pilot flying on instruments follows the on-.course beam of the inter-city airways until he reaches the " cone of silence " near his destination. At this point he swings the ship by compass until he picks up the landing beam, which has nothing at all to do with the on-course beam. The landing track is not difficult to find, as one might presume, since the beam fans out after leaving the localizer, and since most systems provide for vertical radio cones that turn on dash lights when crossed. Once on the landing beam, it is only necessary to fly carefully, keeping the two needles at zero-zero and watching air speed and turn indicators to avoid slips and stalls. Another light flashes, meaning that the ship has passed a second vertical cone and is only about forty feet above the ground. The pilot cuts his motors and flattens the glide. Even with wheels and flaps down, the plane is skimming along at about ninety miles an hour — a safe landing speed, but requiring a long runway, even with brakes.

Half a dozen companies are ready with instrument-landing systems. Equipment is similar in principle, but localizers may be permanent or portable, and landing-beam angles may be different for various types of craft. The only drawback is the need for vast landing areas, unobstructed by high objects for several miles from the airport margins. Runways a mile long are an absolute necessity. Only large cities can afford such fields, and too often the established airport is hemmed in by factory chimneys and power lines.[4]

Instrument flying will make aviation not only safer, but faster. If an airport has a normal capacity of twelve arrivals an hour, it is dispatching ships at the rate of one every five minutes. When weather closes in, the airport can safely flag in only about one ship every fifteen minutes, or four an hour. The other ships must circle around until their turn comes for landing. Sometimes planes are "stacked" in many layers above a fog-bound field, and the passenger may be delayed an hour or more. Since speed is the commodity sold by the air-line operator, he is interested in any system that can solve the problem of stacking. Instrument-landing systems do just that.

The new radio altimeter also offered the promise of safer operation. The old altimeter recorded only the distance above sea level, although it could be adjusted for various localities. Thus a pilot flying off his course might skim a mountain peak with only a hundred feet of clearance, while his meter recorded his altitude as three thousand feet. What the pilot is interested in is not his altitude so much as his clearance above obstacles. The new altimeter throws radio waves down and then registers the distance above the ground by the "bounce," or reflection. It is similar to the electrical sounding device used on steamships, and it is so sensitive that it will react violently if a plane flying down the Hudson River crosses over the Washington Bridge at eight hundred feet.

The most advertised method of beating the weather hazard has been high-altitude flying. "Overweather" air transportation was first attempted by Transcontinental & Western Air and by Pan American Airways System. TWA's "Stratoliners" crossed the country at altitudes up to twenty thousand feet, which is high enough to avoid local disturbances. The ships were thirty-three-passenger adaptations of a four-motored "flying fortress" bomber designed and built at the Boeing plant in Seattle. Known as the Boeing 307, these transports cruised at 220 miles an hour in the smooth upper air. To counteract the effects of high altitude, cabins were supercharged to approximate terrestrial pressures. Had the war not drained all available aircraft into military service, TWA's "Stratoliner" would have been the model for many similar transports, for by 1940 air transportation was ready to expand into new fields.

By July 1938, operators were ready to emulate the railroads by building a great terminal in New York City. Within a year this Grand Central of the air lines began to bustle with activity. Appropriately enough, the Union Air Terminal faced the country's largest railroad station, across Park Avenue at Forty-second Street. The building was completed just in time to accommodate the enormous increase in passenger traffic.

The growing popularity of air travel was accompanied by a growing independence of mail payments. When the private operators took over the air lines in 1926, they were entirely dependent upon mail subsidy for revenue. At the time of the cancellations, great air lines were getting as much as seventy per cent of their income from Uncle Sam. By 1941, however, mail amounted to less than one third of the revenue. It still represented the difference between profit and loss, and no line could have got along without it, but no longer could operators be accused of living off government subsidies. There was no subsidy. Furthermore, the lines had developed another source of income. This was air express, which for many years furnished a small percentage of revenue, but which became of considerable importance with the all-out defense program.

Air express was almost as old as the air lines. It was started in September 1927, largely upon the suggestion of Robert E. N. Cowie, president of the American Railway Express Company. Cowie had been trying to arouse interest in air express since 1921. The subject has been ignored heretofore in this book because it was not a very important factor in the development of the air lines, and because it accounted for only 2.6 per cent of total air-line revenue up to 1936.[5] Since then, however, it has grown faster than either mail or passenger traffic, and with the development of special express planes this service may some day be the big money-maker for the operators.

Before 1936 all air express was carried by two companies. The larger was Railway Express Agency, owned jointly by the railroads, which had agreements with fourteen air-line operators. Railway Express picked up and delivered parcels sent over this air-line system. It kept all accounts, paid part of the advertising, and provided a C.O.D. service. Its " take " from air-express traffic was 12.5 per cent, after subtracting out-of-pocket expenses. What was left went to the operators.

The other big agency was General Air Express, which was an association representing six air lines. It was not a corporation, since the terms of the Black-McKellar-Mead Law prohibited air-mail operators from owning stock in any corporation connected even remotely with commercial aviation. Otherwise General Air Express operated much as did Railway Express. After 1936 there was a shake-up in the express business. Railway Express won away American Air-lines and Eastern Air Lines, leaving only TWA and three small lines to General Air Express.

It cost the customer from two to eight times as much to send a package by air as by rail. Up to one pound, even the air-mail rate was less than air express.[6] Its only advantage was the efficient ground service of the express companies. Air express was largely an " emergency " business, where speed was at a premium, but lower rates might have made the service more attractive to regular patrons.

Two improvements were needed before air express could be important. One was the development of special cargo ships, capable of carrying larger bulk loads more efficiently and at lower cost. Another requirement was the development of a specialized feeder service. Operators soon discovered that a large percentage of air express originated in "off line" communities. Mail-order merchandise for impatient farm women, machinery for out-of-the-way oil fields and lumber mills, special dies for small-town manufacturers were the kind of packages that might be labelled "Air Express." Important operators, notably American Airlines and TWA, were experimenting with special cargo ships when the defense efforts halted development. An efficient feeder service was already expanding before defense could strangle it, and this was a big factor in the increase of air-express business.

One of the new developments in the air-line feeder system was aerial pickup, invented years before by Dr. Lytle S. Adams of Irwin, Pennsylvania, and Dr. Godfrey L. Cabot of Boston. The two scientists were convinced that mail planes sooner or later would pick up and deliver mail and express from small communities "on the fly," much as the fast mail train snatches sacks of letters without stopping. At first they dropped packages by parachute. Later they found that by swooping low they could deliver packages much more conveniently, and just as safely, in shock-proof cartons. Picking up the sacks from a moving plane was more of a problem. They solved it by trailing a hook which engaged a rope stretched between two uprights. The rope was attached to the mail sack, and a system of springs, together with the friction of the hook sliding along the rope, prevented sudden strain. Although crude aerial pickup was amazingly successful, Richard C. du Pont, member of the wealthy Wilmington dynasty and a soaring pilot of great ability, was interested in this plan of bringing air service to isolated communities, and he formed All-American Aviation, Incorporated. In May 1939 the CAA granted All-American a temporary certificate to carry mail and express over a circuit in Pennsylvania, West Virginia, Delaware, and New Jersey. The " milk route " clicked from the start. For the first time villages enjoyed the air-mail advantages of the big cities. All-American's smallest way-station was Glenville, West Virginia; population, 588. The largest was Wilmington; population, 113,000.

Equipment consisted of small, sturdy Stinson " Reliant " monoplanes. Pilots flew the ships over a 1,500-mile course. Swooping over a " depot " (any plot of ground large enough to hold the uprights) at a hundred miles an hour, the pilot signals his assistant to drop the delivery sack. A moment later the trailing hook engages the rope on the incoming sack, and the assistant reels in his cargo. Already the ship is heading for the next depot, scuttling along with the wind at a hundred and thirty miles an hour. In two years of operation there was not a single serious accident. Once a plane nosed over in the snow on a take-off. Occasionally the trailing hook hit the ground and lashed back — once plummeting through a wing. Engineers solved that problem by substituting a long pole for the trailing rope, and though this meant flying closer for pickups, pilots were by then experienced enough to manage all right.

Aerial pickup meant that instead of 288 communities on the air-mail route, 1,440 were now potential mail stops. It meant not only another opportunity for the promoter, but new profits for the main lines. All-American increased its volume of traffic every month. In April 1941 it was carrying 15,000 pounds of mail a month.[7] It needed only a twenty-thousand-pound volume to show profit, and such volume was inevitable. Encouraged by this success, ten other operators applied to the CAB for certificates in June 1941.

The development of aerial pickup might be called the lowest rung on the transportation ladder. The topmost rung was the transcontinental super-service, with giant sky-liners spanning the country in two or three hops, and at altitudes of eighteen thousand feet or more. Just below was the inter-city transport, providing fast service for the passenger traveling only a few hundred miles. Below that was the feeder service, which could be developed not only for the transportation of mail, but as a " local " passenger commuting system, with small ships capable of landing in small fields close to business districts. The picture is not complete, but details of it are rapidly emerging.

Development of such an air-line system would have gone on much faster had the European war not interfered. The first effect of the war was the curtailing of all route expansion. That was no great hardship, since it meant that operators could begin to realize profits on investments without fear of being outmoded or outwitted by rivals. It was only when the United States began " all-out " defense that the air lines suffered.

Early in the summer of 1940 President Roosevelt announced his plan for an air force of 50,000 planes. To the average citizen, who had read of the Luftwaffe successes, this program was reassuring, and that may have been its main purpose. To the men in the aircraft industry, the 50,000-plane program was just loose talk. The United States had yet to produce its 50,000th plane in more than thirty years of aircraft-manufacturing — including the building spree of 1917 and 1918. As best he could, the aircraft-builder buckled down to the task. There was the same confusion as in 1917. Many of the mistakes of the First World War were repeated. There was the same greed and the same selfishness, at the expense of the public. Yet planes did begin to appear. Of all the defense efforts, the aircraft program was the most successful. But it was not enough. At the end of the first year about 10,000 planes had left the shops, as near as expert guessers could determine. That was far from the 50,000 goal, but it was a good start.

By this time civil aviation was beginning to feel the squeeze. Operators found they could get no more equipment, although they needed ships desperately as traffic swelled. British and American military men insisted that every new transport was a bomber wasted. This made good sense to many intelligent readers, for why should the air lines drain away equipment when Great Britain was fighting for her life, and the United States was girding for trouble, should Hitler win.

What these critics failed to see was the air-line picture of 1940. They appeared to believe that the air lines would leave few planes for military purposes. Nine out of ten queried as to the number of transport planes in the United States would have thought in terms of vast fleets. The air-line advertiser liked to have the public think that way. But when Hitler marched into Poland, there were less than 300 transports of all types in the whole United States. There were exactly 358 when the defense program began. All the dozen operators asked was 40 additional planes, to be prorated among them. In terms of 50,000 planes, that did not appear to be exactly a " drain."

Of course the President was referring to small trainers as well as to bombers and battle planes when he made his demand on the industry. Operators were willing to admit that big transports took time to build. They also admitted that the Allies should have every single bomber available. What they did not admit was their subordinate place in the defense picture. Air lines fulfilled a vital function in the preparedness effort. Arsenals, tank factories, powder plants, foundries, and mills were building in every section of the country. Government officials, engineers, and designers had to move fast to supervise and create. A day's delay in the return of important plans from Washington might hold up battle planes poised for the flight that would relieve some British town of further bomb destruction. The air lines were absolutely essential, and every transport ship was needed to turn the tide. That official Washington depended upon the skyliners is attested by the fact that 156 transports leaving the capital every day could not begin to supply the demand for seats. In April 1941, defense authorities saw the light. Though Britain and the United States needed big ships more than ever, the Office of Production Management released 30 transports to the air lines.

War is not good for the air lines, but when it is over, they are ready to expand into a transportation system such as an H. G. Wells might dream about. Pan American Airways already has a standing order for 40 mammoth clipper ships, capable of flying eighty passengers on daily round-trip flights to Europe. Domestic operators have their eyes on skyliners twice as large as the 1941 transport planes, which will carry forty passengers across the country at twenty to thirty thousand feet.

Yet even the war cannot stifle the lusty air lines. They are too young, too obstreperous to be held down long. Air transportation is just beginning. The men who saw it grow from nothing still move in and out of the scenes. Orville Wright, co-inventor of the device that has become, to his horror, an engine of destruction, is still active in the industry. Glenn L. Martin, Donald Douglas, Reuben Fleet, William E. Boeing, and W. B. Stout, who nursed aircraft through the bamboo-and-piano-wire days are still leaders or interested spectators. Even the old pilots are still on the job. Jack Knight, who carried the first night mail, still flies on the west coast for United Air Lines. Leon Cuddeback, who carried the first mail over CAM–5, is a district official of the CAB safety bureau. When David Davis sold his marvelous "Davis Wing" to the Consolidated engineers at San Diego, the man who introduced him to President Fleet was Walter Brookins, the Wrights' first civilian pupil.

An industry as young as that does not need to worry about withering away. It has just begun to live.

Appendix I

THE FIRST AIR–MAIL LAW

(KELLY ACT)

AND AMENDMENTS

H.R. 7064 (The Kelly Act) *An act to encourage commercial aviation and to authorize the Postmaster General to contract for Air Mail Service.*

Be it enacted, etc., That this act may be cited as the Air Mail Act.

SEC. 2. That when used in this act the term "air mail" means first-class mail prepaid at the rates of postage herein prescribed.

SEC. 3. That the rates of postage on air mail shall be not less than 10 cents for each ounce or fraction thereof.

SEC. 4. That the Postmaster General is authorized to contract with any individual, firm, or corporation for the transportation of air mail by aircraft between such points as he may designate at a rate not to exceed four fifths of the revenues derived from such air mail, and to further contract for the transportation by aircraft of first-class mail other than air mail at a rate not to exceed four fifths of the revenues derived from such first-class mail.

SEC. 5. That the Postmaster General may make such rules, regulations, and orders as may be necessary to carry out the provisions of this act: *Provided,* That nothing in this act shall be construed to interfere with the postage charged or to be charged on Government operated air-mail routes.

Approved, February 2, 1925.

H.R. 11841 *An Act to amend section 4 of the Air Mail Act of February 2, 1925, so as to enable the Postmaster General to make contracts for the transmission of mail by aircraft at fixed rates per pound.*

Be it enacted, etc., That section 4 of the Air Mail Act of February 2, 1925, is amended to read as follows:

" That the Postmaster General is authorized to contract with any individual, firm, or corporation for the transportation of air mail by aircraft between such points as he may designate, and to further contract for the transportation by aircraft of first-class mail other than air mail at fixed rates per pound, including equipment, under such rates, rules, and regulations as he may prescribe, not exceeding $3 per pound for air mail for the first 1,000 miles and not to exceed 30 cents per pound additional for each additional 100 miles or fractional part thereof for routes in excess of 1,000 miles in length, and not exceeding 60 cents per pound for first-class mail other than air mail for the first 1,000 miles, and not to exceed 6 cents per pound additional for each additional 100 miles or fractional part thereof for routes in excess of 1,000 miles in length. Existing contracts may be amended by the written consent of the contractor and the Postmaster General to provide for a fixed rate per pound, including equipment, said rate to be determined by multiplying the rate hereinabove provided by a fraction, the numerator of which is the percent of revenues derived from air mail to which the contractor was previously entitled under the contract, and the denominator 80."

Approved, June 3, 1926.

H.R. 8337 *An act to amend the Air Mail Act of February 2, 1925, as amended by the act of June 3, 1926.*

Be it enacted, etc., That section 3 of the Air Mail Act of February 2, 1925 (U.S.C., title 39, sec. 463), as amended by the act of June 3, 1926, is hereby amended to read as follows:

" Sec. 3. That the rates of postage on air mail shall not be less than 5 cents for each ounce or fraction thereof."

Sec. 2. That after section 5 of said act a new section shall be added:

" Sec. 6. That the Postmaster General may by negotiation with an air-mail contractor who has satisfactorily operated under the authority of this act for a period of 2 years or more, arrange with the consent of the surety for the contractor and the continuation of the obligation of the surety during the existence or life of the certificate provided for hereinafter, for the surrender of the contract and the substitution therefor of an air-mail route certificate, which shall be issued by the Postmaster General in the name of such air-mail contractor, and which shall provide that the holder shall have the right of carriage of air mail over the route set out in the certificate so long as he complies with such rules, regulations, and orders as shall from time to time be issued by the Postmaster General for meeting the needs of the Postal Service and adjusting air-mail operations to the advances in the art of flying: *Provided,* That such certificate shall be for a period not exceeding 10 years from the beginning of carrying mail under the contract. Said certificate may be canceled at any time for willful neglect on the part of the holder to carry out such rules, regulations, or orders; notice of such intended cancelation to be given in writing by the Postmaster General and 60 days provided to the holder in which to answer such written notice of the Postmaster General. The rate of compensation to the holder of such an air-mail route certificate shall be determined by periodical negotiation between the certificate holder and the Postmaster General, but shall never exceed the rate of compensation provided for in the original contract of the air-mail route certificate holder."

Approved, May 17, 1928.

Appendix II

THE McNARY–WATRES ACT

H.R. 11704 (The Watres Act) *An act to amend the Air Mail Act of February 2, 1925, as amended by the acts of June 3, 1926, and May 17, 1928, further to encourage commercial aviation.*

Be it enacted, etc., That section 4 of the Air Mail Act of February 2, 1925, as amended by the act of June 3, 1926 be amended to read as follows:

" SEC. 4. The Postmaster General is authorized to award contracts for the transportation of air mail by aircraft between such points as he may designate to the lowest responsible bidder at fixed rates per mile for definite weight spaces, 1 cubic foot of space being computed as the equivalent of 9 pounds of air mail, such rates not to exceed $1.25 per mile: *Provided,* That where the air mail moving between the designated points does not exceed 25 cubic feet, or 225 pounds, per trip the Postmaster General may award to the lowest responsible bidder, who has owned and operated an air-transportation service on a fixed daily schedule over a distance of not less than 250 miles and for a period of not less than 6 months prior to the advertisement for bids, a contract at a rate not to exceed 40 cents per mile for a weight space of 25 cubic feet, or 225 pounds. Whenever sufficient air mail is not available, first-class mail matter may be added to make up the maximum load specified in such contract."

SEC. 2. That section 6 of the act of May 17, 1928, be amended to read as follows:

" SEC. 6. The Postmaster General may, if in his judgment

the public interest will be promoted thereby, upon the surrender of any air-mail contract, issue in substitution therefor a route certificate for a period of not exceeding 10 years
from the date service started under such contract to any
contractor or sub-contractor who has satisfactorily operated an air-mail route for a period of not less than 2 years,
which certificate shall provide that the holder thereof shall
have the right, so long as he complies with all rules, regulations, and orders that may be issued by the Postmaster
General for meeting the needs of the Postal Service and adjusting mail operations to the advances in the art of flying
and passenger transportation, to carry air mail over the
route set out in the certificate or any modification thereof
at rates of compensation to be fixed from time to time, at
least annually, by the Postmaster General, and he shall publish in his annual report his reasons for the continuance or
the modification of any rates: *Provided,* That such rates
shall not exceed $1.25 per mile. Such certificate may be
canceled at any time for willful neglect on the part of the
holder to carry out any rules, regulations, or orders made
for his guidance, notice of such intended cancelation to be
given in writing by the Postmaster General and 45 days allowed the holder in which to show cause why the certificate
should not be canceled."

SEC. 3. That after section 6 of the said act as amended, additional sections shall be added as follows:

" SEC. 7. The Postmaster General, when in his judgment
the public interest will be promoted thereby, may make any
extensions or consolidations of routes which are now or
may hereafter be established.

" SEC. 8. That the Postmaster General in establishing routes
for the transportation of mail by aircraft under this act may
provide service to Canada within 150 miles of the international boundary line, over domestic routes which are now
or may hereafter be established and may authorize the carrying of either foreign or domestic mail, or both, to and

from any points on such routes and make payment for services over such routes out of the appropriation for the domestic air-mail service: *Provided,* That this section shall not be construed as repealing the authority given by the act of March 2, 1929, to contract for foreign air-mail service.

" SEC. 9. After July 1, 1931, the Postmaster General shall not enter into contracts for the transportation of air mail between points which have not theretofore had such service unless the contract air-mail appropriation proposed to be obligated therewith is sufficient to care for such contracts, and all other obligations against such appropriation, without incurring a deficiency therein."

Approved April 29, 1930.

Appendix III

DETERMINATION OF PASSENGER SUBSIDY ELEMENT IN AIR–MAIL PAYMENTS FOR FISCAL YEARS 1931–3*

Item	1931	1932	1933	1934
MAIL IN TON MILES	3,398,785	3,137,968	2,417,796	8,954,549
REVENUE IN PASSENGER TON MILES	3,747,804	7,710,550	10,936,600	22,394,954
TOTAL TON MILES	7,146,589	10,848,518	13,354,396	31,349,503
NET OPERATING EXPENSE	18,534,025	24,621,288	23,861,596	67,016,909
EXPENSE OF AIR-MAIL TRANSPORT	8,814,438	7,121,785	4,320,111	20,256,334
ESTIMATED FAIR PROFIT ON HANDLING MAIL	661,083	534,134	324,008	1,519,225
EXPENSE OF MAIL TRANSPORTATION PLUS FAIR PROFIT	9,475,521	7,655,919	4,644,119	21,775,559
AIR-MAIL PAYMENTS TO CARRIERS	16,943,606	19,938,123	19,400,265	56,281,994
ESTIMATED PASSENGER SUBSIDY	7,468,085	12,282,204	14,756,146	34,506,435
PASSENGER SUBSIDY PER PASSENGER MILE	19.9 cents	15.9 cents	13.5 cents	15.4 average

* Paul T. David: *Economics of Air Mail Transportation* (Washington, 1934), p. 167. By special permission of the Brookings Institution.

In the first item, the former weight basis has been reduced by dividing pound miles by 2,000 (2,000 lbs. = 1 ton). The ton mile is used as common denominator in computing mail and passenger loads. In the same way, passengers have been reduced to ton miles by dividing the number of passengers per mile by 10 (arbitrarily assuming 10 men to the ton — a high figure, but done to give a little leeway because mail can be dumped into a pit, while passengers must have considerably more space). Together these figures give the total ton miles. The net operating expenses are found by figuring up the total operating expenses of the carriers and adjusting by subtracting non-scheduled flying operations. The expense of air-mail transportation is computed by allocating a share of net operating expense to air mail in such a way that it would have the same ratio to total expense that mail ton miles would have to total ton miles. A " fair profit " is then estimated for handling the mail. This is figured at 7.5 per cent of the expense of air-mail transportation, since it was shown in three years of operation that this amount would have given a return of 10 per cent on operating assets, less accrued depreciation. Estimated fair profit is then added to estimated expense of air-mail transportation to obtain an estimate of fair compensation for mail transportation during the preceding three years. Such payments would have resulted in operation at a loss, in most cases, but the air lines were given additional payments. The excess of payments over fair compensation over the three years is shown by this computation to be $34,506,435, when the estimated fair compensation for mail service is compared with the actual payments to the carriers. David concludes: " It is believed that any excess over fair compensation is in effect, if not intentionally, a subsidy to passenger transportation." Note that the ratio of estimated passenger subsidy to fair compensation for mail service grew rapidly during these years because of the increase in total payments in the face of declining volume of mail and an increase in passenger traffic. However, the increase in passenger traffic has brought a decline in the average subsidy per passenger mile from 19.9

to 13.5 cents, although the total passenger subsidy nearly doubled over this same period. And even in 1933 the subsidy per passenger mile was more than twice the average passenger fare, which on most lines was about 6 cents a mile. According to these figures air mail cost the taxpayer about $34,506,435, or about $11,500,000 a year, during the years that Postmaster General Brown was building an air system. Even Representative Clyde Kelly, who had no reason to like Brown, backed the policy of government aid to the air lines. Said Kelly: " We have spent $73,000,000 over the entire life of the air mail service, and never was there a better expenditure in the history of Congress." Furthermore, a depression-minded group of lawmakers had already slashed air-mail appropriation by 30 per cent when Black began his investigation.

Appendix IV

AIR–MAIL ROUTE MILEAGE AND EXTENSIONS[1]

APPENDIX IV

AIRMAIL ROUTE MILEAGE AND EXTENSIONS[1]

Date of Original Contract	Routes Grouped as to Present Holdings	Route	Original Mileage	Extension Mileage	Date of Extension
	United Air & Transport Corp.:				
Oct. 7, 1925	*Chicago to Dallas & Fort Worth*	3	965	73	July 5, 1921
Apr. 2, 1927	*New York via Cleveland to Chicago*	17	736		
Oct. 7, 1925	*Salt Lake City via Boise to Pasco*	5	548		
Aug. 21, 1929	*Pasco to Seattle and Spokane*	32	469		
Jan. 29, 1927	*Chicago to San Franciso*	18	2,030	259	Jan. 16, 1932
Dec. 31, 1925	*Seattle to Los Angeles*	8	1,238	32	Oct. 15, 1928
				120	July 1, 1930
	Total		5,956	484	
	Cord Corporation (American Airways, Inc.):				
Oct. 7, 1925	*Boston via Hartford to New York*	1	200	204	Aug. 1, 1931
do	*Chicago via Springfield to St. Louis*	2	276	269	July 20, 1931
Oct. 10, 1927	*Cleveland to Louisville*	16	351	166	Mar. 2, 1931
July 27, 1927	*Albany to Cleveland*	20	463	162	Feb. 12, 1933
				671	June 15, 1931
				148	Aug. 1, 1931
Aug. 17, 1927	*Dallas & Fort Worth via Houston to Galveston*	21	333		
do	*Dallas via Waco, Austin, and San Antonio to Brownsville*	22	547		
Aug. 19, 1927	*Atlanta via Birmingham and Mobile to New Orleans*	23	488		
July 13, 1928	*New Orleans via Beaumont to Houston*	20	325		
Nov. 17, 1927	*Chicago via Indianapolis to Cincinnati*	24	274		
May 9, 1928	*St. Louis via Kansas City to Omaha*	28	404		
May 5, 1928	*Bay City to Chicago*	27	867	213	Feb. 11, 1933
				167	Feb. 10, 1933
				33	Nov. 27, 1928
				141	Apr. 1, 1929
				151	June 16, 1930
				86	Dec. 6, 1930
Aug. 9, 1928	*Chicago to Atlanta*	30	810	544	June 5, 1931

[1]Black Committee, pp. 1483–5.

Contractor to Whom Route Sublet	Remarks
	Tulsa to *Ponca City.*
	See rt. 32.
	Consolidated with rt. 5, contract let at 9 cents per lb.; upon consolidation took rate of pay of rt. 5.
	Omaha to *Watertown,* see rt. 30.
	Oakland to *San Jose* (discontinued).
	Los Angeles to *San Diego.*
Pan American Airways Co.	*Boston* to *Bangor* (discontinued Sept. 30, 1931).
	St. Louis to *Memphis,* see rt. 33.
	Consolidated May 15, 1931 with rt. 20; see rt. 20.
	Louisville to *Nashville,* see rt. 20.
	Consolidated May 15, 1931 with rt. 16.
	Albany to *Boston.*
	Nashville to *Fort Worth.*
	Albany to *New York City.*
	Original rt. 20 extended from *Albany* to *Cleveland.* With it was consolidated, May 15, 1931, rt. 16 extended from *Cleveland* to *Louisville,* extended on Mar 2, 1931 from *Louisville* to *Nashville,* making one route from *Cleveland* to *Nashville.* The result of the consolidation of rts. 20 and 16 was then known as rt. 20, *Albany* to *Nashville.* This route was then extended on June 15, 1931 from *Albany* to *New York City* and on Feb. 12, 1933 from *Albany* to *Boston,* making rt. 20 extend from *Boston* and *New York* to *Fort Worth.*
	Consolidated with rt. 30, July 15, 1930, see rt. 30.
	Detroit to *Buffalo.*
	Detroit to *Columbus* (discontinued).
	Flint and *Pontiac* added.
	Detroit to *Toledo* to *Cleveland.*
	Pontiac to *Muskegon* (discontinued).
United States Airways (Boeing Air Transport, Inc.) See United Aircraft & Transport Corp., route 18.	*South Bend* and *Fort Wayne* added (discontinued).
	Kansas City to *Denver.*

AIRMAIL ROUTE MILEAGE AND EXTENSIONS *(continued)*

Date of Original Contract	Routes Grouped as to Present Holdings		Route	Original Mileage	Extension Mileage	Date of Extension
Sept. 16, 1930			33	2,405	198	June 15, 1931
					164	do
					305	do
					315	Aug. 1, 1931
					219	do
		Total		7,752	4,156	
	General Motors Corporation					
Feb. 28, 1927	*New York to Atlanta*		19	803		
Nov. 19, 1927	*Atlanta to Jacksonville*		25	619	581	Apr. 1, 1931
					93	July 10, 1931
					51	July 15, 1931
					147	July 20, 1931
					129	Mar. 1, 1929
					18	July 5, 1928
					172	Dec. 1, 1932
Oct. 7, 1925	*Salt Lake to Los Angeles*		4	651	120	June 1, 1930
Oct. 7, 1927	*Cheyenne to Pueblo*		12	204	291	Aug. 1, 1931
					276	do
					{ 315	{ do
					{ 219	{ do

Contractor to Whom Route Sublet	Remarks
	Original rt. 30 extended *Chigago* via *Evansville* and *Nashville* to *Atlanta* with a spur line connecting *Evansville* and *St. Louis.* With this was consolidated, July 15, 1930, rt. 28 which extended from *St. Louis* via *Kansas City* to *Omaha*; henceforth this consolidation is known as rt. 30., *Atlanta* to *Omaha.* On June 5, 1931 this route was extended from *Kansas City*, a stop on the line, to *Denver*, and this extension, 544 miles, sublet by American Airways, Inc., to United States Airways, an independent concern which had been operating a passenger service between *Kansas City* and *Denver* for some time. On Jan. 16, 1932 this route was extended from *Omaha*, its western terminal at which point it connected with Boeing Air Transport, Inc. to *Watertown,* 259 miles. This portion was sublet by American Airways to Boeing Air Transport, Inc.
	Memphis to *Jackson.*
	Jackson to *New Orleans.*
	Phoenix to *San Diego* (discontinued).
Western Air Express, Inc. do	*Fort Worth* to *Amarillo.*
	El Paso to *Albuquerque.*
	Original rt. 33, the Southern Transcontinental, was let Sept. 16, 1930, and extended from *Atlanta* to *Los Angeles.* On June 15, 1931 it received extensions from *Jackson,* a stop on the line to *Memphis* and to *New Orleans.* These extensions formed a route running north from *New Orleans* to *Memphis,* which was joined July 20, 1931 with an extension of route 2 from *St. Louis* to *Memphis.* In this manner rt. 2 was extended to form a through route *Chicago* to *New Orleans.* On Aug. 1, 1931 two more extensions were granted; one from *Fort Worth* whose extension of rt. 12, Aug, 1, 1931, from *Pueblo* to *Amarillo,* the *Fort Worth–Amarillo* extension of rt. 33 connected, giving in effect a route from *Pueblo* to *Fort Worth.* A similar combination was made this same date between the extension of rt. 33 from *El Paso* to *Albuquerque,* Western Air Express being the contractor for the two extensions south from *Pueblo* and the subcontractor for the connecting extensions of rt. 33.
	This route consolidated with rt. 19, Jan. 27, 1930; consolidated route known as *New York* to *Miami,* rt. 19, *Richmond* to *Jacksonville.*
	New York to *Atlantic City* (discontinued).
	Philadelphia to *Atlantic City* (discontinued).
	Washington to *Atlantic City* (discontinued).
	Daytona Beach to *Tampa.*
	Tampa to *St. Petersburg.*
	Charlotte to *Augusta* (suspended).
	Los Angeles to *San Diego.*
	Pueblo to *Amarillo* (suspended) see rt. 33.
	Pueblo to *Albuquerque,* see rt. 33.
{ This mileage not included in group total. }	{ *Fort Worth* to *Amarillo* (suspended) see rt. 33. *El Paso* to *Albuquerque* (suspended), see rt. 33. }

AIRMAIL ROUTE MILEAGE AND EXTENSIONS *(continued)*

Date of Original Contract	Routes Grouped as to Present Holdings	Route	Original Mileage	Extension Mileage	Date of Extension
Sept. 30, 1930	*New York to Los Angeles*	34	3,339		
				285	Feb. 1, 1933
				353	do
	Total		5,616	2,516	
	Pittsburgh Aviation Industries Corp.				
Mar. 27, 1926	*Cleveland to Pittsburgh*	11	140	195	June 8, 1931
	National Parks Airways				
Dec. 30, 1927	*Great Falls to Salt Lake City*	26	509		
	Northwest Airways of Michigan				
1926	*Chicago to Twin Cities*	9	407		
				125	Dec. 15, 1928
				104	Mar. 9, 1930
				382	Feb. 2, 1931
				143	May 30, 1931
				190	June 2, 1931
				394	Mar. 2, 1933
				253	do
	Total		407	1,621	
	Grand Total Mileage		20, 240	8,972	

AIRMAIL ROUTE MILEAGE AND EXTENSIONS *(continued)*

Contractor to Whom Route Sublet	Remarks
	Mileage includes spur line *St. Louis* to *Tulsa*. *Columbus* to *Chicago*. *Los Angeles* to *San Francisco*.
Kohler Aviation Corp.	*Pittsburgh* to *Washington*. Unaffiliated and independent. Cha. Dickinson awarded contract Jan. 11, 1926, which was canceled Sept. 30, 1926. Route readvertised and contract awarded Northwest Airways. *Milwaukee* to *Green Bay* (discontinued). *Chicago* to *Madison* (discontinued). *St. Paul* to *Pembina*. *St. Paul* to *Duluth* (suspended). *Fargo* to *Mandan*. *Bismarck* to *Billings*. *Milwaukee* to *Detroit*. Contract sublet as shown to Kohler, who had been operating a passenger service over this route for some time.

Appendix V

AIR LINES IN THE
UNITED STATES

All-American Aviation, Inc.: Strictly mail, using aerial pickup. See last chapter for details.

American Airlines (see Index): Organized as American Airways, an operating subsidiary of Aviation Corporation, in 1929 from a patchwork air-line system. Came under control of E. L. Cord when he emerged as head of Aviation Corporation, following a financial battle. Name changed to American Airlines and flying operations separated from manufacturing interests, according to law, following the cancellation of the air-mail contracts in 1934 and the re-letting of new contracts under the Air Mail Act of June 1934. Emerged from cancellation period in improved condition, and with appointment of C. R. Smith as president in 1935 embarked on prosperous course. Introduced Douglas Sleeper service, script fares (purchase of large block of flying time at fifteen-per-cent reduction), and superb equipment to lure traffic. Carried 31.5 per cent of all passenger traffic in the country by 1936, and flew more passenger miles than any other air line in the world. Accident record one of the best. Listed as transcontinental line, but actually gets most of its traffic on transverse and short-haul routes. Average passenger travels 382 miles on American, as against 516 on United and 496 on TWA. Serves 63 cities with combined population of 24,000,000 — leaving only 66 per cent of population to be served by all other air lines combined. Headquarters at North Beach (La Guardia)

Airport, New York. Ranked tenth in June 1941, along with best railroad and bus companies, as a passenger-carrier.

Braniff Airways (see Index): Organized in 1930 by the brothers Paul and Tom (financial backer) Braniff, of Oklahoma City, as successor to former line sold to the Universal (American Airways) system in 1929. Operated at loss as a non-mail, passenger service until new air-mail contracts relet, following the cancellation of the old contracts in February 1934. Braniff one of few " Independents " (non-mail-carrying operators) to survive, and only large air line using personal name for a title. Picked up old National Air Transport and United Air Lines route from Chicago to Dallas and Fort Worth on low bid for the new contracts in 1934. Absorbed Long & Harman air lines in 1935, to extend service to Brownsville, Houston, and Corpus Christi, thereby becoming a " Great Lakes to the Gulf " airway and the sixth largest air line in the country. Showed profit every year since 1935, except 1937. Taps fastest growing section in United States and has connections with Latin-American trade at Brownsville terminus of Pan American Airways System. Largely dependent on mail for income (45 per cent), but passenger traffic well above average for the industry as a whole (75.6-per-cent increase in passenger revenue for Braniff; 65.2 for industry). Stiff competition with American Airlines for Texas-Chicago traffic; with TWA between Kansas City and Chicago; and with Eastern Air Lines between Houston, San Antonio, Corpus Christi, and Brownsville. High load factor (proportion of seats filled) indicates successful competition. Flying terrain partly responsible for excellent safety record. Has one of the shortest hauls per passenger in the industry.

Chicago & Southern Air Lines: Successor to Pacific Seaboard Air Lines, organized in 1933 to carry only passengers between Los Angeles and San Francisco. Bid on the route between Chicago, St. Louis, and New Orleans when new air-mail contracts advertised, following cancellation period,

and won route from veteran operators when underbid by
only one cent, although company had never been out of
sight of the Pacific before. Changed name to Chicago &
Southern in summer of 1934. New, young, aggressively
managed, began making profits in 1938. One of safest flying routes in the country. Connects important Mississippi
Valley centers, with branch from Memphis to Shreveport
and Houston. Has no competitors on main route, except
American Airlines over Chicago and St. Louis route. Average passenger haul longer than any line except United,
TWA, and Eastern Air Lines.

Continental Air Lines: Successor to Western Air Express
and Wyoming Air Service, which pioneered this transverse
route in days before cancellation of first air-mail contracts.
El Paso and Pueblo section went to Varney Speed Lines
when route put up for rebidding in 1934. Name changed to
Varney Air Transport, and then to Continental Air Lines
in 1937. Same year, Wyoming Air Service sold the Pueblo-
Denver link. With small, six-place Lockheed ships, Continental began to show profit in 1938, and replacement with
larger equipment increased percentage of revenue.
Branches from Pueblo to Wichita and to Roswell, New
Mexico, added to revenue in 1940, but because of sparsely
settled territory, still 75 per cent dependent upon mail for
income. In 1939–40 had smallest operating revenue in the
industry. About 80 per cent of passenger traffic local. Load
factor low, but line valuable because other means of transportation inadequate. Headquarters Denver.

Delta Air Lines: Organized in June 1929, when C. E.
Woolman turned from crop-dusting to air transportation.
Delta began by carrying passengers from Birmingham to
Dallas. Lost money when unable to obtain a mail contract,
and sold out to American Airways. Woolman went back
to crop-dusting. When routes were readvertised after the
air-mail contract cancellations of 1934, Woolman returned
to air transportation with very little equipment and not

much back of him, except nerve. Won Charleston-Augusta-Atlanta-Birmingham-Shreveport-Dallas route. Controlling interest bought by C. E. Faulk, former publisher of the Monroe (Louisiana) *News Star* and *Morning Post,* with Woolman as general manager. Started out with second-hand Stinsons (safe enough, but uneconomical), but began to make money when Lockheed "Electras" substituted in 1936. Standardized on Douglas DC–3's in 1941 and began to boom. Won Atlanta-Knoxville-Cincinnati route in 1941. Passenger traffic increase in June 1941, 800 per cent above entire 1936 fiscal showing. With no competition on main route, perfect safety record, and one of the lowest passenger-fare schedules in the industry, Delta began to improve low load factor (ratio of passengers to seats) after the adoption of the DC equipment. Dependent on mail for 48.9 of income. Crop-dusting still accounts for large part of revenue.

Eastern Air Lines (see Index): Pioneered by Harold Pitcairn, the East Coast airway (Pitcairn Aviation, Incorporated) went to North American Aviation Company, holding agency for a score of air-line and aircraft properties, in 1929. North American Aviation changed name of operating subsidiary to Eastern Air Transport. Original line between New York and Richmond, via Washington, with two antennæ branching south, one to Atlanta, the other to Jacksonville (both to Miami later). After reletting of air-mail contracts, following cancellation period of February 1934, name changed to Eastern Air Lines, but unlike other operating companies which were forced to split from parent companies by Air Mail Act of 1934, Eastern Air Lines stayed in North American fold. In March 1938 Captain E. V. Rickenbacker, former vice president of North American Aviation and general manager of EAL, became head of the company, when North American retired from transportation to concentrate on manufacture. Under Captain Rickenbacker, Eastern Air Lines became one of most successful air lines in world. Profits up every year since

1934. Only line to make money every single month — a record. In June 1941 ranked with top fifteen passenger-carriers, including railroads and bus lines. Absence of competition on main line, low operating costs, and high fares account for profit. Winter tourist trade to Florida nullifies usual winter slump. Worst month (August) only about 36 per cent under best month (March) in traffic. Since heaviest traffic comes while other lines in winter slump, EAL leases extra equipment from them at this time, thereby saving on depreciation charges. Helps explain why EAL has lowest operating cost per seat mile in industry. One of biggest and most profitable lines, receives only about 20 per cent of income from mail. Routes now reach most important centers of South and East. One airway stretches from New York to Brownsville, via Atlanta and New Orleans. Another route from Chicago to Miami, via Louisville, Atlanta, and Jacksonville. An important branch reaches from Memphis to Tampa, via Birmingham, Montgomery, and Tallahassee; another branch connects St. Louis with the Chicago-Atlanta route at Nashville. Much of traffic still goes over the New York-Washington-Richmond-Charleston-Miami airway.

Inland Air Lines: Organized as Wyoming Air Service in 1930, name changed in 1938, following a reorganization of the company. Wyoming picked up mail routes from Cheyenne to Pueblo and to Great Falls in 1934, following the cancellation period. Sold the short Cheyenne-Denver section in 1937 to allow United Air Lines to touch Denver as a transcontinental stop. Denver-Pueblo section went to Continental the same year. Wyoming received $243,000 for these sections, which enabled it to get on a sound financial footing. Called Inland Air Lines after April 1938, when absorbed Cheyenne-Huron route through the Black Hills of the Dakotas. Smallest passenger revenue and highest mail ratio in industry. Low load factor accounted for by thinly populated territory. Provides fast service hitherto lacking in country of vast distances. Fare scale next to lowest in industry. Operating costs very low. On pound-mile basis receives second highest mail pay in industry.

Mid-Continent Airlines, Inc.: Founded as Tri-State Air Lines in 1928 by A. S. Hanford, Jr., backed by father, wealthy merchant. Originally a non-mail passenger service between Minneapolis, Sioux City, and Omaha. When airmail contracts put up for rebidding, reorganized as Hanford Tri-State Airlines. Won Air Mail Route 16, Winnipeg-Fargo-Minneapolis-Chicago; and AM–26, Minneapolis to Kansas City, via Sioux City and Omaha, and connecting with Bismarck and Sioux Falls branch. Route 16 sold to Northwest Airlines December 31, 1934. From June 1934 until July 1, 1936 line controlled by A. S. Hanford, Sr., but after death of son in airplane accident, elder Hanford relinquished control to Thomas Fortune Ryan III, although still holding a substantial interest. Name changed to Hanford Airlines until August 1938, when became Mid-Continent Airlines. Main office at Kansas City. Connects with four larger systems: Northwest Airlines at Minneapolis and Bismarck; United Air Lines at Omaha; TWA at Kansas City; and American Airlines at Tulsa (to which it was extended in September 1934). Main routes Minot, North Dakota, to Tulsa, via Kansas City; and Twin Cities to Tulsa, via Des Moines, with branch from Des Moines to St. Louis. One of the three lines most heavily dependent upon air-mail payments, Mid-Continent lost money until 1939. New routes to St. Louis and Twin Cities raised low load factor and added to passenger revenue. Fares third lowest in industry. Operating costs per seat mile fourth highest, but being reduced steadily with adoption of more economical equipment. Since acquisition of new routes and planes (super-speed Lockheed " Lodestars ") Mid-Continent on road to prosperity.

National Airlines: Started in 1934 after winning new mail contracts. Field of operations almost entirely in Florida (Daytona Beach to St. Petersburg; Miami to St. Petersburg). In 1938 won a route from Jacksonville to New Orleans; and in 1940 connected this route with Daytona Beach. Smallest operating revenue in industry, but increase in passenger revenue up 109.6 per cent, as compared with 65.2 for industry as a whole. Efficient operation explains profit from low operating revenue.

Northeast Airlines: Incorporated in 1931 as Boston-Maine Airways, under contract to Pan American Airways at fixed rentals. Discontinued in 1932. Operated 1933–7 by National Airways (not to be confused with the Florida enterprise). Control passed to Boston & Maine and Maine Central railroads in 1937. Main routes Boston-Burlington-Montreal (as Central Vermont Airways) and Boston-Bangor-Caribou. About 85 per cent of traffic focused at Boston. Became Northeast Airlines in 1940. Extended to Moncton, New Brunswick, same year. Main base at East Boston. President is Paul F. ("Dog") Collins, veteran war pilot and former executive of Transcontinental Air Transport and Ludington Lines. Traffic seasonal because of adverse weather. Explains why fares and operating costs third highest. Mail pay, on pound-mile basis, highest in industry.

Northwest Airlines: Organized in 1926 by Charles Dickinson, predecessor of present line was mail route between Chicago and Twin Cities. Purchased by Northwest Airways in October 1926. By series of extensions granted by both Republican and Democratic postoffice administrations, company slowly added to mileage until by end of 1934 reached Spokane and Seattle, with branches to Winnipeg (purchased from Hanford) and to Duluth. Completion of lighted airway to Seattle made Northwest fourth great primary route running east and west (others: United, TWA, and American). Has lowest passenger fare per mile in industry. Serves territory thinly populated and severely lashed by winter gales, but saves considerable travel time in country of vast distances and maintains high standards of safety, despite weather hazards. Passenger traffic shows increases every year, but line is primarily a mail-carrier (about one half of revenue) although, on a pound-mile basis, only four lines receive lower payments. Headquarters at St. Paul.

Pennsylvania-Central Airlines Corporation: Airway pioneered by Clifford Ball, who carried mail in 1927 between Pittsburgh and Cleveland. Ball bought out by Pennsylvania Air Lines in November 1930. Company became a subsidiary of Pittsburgh Aviation Industries Corporation, which had minor part in the merger of Transcontinental Air Transport and Western Air Express to form the central transcontinental route. Major H. S. Martin, former president of PAIC, head of Pennsylvania Air Lines until Air Mail Act of 1934, following cancellation period, brought about reorganization with C. Bedell Monro as president. In rebidding on new mail contracts, PAL lost the Washington-Detroit route to a competitor, Central Airlines, but won the Kohler route from Milwaukee to Detroit. Central Airlines backed by old PAIC competitor (outgrowth of Pittsburgh Airways, which tried to wrest original mail contracts from PAIC and bucked merger of TAT, WAE, and PAIC as Transcontinental & Western Air, the central transcontinental airway) . Backed by John and Richard Coulter, sons of Greensburg, Pennsylvania, coal magnate, Central Airlines managed by Jim Condon, co-operator of former Pittsburgh Airways. Pennsylvania Air Lines & Transport Corp. (the new name, following passage of Air Mail Act of 1934) and Central Airlines battled for two years. PAL, as veteran operator, had passenger traffic, but Central had mail. Neither made money. PAL tried to buy out rival, but prevented by terms of Air Mail Act. After Ohio valley flood of March 1936, Central ready to sell out, and government approved. Merged November 1, 1936, to become Pennsylvania-Central Airlines Corporation. PCA became fourth largest passenger-carrier. Heaviest traffic on main line, Nor-folk-Washington-Pittsburgh-Cleveland-Detroit. Branches to Chicago and Milwaukee, with passenger service Pitts-burgh-Baltimore and Pittsburgh-Buffalo. Granted Bir-mingham-Knoxville-Charleston-Pittsburgh branch late in 1940. As quickest service between Washington and the booming manufacturing cities of Middle West, PCA prof-ited more than any other line from rearmament and defense activity. One of safest lines in country (no accident until August 31, 1940), despite bad flying terrain. No competi-tion on main route. Fares and operating revenue about average. A prosperous line.

Transcontinental & Western Air, Inc. (see Chapter 14, Index): Formed by merger of Transcontinental Air Transport (organized in 1928 as a non-mail, air-rail pas-senger line), Western Air Express (one of the first five air-mail contractors), and Pittsburgh Aviation Industries Cor-poration (which pioneered state of Pennsylvania), TWA began to operate the central transcontinental airway late in 1930. Reorganized after cancellation of air-mail con-tracts in 1934, line appeared with only an " Inc." added to original name and won old route at lower rate of pay. Sandwiched between two other transcontinental lines, and inadequately served by feeder systems, TWA never big money-maker, but stands out as an efficiently operated com-pany. Has served as training school for other lines in main-tenance and operation. Pioneered with super air liners (Douglas DC–2's in 1934; Boeing four-motored " Strato-liners " in 1939), " overweather " flying, twenty-four-hour coast-to-coast service, many safety devices. Has made a little money every year since 1935. Controlled at various times by North American Aviation Company, General Motors, and Wall Street banking houses. Now controlled by Presi-dent Jack Frye, Vice President Paul Richter, and Round-the-World Flyer Howard Hughes (who owns largest block of stock — about 30 per cent). Has second longest passenger-trip average. One of lowest operation costs, based on seat mile. Fares below average.

United Air Lines (see Index): Pioneered by the government mail flyers in the early twenties, " the main line " was handed over to private operators in 1927. Western section went to Boeing Air Transport; eastern leg to National Air Transport (which also flew from Chicago into Texas). Route consolidated by United Aircraft & Transport, holding company which controlled air lines, plane factories, and engine plants. Varney line from Salt Lake City to Pacific Northwest, and Pacific Air Transport flying between Seattle and San Diego added to system. Lost mail contracts after cancellations of 1934, but regained them after air lines split from manufacturing affiliates. Dominated industry until 1931–2, when some traffic drained away by new competitors. Still heaviest mail-carrier and most direct east-west route for transcontinental passenger traffic, which accounts for its longest average passenger-trip record. Lowest mail payments on pound-mile basis. With its Seattle to San Diego division and extensions into the Pacific Northwest, dominates the west coast.

Western Air Lines (see Index): Until April 17, 1941 known as Western Air Express Corporation, one of the original five private mail contractors over the route between Los Angeles and Salt Lake City back in 1926. Started non-mail, passenger route Los Angeles to Kansas City, which became western leg of Transcontinental & Western Air, the central coast-to-coast airway in 1930–1. Other sections operated as Western Air Express until cancellation of the air-mail contracts in 1934. When new contracts advertised, bid on, and won, original Los Angeles to Salt Lake City route. Extended to Great Falls, with acquisition of National Parks Airways in 1935. Won further extension to Lethbridge, Canada, in March 1941.

Appendix VI

CHRONOLOGY

1796–1809 *Sir* GEORGE CAYLEY *learns many secrets of aerodynamics and is first to point out the advantages of " streamlining."*

1835, *July 4* RICHARD CLAYTON *carries first aerial mail (unofficial) in the United States in a balloon at Cincinnati.*

1843 WILLIAM SAMUEL HENSON *actually flies a heavier-than-air power* model *for a distance of about forty yards, but steam engines of his day have too high a power-weight ratio to permit successful man-carrying flights.*

1859, *August 17* JOHN WISE *and* JOHN LAMOUNTAIN *carry what is believed to be the first official air mail in balloon* Jupiter, *at Lafayette, Indiana.*

1896, *May 6* Dr. S. P. LANGLEY *makes successful flight with steam-propelled model, and is granted $50,000 by the United States government for further experimentation.*

1900, *October* The WRIGHT *brothers begin their gliding experiments, leading to the first successful airplane flight.*

1903, *October 7* Dr. LANGLEY'S *" Aerodrome" fails on first test.*

1903, *December 8* Second attempt to fly the " Aerodrome" ends in disaster, and the public is so disillusioned that it refuses to believe news of the first successful flight, only nine days later.*

393

1903, *December* 17   ORVILLE WRIGHT *makes first controlled flight in power-driven, heavier-than-air craft, Kitty Hawk, North Carolina.*

1906, *February* 27   Dr. LANGLEY *dies, disillusioned and bitter over his failure and the attendant ridicule. Later honored by grateful government.*

1910, *June* 14   *Representative* MORRIS SHEPPARD *introduces first air-mail bill, presaging the importance of postal payments in the development of air transportation.*

1910, *December* 31   *Death of* ARCH HOXSEY, *the typical " birdman."*

1911, *September 17 to December* 10   C. P. RODGERS *is first to fly across the North American continent — twenty years before the route taken over by air lines.*

1911, *September 23 to October* 2   EARLE OVINGTON *carries first airplane mail in Blériot monoplane* Queen, *from Nassau Boulevard, Long Island.*

1912, *May* 30   WILBUR WRIGHT *dies of typhoid fever, thereby breaking a remarkable partnership.* ORVILLE *starts to retire from the aviation business.*

1912, *April*   *Connecticut is first to pass legislation regulating the licensing of planes and pilots.*

1914, *January* 1   *First air line in the United States — the St. Petersburg-Tampa Air Boat Line.*

1916, *February* 12   *First bids for air-mail routes advertised by the Postoffice Department, but no contracts signed because of difficulty in obtaining equipment while war takes all available material.*

1916, *November* 2   VICTOR (" SWEDE ") CARLSTROM *flies first mail from Chicago to New York, consigned to German submarine* Deutschland.

1918, *May* 15   *First regular air-mail service started by the postoffice and U. S. Army between New York and Washington.*

1918, *August* 12   *In the midst of war, the Postoffice De-*

partment takes over complete control of air-mail service.

1918, December 12   *Postoffice Department frustrated in dangerous attempt to start service between Chicago and New York.*

1919, March 3   EDWARD HUBBARD *and* W. E. BOEING *carry first mail under private contract and establish first foreign mail route, between Seattle and Victoria.*

1919, May 15   *Postoffice Department starts Chicago-Cleveland mail service on first anniversary of regular air-mail flights.*

1919, July 1   *New York to Chicago mail service started by daylight only.*

1919, July 27   *First air-line strike settled by compromise between pilots and Postoffice Department.*

1919, October   *Lieutenant* BELVIN W. MAYNARD *wins army cross-country race against 64 rivals, feeling out the possibilities of a transcontinental air service.*

1919, November 1   *Aeromarine-West Indies Airways, one of the important pioneer air lines, begins passenger service from Miami to Havana.*

1920, May 15   *New York to Chicago mail service extended to Omaha on second anniversary of air mail.*

1920, September   WILLIAM B. STOUT'S *" Bat Wing," forerunner of the modern air transport, tested by* BERT ACOSTA.

1920, September 8   *Postoffice Department establishes regular service between New York and San Francisco.*

1921, February 22   JACK KNIGHT'S *famous flight, with mail, crossing the unlighted airways for the first time at night.*

1922, January 26   *Senator (later Representative)* JAMES W. WADSWORTH *and Representative* SAMUEL E. WINSLOW *introduce bill that eventually becomes Air Commerce Act of 1926.*

1923, February 1   *Collier trophy awarded to U. S. Air*

Mail Service for year's greatest achievement in aviation.

1923, *August* 21   *Lighted transcontinental airway tested out in four days of successful operation. Regular cross-country night mail held up by lack of appropriations.*

1924, *February* 9   *Air Mail Service wins Collier trophy second time.*

1924, *July* 1   *Regular twenty-four-hour mail service established on New York-Chicago-San Francisco route, with completion of the lighted airway from Chicago to Cheyenne.*

Postoffice Department divides transcontinental route into three zones, with eight cents postage charged for each zone.

1924, *September* 28   *U. S. Army Air Service completes round-the-world flight in three Douglas cruisers. Public reassured as to the reliability of aircraft.*

1925, *February* 2   *Passage of the Kelly Bill, which becomes the first Air Mail Act, providing for the transference of air-mail operations to private contractors.*

1925, *May* 1   *Organization of National Air Transport.*

1925, *July* 1   *Organization of Western Air Express.*

Postmaster General NEW *authorizes overnight service over the difficult " graveyard run," New York to Cleveland. Entire country now spanned by night mail planes.*

Organization of Pratt & Whitney, which opens doors August 1 and begins producing famous " Wasp " engines in the following March.

1925, *September* 17   *President's Aircraft (Morrow) Board, using data from a score of previous surveys, paves way for passage of sadly needed government regulations, and starts commercial aviation on its way.*

1925, *October* 7   *First five contracts for private operation of mail service on feeder routes let by Postmaster Gen-*

eral NEW. *They are: Colonial Air Transport, Robert-son Aircraft Corporation, National Air Transport, Western Air Express, and Walter T. Varney.*

1926, *February* 15   FORD *line carries first domestic mail under private contract, Detroit to Cleveland, in newly designed, Liberty-powered, Stout transport.*

1926, *April* 1   *Florida Airways begins service.*

1926, *April* 6   *Varney Air Lines is first of five original mail contractors to begin mail service, Elko, Nevada, to Pasco, Washington.*

1926, *April* 15   *Robertson Aircraft Corporation begins mail service, St. Louis to Chicago.*

1926, *April* 17   *Western Air Express begins mail service, Los Angeles to Salt Lake City.*

1926, *May* 12   *National Air Transport begins mail service, Chicago to Dallas and Fort Worth.*

1926, *May* 20   *Passage of the Bingham-Merritt-Parker Bill as the Air Commerce Act of 1926, " legislative corner-stone of American civil aviation."*

1926, *June* 3   *Second Air Mail Act (first amendment to Kelly Act), making weight rather than postal revenue the basis of payments to operators.*

1926, *June* 7   CHARLES DICKINSON *begins service between Chicago and Twin Cities.*

1926, *July* 6   *Philadelphia Rapid Transit air line, carrying passengers from Washington to the Philadelphia World's Fair, teaches valuable lessons in air-line operation.*

1926, *August* 10   WILLIAM P. MACCRACKEN *appointed Assistant Secretary of Commerce for Aviation.*

1926, *September* 15   *Pacific Air Transport begins mail service, Seattle to Los Angeles.*

1926, *October* 1   *Northwest Airways succeeds* CHARLES DICKINSON *in operation of the Chicago to Twin Cities route.*

1926, *December* 9   *Postmaster General* NEW *announces*

ten-cent postal rate, and abolition of the zone system, effective February 1, 1927.

1926, *December* 31 *Air Commerce Act officially in effect, but administrators so hard pressed in licensing all planes and pilots for first time that regulations lapse until late spring.*

1927, *January* 13 SHIRLEY SHORT *wins* 1926 *Harmon trophy for his splendid record as an air-mail flyer.*

1927, *January* 15 BOEING *and* HUBBARD *shock rivals by their low bid for the Chicago to San Francisco route, about to be transferred from postoffice to private management.*

1927, *January* 28 BOEING *wins the " Columbia " main line.*

1927, *February* 28 *Pitcairn Aviation Company gets New York to Atlanta mail route.*

1927, *April* 2 *National Air Transport gets New York to Chicago section of main transcontinental line.*

1927, *April* 15 *Colonial Air Transport carries first night passengers from Boston to New York.*

1927, *April* 21 CLIFFORD BALL *flies mail from Pittsburgh to Cleveland.*

1927, *May* 20–1 C. A. LINDBERGH *flies* 3,610 *miles from New York to Paris in Ryan Whirlwind* Spirit of St. Louis, *setting off the spark for an aviation boom.*

1927, *July* 1 *Boeing Air Transport takes over the operation of the Chicago to San Francisco section of the transcontinental line.*

1927, *August* 20 *St. Tamany-Gulf Coast Airway starts passenger service between Atlanta and New Orleans.*

1927, *August* 31 *Postoffice Department relinquishes last of its mail routes to private operators, and National Air Transport begins service from New York to Chicago, connecting there with its Dallas and Fort Worth route and with Boeing Air Transport.*

1927, *September* 1 *Colonial Air Transport, National Air*

Transport, and Western Air Express sign up with American Railway Express Company for package service.

1927, October 10   *Continental Air Lines (upon which Universal Aviation Corporation built) organized to carry mail and passengers from Cleveland to Louisville.*

1927, October 16   *Death of* CHARLES M. MANLY, *who built motors for Langley and who flew the " Aerodrome" on its ill-fated flight.*

1927, December 17   EMBRY-RIDDLE *starts Cincinnati-Chicago mail service.*

1927, December 30   ALFRED FRANK *starts Salt Lake City to Great Falls route.*

1928, March 4   *Postmaster General* WALTER FOLGER BROWN *comes in with* HOOVER *administration. Becomes czar of civil aviation.*

1928, May   *First* BRANIFF *line started (soon bought by Universal, but reappears after passage of Watres Act in 1930) .*

1928, May 17   *Third Air Mail Act (second amendment to Kelly Act) reducing air-mail postage to five cents, with no decrease in payments to operators, and providing for air-line franchises in the form of ten-year certificates.*

1928, July 30   *Organization of Universal Aviation Corporation.*

1928, December   *Organization of United Air Lines.*

1929, January 26   *Collier trophy awarded to* WILLIAM P. MACCRACKEN *and Major* CLARENCE M. YOUNG *for the efficient administration of the aeronautics branch of the Department of Commerce.*

1929, July 4   *Transcontinental Air Transport begins forty-eight-hour air-rail passenger service from New York to Los Angeles.*

1929, July 10   *North American Aviation buys Pitcairn*

Aviation and renames the route between New York and Miami Eastern Air Transport.

1929, *November* 7   *First five mail contracts due to expire, but extended six months by Postmaster General* BROWN, *pending passage of the Watres Act.* BROWN *later accused of thereby favoring the " big boys."*

1930, *January* 25   *Organization of American Airways.*

1930, *April* 29   *Passage of the McNary-Watres Bill, providing payments to operators on a space-mile basis, and giving almost unlimited powers to the Postmaster General.*

1930, *May* 19   *Beginning of the " Spoils Conferences," in which air-line operators and the Postmaster General were charged with carving up the air-line map in favor of certain privileged operators.*

1930, *July* 24   *Comptroller General* JOHN R. MCCARL *snags the Postmaster General by deciding that air lines cannot be extended more than their " basic lengths," following the petition of Northwest Airways for an extension from Twin Cities to Winnipeg.*

1930, *August* 15   *Pittsburgh Airways, United States Air Lines, and Ohio Transport agree to form United Avigation Company to bid on the central transcontinental route, coveted by Transcontinental & Western Air. Leads to later charges of favoritism.*

1930, *August* 25   *Bids called by Postmaster General on central and southern transcontinental routes, won respectively by TWA and American Airways.*

1930, *September* 1   *Ludington Lines begins passenger service between New York, Philadelphia, and Washington " every hour on the hour."*

1930, *October* 9   *Comptroller General* MCCARL *challenges the award of the central airway to Transcontinental & Western Air over the low bid of United Avigation.*

1931, *February* 13   *Transcontinental Air Transport, Western Air Express, and Pittsburgh Aviation Industries*

Corporation complete final details for merger into Transcontinental & Western Air.

1931, *April* 1   *Organization of the Air Line Pilots Association.*

1931, *June* 2   *Northwest Airways granted extension to Mandan, North Dakota, much to the annoyance of rivals.*

1931, *June* 15   *American Airways granted extension from Nashville to Dallas and Fort Worth, and from St. Louis to New Orleans, against great protest of " Independents."*

1931, *August* 1   *American Airways granted extension from El Paso to Albuquerque and from Boston to Bangor.*

1932, *February*   *Pilots of* E. L. CORD'S *Century Air Lines strike.*

1932, *June* 16   *United Air Lines forced to take Omaha-Watertown extension by Postmaster General.*

1933, *February* 1   *TWA granted Columbus-Chicago extension.*

    Eastern Air Transport buys Ludington when latter line fails to win mail contract on offer to charge Post-office Department 25 cents a mile, as against EAT's 89-cent bid.

1933, *February* 11   *American Airways granted extension from Boston to Albany.*

1933, *March* 2   *Northwest Airways granted extension from Mandan to Billings.*

1933, *April*   *Postmaster General* JAMES A. FARLEY *calls a series of meetings, which his critics charge had same general purpose as the " Spoils Conferences" he so bitterly denounced.*

1933, *April* 29   *Air-line operators receive questionnaire, indicating pending investigation by the Senate.*

1933, *September* 20   EUGENE VIDAL *becomes director of aeronautics branch, which critics charge is falling to pieces.*

1934, *February* 9 *Postmaster General* FARLEY *cancels vital air-mail contracts and President* ROOSEVELT *orders army to carry mail within ten days.*

1934, *February* 18–19 JACK FRYE *and Captain* E. V. RICKENBACKER *carry last load of contracted mail across continent in new Douglas transport, to break the air speed record.*

1934, *February* 19 *The army carries the mail, with disastrous results.*

1934, *March* 10 *President* ROOSEVELT *announces that air mail is to be returned to private contractors on different basis.*

1934, *March* 26 *Senator* PAT MCCARRAN *proposes bill for a separate aviation Authority. Voted down, but essentially the Civil Aeronautics Act of* 1938.

1934, *April* 20 *Bids opened on first contracts to be let since cancellation by the Postmaster General.*

1934, *May* 8 *United Air Lines and Transcontinental & Western Air begin service under new mail contracts.*
     JACK FRYE *breaks air speed record by carrying mail from Los Angeles to New York in eleven hours and thirty minutes.*

1934, *June* 1 *Last of new contracts let to private operators after army interlude.*

1934, *June* 12 *Air Mail Act of* 1934 *takes place of Watres Act and provides for a Federal Aviation Commission to prescribe for the ailing industry.*

1934, *July* 1 *Aeronautics branch of the Department of Commerce reorganized and named Bureau of Air Commerce.*

1935, *January* 22 102 *recommendations of Federal Aviation Commission incorporated in new McCarran Bill.*

1935, *May* 6 *Air-line crash near Kirksville, Missouri, kills Senator* BRONSON CUTTING *and leads to an investigation of aeronautics bureau.*

1935, *August* 14 *Mead Bill becomes Air Mail Act of* 1935, *granting more mileage, adherence to accepted labor practices, three-year contracts for greater stability, and the curbing of "off-line" service to end dangerous competition. Operators maintain legislators make it illegal to show a profit.*

1936, *February* 1   *Twenty-two lines consolidate express business under Railway Express agency.*

1936, *February* 16   *American Airlines begins sleeper service.*

1936, *June* 27   *Postoffice Department settles claims of Northwest Airways, Western Air Express, TWA, and American Airways arising out of cancellations for $601,511.08.*

1936, *November* 1   *Pennsylvania Air Lines and Central Airlines merge to form Pennsylvania-Central Airlines, fourth longest system.*

1937, *November* 1   *Revised Civil Air Regulation effective.*

1938, *April* 22   *Captain* E. V. RICKENBACKER *and associates buy Eastern Air Lines from North American Aviation Company for $3,500,000.*

1938, *June* 23   *McCarran-Lea Bill becomes Civil Aeronautics Act of 1938 — most important legislation in history of civil aviation.*

1938, *August* 22–3   *Civil Aeronautics Act, creating an Authority for civil aviation, becomes effective.*

1939, *March* 5   *All-American Aviation successfully demonstrates aerial pickup service, thereby putting small towns on mail routes. Begins regular service March* 10.

1939, *March* 26   *Eight killed in crash near Oklahoma City, marking last fatal accident for a period of seventeen months — a record even the Pullman train could not surpass.*

1939, *April* 12   ROBERT H. HINCKLEY *becomes new chairman of the Civil Aeronautics Authority.*

1940, *June* 11   *Control of commercial aviation transferred* from *Civil Aeronautics Authority to Civil Aeronautics Board*, *to the consternation of the industry.*

1940, *August* 31　*Senator* ERNEST LUNDEEN *of Minnesota and 24 others killed in crash near Lovettsville, Virginia, ending seventeen months of air-line operation without a fatality.*

1941, *July* 14　*Commissioner* RICHARD H. AKERS, *of U. S. Court of Claims clears government and industry of fraud and collusion, as charged during 1933–4 air mail cancellation period.*

Appendix VII

BIBLIOGRAPHICAL NOTES

A number of books, periodicals, newspapers, and documents were helpful in gathering material for this history. It would probably be of little value to list every reference cited in the footnotes, but the following deserve special mention.

BOOKS

Aircraft Yearbook. Boston and New York: Aeronautical Chamber of Commerce; 1918– . The standard reference book for any study of aviation. Contains annual report on conditions of industry, including statistics on mail and traffic. There is a special section on air transportation and airport maintenance.

DAVID, PAUL T.: *Economics of Air Mail Transportation.* Washington: Brookings Institution; 1934. A scholarly and careful study of the vital relationship between air mail and commercial aviation preceding the air-mail contracts cancellation period.

FREUDENTHAL, ELSBETH E.: *The Aviation Business.* New York: Vanguard Press; 1940. Written by a financial analyst, this book describes and severely criticizes the management of both commercial and military aviation.

JANE, FRED T.: *All the World's Air Ships.* London: Sampson, Low, Marston & Company; 1909– . Especially valuable in comparing specifications of planes in the early days, when commercial and military craft were similar.

LEDERER, JEROME: *Safety in the Operation of Air Transportation.* Burlington: Lane Press; 1939. Written by the director of the Safety Bureau, under the Civil Aeronautics Board, this is the publication of a lecture delivered under the James Jackson Cabot Professorship of Air Traffic Regulation and Air Transportation at Norwich University.

RHYNE, CHARLES S.: *Civil Aeronautics Act of 1938 Annotated.* Washington: National Law Book Company; 1939. The best book describing events leading up to the passage of this important act.

ROHLFING, CHARLES C.: *National Regulation of Aeronautics.* Philadelphia: University of Pennsylvania; 1931. Submitted as a thesis for an advanced degree, this detailed study of air legislation covers the early years of commercial aviation. It of course does not include all the important laws and regulations affecting the air lines since the cancellation of the air-mail contracts in 1934.

ROSS, DONALD, and WELD, DAVID: *Aviation: Manufacturing — Transportation.* New York: White, Weld & Company; 1940. A valuable reference work, particularly the section by Mr. Weld, since it analyses and describes briefly each of the air lines.

WARNER, EDWARD PEARSON: *Early History of Air Transportation.* York: Maple Press; 1937. The best short history of commercial aviation up to the cancellation period. Publication of a lecture given at Norwich University under the sponsorship of the James Jackson Cabot Professorship of Air Traffic Regulation and Air Transportation.

WARNER, E. P.: *Technical Development and Its Effect on Air Transportation.* York: Maple Press; 1938. This authoritative digest of a lecture at Norwich University was written by the vice chairman of the Civil Aeronautics Board, who was formerly a teacher at Massachusetts Institute of Technology, and editor of *Aviation.*

PERIODICALS

Excellent references and sources of information are the trade journals, especially *Aviation,* which has been a reputable organ of the industry for a quarter of a century; *Aero Digest,* written in a more popular and critical vein; the authoritative *Aeronautical Review. Popular Aviation* occasionally has articles of value to the historian.

The most valuable periodical outside the orbit of the trade journals is *Fortune,* which frequently contains complete and, on the whole, very reliable accounts of various phases of aviation. Of particular value were the articles "Aviation and the Air Mail," Volume IX, May 1934; "Aviation: Dollars in the Air," same issue; "United Aircraft & Transport: No. 1 Airplane Company," Volume V, April 1932.

Wayne L. McMillen, assistant to the president of American Airlines, has an authoritative series of articles in the *Journal of Land and Public Utilities.* Entitled "Air Express in the United States," the articles appear in Volume XI, August and November 1935; Volume XII, February and August 1936.

The magazine *U. S. Air Services* had a number of valuable articles about the early days of commercial aviation.

Time magazine has an excellent section keeping up on trends in both commercial and military aviation.

NEWSPAPERS

The most reliable newspapers for reporting aviation matters since the cancellation period are the New York *Times* and the New York *Herald Tribune.* Both papers enjoy a high reputation among responsible aviation authorities. The *Herald Tribune's* former aviation editor was later a member of the Air Safety Board, until it was reorganized in 1940.

DOCUMENTS

So many documents were used in gathering source material for this history that no attempt will be made to cite all of them. For reports on the technical progress of aviation, the annual reports of the *National Advisory Council for Aviation* are valuable. Various air-mail and air-commerce legislation appears in the *Statutes at Large*. The records of the Congressional hearings before the House and Senate postoffice committees furnished a wealth of material. The annual report of the Postmaster General also contains interesting statistics describing progress in commercial aviation. A number of Senate and House investigations provide valuable testimony. The investigation quoted most frequently in this history is the probe conducted by the so-called " Black Committee." Listed as the Hearings before the Special Committee Investigating the Air Mail and Ocean Mail Contracts (Honorable Hugo L. Black, chairman), the testimony appears in nine parts published by the Government Printing Office at Washington in 1934.

INTERVIEWS

While books, periodicals, newspapers, and documents provided background and information, much of the data used in this text came from interviews with a score or more persons who figured prominently in the development of the commercial aviation industry. Included in this list are ORVILLE WRIGHT, ROY KNABENSHUE, C. M. KEYS, COLONEL PAUL HENDERSON, WALTER FOLGER BROWN, WILLIAM P. MACCRACKEN, JR., F. B. RENTSCHLER, C. R. SMITH, PAUL RICHTER, CLIFFORD BALL, GEORGE R. HANN, C. BEDELL MONRO, FRANK L. JONES, JUSTICE HUGO BLACK, DAVID L. BEHNCKE, MAJOR WILLIAM B. ROBERTSON, W. I. DENNING, and many others. There was also extensive correspondence with many persons associated with the air lines.

Notes

CHAPTER 1

[1] Air Transport Association of America: *Little Known Facts about the Air Transport Industry,* Vol. III, p. 21 (April 15, 1941).

[2] J. E. Hodgson: "Sir George Cayley's Work in Aeronautics," from a paper read before the Newcomen Society in London, and published by the *Journal of the Royal Aeronautical Society,* August 1923, in *Aviation,* Vol. XV, p. 744 (December 17, 1923).

[3] Anonymous: "Scientific Events," *Science,* Vol. LXI, p. 533 (May 22, 1925). Clement Ader died in 1925 at the age of eighty-four. An electrical engineer, he observed the flight of birds and began his first flying machine, the "Eole," in 1886. His reputation is based upon the performance of his third craft, the "Avion," which, according to some witnesses, left the ground on October 4, 1897. The fact that the French government did not continue its interest, however, indicates that the "Avion" was not all that it was claimed to be. Ader retired from aviation in disgust, but later he was honored as a pioneer. The "Avion," at last report, was on exhibition at the Musée des Arts et Métiers. Ader is now recognized in France as "the father of aviation," and all French planes are known as Avions.

[4] The model is now on display, along with Langley's other machines, in the National Museum, Washington, D. C.

[5] The Langley data have been preserved by the Smithsonian Institution. A considerable amount of semi-confidential material on the early designers, including correspondence, is available to serious students.

[6] C. Fayette Taylor: "History of the Aeronautical Engine," *Aviation,* Vol. XXI, pp. 284–6 (March 22, 1926). Modern radial motors have a weight-horsepower ratio of nearly 1:1.

⁷ Mr. Paul E. Garber, who is in charge of the aeronautical section, National Museum, Washington, D. C., takes exception to the phrase " clumsy contraption." He points out that the " Aerodrome " was well built and cleverly designed. It is, indeed, as graceful and strong as a fine racing yacht, and the Wright machine, in comparison, is jerry-built. Granting all this, the machine that visitors view today in the old museum must appear unwieldy in comparison with modern ships.

⁸ Editorial, " Prof. Langley's Bird," Washington *Post,* Vol. 9, p. 6, Thursday, October 8, 1903, and p. 1, October 9, 1903.

⁹ Fred Kelly: " How the Wrights Began," *Harper's,* Vol. 179, p. 482 (October 1939).

¹⁰ Oliver Gramling: *AP: The Story of News* (New York, 1940), p. 205.

¹¹ Mark Sullivan: *Our Times,* Vol. II (New York, 1927), pp. 588–90.

¹² Interview with Roy Knabenshue, Washington, D. C., August 3, 1939. The Wright Exhibition Company was the agency that demonstrated the Wright plane at flying meets and before the public.

¹³ Interview with Orville Wright, Dayton, Ohio, June 9, 1939. The younger Wright believes that Dr. Langley's successor had no right to permit Curtiss to make a flight in the " Aerodrome " in 1915. Curtiss was a rival of the Wrights, and he was trying to nullify a basic patent held by the Wrights. Curtiss hoped to show that if a plane, designed earlier than the Wright ship, could fly, then the Wrights had no such basic patent as they claimed. Because of the Curtiss flight in the " Aerodrome," and the implication by the Smithsonian Institution that the " Aerodrome " was the first airplane, the Wrights refused to donate their craft to its rightful place in the National Museum. " How could we turn over our machine to such an institution? " Orville asks. " For if the Institution could prove that the Langley machine was ' capable of flight,' could they not prove that ours was incapable of flight? " Furthermore, Orville maintains that the flight of the " Aerodrome " at Hammondsport proved nothing, since a new motor and thirty structural changes had improved the efficiency of the craft just enough to make flight possible. Because of their feud with the Smithsonian Institution, the Wrights loaned their historic plane to the Kensington Museum in England. During the 1940 bombings it was stored underground. It is erroneous to believe that the Wrights had any quarrel with Dr. Langley during all this bickering, however. Actually, says Orville, Langley's experiments were an inspiration to the Wrights, and they admitted their indebtedness to the designer of the " Aerodrome."

CHAPTER 2

[1] Mark Sullivan: *Our Times,* Vol. II (New York, 1927), p. 599.

[2] Anonymous: " La Machine volante des frères Wright," *L'Aérophile,* Vol. XII, p. 16 (January 1904). This is a full description of the Wright machine, written immediately after the Kitty Hawk flight. Important letters of the Wrights to foreign pioneers appear also in " Les Frères Wright et leur aéroplane à moteur," *L'Aérophile,* Vol. XIII, p. 265 (December 1905).

[3] Interview with Orville Wright, Dayton, Ohio, June 9, 1939. Miss Mabel Beck, who is familiar with the early history of aviation, as the confidential secretary of the Wrights, holds that the quotation from the interview is utterly inadequate in describing the situation at that time. Wrote Miss Beck in a letter dated September 30, 1941:

". . . the aviation activity in France, which culminated in the first flight in Europe by Santos-Dumont in October, 1906, was not an independent movement on the part of the French, but was started by the publication in Europe of the early Wright experiments in America. Their early machines were all based on the Wright. While there had been considerable activity in France in the latter part of the nineteenth century, the many failures discouraged the experimenters, and interest in the subject of heavier-than-air [flight] was practically dead at the beginning of this century. The Aero Club of France and the French aeronautical papers concerned themselves almost exclusively with matters pertaining to lighter-than-air at that time.

" I believe the first European publication of anything concerning the Wright brothers' experiments appeared in the " Illustrierte Aeronautische Mittheilungen " (Berlin) of July, 1901, which contained a photograph of the Wright 1900 glider. Captain Ferber, an officer in the French artillery, reading of these experiments in " Mittheilungen," became interested and wrote to Octave Chanute of Chicago to get some information about the Wright brothers. Ferber then became actively interested and built what he called Wright and Chanute-Wright types of gliders. Many accounts of these appeared in French publications at the time.

" ' L'Aerophile,' the official journal of the Aero Club of France, of February, 1903, in referring to the people who were experimenting in heavier-than-air [machines] makes this statement: ' There are actually five in the world, MM. Chanute and Herring of Chicago, MM. Orville and Wilbur Wright, of Dayton, Ohio, U. S. A., and Captain Ferber of Nice.'

" Mr. Chanute, who had visited the Wright camp at Kitty Hawk in

1901 and 1902, went to Europe in the early part of 1903 in the inter-ests of the St. Louis Exposition to induce Santos-Dumont to bring his dirigible to the fair. While in Paris on the second of April, 1903, he gave a talk before the Aero Club of France, in which he exhibited photographs of the Wright gliders and described the Wright method of maintaining control. Ferber on page 22 in ' Les Progres de l'Avia-tion Par Le Vol Plane,' published in 1904, in referring to this address by Mr. Chanute says: ' Sa conference du 2 avril fut une revelation et un triomphe.'

"Mr. Chanute was asked at this time by the editors of ' l'Aero-phile' and the ' Revue Generale des Sciences' to contribute articles on aviation. The article for the ' Revue of Sciences' (November, 1903) contained photographs and descriptions of the 1902 Wright glider. The article for ' l'Aerophile' (August, 1903) contained photographs and drawings. Interest was immediate and Ferber wrote in January, 1904, ' Archdeacon is very active and hence I believe that not fewer than six apparatus of the 1902 Wright type are now being built in France.'

" The French in copying the Wright machine made what they thought would be improvements. The results were not as good as had been claimed for the Wrights by Chanute. Chanute had told them that the Wrights were able to glide with a descent of one in ten. The French began questioning in print the accuracy of Chanute's accounts, and accused him of exaggeration. Esnault-Pelterie, one of the French pioneers, said the way to settle the matter would be to build a Wright machine exactly according to the drawings and de-scription given to them by Chanute. This he did in 1904 and found that what Chanute had told them was true. (See ' l'Aerophile,' June, 1905, ' Experiences d'Aviation, executees en 1904, en verification de celles des freres Wright.')

"Voisin, who after Santos-Dumont was the first in Europe to make a power flight, got his first experience in aviation flying a Wright glider for Archdeacon. (See ' L'Aviation, ses debuts — son developpement,' Berger-Levrault & Cie, Paris, Juliet, 1908.)

"Voisin later went into the business of building, and it was in planes of his make that Delagrange, Farman, and many of the early French experimenters did their flying.

"If you will examine French publications of that time I think you will find that all of the French experiments started from Mr. Cha-nute's lecture of April, 1903. The situation at that time was very different from what the public now generally believes it to have been. The writers today seem to think that the movement in France was independent of America, and that the French were barely beaten by the Americans. There was no motor flight in Europe until October, 1906, more than three years after Chanute's disclosure of the Wright designs and invention."

⁴ The rotary engines survived up to about 1918. They were air-cooled motors, similar in appearance to the modern radial, with cylinders set spoke-wise around a central hub, so as to present the largest possible area to the air flow. The rotary differed from the radial in that the entire motor revolved with the propeller.

⁵ Charles C. Turner: *Aerial Navigation of Today* (second edition, London, 1910), opposite p. 276.

⁶ Anonymous: " Fastest Mile Dash," New York *Tribune,* Vol. LXIX, p. 1 (March 17, 1910).

⁷ Anonymous: "Airship for French Army," New York *Tribune,* Vol. LXX, p. 1 (September 6, 1910).

⁸ William Menkel: " The Aeroplane — A Year's Marvelous Progress," *Review of Reviews,* Vol. XLIV, p. 177 (August 1911).

⁹ Anonymous: " Roosevelt Goes Up in Aeroplane," New York *Tribune,* Vol. LXX, p. 1 (October 12, 1910).

¹⁰ Anonymous: " Wright Aviators Must Obey Orders," New York *Tribune,* Vol. LXX, p. 1 (December 4, 1910).

¹¹ Interview with Mrs. Virginia S. Smith, Staunton, Illinois, cousin of the flyer, June 7, 1939.

¹² Ibid.

CHAPTER 3

¹ A full discussion of this phase will be found in Chapter iv.

² P. E. Fansler: " The First Commercial Air Line," *Aero Digest,* Vol. XV, p. 58 (December 1929).

³ Anonymous: *The Flight across the Atlantic,* released by Department of Education, Curtiss Aeroplane & Motor Corporation (New York, 1919).

⁴ Elsbeth E. Freudenthal: *The Aviation Business* (New York, 1940), pp. 22–4.

⁵ Grover C. Loening: *Our Wings Grow Faster* (New York, 1935), p. 65.

⁶ *Minority Report,* Committee on Military Affairs, United States Senate, April 10, 1918, as reported in " Senate Investigation of the War Department," *Aerial Age,* Vol. VII, p. 262c (April 15, 1918).

⁷ Major H. B. Hickam: " The Truth about Our Aeroplane Record," *Current History,* Vol. XV, pp. 47–57 (October 1921).

⁸ Ibid. (See also *Congressional Record,* Vol. LVII, Part I, pp. 883–914.)

⁹ Freudenthal, op. cit., pp. 28–32.

[10] United States Department of Justice: " Report of the Aircraft Inquiry," signed by Charles E. Hughes (Washington, 1919).

[11] Ibid.

[12] Anonymous: " The Hughes Report," *Aerial Age,* Vol. VIII, pp. 462–72 (November 11, 1918).

[13] Ibid. (Much of this report is concerned with this phase. Telegrams and letters were used as evidence to show that Colonel Deeds was influenced by his pre-war associations.)

[14] Ibid., p. 466.

[15] Ibid.

[16] Ibid.

[17] *Hearings,* " Committee on Military Affairs" (Thomas Committee), United States Senate, 65th Congress, Second Session, Vol. II, 1918.

[18] See note 12.

[19] Ibid., p. 996.

CHAPTER 4

[1] *A Brief History of the Air Mail Service,* published by the Second Assistant Postmaster General, Information Service, Washington, no date given.

[2] Ibid.

[3] Not until 1916 did the mail travel so far by air.

[4] Records of the flight are to be found in the Tippecanoe County Historical Association Museum, State Library, Indianapolis, Indiana. (Wise was drowned in Lake Michigan, after a forced landing, in 1879.)

[5] Richard B. Wetherill: " The First Official Air Mail," *Indiana Magazine of History,* Vol. XXXV (December 1939).

[6] Advertisement in Lafayette *Daily Courier,* August 15, 1859. (The flight was scheduled for the 15th, but trouble with the inflating apparatus delayed the ascension.)

[7] *A Brief History of the Air Mail,* p. 8.

[8] Ibid.

[9] Edward Pearson Warner: *The Early History of Air Transportation* (Norwich University, 1937), p. 4. There were only nine citations under " Transportation," six under " Commerce," and two each under " Aerial Routes " and " Travel."

[10] Data available at United States National Museum, Washington.

[11] Paul T. David: *Economics of Air Mail Transportation* (Washington, 1934), p. 3.

[12] Undated mimeographed report of Second Assistant Postmas-

ter General entitled: " A Brief History of the Air Mail Service," released by Postoffice Department information division.

¹³ *Congressional Record,* Vol. XLVIII, Part V, pp. 5063–5 (April 20, 1912).

¹⁴ *Hearing,* Report on HR 3393, House of Representatives, 63d Congress, First Session, p. 50, April 21, 1913.

¹⁵ New York *Times,* Part I, p. 16 (February 13, 1916).

¹⁶ David, p. 9.

¹⁷ Carlstrom was killed the following May, while flying at Newport News.

¹⁸ Warner, op. cit., p. 5.

¹⁹ Early air-mail records appear in *Aerial Age,* Vol. VII, p. 1119, (August 19, 1918), and in succeeding issues.

²⁰ Letter of Otto Praeger: " Advantages of Sending Mail by Aeroplane," *Aerial Age,* Vol. VII, p. 578 (June 3, 1918).

CHAPTER 5

¹ The newspapers and periodicals poked fun at these antics, but the criticisms were good-natured, and the general tone of the articles appears to be one of encouragement.

² Edward Pearson Warner: *The Early History of Air Transportation* (Norwich University, 1937), p. 8.

³ Lieutenant Edgerton's log book is preserved in the aeronautical section of the National Museum, Washington, D. C.

⁴ From an interview with James Clark Edgerton, Washington, D. C., August 12, 1940.

⁵ See successive issues of *Aerial Age,* beginning Vol. VII, p. 1119 (August 19, 1918).

⁶ *Hearings,* Committee on the Post Office and Post Roads, House of Representatives, 65th Congress, Second Session, pp. 48–61, 67–8, December 4, 1918.

⁷ Ibid., p. 50.

⁸ Warner, op. cit., p. 20.

⁹ Ibid.

¹⁰ *Hearings,* " Air Service Unification," Committee on Military Affairs, House of Representatives, 68th Congress, Second Session, p. 102.

¹¹ Donald Wilhelm: " Flying the Mail," *World's Work,* Vol. XLII, pp. 49–59 (May 1921).

¹² Letter from Jack Knight, dated New York, January 15, 1941.

¹³ Warner, op. cit., p. 19.

CHAPTER 6

[1] Paul T. David: *Economics of Air Mail Transportation* (Washington, 1934), p. 27.

[2] Paul F. Collins: "The Air Mail," *Liberty*, April 20, 1929, p. 38.

[3] *Hearings*, "Testimony of Col. Paul Henderson," Select Committee of Inquiry into the Operations of the United States Air Services, House of Representatives, 68th Congress, First Session, p. 279, December 17, 1924.

[4] Anonymous: "Air Mail Invites Bids for New Mail Planes," *Aviation*, Vol. XVI, p. 422 (April 21, 1924).

[5] G. W. Carr: "The De Haviland Airplane and Its Modifications," *U. S. Air Services*, Vol. IX, p. 21 (January 1924).

[6] The translation of William Beloe reads: "Neither snow, nor rain, nor heat, nor darkness, are permitted to obstruct their speed," Bartlett's *Familiar Quotations* (eleventh edition, Boston, 1938), p. 969.

[7] Edward Pearson Warner: *The Early History of Air Transportation* (Norwich University), p. 23.

[8] David, p. 32.

[9] Ibid., p. 34.

[10] Warner, op. cit., p. 25.

[11] Interview with Colonel Paul Henderson, Washington, D. C., August 14, 1940.

[12] Warner, op. cit., p. 26.

[13] Letter from Colonel Paul Henderson, dated Washington, D. C., January 13, 1941.

[14] Lieutenant D. L. Bruner and Lieutenant H. R. Harris: "The First Night Airways," *U. S. Air Services*, Vol. IX, p. 7 (June 1924).

[15] Charles C. Rohlfing: *National Regulation of Aeronautics* (Philadelphia, 1931), p. 12.

[16] Charles A. Lindbergh: "He Does It Again," *National Aeronautic Association Review*, Vol. IV, pp. 174–5 (November 1926). (Reprinted by permission of the publishers.) Another account written by Lindbergh appears in the October issue of the magazine. While these accounts were written after the transference of air mail to private operators, the conditions described are so nearly those of the period discussed here, that they are included for this purpose.

CHAPTER 7

[1] Letter from Colonel Paul Henderson, Washington, D. C., January 13, 1941.

[2] Ibid.

[3] P. E. Fansler: "The First Commercial Air Line," *Aero Digest,* Vol. XV, p. 58 (December 1929).

[4] *Aircraft Yearbook* (Boston, 1921), pp. 11–13.

[5] *Hearings,* "Testimony of Charles F. Redden," Select Committee of Inquiry into the Operations of the United States Air Services, House of Representatives, 68th Congress, Second Session, pp. 1024–33, January 16, 1925.

[6] In 1920 the fare from Miami to Havana was $75. By the end of 1922 it was only $50, and passengers were taking the trip for the convenience, not just for the novelty.

[7] The significance of the Aeromarine company is greater than the space given to it here would imply. As an operating experiment it was far more important than the Seattle or New Orleans ventures, according to Colonel Henderson.

[8] *Aircraft Yearbook* (New York, 1923), p. 16.

[9] *Hearings,* "Air Service Unification," Committee on Military Affairs, House of Representatives, 68th Congress, Second Session, p. 6, January 8 to February 17, 1925.

[10] Ibid.

[11] *Hearings,* "Testimony of Major Edward V. Rickenbacker," Select Committee of Inquiry into Operations of the United States Air Services (hereafter called the *Lampert Committee*), House of Representatives, 68th Congress, Second Session, p. 2158. (Rickenbacker is referred to throughout this history as "Captain" Rickenbacker, the title by which he is better known.)

[12] *Lampert Committee,* pp. 1221–36. This is the Aviation Mission report of a European survey submitted to Newton D. Baker, Secretary of War, by Benedict Crowell.

[13] *Lampert Committee,* "Testimony of Howard E. Coffin," p. 1264.

[14] See note 5.

[15] Anonymous: "Rickenbacker Speaks," *Aero Digest,* Vol. IV, p. 362 (June 1924)..

[16] *Lampert Committee,* "Testimony of Colonel Paul Henderson," p. 284.

CHAPTER 8

[1] *United States Statutes at Large,* Vol. XLIII, Part I, p. 805.

[2] L. D. Gardner: "Publisher's News Letter," *Aviation,* Vol. XVIII, p. 445 (April 20, 1925).

[3] James G. Woolley and Earl W. Hill: *Airplane Transportation* (Hollywood, 1929), pp. 319–25.

[4] *Aircraft Yearbook* (New York, 1925), pp. 114–15.

⁵ For a discussion of proposed legislation, see Charles C. Rohlfing: *National Regulation of Aeronautics* (Philadelphia, 1931) , pp. 21–30.

⁶ Ibid.

⁷ Anonymous: "Merritt Bill Amends Bingham Bill," *Aviation*, Vol. XX, p. 404 (March 22, 1926) .

⁸ *Twelfth Annual Report of the National Advisory Committee for Aeronautics* (Washington, 1926) , p. 11.

⁹ Ibid.

¹⁰ *Hearings,* Select Committee of Inquiry into the Operations of the United States Air Services, House of Representatives, 68th Congress, Second Session, October 1924 to January 1925.

¹¹ *Aircraft,* Hearings Before the President's Aircraft Board, September 21 to October 16, 1925, four volumes.

¹² The chairman of the committee was Dwight Morrow, of the House of Morgan, and later the father-in-law of hero Charles A. Lindbergh. Other members of the group were: Major General James G. Harbord; Rear Admiral Frank F. Fletcher (retired) ; Howard Coffin; Colonel Hiram Bingham, of the Senate Committee on Military Affairs, and author of the Bingham Bill; James S. Parker, of the House Commerce Committee, and sponsor of air-commerce legislation; and William F. Durand.

¹³ *Message of the President of the United States,* transmitting the report of the President's Aircraft Board (Morrow Board) , to the 69th Congress, First Session, December 10, 1925, in Senate Document No. 18.

¹⁴ Ibid.

¹⁵ *Annual Report of the Director of Aeronautics to the Secretary of Commerce* (Washington, 1927) .

¹⁶ Anonymous: "MacCracken to Head Civil Aviation Bureau," *Aviation,* Vol. XXI, p. 322 (August 23, 1926) ; and Hon. William P. MacCracken: "Civil Aeronautics Takes Off," *National Aeronautics Association Review,* Vol. IV, p. 135 (September 1926) .

CHAPTER 9

¹ Ralph W. Cram: "American Aviation's Greatest Year," *Aero Digest,* Vol. VII, p. 519 (October 1925) .

² Robert W. Marks: "Detroit DaVinci," *Saturday Evening Post,* December 7, 1940, p. 21.

³ Anonymous: "National Air Transport Organized," *Aviation,* Vol. XVIII, p. 598 (June 1, 1925) .

⁴ From an interview with Clifford Ball, Pittsburgh, August 1, 1940.

⁵ The Daniel Guggenheim Fund for the Promotion of Aeronautics

was established in January 1926, with a capital of $2,500,000. The trustees used the income to help many worthy causes in the interests of aviation.

⁶ Edward Pearson Warner: *The Early History of Air Transportation* (Norwich University, 1937), p. 53.

⁷ J. D. Bowersock: "The Rise of an Airline Magnate," Kansas City *Star*, May 7, 1939, Section C, p. 1.

⁸ Interview with Paul Richter, Kansas City, May 23, 1940.

CHAPTER 10

¹ Edward Pearson Warner: *The Early History of Air Transportation* (Norwich University, 1937), p. 50.

² *United States Statutes at Large*, Vol. XLIV, Part II, p. 693.

³ Anonymous: "Air Mail Ace Wins Harmon 1926 Trophy," New York *Times*, January 14, 1927, p. 3; and Howard Mingos: "Only the Mail Planes Came Through," New York *Times*, March 6, 1927, Section 4, p. 4.

⁴ William E. Boeing: "Air Transportation," *Aero Digest*, Vol. XIV, p. 37 (January 1929).

⁵ *United States Statutes at Large*, Vol. XXXV, Chapter 321, Part I, Sec. 226, p. 1088.

⁶ *Annual Report of the Director of Aeronautics to the Secretary of Commerce for the Fiscal Year Ended June 30, 1928* (Washington, 1928), p. 3.

⁷ *Hearings*, "Testimony of Charles W. Deeds," Special Committee on Investigation of Air Mail and Ocean Mail Contracts, United States Senate, 73d Congress, Second Session, Part I, September 26, 1933, p. 1695. (The "stock dividend" mentioned here appears to be in reality a stock split, but the former term is used throughout the hearing.)

⁸ Paul T. David: *Economics of Air Mail Transportation* (Washington, 1934), p. 75.

⁹ *Little Known Facts about the Scheduled Air Transport Industry* (third edition, Chicago, 1941), Chart 17, p. 12.

¹⁰ Warner, op. cit., p. 55.

¹¹ *United States Statutes at Large*, Vol. XLV, Part I, Chapter 603, p. 594.

¹² David, p. 83.

¹³ Talbot O. Freeman: "What Price Merger," *Aviation*, Vol. XXVII, p. 1105 (December 7, 1929).

CHAPTER 11

1 E. P. Warner: "Commercial Aviation — Illusion or Fact," *Yale Review*, Vol. XX, p. 707 (June 1931).

2 Ibid., p. 708.

3 Ibid.

4 Interview with Colonel Paul Henderson, Washington, D. C., August 14, 1940.

5 Interview with F. B. Rentschler, Hartford, Connecticut, August 9, 1940.

6 *Statement of F. B. Rentschler,* before the Temporary National Economic Committee, Washington, D. C., May 18, 1939, as reprinted and issued to stockholders of United Aircraft Corporation by President Donald L. Brown.

7 Ibid.

8 Interview with C. M. Keys, New York, August 5, 1940.

9 Anonymous, "Number One Airplane Company," *Fortune,* Vol. V, p. 127, April 1932.

10 Interview with F. B. Rentschler.

11 *Moody's Manual of Investments: Industrial Securities* (New York, 1933), p. 2509.

12 *Hearings,* "Testimony of D. M. Sheaffer," Special Committee on Investigation of the Air Mail and Ocean Mail Contracts, United States Senate, 73d Congress, Second Session, p. 1556.

CHAPTER 12

1 George Svehla: "Survey of Civil Aviation in the Southwest," *Aero Digest,* Vol. XVII, p. 35 (August 1930).

2 Ibid.

CHAPTER 13

1 L. D. Gardner: "News Letter," *Aviation,* Vol. XXII, p. 192 (January 24, 1927).

2 *Hearings,* "Testimony of Walter Folger Brown," Special Committee on Investigation of the Air Mail and Ocean Mail Contracts (hereinafter called the *Black Committee*), United States Senate, 73d Congress, Second Session, p. 2569.

3 Anonymous: "Aviation and the Air Mail," *Fortune,* Vol. IX, p. 142 (May 1934).

4 Interview with Colonel Paul Henderson, Washington, D. C., August 14, 1940.

5 *United States Statutes at Large,* Vol. XLVI, Part I, Chapter 223.

6 *Black Committee,* op. cit., p. 2580.

[7] Interview with Walter Folger Brown, New York, August 19, 1940.

[8] *Fortune*, Vol. IX, p. 142 (May 1934).

[9] *Black Committee*, op. cit., p. 2451.

[10] *Aircraft Yearbook for 1932*, p. 26.

[11] See James G. Woolley and Earl W. Hill: *Airplane Transportation* (Hollywood, 1929), pp. 42–3, for data on foreign subsidies.

[12] White, Weld & Company: *Aviation, An Appraisal of the Aeronautical Industry* (New York, May 1940), Sec. II, p. 9.

[13] A more reliable definition of subsidy is given in Appendix III.

[14] *Hearings*, Air Mail, "Testimony of W. Irving Glover," Committee on the Post Office and Post Roads, House of Representatives, 72d Congress, First Session, pp. 6–7.

[15] *Fifteenth Annual Report*, National Advisory Committee for Aeronautics (Washington, 1930), p. 88.

CHAPTER 14

[1] *Hearings*, "Testimony of D. M. Sheaffer," Special Committee on the Investigation of Air Mail and Ocean Mail Contracts (hereinafter called the *Black Committee*), United States Senate, 73d Congress, Second Session, pp. 1549–57.

[2] Ibid., p. 1550.

[3] *Black Committee*, "Testimony of Hainer Hinshaw," p. 1592. (Hinshaw was Washington representative for American Airways. He became secretary of the National Republican Committee.)

[4] *Black Committee*, "Testimony of James G. Woolley," p. 2849.

[5] *United States Statutes at Large*, Vol. XLIII, Part I, p. 806.

[6] *Black Committee*, "Testimony of Walter Folger Brown," p. 2352.

[7] *Black Committee*, "Testimony of D. M. Sheaffer," pp. 1549–50.

[8] Ibid.

[9] *Black Committee*, "Testimony of Karl Crowley," pp. 2735–6.

[10] Letter from George R. Hann, Pittsburgh, June 24, 1941.

[11] *Black Committee*, "Testimony of Theodore Taney," p. 1614.

[12] Interview with George R. Hann, Sewickley, Pennsylvania, June 22, 1941.

[13] *Congressional Record*, "Speech of Hon. Simeon D. Fess," Vol. LXXVIII, Part VII, p. 6981.

[14] Interview with George R. Hann, Pittsburgh, July 30, 1940.

[15] *Black Committee*, "Testimony of D. M. Sheaffer," p. 1568.

[16] Letter from R. W. Robbins, Belvidere, Kansas, May 19, 1941.

[17] *Black Committee*, "Testimony of W. F. Brown," p. 2419.

[18] *Black Committee,* " Testimony of D. M. Sheaffer," p. 1640–2.

[19] Ibid.

[20] Interview with Stewart Dunn, Pittsburgh, August 1, 1940.

[21] *Black Committee,* " Testimony of Larry King," p. 1516–20.

[22] Interview with Walter Folger Brown, New York, August 1940.

[23] *Hearings,* Air Mail, " Testimony of Karl Crowley," Committee on the Post Office and Post Roads (hereinafter called the *Mead Committee*), House of Representatives, 73d Congress, Second Session, p. 231.

[24] Ibid., p. 230.

[25] *Mead Committee,* " Testimony of Captain Thomas B. Doe," p. 152.

[26] Anonymous: " U. S. Aviation and the Air Mail," *Fortune,* Vol. IX, p. 144 (May 1934). (If Pop Hanshue did not make this statement, at least it was the kind of thing he *would* have said, his associates relate.)

CHAPTER 15

[1] Letter from C. E. Woolman, dated Selman Field, Monroe, Louisiana, March 30, 1940.

[2] *Hearings,* " Testimony of Walter Folger Brown," Special Committee on Investigation of Air Mail and Ocean Mail Contracts, United States Senate, 73d Congress, Second Session, p. 2451.

[3] Ibid., p. 2452.

[4] Ibid., " Letter of December 10, 1929, to Postmaster General," pp. 1502–4.

[5] Ibid.

[6] Ibid., " Testimony of Erle P. Halliburton," pp. 1489–1500.

[7] Ibid.

[8] Ibid.

[9] Ibid., " Testimony of Walter Folger Brown," p. 2450.

[10] Ibid., " Letter of E. P. Halliburton to Hon. Patrick J. Hurley, August 5, 1930," pp. 1499–1500.

[11] Ibid., p. 1495.

[12] Ibid., " Testimony of Karl Crowley," pp. 2733–6. The subsidiary of American Airways involved in this transaction was Robertson Aircraft Corporation, one of the five original contractors, and well qualified to meet the night-flying requirement. The agreement between Halliburton and American Airways, owner of Robertson, provided for a loan of $250,000 in Liberty Bonds, which American was to furnish Robertson as a binder. If Robertson and SAFEway won the mail contract, they were to assign it to a new corporation, to be called Southern Air Fast Express, later actually incorporated as

Southern Transcontinental Airways, Inc. The stock of this new company was to be divided between Halliburton and Robertson and placed in escrow in the Commercial National Bank & Trust Company, New York. The stock was to remain there until either American Airways took up its option, for which it had already provided a $250,000 binder, or until Halliburton took over the company, in case American forfeited its option. In either case, Halliburton was to make no more charges regarding the illegality of the night-flying clause.

¹³ Ibid.

¹⁴ Anonymous: " U. S. Aviation and the Air Mail," *Fortune,* Vol. IX, p. 144 (May 1934).

CHAPTER 16

¹ Anonymous: " Airline in the Black," *Fortune,* Vol. XIX, p. 115 (February 1939).

² Anonymous: " Cohû for Coburn," *Time,* Vol. XIX, p. 43 (March 28, 1932).

³ *Hearings,* Special Committee on Investigation of the Air Mail and Ocean Mail Contracts, United States Senate, 73d Congress, Second Session (hereinafter called the *Black Committee*). See chart, pp. 1483–5.

⁴ *Black Committee,* " Testimony of W. F. Brown," p. 2393.

⁵ *Black Committee,* " Testimony of Temple Bowen," p. 1829.

⁶ Ibid., p. 1831.

⁷ Ibid. (See also *Fortune,* as in note 1 of this chapter.)

⁸ *Black Committee,* " Testimony of F. G. Coburn," pp. 1678–9.

⁹ *Black Committee,* " Testimony of Major W. B. Robertson," p. 1720.

¹⁰ Interview with Major William B. Robertson, St. Louis, August 26, 1940.

¹¹ *Black Committee,* " Testimony of Major W. B. Robertson," p. 1722.

¹² *Black Committee,* " Testimony of Frank Robertson," p. 1891.

¹³ *Black Committee,* " Testimony of William Sacks," p. 1868.

¹⁴ *Annual Report of the Postmaster General for 1933,* Appendix, Table 48, pp. 106–8. See also ibid., p. 22.

¹⁵ London *Times,* June 14, 1892, p. 8.

¹⁶ David Weld: " A Review of the Air Transportation Industry " (White, Weld & Company, New York, 1940), p. 9. (The actual payment was $1.094.)

¹⁷ *Annual Report of the Postmaster General for 1933,* p. 22. (The report shows payments of 79 cents in 1931; 62 cents in 1932.)

18 *Hearings,* Air Mail, " Letter of Hon. James A. Farley to Hon. Hugo L. Black," Committee on the Post Office and Post Roads, House of Representatives, 73d Congress, Second Session, Part II, pp. 86–8.

CHAPTER 17

1 Interview with Fulton Lewis, Jr., Washington, D. C., July 1939.

2 Letter from Walter Folger Brown, New York, May 12, 1941.

3 Anonymous: " Plane Every Hour," *Time,* Vol. XVI, p. 46 (September 8, 1930) .

4 See note 6, Chapter xiii.

5 *United States Statutes at Large,* Vol. XLI, Section 406, pp. 480–2.

6 *Report of the Federal Co-ordinator of Transportation,* House Document Number 89, 74th Congress, First Session, 1934, pp. 1–56.

7 Anonymous: " Number One Airplane Company," *Fortune,* Vol. V, p. 131. (April 1932) .

8 *Hearings,* Air Mail, " Testimony of Hainer Hinshaw," Special Committee on Investigation of the Air Mail and Ocean Mail Contracts, United States Senate, 73d Congress, Second Session, p. 1587.

9 *Hearings,* Committee on the Post Office and Post Roads, House of Representatives, 73d Congress, Second Session, p. 153.

10 Editorial, " Breakers Ahead," *Aviation,* Vol. XXX, p. 665 (December 1931) .

11 Interview with Justice Hugo L. Black, Washington, D. C., August 14, 1940.

12 Interview with Colonel Paul Henderson, Washington, D. C., August 14, 1940.

CHAPTER 18

1 *Hearings,* " Testimony of W. P. MacCracken, Jr.," Special Committee on the Investigation of the Air Mail and Ocean Mail Contracts (hereinafter called the *Black Committee*) , United States Senate, 73d Congress, Second Session, p. 2196.

2 Letter from W. P. MacCracken, Jr., dated July 24, 1941, Washington, D. C.

3 Interview with W. P. MacCracken, Washington, August 12, 1940.

4 *Black Committee,* " Testimony of F. B. Rentschler," p. 1801. See footnote 7, Chapter X.

5 Ibid.

6 There is no hesitancy in admitting the presence of a lobby.

7 There was a provision for the granting of route certificates in the Air Mail Law Amendment of May 17, 1928, but neither the air-line executives nor Postmaster General Harry S. New took advantage of

the clause. The law left the initiative to the operators, and although they coveted the stability that would have been theirs with the acceptance of the ten-year certificates, they knew that they would be given lower payments if they entered into negotiations, for the law provided only for lower rates.

[8] Note that while Postmaster General Brown later bore the blame for extravagance in the awarding of air-mail contracts, it was Postmaster General New who failed to reduce payments under the terms of the Air Mail Amendment of May 17, 1928. Postmaster General Brown, on the other hand, worked hard to pass the McNary-Watres Act, which enabled him to issue certificates on his own initiative and thereby negotiate for lower payments.

[9] *Black Committee,* " Testimony of Colonel Paul Henderson," p. 3078.

[10] *Hearings,* Air Mail, " Letter of Hon. James A. Farley to Hon. Hugo L. Black," Committee on the Post Office and Post Roads, House of Representatives, 73d Congress, Second Session, pp. 86–8.

[11] Anonymous: " Morell Charges FDR on Mail ' Subsidy ' to Press," *Editor & Publisher,* Vol. LXXI, p. 9 (January 22, 1938) .

[12] Anonymous: " More Needling," *Editor & Publisher,* Vol. LXXI, p. 22 (January 15, 1938) .

[13] Paul T. David: *Economics of Air Mail Transportation* (Washington, 1934) , p. 167.

CHAPTER 19

[1] *Hearings,* Air Mail, " Letter of Hon. James A. Farley to Hon. Hugo L. Black," Committee on the Post Office and Post Roads, House of Representatives, 73d Congress, Second Session, pp. 86–7.

[2] The familiar remark is associated with Harry M. Daugherty at the time he was engineering Harding's nomination for President. See Mark Sullivan: *Our Times,* Vol. VI (New York, 1935) , p. 37.

[3] *Hearings,* " Testimony of William McKee," Special Committee on Investigation of the Air Mail and Ocean Mail Contracts (hereinafter called the *Black Committee*) , United States Senate, 73d Congress, Second Session, pp. 1443–57.

[4] Ibid., p. 1448.

[5] Ibid., p. 1450.

[6] *Black Committee,* " Testimony of Colonel Paul Henderson," p. 3005.

[7] *Black Committee,* " Testimony of F. G. Coburn," pp. 1658–60.

[8] Anonymous: " Brown Asks Plans for New Air Routes," New York *Times,* May 20, 1930, p. 23.

⁹ Editorial: "Postmaster General Brown and the Proposed Air Routes," *Aero Digest,* Vol. XVI, p. 70 (June 1930).

¹⁰ Brice Clagett: "The New Air Mail Law," *Aviation,* Vol. XXIX, p. 23 (July 5, 1930).

¹¹ *Black Committee,* "Testimony of Karl Crowley," pp. 2789–90.

¹² *Black Committee,* "Testimony of J. A. Farley," p. 2704.

¹³ *United States Code,* Title 39, Sec. 434, 1934 edition.

¹⁴ *Black Committee,* "Testimony of J. A. Farley," p. 2705.

CHAPTER 20

¹ *Hearings,* Air Mail, "Testimony of General Benjamin Foulois," Committee on the Post Office and Post Roads, House of Representatives, 73d Congress, Second Session, p. 97.

² Anonymous: "U. S. Aviation and the Air Mail," *Fortune,* Vol. IX, pp. 85 ff. (May 1934).

³ *Hearings,* Air Mail, Committee on the Post Office and Post Roads, House of Representatives, 73d Congress, Second Session, pp. 88–9.

⁴ *Aircraft Yearbook,* Vol. XVII, pp. 144–7.

⁵ *Hearings,* Air Mail, "Testimony of General Benjamin Foulois," Committee on the Post Office and Post Roads, House of Representatives, 73d Congress, Second Session, p. 98.

⁶ Letter, "Will is Stunned," Kansas City *Star,* February 12, 1934, p. 1.

⁷ Colonel Shaughnessey restricted service for three and a half days, but only to make a quick survey.

⁸ *Hearings,* "Testimony of Colonel Charles A. Lindbergh," Committee on the Post Office and Post Roads, United States Senate, 73d Congress, Second Session, March 16, 1934, pp. 148–52.

⁹ *Aircraft Yearbook,* Vol. XVII, pp. 124–5.

CHAPTER 21

¹ From correspondence with W. R. Beattie, of Braniff Airways, April 1940.

² *Hearings,* "Testimony of William I. Denning," Special Committee on Investigation of the Air Mail and Ocean Mail Contracts (hereinafter referred to as the *Black Committee*), United States Senate, 73d Congress, Second Session, pp. 3294 ff.

³ Ibid., p. 3316.

⁴ Ibid., p. 3288.

⁵ *Black Committee,* "Letter of T. E. Braniff to W. I. Denning," p. 3322.

⁶ *Black Committee,* " Testimony of James A. Farley," pp. 2698–2703.

⁷ Ibid.

⁸ Ibid., pp. 2707–8.

⁹ Ibid.

¹⁰ *Black Committee,* " Testimony of Walter Folger Brown," p. 2677.

¹¹ Ibid., pp. 2677 ff.

¹² James A. Farley: *Behind the Ballots* (New York, 1938), p. 269.

¹³ For obvious reasons, the name of the correspondent must be withheld.

¹⁴ *Behind the Ballots,* p. 334.

¹⁵ *Black Committee,* " Testimony of Walter Folger Brown," pp. 2569–74.

CHAPTER 22

¹ Charles S. Rhyne: *The Civil Aeronautics Act of 1938 Annotated* (Washington, 1939), p. 26, n. 66.

² E. Dillon Smith: *Air Mail Transport* (New York, 1937), pp. 11–14.

³ Anonymous: " Unfinished Business," *Fortune,* Vol. XIX, September 1934, p. 168.

⁴ Ibid.

⁵ Ibid.

⁶ Rhyne, op. cit., pp. 45–6.

⁷ *United States Statutes at Large,* Vol. XLIX, Part I, p. 614.

CHAPTER 23

¹ Anonymous: " Airline in the Black," *Fortune,* Vol. XIX, p. 116 (February 1939).

² *Hearings,* " Testimony of Colonel Paul Henderson," Special Committee on Investigation of Air Mail and Ocean Mail Contracts, United States Senate, 73d Congress, Second Session, p. 1486.

³ From a report loaned by P. M. Willcox, secretary of United Air Lines.

⁴ Interview with C. Bedell Monro, Allegheny County Airport, Pittsburgh, July 30, 1940.

⁵ Ibid.

CHAPTER 24

1 Charles S. Rhyne: *The Civil Aeronautics Act of 1938 Annotated* (Washington, D. C., 1939), p. 62. (This is the outstanding study of events leading up to the passage of the law.)

2 Ibid., p. 52.

3 Letter from Senator Pat McCarran, dated Washington, April 24, 1941.

4 Symposium, *Aviation*, Vol. XXXVII, p. 54 (July 1938).

5 Ibid.

6 Editorial: " A Law at Last," *Aviation*, Vol. XXXVII, p. 19 (July 1938).

7 Rhyne, op. cit., pp. 75–6.

8 Ibid.

9 Ibid., p. 78, n. 279.

10 Editorial, *Aviation*, Vol. XXXVII, p. 19 (August 1938).

11 Ibid.

12 Editorial: " A Law at Last," *Aviation*, Vol. XXXVII, p. 19 (July 1938).

CHAPTER 25

1 Anonymous: " AM23-3: NK to GX," *Fortune*, Vol. XIX, p. 112 (February 1939).

2 *Aircraft Yearbook*, Vol. XVI, p. 66.

3 Edward Pearson Warner: " Aviation in 1940," *Yale Review*, Vol. XXIX, p. 732 (Summer 1940).

4 Ibid., p. 735.

5 Ibid. (See also charts of Air Transport Association on adjoining pages of text.)

6 Ibid., p. 738.

7 E. P. Warner: *Technical Development, and Its Effect on Air Transportation* (Norwich University, 1938), p. 2.

8 Ibid.

9 Ibid.

10 Ibid., p. 4.

11 Ibid.

12 Anonymous: Sketch, *L'Aérophile,* Vol. XIV, p. 99 (April 1906).

13 Warner: *Technical Development*, pp. 13–18.

14 Ibid., pp. 19–20.

15 Warner: *Technical Development*, p. 40.

CHAPTER 26

[1] William B. Stout: "Planes of Yesterday," *Aviation,* Vol. XXXI, p. 166 (April 1932).

[2] Ibid.

[3] James G. Woolley and Earl W. Hill: *Airplane Transportation,* (Hollywood, 1929), p. 105.

[4] C. Fayette Taylor: "History of the Aeronautical Engine," *Aviation,* Vol. XXI, pp. 284–6 (August 16, 1926).

[5] Charles L. Lawrance: "Modern Aircraft Engine Development," *Aviation,* Vol. XX, p. 411 (March 22, 1926).

[6] In April 1941 an airliner crashed on the take-off near Charleston, West Virginia. It was one of the few proved cases of transport engine failure. No one was killed.

[7] Interview with Paul Richter, vice president of Transcontinental & Western Air, Kansas City, May 1940.

[8] Virtually every foot of pipe and every pound of machinery carried into the Barco oil fields of Colombia was transported in such ships.

[9] John T. Nevill: "Ford Motor Company and American Aeronautic Development," *Aviation,* Vol. XXVI, p. 2073 (June 15, 1929).

[10] Ibid. (The complete story is told in subsequent issues.)

[11] Nevil, *Aviation,* Vol. XXXVII, p. 44 (July 6, 1929).

[12] Anonymous: "Success at Santa Monica," *Fortune,* Vol. XI, p. 175 (May 1935).

[13] Ibid., p. 178.

CHAPTER 27

[1] Jerome Lederer: *Safety in the Operation of Air Transportation* (Norwich University, 1939), p. 23. (Lederer became director of the safety division, when civil aeronautics was returned as a bureau of the Department of Commerce in 1940.)

[2] David Weld: *Aviation — Manufacturing, Transportation* (White, Weld & Company, May 1940), p. 22.

[3] Kenneth Brown Collings: "Annual Report on Air Safety," *American Mercury,* Vol. XLVI, p. 24 (January 1939).

[4] Ibid.

[5] *Report of the Secretary of Commerce,* filed June 14, 1935 with the Bureau of Information. Accident reports are available to the public.

[6] C. B. Allen: "Why Do Air Liners Crash," *New Republic,* Vol. XCI, p. 35 (May 19, 1937).

[7] *Hearings,* " Testimony of John B. Lynn," Special Committee Investigating the Air Mail and Ocean Mail Contracts, United States Senate, 73d Congress, Second Session, pp. 3533–9.

[8] Kenneth B. Collings: " A Year without Death," *American Mercury,* Vol. L, p. 60 (May 1940). See also footnote 3.

[9] Figures submitted by T. J. Guold, assistant to the conservation engineer of the Equitable Life Assurance Society, July 8, 1941.

[10] Interview with Frank L. Jones, vice president of the Equitable Life Assurance Society of the United States, and executive head of the New York division of the National Safety Council, New York, July 7, 1941.

[11] Air Transport Association of America: *Little Known Facts,* Vol. III, Chart 41, p. 21 (April 1941).

CHAPTER 28

[1] Editorial: " Back to the Dark Ages," *Aviation,* Vol. XXXIX, p. 27 (May 1940).

[2] Anonymous: " Aviation News," *Aviation,* Vol. XXXIX, p. 80 (June 1940).

[3] C. H. Maxwell: " Zero-Zero — But Safe," *Popular Aviation,* Vol. XXVII, p. 14 (August 1940).

[4] Interview with Robert Knight, chief of the air transport section, Civil Aeronautics Board, Washington, D. C., August 14, 1940.

[5] William Barclay Harding: *The Aviation Industry* (New York, 1937), p. 50.

[6] Wayne L. McMillen: " Air Express Service in the United States," *Journal of Land and Public Utility Economics,* Vol. XI, p. 369 (November 1935).

[7] Anonymous: " Wings for Rural Mail," *Time,* Vol. XXXVII, p. 78 (April 28, 1941).

Index